Social Work and Social Justice

Social Work and Social Justice

Concepts, Challenges, and Strategies

MICHAEL REISCH

AND

CHARLES D. GARVIN

OXFORD
UNIVERSITY PRESS

OXFORD
UNIVERSITY PRESS

Oxford University Press is a department of the University of Oxford. It furthers
the University's objective of excellence in research, scholarship, and education
by publishing worldwide. Oxford is a registered trade mark of Oxford University
Press in the UK and certain other countries.

Published in the United States of America by Oxford University Press
198 Madison Avenue, New York, NY 10016, United States of America.

© Oxford University Press 2016

First Edition published in 2016

Library of Congress Cataloging-in-Publication Data
Reisch, Michael, 1948– author.
Social work and social justice : concepts, challenges, and strategies / Michael Reisch
and Charles D. Garvin.
    pages cm
Includes bibliographical references and index.
ISBN 978-0-19-989301-0 (alk. paper)
1. Social service—Moral and ethical aspects.   2. Social justice.   3. Social service—Practice.
4. Social workers—Professional ethics.   I. Garvin, Charles D., author.   II. Title.
HV10.5.R45 2016
179'.93613—dc23
2015032263

9 8 7 6 5 4 3 2 1
Printed by Sheridan, USA

Contents

Preface

THE *CODE OF ETHICS* of the National Association of Social Workers has established the pursuit of social justice as one of the core values of the profession. Similarly, the curriculum guidelines of the Council on Social Work Education (CSWE) require all social work programs to educate their students to overcome social and economic injustice and combat oppression. Despite this powerful social justice rhetoric, there is still considerable confusion and ambiguity about how to translate these values into practice. Few texts today provide guidance regarding the practical and ethical challenges involved.

In fact, most social work literature that addresses the issue of social justice emphasizes the amelioration or eradication of injustice. The knowledge and skills to achieve this goal, however, are necessary but insufficient tools to create a more socially just world. Both history and contemporary events demonstrate that socially just ends cannot be realized and sustained unless they are achieved through socially just means. A distinguishing feature of this book, therefore, is its emphasis on the complementary nature of socially just goals and processes.

This book is our attempt to fill this gap in a creative way by conveying the importance of social justice work, illustrating its complexity, and discussing how to negotiate the challenges involved. We have tried to go beyond a presentation of abstract social justice concepts and goals to include illustrations of practices that produce socially just results through the use of socially just means at the interpersonal, organizational, community, and societal levels.

Because of the CSWE mandate that social work curricula focus on the implementation of social justice, this book can be used either as a text or as a major resource for courses that focus on social work practice at the Master of Social Work (MSW) and advanced Bachelor of Social Work (BSW) level, particularly practice courses taught in the foundation (first year) curriculum. Alternately, the book could be used in courses on multiculturalism or diversity in which social justice content is increasingly seen as critical. In addition, the book could be used as a supplementary text for courses on social policy, policy practice, or human behavior. The inclusion of theoretical, conceptual, and historical material makes the book especially suitable for PhD courses that focus on social work theory and philosophy. These exist in virtually all doctoral programs.

Finally, the book can be used in departments of community/applied psychology, applied anthropology or sociology, counseling, or public health and in schools of public policy, nursing, or education. In addition, practitioners and scholars who wish to orient their work to social justice issues will find this book an important resource. The former are likely to be especially attracted to the case studies in the book that present social justice concepts in concrete ways.

Over many years, the authors have developed the ideas and frameworks for this book through teaching relevant courses; engaging in various types of research; and participating in direct practice, community-based change projects, and policy advocacy in diverse sociocultural contexts. We have taught at the baccalaureate, masters, and doctoral levels about the history of social welfare and social action, theories and knowledge for social justice and social change, interpersonal practice, group work, mental health and stigma, race, gender and ethnic issues in intervention, community organizing and community development, contemporary social policy and policy practice, and organizational change. We have also conducted numerous workshops on social justice goals for a wide range of groups and organizations in various areas of the United States and other nations. We have been involved in local, state, national, and international task forces and workgroups, and we have provided consultation to nonprofit social service agencies, advocacy groups, government departments, community-based organizations, political campaigns, colleges, and universities. We have used a considerable amount of the material to be included in the book in our courses, as well as in conference presentations and workshops.

Personal Reflections

Although we are of different generations, the paths that led to our commitment to social justice and the way we conceive it have many similarities.

Charles's Reflection

One of my earliest recollections from when I was in grade school was a family gathering. Many of my relatives were shopkeepers, but my father was a factory worker at a General Motors factory who had only completed the eighth grade. When other family members criticized their employees for being lazy and alcoholic, my father said, "We working people see this differently!" I knew of his strong identification with workers as we lived through several strikes when we had to struggle to meet our basic needs.

Later in high school, I joined a Zionist group because I was very conscious of the Holocaust. I soon left this organization for a left-wing organization that had a broader focus on fighting oppression of all groups, especially those we now call "people of color." I continued to be a member of this organization as a junior college student. One day, near the college, I was distributing leaflets that opposed the reinstitution of the draft. The dean of the college had the police haul me into his office, where he admonished me for my "un-American" views.

About that time, I volunteered at the Henry Booth (Settlement) House in Chicago, where I quickly became convinced I wanted a career in social work. The settlement was located in one of the most impoverished, primarily African American communities in Chicago. I soon became deeply concerned about the plight of the neighbors.

As a result, I changed my major at the University of Chicago from sociology to social work. I also became the editor of the student paper and frequently incurred the wrath of the administration because of the paper's editorials, which often dealt with social justice issues. After I received my MSW during the Korean War, I was drafted into the Army. The Army learned of my political views and put me through basic training three times while it pondered my fate. I guess it decided I was not a dangerous subversive because I was eventually used as a social worker for the remainder of my service.

After the Army, I worked for a dozen years in settlements and community centers until I decided I was ready to teach others and I entered the doctoral program at the University of Chicago. Subsequently I accepted an offer to teach at the University of Michigan. I like to think that my teaching and research, which were largely about work with groups, reflected my views about what we now refer to as social justice. For example, I taught a group work course in which all the readings were derived solely from feminist authors.

Since I became an Emeritus Professor in 2002, I have continued to be active in community social action efforts. I decided that all my subsequent writings will be focused on social justice—thus this book.

Michael's Reflection

I grew up in a working-class, union household during the McCarthy era, in which the fear of communism produced widespread political repression, and I came of age during the tumultuous 1960s. My parents, grandfathers, and several of my aunts and uncles belonged to different labor unions. Although none of my family members were radicals, for the most part they were strong supporters of the New Deal and of workers' rights. Although we disagreed on issues, ranging from civil rights to the Vietnam War, my family was united in the belief that unions improved the lives of working people. As a result, the idea of "fairness" was instilled in me since I was a small child.

As a high school and college student, I belonged to several unions required for summer or full-time employment and became involved in civil rights, anti-war, and other social change organizations. As I read more about history, politics, and economics, my working-class background informed my perspective on contemporary events and shaped my career choices, my activism, and, eventually, my scholarship. Travel to other countries has broadened my ideas about social justice and its complex meaning and implications.

Throughout my career, I have attempted to balance my professional work with social and political activism. I have collaborated with labor unions, churches, and civil rights groups to protest cutbacks in social welfare spending and to expand social protections for our society's most vulnerable populations. I have directed several local and statewide coalitions that advocated on behalf of these populations, served as president of a national children's advocacy organization based in California, and directed or consulted on the political campaigns of progressive candidates.

My family background and political views have consistently informed my research and scholarship on the history of social welfare and social work, the impact of welfare reform, the causes and consequences of poverty and inequality, and the future of the welfare state. I am interested in how social work's status aspirations have diverted the profession from its social justice mission and how economic globalization and the transformation of the welfare state have undermined people's well-being. I believe the goal of social justice is more important than ever today and hope this book will make a modest contribution to that goal.

Acknowledgments

WE COULD NOT have written this book without the support, encouragement, and assistance of family, friends, and colleagues. Our colleagues at the University of Michigan, Professors Beth Reed and Mieko Yoshihama, contributed many stimulating ideas in our frequent discussions about an earlier version of this work. We thank them for their generosity in allowing us to incorporate some of the ideas we developed collectively into the book. Professors Edith Lewis and Robert Ortega drew upon their extensive practice and research experience in coauthoring two of the most important chapters—on practice with individuals and families and on practice with groups. Several graduate research assistants at the University of Maryland—Katie Januario, Pamela Parnell, Dawn Philip, Meredith Slater, and Todd Vanidestine—proved to be indefatigable and consistently reliable aides. Our editors at Oxford University Press, Maura Roessner and Dana Bliss, were always supportive and extraordinarily patient. We thank them and the other staff at Oxford for their assistance in seeing this project through to its completion. Any errors in the manuscript are entirely ours. Finally, we thank our families, who stuck with us through the long process of researching and writing this book. We dedicate the book to them with love and boundless appreciation.

Michael Reisch, University of Maryland
Charles D. Garvin, University of Michigan

About the Authors

MICHAEL REISCH, PhD, is the Daniel Thursz Distinguished Professor of Social Justice at the University of Maryland. A former Woodrow Wilson Fellow and Fulbright Scholar, he previously held faculty and administrative positions at the University of Michigan, the University of Pennsylvania, San Francisco State University, and the State University of New York at Stony Brook, and he was a visiting professor at the University of California, Berkeley, the New Bulgarian University in Sofia, the Chinese University of Hong Kong, and the University of Queensland in Australia. His 30 books and monographs include *Social Policy and Social Justice*; *The Road Not Taken: A History of Radical Social Work in the U.S.*; *From Charity to Enterprise: The Emergence of American Social Work in a Market Economy*; *Social Work in the 21st Century*; *The Routledge International Handbook of Social Justice*; and *The Handbook of Community Practice*. Some of his many publications and conference papers have been translated into 10 languages, and he has lectured widely in Asia, Australia, Europe, and Latin America.

He has held leadership positions in local and national professional, advocacy, and social change organizations. He has been honored for this work by the Maryland General Assembly, the San Francisco Board of Supervisors, and several nonprofit organizations and universities. In 2013, he was named "Social Work Educator of the Year" by the Maryland Chapter of the National Association of Social Workers, and in 2014 he received both the "Teacher of the Year" award from the University of Maryland, Baltimore, and the Significant Lifetime Achievement Award from the Council on Social Work Education.

CHARLES D. GARVIN received his master's degree in social work in 1951 and PhD in social work from the University of Chicago in 1968. He was a professor of social work at the University of Michigan from 1965 until he became Professor Emeritus in 2002. He is author of numerous texts and more than 100 articles and book chapters on social work, social work education, group work, social work practice, and research. His current work deals with integrating the concept of social justice into all social work activities. In 2013, he received the Significant Lifetime Achievement Award from the Council on Social Work Education.

EDITH A. LEWIS, MSW, PhD, is Emerita Associate Professor of Social Work and Women's Studies at the University of Michigan. Her career has focused on enhancing social justice and social change by integrating the strengths of families of color in professional practice, theory, and research. Her primary research interests concern how women of color offset personal, familial, community, and professional role strain. She has studied such topics as the intersections of gender and ethnicity in the lives of women of color; an intervention project for pregnant, substance-dependent women; and the successful methods used by Ghanaian women in community development projects. She is currently evaluating a global exchange effort between the University of Michigan and a university in West Africa.

ROBERT ORTEGA is Associate Professor in the University of Michigan School of Social Work. His research interests are in the areas of child welfare, relationship development, group work practice, treatment interventions, and service utilization, particularly in the areas of mental health and child welfare. He has presented and written on these topics with a special focus on diversity, social justice, and cultural responsiveness in research and practice. He also serves as a consultant on several national research projects and with organizations focusing on social work education, child welfare, and social justice issues. In 2013, he received the Distinguished Recent Contributions to Social Work Education Award from the Council on Social Work Education.

Social Work and Social Justice

Historical, Conceptual, and Theoretical Foundations of Social Justice

Part I provides the historical, conceptual, and theoretical foundation for the application of social justice principles to social work practice presented in Part II. The chapters in Part I emphasize the relationship of theories and concepts to the development of social welfare and social work and to the institutions and practices that emanate from a society's efforts to achieve and sustain social justice goals, however they are defined. The integration of diverse and sometimes conflicting approaches to social justice throughout these chapters is designed to promote critical thinking and underscore the value of incorporating such perspectives into practice. Case examples or historical illustrations are used to illuminate how social justice concepts have been or could be applied to the real world.

Chapter 1 contains an overview of our goals and underlying assumptions, including the overriding importance of social justice in social work practice and the role of critical theories in providing a foundation for that practice. One of our basic assumptions is that social justice concepts need to be incorporated into both practice goals and processes. Another is the value of creating spaces in which we can practice social justice skills effectively and ethically. We briefly outline the multiple ways in which inequalities and injustices are sustained and re-created, and we suggest some ways in which practitioners can recognize these patterns. We also discuss the importance of understanding our identities and group memberships from an intersectional perspective that acknowledges the complex and interactive roles that race, class, gender, sexuality, ethnicity, nation, religion, ability status, gender expression, and age play in shaping people's lives and experiences. In addition, we examine how these concepts possess both an intrinsic meaning and one derived from their social construction. Finally, we acknowledge the dynamic and dialectical nature of the issues involved in social justice-oriented work, the various and sometimes competing visions of justice that exist, the multiple dimensions that are important to consider when conceptualizing justice, and the ways in which conceptions of change and power shape social justice goals and processes.

Chapter 2 examines the historical evolution of social justice concepts and theories, with a particular focus on alternative (non-Western) perspectives. One of the shortcomings of most books on social justice and social work published in the United States is the absence of such alternative perspectives. This produces a serious problem as US society becomes increasingly multicultural because it forces marginalized and excluded populations to adopt dominant conceptions of social justice that are often at odds with their own. A major theme in this chapter is the distinction between group-specific and universal concepts and theories of social justice. We emphasize the common and differential conceptions of social justice that have emerged in different cultures and eras and how these different conceptions shaped the institutions through which social justice could be achieved.

Chapter 3 analyzes the influence of social justice on the development of the social work profession in the United States. The profession of social work has long struggled with the translation of concepts of social justice into social policies, programs, and practice frameworks. In this chapter, we trace the major features of this struggle and the contributions of key individuals and groups to its development. Among the factors discussed is the impact of religious and secular ideologies, the evolution of the profession's "vocabulary" of social justice, the emergence of practice theories and principles that reflect social justice concerns, and the impact of professionalism on the social justice mission of social work. The chapter concludes with a critique of the profession's current approach to social justice, including the distinction between human rights and social justice perspectives on practice, an analysis of some persistent dilemmas in putting social justice rhetoric into practice, and some suggestions as to how social work's ethics and practice could be adapted to 21st-century realities.

Chapter 4 provides an overview of the major theories and concepts that underlie socially just practice across all methods and in all settings. An integrative theme in this chapter is that the institutional structure and cultural processes in all societies have the potential to create (or re-create) inequalities and injustice. This requires practitioners to engage in ongoing reflection, critical thinking, and active struggle to attain and sustain socially just goals.

Another important issue discussed in this chapter is the need to address diversity and differences among peoples and cultures, as they are reflected in their values, goals, patterns of interaction, planning and action styles, definition of need, help-seeking behavior, and change agendas. These differences, which often create miscommunication and misunderstanding, can arise from groups' historical experiences, locations in social hierarchies, cultural norms and values, and other factors. This chapter includes a concise analysis of the multiple ways that historical and cultural forces shape how these differences are constructed and maintained.

In addition, this chapter discusses the importance of theorizing as a tool for effecting change; reviews theories about power; and discusses how different forms of power interact with each other to create a maldistribution of resources, status, and privilege. In addition, the chapter describes the processes by which people and systems change and grow and how the various sources of resistance that frequently block change and growth emerge. A goal of this chapter is to enable readers to appreciate and anticipate multiple forms and types of resistance and to overcome that resistance in a variety of ways to create desired change.

Other important concepts that are introduced in Chapter 4 are intersectional humility and critical structural thinking. These involve new "habits of mind," which we believe are critical elements of practice in a complex multicultural society and multipolar world. Finally, we introduce the concept of praxis, which employs iterative and interactive cycles of theorizing, acting, and reflecting in order to deepen critical consciousness, increase insights about social justice, and identify and reduce barriers to justice. The application of praxis to various practice methods is further discussed in Part II.

1

Introduction

BACKGROUND, THEMES, AND GOALS

Goals of the Chapter

Given the complexity of the underlying concepts we attempt to apply to practice in this book, it is essential that we define some of the important terms we will use in subsequent chapters. The most important concept is *social justice*, and we devote much of this chapter to discussing the complex dimensions of this concept. We then discuss some of the assumptions that underlie the application of social justice to social work practice.

In this chapter and throughout the book, we also emphasize the importance of critical consciousness. We define this term and discuss its relationship to identity issues and group memberships such as race, gender, sexuality, ethnicity, class, nationality, religion, ability statuses, gender expressions, and age. We discuss how these terms are social constructions and the implications of this phenomenon. Because identity issues are increasingly complex, we apply an intersectional perspective and discuss its implications for practice.

In addition, we discuss the concepts of change and power, their connection to social justice, and their impact on individual and group identity and relationships. One way in which this interaction occurs is through intergroup *dialogue* and the application of *praxis*. We discuss the implications of these terms for social work theory and practice, particularly in Chapter 4. In addition, we discuss how social injustices are maintained and how barriers to social justice must be recognized and addressed by social workers in all forms of practice. At the conclusion of this chapter, we introduce the other chapters in the book in which these issues are explicated in more detail.

Defining Social Justice

Defining social justice is a complex task because this concept often reflects many conflicting dimensions and ideological perspectives (Reisch, 2002). John Rawls (1971/1999), one of the most cited writers on this subject, emphasizes the following two principles:

> Each person is to have an equal right to basic liberties compatible with similar liberties for others. . . . Social and economic inequalities are to be arranged so that they are both (a) reasonably expected to be to everyone's advantage and (b) attached to positions and offices open to all. (pp. 151–152)

An underlying assumption of Rawls's (2001) theory of justice is that "all social values . . . are to be distributed equally unless an unequal distribution of any, or all, of these values is to everyone's advantage" (p. 62).[1] According to Reisch (2002),

> From these principles of justice, Rawls articulated a "principle of redress" which established the philosophical basis for social justice policies directed toward a more just distribution of social goods. . . . As stated by Rawls, the principle seems particularly well-suited to the social work profession's goal of eliminating racial, gender, and economic inequalities. (p. 346)

This principle has significant implications for policy and practice. Rawls (1971/1999), as quoted in Reisch (2002), states,

> Undeserved inequalities call for redress; and since inequalities of birth and natural endowment are undeserved, these inequalities are somehow compensated for. Thus, the principle holds that in order to treat all persons equally, to provide genuine equality of opportunity, society must give more attention to those with fewer native assets and to those born into the less favorable social positions. The idea is to redress the bias of contingencies in the direction of equality. (p. 100)

These principles also apply more broadly to the basic structure of society. They are intended to govern the assignment of rights and duties and to regulate

---

1. See Reisch's (2002, pp. 346–347) summary of Rawls's definitions and the problems with these definitions.

the distribution of social and economic advantages. As their formulation suggests, they presuppose the division of the social structure into two more or less distinct parts, the political and the socioeconomic, with the first principle applying to the former and the second to the latter.

The first principle represents those aspects of the social system that specify the equal or unequal liberties of citizenship; the second principle refers to those aspects of the social system that produce either social and economic equalities or inequalities. According to this formulation, the basic liberties of citizens are, generally speaking, political liberty (e.g., the right to vote and be eligible for public office) and civil liberties such as freedom of speech and assembly, liberty of conscience and freedom of thought; freedom of the person and the right to possess (personal) property; and freedom from arbitrary arrest and seizure as defined by the concept of the rule of law. According to Rawls's first principle, these liberties, which are largely embodied in the Bill of Rights of the US Constitution, must be applied equally to all citizens in a just society in order to ensure that they have the same basic rights.

Rawls's second principle applies, in the first approximation, to the distribution of income and wealth and to the design of organizations and institutions that make use of differences in authority and responsibility, or chains of command. Although the distribution of wealth and income need not be equal, any inequalities that exist must be to everyone's advantage, and positions of authority and offices of command must be accessible to all.

According to Rawls (1971/1999),

the two principles . . . are a special case of a more general conception of justice that can be expressed as follows: All social values—liberty and opportunity, income and wealth and the bases of self-respect—are to be distributed equally unless an unequal distribution of any, or all, of these values is to everyone's advantage. (pp. 61–62)

Applying Social Justice to Social Work Practice

This discussion of the definition of social justice requires some elaboration as we embark on our effort to link social justice to the theories and practices of social work. Here, we discuss some of the complexities we will encounter.

First is that socially just social work practice relates to both *processes* and *outcomes*. Processes include all of the activities in which social workers engage and the responses of other individuals and larger entities to these activities. They also include planned activities and reactions as well as unintended and unforeseen ones. In addition, processes may be initiated by a single word, an emotional expression, or a succession or combination of these actions; responses may be reflected by the same range of actions. Although a practitioner can hardly contemplate each of these possibilities before acting, it behooves the critically conscious social worker to reflect seriously on them. The social justice implications of such processes include the following:

- What does each component of the process reveal about the power differentials between the individuals or systems involved? A question can be viewed as a simple request for information, as an intrusion on the privacy of a less powerful person by a more powerful person, or as an implicit demand that the less powerful person comply with something (Have you done the dishes today?) or a request for further direction by the less powerful person (Do you want me to rinse them first?).
- Do the actions of the workers and others with whom they are involved (e.g., recipients of services, colleagues, other agency personnel, and political officeholders) reflect attention to oppressive social conditions, empowerment of service recipients, and respect for the rights of all concerned?
- Has the worker sought to inform his or her actions by a critical reflection on the sources of the injustices he or she intends to address and their likely impact on others?
- What roles is the worker enacting in these exchanges (e.g., mediator, expert, enabler, and leader), and do these roles reflect the rights and needs of others, respect for them, and non-abuse of the worker's power?

The Impact of Culture and Context

The worker's understanding and application of the concepts of social justice occur within the contexts of people's cultures, the social structures of which they are part, their personal philosophies and beliefs, as well as the dominant philosophies and beliefs of their culture and the historical evolution of these cultures, structures, and philosophies. In Chapter 2, we discuss in detail and through a multinational lens some of these issues of cultural and structural variations in how social justice is defined and applied.

Although Rawls's extensive treatment of social justice discusses the implications of the concept for both individuals and groups, some cultures primarily focus on the application of social justice to individuals (e.g., the United States), whereas others emphasize social justice in terms of its collective or communal impact. This distinction represents a complex issue for social workers because of the potential conflict between an individual's goal and those sought by the community or society. A contemporary example is the conflict over Affirmative Action: Some Americans believe that a society should provide all individuals with equal opportunities to attain their educational or occupational goals without reference to their demographic characteristics or history. Others argue that true equality of opportunity for some social groups (e.g., African Americans, people with disabilities, and women) can only occur if society makes targeted efforts to overcome previous conditions of oppression (Babkina, 2004; Kellough, 2006; Kennedy, 2013; Sterba, 2009). Another contemporary example is the conflict over whether parents should be required to immunize their children against communicable diseases.

Marxism and Social Justice

In our discussion and application of social justice, we take note of the Marxist idea that "the roots of injustice lie ... in the political–economic structure that was based on subjugation, discrimination, exploitation, and privilege" (Berlin, 1996, as quoted in Reisch, 2002). Marx and colleagues posited that the primary driving force in all history is class struggle and that over many centuries such struggles led to the transformation of society from primitive communism (or collectivist societies) to hierarchical societies characterized by slavery and feudalism and then to the class divisions of contemporary postindustrial countries. According to Marx, each set of social conditions reflected the class conflicts of the period. Through a dialectical process, these conflicts produced new social conditions that contained a different configuration of these conflicts (e.g., aristocrat and serf in feudal society and capitalist and worker in industrial society). Marx believed that the ultimate resolution of this dialectical process would be the creation of a communist society in which class conflicts would no longer exist.

Although many historians and political social theorists at all points of the ideological spectrum take issues with various aspects of Marx's analysis and predictions, his assessment of how structural conditions produce and sustain injustices is still valid today. As Reisch states,

> Marx rejected the idea that injustice was the by-product of natural human competition, selfishness, and aggression. He asserted that the roots of injustice lie, instead, in the political–economic structure that was based on subjugation, discrimination, exploitation, and privilege (Berlin, 1996). Justice would prevail, therefore, when individuals received what they needed on the basis of their humanity and not merely what they deserve

on the basis of their social class origin or productivity. (Marx, 1964, as quoted in Reisch, 2002, p. 345)

Social Justice and the Distribution of Social Goods

Most definitions of social justice incorporate various means of achieving an equitable distribution of societal goods—tangible and intangible. Despite ongoing philosophical and political disputes over the meaning of social justice, there is broad agreement on this principle (Reisch, 2002). Miller (1976) states that social justice incorporates

> the distribution of benefits and burdens throughout a society, as it results from the major social institutions such as property systems and public organizations. It deals with such matters as the regulation of wages and . . . profits, the protection of persons' rights throughout the legal system, the allocation of housing, medicine, welfare benefits, etc. (p. 222)

In recent decades, feminist philosophers such as Nussbaum (1999) and Held (1995) added a gender dimension to contemporary views of social justice. This perspective is particularly relevant to social work practice due to the long-standing oppression of women, the different ways that women view the conditions of existence, the continuing presence of social structures that support male hegemony, and the cultural norms that influence male–female interaction.

Social Work's Evolving Conception of Social Justice

For more than a century, "the pursuit of social justice has been a core value of the social work profession in the United States, providing an alternative to the concept of social welfare as charity" (Reisch, 2002, p. 347). Reisch notes, "The creation of greater social solidarity (fraternity or humanity) implied in the goals of multiculturalism and social justice, requires the reassertion of the ideas of collective responsibility, a community of need, and public virtue" (p. 347). This includes citizenship requirements that recognize our communitarian and collective security needs without neglecting equal attention to the value of liberty and justice for all. As discussed in Chapter 3, this perspective first emerged during the Progressive Era (~1890–1917) through the combined influences of religious and secular ideas. As Garvin (1997) notes,

A more rigorous reform thrust, however, was provided by the introduction of the settlement house into the United States, inspired by similar institutions developed in England. Stanton Coit, after a visit to Toynbee Hall in London, established the Neighborhood Guild on the lower east side of New York in 1886. The settlement idea spread rapidly and in 1891 there were six settlements in the United States; by 1900 there were more than 1400. (p. 25)

The idea underlying the settlement house movement was that people interested in addressing the problems of the poor could understand them better by participating in their community life. In contrast to many other social services that emphasized adjustment to the social order, settlement houses combined efforts to change social conditions with a variety of programs to ameliorate the specific problems of their communities (Garvin, 1997).

As Berman-Rossi and Miller (1994) note, however, the settlement house movement was also a product of its times. Settlements had "uneasy, ambivalent relations with and virtual neglect of service to African Americans during their early years" (Berman-Rossi & Miller, 1994, p. 78). Unfortunately,

the historic "truth" appears to be that the "preferred" groups served by the settlements were the European immigrants, not African American migrants. Europeans were apparently thought to be better able to identify with and be influenced by the social and cultural ideals of the settlements, their leadership, and their "settlers." The goal of assimilation was apparently intended for European Americans only. This indeed is an unsettling irony to contemplate and rationalize. In the main, African Americans were not sought or encouraged to use settlement services, particularly settlements where whites were ubiquitously present. (p. 78)

This analysis underscores a basic point about efforts to achieve social justice. Despite our best hopes, struggles for social justice will not create a permanently socially just society. Rather, each successful struggle reveals new injustices or may even create new unjust social conditions and sources of social injustice. This reflects the dialectical nature of social change that continues to the present.

The experience of one of the authors, who began his social work career as a settlement worker in the post–World War II period (1948–1955), illustrates how the settlement movement reflected local social conditions. He worked in a settlement house in an African American community in Chicago. The majority of the staff was African American, and the settlement engaged in such social change activities as the formation of block clubs, the presentation of testimony before the city council on the need for social changes, the promotion of peace activities such as opposition to US involvement in the war in Korea, and efforts to empower youth through leadership training. Much still remained to be done. This author had occasion to visit a settlement in Augusta, Georgia, in 1953. Whereas the members and the program director were African American, the director was White and the program director somewhat sadly noted that the director never asked to accompany her to city-wide meetings.

Thus far, in our discussion of the concept of social justice, we have utilized a series of assumptions that we now describe in more detail.

Underlying Assumptions

We developed our practice framework based on the following assumptions about social justice:

1. Social justice values and precepts must be incorporated into all practice goals and processes.
2. The conditions that produce social justice or injustice are often complex, evolving, conflict-laden, and ever changing.
3. Different persons view these multifaceted conditions through different interpretive lenses. These conditions often involve multiple systems that are constantly evolving. The following case is an example of this complexity. This case illustrates how one person's experiences may lead to an increased consciousness of existing conditions and, potentially, to forming relationships with others who have similar concerns in order to take action to rectify injustice.

Case Example: Sarah Smith

Sarah Smith is an African American woman who had recently been denied the right to vote in a statewide election because she lacked the required identification—in this case, her birth certificate. This barrier to her ability to exercise her civil right resulted from a recent action of the state legislature that made such identification a requirement. Sarah was aware that her next door neighbor who was White had not had such difficulty. Although the proponents of the legislation argued that it was designed to prevent voter fraud, there had been no recent incidents of documented voter fraud in the state. To many observers, the new law apparently resulted from pressure from the local Tea Party organization and the support of the governor and key legislators, who feared that a large African American turnout would jeopardize their election chances. Sarah did not have a birth certificate because she was born at home and the attending persons failed to submit the necessary paperwork. Sarah had been urged to vote by the National Association for the Advancement of Colored People (NAACP) chapter in her city, of which she was the treasurer.

The NAACP chapter had been represented at a national meeting by Sarah when the issue of increasing the African American vote was a major item on the agenda. She had many ideas about how to increase the number of voters but was stymied by the new legislation. There were also disagreements among the attendees as to how best to tackle the new law. Some thought it was a lost cause and they should work to influence the current legislators and governor to support measures to simplify the registration of voters. Several said they would not vote if given the chance because they disapproved of all the competitors for legislative positions. Others thought they should go back to the civil rights struggles of the 1960s for ideas because of the support they got from radical White youth.

When Sarah got home, her partner thought they should just give up on the United States and move to some other country, such as Canada. One of her children said he could not care less about the issue because he had more important things to think about!

---

4. Power is always relevant, and power analyses must be recurrent. In all situations in which social justice issues are being considered, power issues are involved. These issues are ever changing; therefore, an analysis of these power issues and their impact on the development of change strategies must be an ongoing process. These power issues include the type and amount of power possessed by service recipients, practitioners, and other key actors. The source of this power may be a formal position (e.g., an agency executive, legislator, or officer in a change organization), the possession of money or other valued resources, the ability to inflict pain (a fine, termination of employment, punishment ordered by a court, or possession of greater physical strength), personal social status or charisma, or the possession of valuable knowledge and expertise (French & Raven, 1959). This power may not be drawn upon in a given instance, but when it is used to affect an outcome, it is referred to as "influence." In addition, the way service users and practitioners apply their power may produce different effects and reflect different degrees of readiness to engage in action and tolerate conflict. It may also involve different costs, benefits, and risks in taking action. Garvin et al. (1985) proposed the following ordering of strategies that they hypothesized would create different degrees of conflict in such situations:

   - *Avoidance*: The participants use their ability (or power) to remove themselves from the situation.

- *Alternative reactions*: The individual changes his or her behavior without making any demand of the other person. This change is presumed to lead to a change in the other. An example of this is a teacher who resolves to respond to her student's aggressive behavior assertively although she had been aggressive before. She anticipates that the student will respond to this behavior and use it as a model for his own.
- *Manipulation of the social or physical situation*: An example is a student who had a hostile teacher. His parent asked that he be moved to another classroom in which the teacher was known to be a very kindly person.
- *Interpretation*: This involves *explaining* to another the causes or consequences of either his or her own behavior or the behavior of the other. An example is the decision of a group to explain to an agency that their room assignment to the nursery is leading to others ridiculing the group.
- *Education*: The individual who seeks a change in the behavior of others may have determined that his or her behavior was due to a lack of information. An example is a group of ex-offenders who determined that their difficulty gaining employment was due to ignorance in the community about their abilities and trustworthiness. They obtained the support of a newspaper reporter who agreed to write a series of articles educating the public about this issue and that will include interviews with members of the group.
- *Evaluation*: This involves gathering information that may influence the behavior of others. An example is a group that gathered interviews with a representative sample of people whose unemployment benefits were discontinued. These data revealed all of their efforts to find new employment. They hoped this would counter the statements of legislators that they were lazy and content to live on the "dole."
- *Use of influentials*: This strategy entails the individuals or groups concerned seeking the support of others for their cause, such as legislators, executives, or newspaper editors.
- *Bargaining*: The approach here is to engage in a process with selected others in which the individuals/groups concerned do something in exchange for the actions desired from the other party. For example, union members in collective bargaining may agree to forgo a shortened workweek in exchange for an increase in wages.
- *Confrontation*: This involves actively presenting to other persons or systems the actions they have taken or the results of their actions often accompanied with a request/demand for change. This strategy can lead to

more conflict than the previous ones because it tends to force people to confront how their behaviors or attitudes are problematic to others and should be changed. In one example, a group of parents recognized that a teacher was discriminating against Latino students. They drew up a list of such occasions and arranged to meet with the teacher as a group. They told him that if this behavior continued, they would present a petition to the principal asking for his removal.

- *Use of mass media*: People, in seeking social justice, can contact newspapers or TV stations (or a website on the Internet or a large number of people whose e-mail addresses they have obtained). They may also create their own website to report an injustice and/or a demand for a change in the actions of other individuals/systems.

- *Passive resistance*: This is a strategy to disrupt the system at which it is directed through non-cooperation with key authorities. People who utilize this approach will refuse to perform tasks or will obstruct other activities such as with "sit-ins." A famous example of this occurred during the modern civil rights era when African Americans sat at lunch counters that were "Whites only" and requested service. They were often dragged away forcefully by law enforcement personnel and arrested. Other examples of this approach are patients in residential centers who refuse to do "make up" work chores. Members of the public may sympathize with these activists when they see that lesser confrontational approaches have been futile.

- *Active resistance*: This involves taking an action likely to be unpleasant or disruptive to a system. Extreme forms include destroying property or committing acts of violence. An example is when war protesters poured blood on draft board records. "The more extreme forms are not considered by most social workers to be professionally acceptable.[2] Nevertheless, social workers should be cognizant of the extremely cruel conditions that have led some clients (sic) to engage in prison riots, university disruptions, or industrial actions." Social justice principles would direct us to look at the systems that are inhumane and that led to such desperate actions.

5. Injustice exists in all societies but takes different forms in different contexts. We know of no society that is completely devoid of any manifestation of injustice. There are, of course, societies in which the injustices inflicted upon citizens are greater than those in other societies. This is likely to be correlated

---

2. For an extended discussion of the ethical issues involved, see Specht (1969).

with such matters as the degree of democracy and income inequality, whether forms of oppression with historical origins still exist, and the extent to which all persons are accorded respect and dignity regardless of their social status or group membership. In some societies, various forms of justice are manifested more than others, such as respect for women, the aged, those with disabilities, those who practice different religions, and children. Each society's culture is likely to promote different definitions of justice and injustice—a topic we discuss in greater detail in Chapter 2. Nevertheless, all societies express ideas about social justice both explicitly and implicitly through the values embodied in their literature, philosophy, theological tracts, laws, and speeches by religious and secular leaders and intellectuals. Other expressions can be found in such cultural artifacts as art, music, and cinema.

6. Social justice is never achieved for all time. Any social change that produces a more socially just situation is not for "all time." New conditions are likely to arise that require further changes to maintain or expand social justice. An example is the passage of Social Security legislation in the 1930s. Because the original law excluded approximately 40% of the workforce from coverage—an exclusion that had a disproportionate impact on workers of color and women—further legislative modifications were needed to make the 1935 Social Security Act more socially just. Similarly, the provision of the Social Security Act that created Aid to Dependent Children did not cover dependency due to their parents' unemployment, necessitating further amendments. A more recent example of policy efforts to promote greater equity is the push for mental health parity—that is, to cover the costs of mental health treatment similarly to the coverage for physical illness.

7. Our social locations and histories limit our ability to recognize mechanisms of injustice or envision a truly just society. At times, social workers are limited in their awareness of social injustices due to their prior experiences or present locations. Social workers who come from the White middle class may be insensitive to cultural and other expressions that insult people of color. Social workers from warm climates may be insensitive to the impact of cold climates, especially as children go to school without warm clothing in winter. Christian social workers may not recognize the impact on people who are Jews or Muslims when their children are taught Christmas songs in school or view Christmas-themed exhibits in their communities, workplaces, or schools. In summary, the forces that contribute to injustice operate sometimes in separate domains and sometimes in conjunction with each other. Conversely, the forces that can be mobilized to work for social justice can be located in different sources and at different societal levels.

Assumptions About Practice

We believe that social justice influences all aspects of practice, including its under-lying values, purposes, methods, assumptions, and the theories that inform it. It is important to stress that in our view of practice, from work with individuals to efforts to create and implement policy change, practitioners interact with individ-uals, families, groups, organizations, communities, and even larger entities. Pincus and Minahan (1973) refer to these entities as "action systems" whose relevance to practice depends on the purpose and goals of a service. For example, practitioners may interact with individuals for many different reasons, such as to help them with personal problems or with their roles in an organization or community or to enhance their influence by virtue of their position of authority (e.g., mayor or legis-lator or as a so-called *collateral* such as a parent or teacher). Similarly, a practitioner might interact with a group whose members have joined to help solve individual problems, with a community group to change some aspect of their community, or with a group that comprises a legislative committee. Finally, a practitioner might approach an organization to obtain a change in policy affecting an individual client or as an employee of that organization to create a more just organizational culture and climate.

Finn and Jacobson (2008) begin their discussion of what they call "just prac-tice" with a consideration of theories of practice that are informed by "critical social and cultural theory":

> The term "practice" in contemporary social theory does not have the same meaning as practice in the traditional social work sense of a series of planned interventions. Rather practice refers more broadly to social action carried out in the context of unequal power relations. Also a post-modern and critical social work practice is primarily concerned with prac-ticing in ways which further a society without domination, exploitation, and oppression. It should focus on how structures dominate and also how people construct and are constructed by changing social structures and relations, recognizing that there may be multiple and diverse construc-tions of ostensibly similar situations. Such an understanding of social relations and structures can be used to disrupt dominant understandings and structures, and as a basis for changing these so that they are more inclusive of different interest groups. (p. 8)

Thus, it should be clear that we do not view social justice as an "add on" to practice but as the underlying ethical, moral, and philosophical basis for everything we do as social workers. We believe that practice that concerns itself with the struggles of people to deal with the issues in their lives, in whatever setting, must seriously incorporate attention to people's history and social contexts. This is true whether the issues relate to the interpersonal relationships in their families, the ways they seek to use groups to effect changes in their communities and organizations, or the manner in which their communities and organizations strive to create and implement policy changes. Thus, we assert that work at any level of the social order (individual, dyadic, family, organization, community, and society) must be informed by what is transpiring at other levels—especially as these developments relate to issues of justice and injustice. In summary, socially just practice is not merely "good practice"; it is practice informed by critical analysis of the role of power, social conditions, and people's multiple social identities and relationships.

Even Actions Taken with Good Intentions Can Have Unjust Consequences

Practitioners should consider that even actions with the best intentions may produce unjust consequences. The following are examples of this unintended, but not uncommon, phenomenon:

- A practitioner sought to help a man reduce his employment-related stress by engaging in an exercise program after work. This overlooked the fact that the man's wife then had no help preparing supper or getting the children ready for bed. When the practitioner and the man realized this, the man decided to use his lunch hour to exercise instead.
- A member of a group was experiencing a crisis and spent the entire group meeting seeking help to resolve it. Several other members also needed time to help them work on serious problems. This was discussed at the end of the meeting, and the group members resolved to hold a longer session the next time and to consider whether, in the future, they will devote an entire session to one member.
- A consultant to an agency met with the director to consider how to resolve a budgetary crisis in the organization. She thought she would reduce the hours of staff and cut the staff's wages. The consultant suggested that she appoint a committee, chosen by the staff, to consider ways of solving the budget issues in order to democratize the decision-making process and increase the likelihood of staff "buy-in" to the outcome.
- A legislative committee was planning to recommend to the full legislature that a greater portion of the budget be devoted to programs for the elderly. Several social workers testifying before the committee were concerned that

this would so consume finite fiscal resources that recommended programs for children would not be enacted. The committee decided to recommend that the tax structure be amended so that both categories of programs would be enacted.

Everything Needed to Maintain a Society Has the Potential to Create Injustice

The creation of a more just society often entails institutional change. These institutions may be located in the educational system; the criminal justice system; the legislative, judicial, and executive systems; and in financial regulatory bodies. They also establish rules for conducting democratic elections, provide public means to support the arts, and protect religious institutions from interference. Each of the institutions created for these purposes may create injustices that must be rectified. The following are examples of this phenomenon:

- In efforts to democratize education, the educational system may create tracking systems that are unfair to certain groups or individuals who, by virtue of social conditions, are streamed into curricula that do not correspond to their aspirations or prior preparation.
- The criminal justice system may punish people based on discriminatory assumptions about which drug offenders should be incarcerated, that certain categories of people are more likely to use illicit substances, or that using certain substances is more dangerous.
- Traditions and cultural norms often maintain executive systems that may unfairly give priorities to White men to the exclusion of women and people of color.

Social Justice and Human Rights

A commitment to the pursuit and attainment of human rights is often contrasted to or considered complementary to the commitment to social justice; however, there are important distinctions.[3] One is that the emphasis on human rights can fail to address structural issues that maintain injustice or impede the pursuit of social justice. As we discuss throughout this book, these issues reflect how societal institutions maintain injustices through the mechanisms employed to distribute resources, power, status,

---

3. For a comprehensive discussion of the origins, definitions, and controversies regarding the concept of human rights, see Reisch, Ife, and Weil (2012).

and opportunities. Recently, changes in the global market system and the political institutions that maintain it have exacerbated long-standing structural inequalities (Reisch, Ife, & Weil, 2012). The interpretation and fulfillment of human rights principles also differ among cultures. (This topic is discussed more extensively in Chapter 3.)

Reisch et al. (2012) describe three traditions that affect how human rights can be defined:

> *Natural* rights are located in our essential humanity, *legal* rights are located in jurisdictions [the various geographical entities and their laws and constitutions], and *constructed* rights are located in cultures and communities. There are elements of all three included in contemporary discussions of human rights. . . . However, a legal rights perspective often dominates the discourse of many practitioners. (p. 80)

Rights also are conceived of under several interconnected social categories— so-called "first-generation rights," or civil and political rights (e.g., the right to vote and to have one's voice heard in the body politic); "second-generation rights," or economic rights and social protections (e.g., to have an adequate income, a job for which one is qualified, and financial and other supports when in age-related retirement); and, more recently, "third-generation rights," or social and cultural rights (e.g., to be given respect, to have one's beliefs respected and protected, as well as one's rights of association with others). Another set of categories relate to whether rights are viewed as individual or collective or both. An individual right, for example, is the right of each person to receive an education commensurate with his or her abilities and interests. In certain circumstances, this may be also construed as a collective right, such as the right of people of color to receive an equal quality public education (Warren in *Brown v. Board of Education*, 1954). These three sets of rights are interconnected (Reisch et al., 2012):

> In the globalized market system of the 21st century, for example, the exercise of economic rights depends on the exercise of other rights— legal, political, and social—if they are to have any validity. The right to gainful employment, for example, has little meaning unless individuals have access to a just legal system which is capable of enforcing this right when it is denied. . . . Another problem with the broadly defined second generation of rights is that "social rights" include both rights which are truly social (i.e., based on the implementation of fairly constructed community norms), such as the right to choose a marriage partner and

the right to receive an education and basic requirements for physical existence—food, water, clothing, shelter, health care—which are more properly called survival rights. Two other categories of rights, which have recently been recognized, do not readily fit within the traditional "three generation" format. These are environmental rights—the right of people to the features of a sustainable and healthy environment . . . and spiritual rights. (p. 82)[4]

How Inequalities and Injustices Are Sustained and Re-created

Our primary view of this issue is that the forces that maintain society and its institutions have the potential to create and re-create both justice and injustices.[5] Of particular importance is what is referred to as the *structural features* of society. We define these features in three ways. The first is related to the physical environment—its features and organization. Second, we include how power and influence are organized and regulated. Third, structures include the composition of the population of a group, community, organization, or society.

Another way of understanding how structures may maintain injustice is by examining the operations of various systems, such as the economic system. Most Western societies are based on private ownership of the means by which commodities (goods and services) are produced and distributed. In its present form, this system has significant social and political consequences: It creates enormous wealth and extensive prerogatives to a small proportion of society and considerable deprivation and lack of power and influence for large numbers of people. Many laws maintain this status quo, as do other more subtle features of societal culture, such as the prioritization of competition over cooperation and the value placed on material success. In the past, but to a considerably lesser extent today, the effects of these institutional forces have been countered and somewhat ameliorated by the activities of labor unions and other activist groups. They promoted legislation that protects workers, prevents the spread of monopolies, and creates a social safety net through such social welfare programs as Social Security, unemployment insurance, and health insurance such as the 2010 Affordable Care Act.

---

4. For an extensive discussion of targeting the environment in social work practice, see the chapter by Garvin and Tropman on practice directed at the environment in their text *Social Work in Contemporary Society* (1998).

5. This topic was originally developed by the authors in work on an unfinished book with Mieko Yoshihama and Beth Glover Reed.

A second critical system is the legal system—the system of laws (legislation, judicial rulings, and administrative regulations) that govern most economic, social, cultural, and political activities in a society. At the national level, this also includes a nation's constitution. At the global level, this includes aspects of international law such as the law of the seas and laws governing the International Court of Justice in The Hague.

The third system is the governance structure, namely who has the right to create and implement new laws/rules and to oversee this implementation. At the national level, this includes all who have authority to promulgate and administer these laws/rules, such as the legislature, judiciary, and the executive. At the group level, this would include the "leader" of the group, although a group governed by democratic principles will have this lodged in the group members as a collectivity.

The last system is composed of the structures and procedures that maintain and govern relationships between various social entities. At the national level, for example, this will include the principle of "due process," in which one entity cannot deprive another of his or her rights without following certain legal procedures. At the family level, this would include any processes that are established, usually by the parents but sometimes by an even older generation, as to how parents and children (and their siblings) are to treat one another. At a group level, this will include rules regarding how members are to interact (e.g., do not interrupt when another is speaking and do not monopolize the conversation). In some therapy groups, there may be a rule that members should not intentionally seek one another out when the session is over and that professional facilitators should not develop intimate relationships with members and should be aware of any feelings they have toward members.

All of these systems and the creations they produce may create injustices or be used to strive for greater justice. For example, at both the national level and the international level, the economic system has produced widening gaps in income and wealth, particularly during the past several decades. This inequality also provides a small segment of society with enormous power to influence elections and the actions of elected officials. A related factor that maintains injustice is the nature of the current global political and economic order. One phenomenon that advantages one nation and disadvantages others is the transfer of industry to poorer nations with low-cost labor. Although workers in developing nations suffer (as do those workers in more affluent nations who are unemployed by this transfer), the owners of industry benefit by the lower costs of production, as Piketty (2014) describes in a comprehensive analysis of the origins of economic inequality and the forces that maintain it.

At a group or organizational level, wealthy members may use their wealth to reward other members for their compliance with their desires, even if it is to the disadvantage of the rest of the group or organization. In the family, if the parents possess all the "wealth" and use it to bribe the children to do things against their best interests, this can create unjust consequences.

As just illustrated, these structures exist at each level of society—in macro systems (nations, states, and cities), mezzo systems (communities, organizations, and sometimes groups), and micro systems (families and individuals). These conditions are maintained by many cultural norms and beliefs—for example, about the relationship between effort and success and the relative merits of people of different races, ethnicities, genders, class, or sexual orientations. Often, individuals and groups internalize these norms and beliefs, and they inadvertently collude in the maintenance of unjust structures, processes, and symbols.

Contesting and resisting these unjust systems are integral aspects of socially just practice. This resistance can be a powerful force for change because it can destabilize the status quo and challenge our meanings and day-to-day interactions. However, when misused, resistance can also become a powerful form of oppression if it leads to violence and attempts to replace one form of dominance with another.

An Intersectional Perspective

This perspective acknowledges the complex and interactive roles that race, gender, sexuality, ethnicity, nation, religion, ability status, gender expression, and age play in shaping people's lives and experiences. Thus, this perspective informs many of the discussions in this book. As the Council on Social Work Education's *Educational Policy and Accreditation Standards* (2008, 2015) states in Educational Policy 2.1.4 "Engage Diversity and Difference in Practice,"

> Social workers understand how diversity characterizes and shapes the human experience and is critical to the formation of identity. The dimensions of diversity are understood as the intersectionality of multiple factors including age, class, color, culture, disability, ethnicity, gender, gender identity and expression, immigration status, political ideology, race, religion, sex, and sexual orientation. Social workers appreciate that as a consequence of difference, a person's life experience may include oppression, poverty, marginalization, and alienation as well as privilege, power, and acclaim. [In addition], social workers recognize the extent to which a culture's structure and values may oppress, marginalize, alienate, or create or enhance privilege and power; gain sufficient self-awareness to eliminate the influence of personal biases and values in working with diverse groups; recognize and communicate their understanding of the importance of

difference in shaping life experiences; and view themselves as learners and engage those with whom they work as informants (pp. 4–5).

There have been criticisms, however, of the use of the concept of intersectionality. Alexander-Floyd (2012), for example, expressed concern about how the concept is used with reference to women of color. A number of other authors support her position, including Berger and Guidroz (2009), Hull, Bell-Scott, and Smith (1982), Crenshaw (1990–1991), and Hancock (2007).

Their criticism centers on how the concept has been used in some research and produced a view of people as fragmented and, therefore, as subject to internal conflicts and other "pathologies" rather than as "whole" individuals who are subject to a variety of social and cultural forces. According to Alexander-Floyd (2012), "A postmodernist approach problematizes identity by suggesting that we all . . . have ruptured identities and fragmented bodies" (p. 2). She also expresses concern about the "flattening of intersectionality"—that is, a failure to recognize the structural sources of inequality (p. 70)—and concludes that "intersectionality is a broad project, focused on *social justice* theorizing and action and has a long and complex history" (p. 5).

It is significant that Crenshaw (1990–1991) begins her analysis of demarginalizing the intersection of race and sex by discussing the Black feminist text *All the Women Are White, All the Blacks Are Men, But Some of Us Are Brave* (Combahee River Collective, 1982). This title "captures the perennial failure of mainstream feminist and antiracist politics to reflect the experience of racism *and* sexism that befalls black women" (Crenshaw, 1990–1991, p. 6). Crenshaw defines three forms of intersectionality: structural, political, and representational. The first refers to the various social structures that in complex ways contribute to injustice. Political intersectionality is reflected in the ways social movements adopt a single focus, whereas representational intersectionality relates to the ways cultural expressions can be oppressive. Crenshaw states, "The objectification and hypersexualization of black women in music, television, and other cultural outlets are commonplace" (p. 8).

In this book, we have occasion to utilize the concept of intersectionality, while attempting to be responsive to these criticisms. If we or others use it in a way that negates the lived experience of people experiencing oppression, we urge the reader to join us in the effort to challenge this and to call us to account when we fail to heed the writings of the scholars and activists whom we have cited previously.

Praxis

Throughout this book, we emphasize the importance of praxis—the dialectical relationship between reflection and action. We encourage readers to examine and validate all of the material in the book through their experience with the "real" world and modify it in an essentially endless cycle.

The rest of the book's chapters expand on and further develop much of this introductory material. Chapters 2 and 3 discuss the historical evolution of theories and concepts of social justice in various societies and cultures; the major ideological, political–economic, and cultural influences on their development; and contemporary critical perspectives on the concept. Particular emphasis is placed on the relationship of these perspectives to the development of social welfare and social work and to the institutions and practices that emanate from a society's efforts to achieve and sustain social justice goals, however they are defined.

The following six chapters examine the many dimensions of socially just practice. The final chapter in Part I, Chapter 4, discusses the theories and concepts that underlie socially just practice in greater detail. The chapters in Part II focus on social justice practice with individuals and families, groups, organizations, communities, and in the areas of policy development and advocacy. We emphasize in these chapters that they are efforts to portray practice when the practitioner is involved with each of these system levels. We attempt to integrate a contextual perspective that views social workers as always cognizant of the impact of each level and the need, at times, to act on any level of practice depending on the goals, purposes, and needs of the practice situation.

The final chapter, while also in a sense a practice chapter, focuses on engagement in socially just research and evaluation. We believe in an empirical base for practice, but we discuss in depth in this chapter how the concept of "empirical" does not imply a narrow positivist perspective but, rather, incorporates through diverse research methods, qualitative and quantitative, the lived experience of people and their narratives.

2

Alternative Concepts of Justice

Introduction

One of the shortcomings of most books on social justice and social work published in the United States is the absence of alternative definitions of social justice that are derived from other cultures. As US society becomes increasingly multicultural, however, inattention to these perspectives compels many oppressed and marginalized populations to adopt mainstream concepts of social justice that are often at odds with their own. It also limits the ability of social workers from the dominant culture to understand the needs and aspirations of their diverse clients and constituents.

This chapter presents some alternative views of social justice, historical and contemporary, and compares and contrasts them with each other and with Western ideas. A theme of this chapter is that different concepts of social justice emerged within different cultures and within different eras for specific purposes. These concepts shaped the strategies developed to achieve social justice and the institutions and policies that emerged from various social justice struggles.

The chapter begins with a discussion of the evolution of religious and secular ideas about social justice in the West. It then provides a selective overview of the evolution of this concept in nations and cultures throughout the world. This global focus is important to include because most contemporary discussions of justice, particularly in the literature of US social work, rest on the following erroneous assumptions: (1) that justice is primarily a Western concept; (2) that the concept emerged only in modern times; (3) that the definition of justice is static; (4) that contemporary views of justice all share the same origins, goals, values, and ideological perspectives; and (5) that whatever societal differences exist regarding the meaning of justice can easily be reconciled in practice through the use of a common framework. Understanding the problems generated by these assumptions is a critical step in developing socially just practices.

Today, in an increasingly interdependent world, the concept of justice requires a more complex and nuanced understanding than is implied—with considerable ambiguity—in the National Association of Social Workers' (NASW) *Code of Ethics* (2015) and the *Educational Policy and Accreditation Statement* of the Council on Social Work Education (2008, 2015). These complexities produce new, previously unacknowledged challenges and require a re-examination of our commitment to justice and how we translate that commitment into practice. The inclusion of multiple perspectives on social justice in this book, therefore, is intended to de-center this important discussion away from Western perspectives and to emphasize the importance of context, culture, and history in the development and implementation of ideas about justice.

Ironically, ideas about justice have been used both to promote greater equality and to sustain or rationalize existing inequalities (Gil, 1998). This suggests that a more nuanced understanding of the multiple meanings and applications of justice is required to grasp the complexities of the 21st-century world. For example, one recent issue is whether social justice and universal human rights are compatible goals. This topic is discussed in Chapter 3.

Twenty-first century concepts of social justice are characterized by significant regional and ideological differences, within and among nations, that have made it difficult to translate the ideals of social justice into policies, programs, and practices within either public or private institutions. This chapter summarizes various contemporary critiques of Western ideas of social justice and discusses attempts to resolve ongoing and newly emerging issues.

To introduce the historical portion of the chapter, we present a 10-part framework of justice derived from a variety of secular and religious sources. The diverse historical examples that follow focus on the relationship between the emergence of concepts of justice and their environmental contexts. The key lesson for practitioners is the importance of contextualizing the meaning and application of social justice in order to move beyond rhetorical appeals to normative concepts to the creation and implementation of justice-oriented practice principles.

The presentation of these historical and contemporary illustrations is intended neither to demonstrate the inevitability of "progress" in the development of concepts about justice nor to argue that certain concepts of justice are superior to others. Rather, it is intended to encourage the reader to apply a critical lens to the examination of current ideas about social justice and their applications to practice. These various theoretical approaches include conscientization, empowerment-oriented and strengths-based practice, structural and critical social work, anti-oppressive practice, and the emerging global movement for sustainable development (Dominelli, 2010, 2012; Freire, 1970; Lavalette, 2011; Mullaly, 2010; Saleeby, 2002; Solomon, 1976). Doing justice today requires a synthesis of such alternative theories and practice methods.

A Social Justice Framework

Constructing a typology of social justice that synthesizes a multitude of different perspectives presents a major challenge because of the enormous amount of relevant material and the difficulty in deciphering the meaning of the material due to linguistic and cultural barriers. Nevertheless, we believe that the construction of such a typology is useful for several reasons. First, it provides some basis for making cross-cultural and cross-national comparisons. Second, it enables us to determine how societies evolved historically and how this evolution shaped their ideas about social justice. Finally, it helps us develop a framework for justice-oriented theory and practice in today's multicultural and multipolar world.

One assumption underlying this chapter is that all societies articulate a conception of justice in some form. That is, their cultures explain or rationalize prevailing patterns of resource and power distribution, existing institutional and status arrangements, interpersonal relationships, and desired social goals. Often, the concept of social justice is implied through the dominant (or hegemonic) culture both directly and indirectly. Direct expressions of a society's concept of social justice are found in its formal theological or ideological tracts, written laws or policies, and official pronouncements by religious or secular leaders. Indirect expressions can be found in a wide range of cultural artifacts (e.g., music, literature, and art), language or vocabulary, customs, rituals, and social mores. Sometimes a society's ideas about social justice can be inferred from the priorities it establishes and from the range of issues that are given lesser attention or are ignored entirely (Finn & Jacobson, 2008; Pelton, 2005).

Although concepts of social justice are both historically and contextually specific, there are several broad generalizations that can be made about how they emerge. Explicit calls for social justice tend to appear under one or more of the following circumstances: (1) When an influential segment of the population becomes increasingly dissatisfied about how prevailing concepts of social justice—under whatever label—are being applied in practice or when a gap appears to exist between a society's rhetoric about social justice and its social reality; (2) when changes in the environment, sometimes due to external forces or threats, lead to challenges about the validity or efficacy of long-standing ideas about social justice; (3) when the interplay of social and cultural forces produced by a society's ideas about social justice leads to the formulation of a new definition of social justice reflected in the appearance of an alternative ideology; and (4) when societal conditions become so oppressive that in order to survive, people seek fundamental changes in existing structural arrangements.

Although concepts of social justice have both universal and culturally specific components, they can be classified along a continuum. On one end of the continuum are views of social justice that focus primarily on the individual and individual liberation. As we will see, these views emphasize personal freedom and the establishment or preservation of civil liberties, such as freedom of speech and religion (Lorenz, 2014; Stoesz, 2014). At the other end of the continuum are concepts that emphasize social justice for all humankind and, in some cases, for all living creatures (Nussbaum, 2006). In between these poles are group-specific conceptions of social justice that focus on the goal of equal justice but apply the principle exclusively to members of a particular community (e.g., Athenian *citizens* in Aristotle's *Politics*, Israelites in the Old Testament, and contemporary followers of fundamentalist Christianity or Islam). A common element in each conception of social justice, however, is a connection between ideas about social justice, cultural beliefs regarding the nature and desirability of change, and a society's views about the relevance of its past for understanding and influencing current realities.

We selected the components of social justice shown in Box 2.1 because they can be applied at both macro and micro levels in social work practice today. The components are framed as questions in a manner that reduces but does not eliminate the potential for cultural bias in the formulation of the "question" itself. As much as possible, we tried to organize these components without assuming the superiority of any underlying concepts or precepts.

A final note on terminology is in order here. Although NASW's *Code of Ethics* (2015) creates an imperative to work for *social* justice, in this book we use the more generic term *justice* and the term *social justice* interchangeably for several reasons. First, the literature on the topic, particularly the historical literature, often does not distinguish between these terms. Second, various cultures incorporate other aspects of justice (e.g., retributive or restorative justice) into their concepts of social justice. Finally, a 21st-century view of social justice needs to integrate components of justice, such as socially just *processes*, that are not traditionally found in narrower definitions of social justice, which often focus solely on its redistributive goals.

The Evolution of Social Justice

This section presents concise descriptions of a broad range of social justice movements and ideas. Although the focus is on the diversity of concepts and their applications, the following generalizations can be made. Think about their implications for practice today:

- Views of social justice often reflect a synthesis of religious and secular ideas and are often a hybrid of indigenous concepts and those imposed by conquerors or colonists.

BOX 2.1

A Social Justice Framework

A. Origins of Social Justice Concepts
   1. What are the ideological and political sources of the society's social justice concepts?
   2. What are the purposes for articulating a concept of social justice?
   3. How do social justice concepts evolve differently in different societies?
B. Comparative Components of Social Justice
   4. How do different societies define social justice, injustice, and a socially just society? How do a society's language, symbols, and cultural artifacts reflect its conception of social justice?
   5. How does a society view the relationship between social justice and rights? Are these rights defined as civil/political, sociocultural, or economic? In what ways are these rights interrelated?
C. Strategies for Creating Change Toward Social Justice Goals
   6. What approaches to creating change are used and preferred (e.g., incremental or revolutionary, violent/nonviolent, and legal/extralegal)?
   7. What are the ideological or practical rationales for such choices?
   8. How do historical circumstances affect the development of change strategies?
D. The Application of Justice
   9. How are a society's social justice concepts *expressed and implemented* through laws, values, customs, institutions, morés, traditions, and social processes? Who has responsibility for their creation, enforcement, and monitoring?
   10. Who are the intended "beneficiaries" of social justice in a society? Is social justice defined in individual or group terms? What prerequisites and obligations are required to be treated justly? How do societies resolve or rationalize conflicts of social justice?

- Social justice concepts are used both to transform existing societal structures, social relationships, and institutions and to rationalize the status quo.
- The historical context, particularly the political–economic and social structures of a society, plays a significant role in the evolution of concepts of justice.

- Social justice concepts reflect both "top-down" and "bottom-up" ideas.
- Social justice concepts range in their focus from individual well-being to universal human rights and from anthropocentric perspectives to those applied to all creatures.
- Concepts of social justice are closely linked to a society's ideas about equality, freedom, authority, and power, which are defined and emphasized differently by different cultures.
- Ideas about social justice are expressed explicitly in laws and reflected symbolically in the various cultural artifacts of every society, sometimes in ways that individuals from other cultures cannot see or fully understand. Recognition of these differences is an important component in the development of socially just practices today.

Religious Ideas of Social Justice

Ideas about social justice have emerged from both religious and secular sources. Each of these interpretations of justice has attempted to explain, justify, or critique prevailing social conditions or to provide an ethical basis for people to behave and organize their lives. Because religious perspectives on social justice appeared earlier and continue to have a powerful influence on contemporary societies, we first discuss some of the major religious ideas about justice.

For millennia, religious values, institutions, and practices have been employed to promote the goal of social justice and to maintain or rationalize injustice and oppression. Although there is some merit to the Marxist assertion that *organized* religion has redirected people's attention away from earthly concerns by deferring socially just outcomes to the afterlife, there is also evidence that many individuals and groups involved in social justice work have been motivated by their religious or spiritual beliefs (Daloz, 2004; Reisch, 2002). Most religions provide guidelines to lead an ethical life that emphasize just conduct toward others; their texts focus on the interconnectedness of people and encourage empathy and compassion for others.

Modern activists such as Mohandas Gandhi, Martin Luther King, Jr., Malcolm X, Cesar Chaves, and Bishop Desmond Tutu were not the first individuals to link religion to social action. Religious leaders as diverse as Moses, Jesus, Muhammed, and Confucius stressed the importance of action in effecting social change (Huddleston, 1989). Therefore, religion has long been connected to the attainment of justice through social and political struggle.

Religions have also frequently emphasized the goals of universal freedom and the creation of a world in which all creatures live in peace, harmony, and mutual respect. Given contemporary religious conflicts, it is particularly ironic that Judaism, Islam, Hinduism, and Buddhism share similar perspectives in this regard, as illustrated by the following quotations:

> They shall beat their swords into plowshares, and their spears into pruning hooks: Nation shall not lift up sword against nation, neither shall they learn war any more. (Isaiah, 2:4)

> The worshippers of the All-Merciful are they who tread gently upon the Earth, and when the ignorant address them, they reply, "Peace!" (Qur'an 25:63)

Many religions also predict the advent of a "golden age" in which justice, peace, and prosperity will prevail. These visions reflect remarkably similar ideals of individual and social justice, and they frequently link the achievement of justice with peace (see Paul's "Letter to Corinthians" in the New Testament). Such ideas guided Gandhi's activism and influenced such famous orations as Abraham Lincoln's second inaugural address and Martin Luther King Jr.'s "I Have a Dream" speech. Major religions—Christianity, Islam, and Confucianism—emerged, in part, in response to widespread violence and anarchy in their environments (Huddleston, 1989).

No religion, however, is inherently committed to social justice. Like secular ideologies and institutions, religious beliefs and the institutions created to promote, sustain, and defend them emerged from specific historical and cultural contexts. Therefore, organized religions have always been highly politicized. That is, they have been and continue to be used both by elites to maintain the status quo, reflecting "a cursory interest in social justice" (Thakur, 1996, p. 45) and a static view of the social order, and by activists to promote radical social change.

One reason for this contradiction is that many modern notions of justice emphasize both social rights and individual autonomy. Based largely on secular and humanist frameworks, they assume that people can correct "wrongs" through their own actions. By contrast, many religions, particularly fundamentalist religions, believe that the world can be changed only through some form of divine intervention in which human agency is reduced to doing God's work (Thakur, 1996). Consequently, adherents of such faiths are far more likely to resist participation in human-inspired justice movements, unless they are designed to *restore* a divinely inspired order. The 1979 Iranian revolution is an example of the latter.

Because there are a vast number of religions in the world, it is impossible to cover their views of justice adequately in a single chapter. Instead, this chapter focuses on some of the major religions of the modern world—Buddhism, Christianity, Confucianism, Hinduism, Islam, Judaism, and Zoroastrianism—and includes some content on indigenous religious traditions as well. Despite their differences, common themes of nearly all religions include the *centrality of righteousness or fairness* (often expressed through different forms of retributive justice); the role of *mutuality or interdependence*; the importance of *adherence to laws, rules, or customs*; and *loyalty* to the tribe, group, or community. The ancient concept of mutuality has influenced thinkers and activists as diverse as Russian anarchists Peter Kropotkin (1902) and Mikhail Bakunin and 20th-century proponents of communitarian ideas. It also underlies the self-help efforts of diverse US communities to create social services that address their particular needs.

To achieve these ends, religions prescribe optimal ways of living and emphasize the importance of right or just actions. For example, Hinduism writes of *karma*, Buddhism stresses the principle of doing no harm, Judeo-Christian texts focus on the difference between good and evil, and the Qur'an prescribes rules to live a proper and moral life. Two major teachings of Hinduism are to seek the truth and lead a harmless life (Thakur, 1996), whereas the Buddhist principle of right livelihood emphasizes the importance of doing no harm—a concept that is reflected in the first axiom of modern Western medicine's Hippocratic Oath.

A focus on prescriptive ways of doing justice, however, was not always present in religious thought. Ancient religions, such as those practiced among the Greeks and the indigenous peoples of the Americas, were less prescriptive. Through the use of oft-repeated myths, they relied more on symbolic narratives that primarily sought to explain phenomena rather than offer guidance on proper living (Connelly, 2014). Although many of their underlying beliefs about the nature of justice remain constant, the narratives used to explain natural phenomena, such as creation myths, express views of morality and, by implication, justice that are often considerably different from those of today (Campbell, 1991).

Among ancient Greeks, for example, it was customary to invite visitors into one's home without asking questions, in case a stranger was a god in disguise. A similar practice toward strangers prevails among Arab peoples. The gods, however, rarely served as teachers of morality or righteousness. In fact, many ancient mythologies depict the gods as being capable of human emotions such as greed, envy, fear, anger, and lust. Thus, while the gods possessed great power, they were also capable of mistakes and immoral actions.

Biblical Conceptions of Justice

Maguire (2014) asserts that expressions of prophetic justice in the Bible symbolized recognition of the importance of establishing social justice principles in societies that were increasingly stratified on the basis of status, power, class, and wealth. Biblical ideas of justice, therefore, focused more on social and distributive justice than on commutative justice—principles that were also embodied in

Islam. Maguire asserts that all religions prioritize social justice in some form; it embodies the strongest moral challenge to human selfishness.

For example, among contemporary religions, what is considered "right" or "just" is expressed in different ways. The Hebrew Torah employs many terms to connote justice—most frequently, *tzedek* or *tzaddakah* (righteousness; or what is true, right, fitting), *mishpat* (judgment), and *ken* (firmness). What binds these nuanced terms is the concept of fairness, which is frequently used in the Old Testament and among rabbinic commentators as the central theme of tales of judgment, punishment, or retribution. In some cases, justice can condone violence, whether by God or man, as recounted in the story of the Hebrews' exodus from Egypt. Of greater significance for this book, it also provides the foundation for Jewish notions of charity and social welfare. As the medieval philosopher Maimonides (1949) wrote, giving charity simply meant meeting the requirement to be righteous or "do justice."

Perhaps the most striking discussion of early Jewish concepts of justice occurs in the book of Genesis when in a most unusual conversation God discusses with Abraham His decision to destroy the cities of Sodom and Gomorrah because of their wickedness.[1] Abraham goes so far as to challenge the divine idea of justice itself:

Will You sweep away the righteous along with the wicked? What if there should be fifty innocent within the city; Will You wipe out the place and not forgive for the sake of the innocent fifty who are in it? Far be it from You to do such a thing, to bring death upon the innocent as well as the guilty, so that the innocent and guilty fare alike.

Then, in the most provocative statement of all, Abraham asks, "Shall not the Judge of all Earth deal justly?" (Genesis 18:23–25). Amazingly, God relents and promises that if Abraham can find even 10 innocents in the city, He will spare it.

This exchange between God and Abraham is one of the earliest reflections in religious thought of the idea of justice. First, it begins to define what is fair or just. In this instance, it expresses the view that persons be judged solely by their conduct and not by their associations. This implies both individuation and personal responsibility. Second, it asserts that God and, by implication, the creatures (i.e., humans), institutions, or laws created in His name or based on His teachings are or should strive to be just. These themes reverberate to the present in religious and secular expressions of justice as both an end and a means to that end.

---

1. This is unusual not only for the ideas about justice it conveys but also because in his defense of the people of these cities, Abraham argues with God nearly as an equal. The implications of his questioning attitude reverberate throughout the history of the Jewish faith and permeate all aspects of Jewish culture to this day.

To ensure the attainment of justice, both Judaism and Christianity imply a contract between God and humankind. In Judaism, the contract is explicit—the covenant between God and Abraham (Genesis 15:18) or between God and Noah (Genesis 9:8-17). The bases of this covenant are amplified in the Ten Commandments and the other laws inscribed in the Torah. These commandments articulate clearly the precepts of a moral daily life, including proper reverence to God and proper behavior toward others.[2]

The emphasis on the latter is particularly striking, even in the language of the Ten Commandments. Whereas the first four commandments stress the importance of honoring God (Exodus 20:2–11), the last six establish basic behavioral standards for a community (Exodus 20:12–17). The authors of the Talmud, the rabbinical commentary on the Torah, asserted that "justice must override all other considerations, even those of mercy" (Telushkin, 1994, p. 398).

The New Testament expanded upon these principles, particularly in the Gospel of Matthew and in Paul's letters, in which justice is often equated with righteousness (Matthew 3:25; Phil. 4:8; 2 Cor 5:14). They are also nearly identical to the ethical guidelines outlined centuries later in the Qur'an. In a similar but less explicit manner, Buddhism expresses an eightfold path to achieve *nirvana*: right view, right thought, right effort, right mindfulness, right concentration, right speech, right action, and right livelihood (Conze, 1964).

It is important to note that although these rules were implemented within theocratic societies, a distinction was made from the outset between obligations to God and obligations to the state or community. Jesus's teaching to "render unto Caesar the things which are Caesar's and unto God the things that are God's" (Matthew 20:21) was later codified into Christian doctrine through Augustine's work, *City of God* (2005). Such distinctions, which appear throughout the Old and New Testaments, and later in the Qur'an, reflect both explicit and implicit conflicts between religious and secular ideas about justice. Prophets and teachers, from Samuel and Jeremiah to Jesus and Muhammed, presented unprecedented challenges to the prevailing political and social order and claimed that their revised moral codes were distinct from, superior to, and took priority over those of kings or the state (Huddleston, 1989).

The later Old Testament prophets and Jesus and the apostles were, in many ways, the ancestors of contemporary activists. Their criticism of kings, religious authorities, and courts addressed the failure of elites to adhere to a higher moral

---

2. The idea of a contract—whether between God and humankind, among humans, or between persons and the state or community—has been a central feature of Western religious and secular thought for more than three millennia. In the Old Testament, Hebrews sacrificed some personal freedoms (e.g., acts that are denounced by God, such as idol worship) in order to gain God's love and protection. A similar emphasis on contract occurs in modern society.

code and their abandonment of their obligations to the people and, by implication, to God (Isaiah 32:1; Jeremiah 23:5). Ordinary persons were required to treat their neighbors as covenant partners, neither oppressing nor being oppressed (Amos 5:6–7, 21–24). In effect, these prophets and preachers argued that there were two components of justice: those established by earthly laws and those established at a higher spiritual level (Thakur, 1996). It was insufficient, therefore, for people (or kings) to obey earthly laws; justice required transcending such laws and acquiring a more nuanced understanding of right and wrong. Two millennia later, these ideas were expressed in secular terms, such as Rousseau's notion of the "general will" and the language of the Declaration of Independence (Smith, 1997). Ironically, during the past three centuries, these Western ideas about justice have rationalized both egalitarian movements and totalitarian regimes (Talmon, 1970).

Justice and Forgiveness

Woven throughout these religious texts, particularly in the latter books of the Old Testament and the New Testament, is another aspect of justice: the relationship of justice to forgiveness (Matthew 5:43–46; Romans 12:9–13, 14; 1 Corinthians 6:7). This is most clearly illustrated in the contrast between the dictum "an eye for an eye, a tooth for a tooth" (principles expressed both in the Old Testament and in the Babylonian Code of Hammurabi) and the following statement by Jesus in the New Testament: "If anyone strikes you on the right cheek, turn to him the other also" (Matthew 5:39).[3] In the Sermon on the Mount, as related in the Gospel according to Matthew, Jesus proposes substituting the idea of loving one's neighbor and hating one's enemy with the proposition "love your enemies and pray for your persecutors, so that you may show yourselves true sons of your Father in heaven" (Matthew 5:43–45).

Seven centuries later, the Qur'an similarly beseeches Muslims to be kind and forgiving to others: "The recompense for an injury is an injury equal thereto (in degree): But if a person forgives and makes reconciliation, his reward is due from Allah for Allah loves not those who do wrong" (Qur'an 42:40). Confucianism also states that we must look to one another with love and understanding: "Virtue is to love men: Wisdom is to understand them" (as quoted in Huddleston, 1989, p. 29). It is important to note, however, that these views were expressed in societies that still defined justice largely in patriarchal and hierarchical terms (Boer & Okland, 2008).

---

3. These oft-quoted statements, however, have a more subtle and sophisticated interpretation. The former implies a limit to punishment rather than merely sanctioning vengeance. The latter reflects a strategic decision in a society torn with social conflict and in which the distribution of power is vastly unequal.

During this period, Greek ideas of justice evolved in a similar direction. One example of this development can be found in Aeschylus's (1956) remarkable *Oresteian* trilogy. Over the course of its three plays, the concept of justice evolves from the *requirement* of vengeance to the *necessity* of forgiveness. In the final play, *The Eumenides*, the chorus is persuaded by the goddess Athene to forswear vengeance for a more merciful approach to the resolution of differences:

> *Let civil war, insatiate of ill,*
> *Never in Athens rage;*
> *Let burning wrath, that murder must assuage,*
> *Never take arms to spill,*
> *In this my heritage,*
> *The blood of man till dust has drunk its fill.*
> *Let all together find*
> *Joy in each other;*
> *And each both love and hate with the same mind*
> *As his blood-brother;*
> *For this heals many hurts of humankind. (pp. 179–180)*

These new approaches to justice represented a radical change in social and cultural norms. They reflected a near universal transformation of the relationship between humans and divinely inspired ideas and an increasingly complex set of social and political relationships in the secular world. Consequently, the institutions that emerged from this new concept of justice went beyond the proscription or prescription of certain behaviors and the institutionalization of punishment for those who violated these rules. They also reflected an attempt to understand *why* people act as they do and to discover how to encourage their best instincts.

Justice and Equality

Perhaps the most revolutionary of all aspects of justice in both Old and New Testaments was the concept that all individuals were created equal. This idea evolved over the course of several millennia leading to the 20th-century Universal Declaration of Human Rights. When it first appeared, the idea of social justice was applied solely to a single people with the goal of addressing the consequences of entrenched inequalities, particularly inequalities of birth. Social justice, however, was not to be applied to outsiders; it focused primarily on issues of economic redistribution among individuals within the same community. For example, in the Pentateuch (the first five books of the Old Testament), justice clearly does

not imply universal equality. Women play an important, if often underappreci-
ated, role in events, but Judaic laws and customs were highly patriarchal, as were
the traditions of almost all cultures in the region. Slavery was also condoned, if
regulated. The emergence of a priestly class and a monarchy reflected an increasingly stratified society dominated by clerical and aristocratic elites. Above all,
the concept of a special covenant between God and the Israelites implied that
justice meant justice for a particular community and not for all humankind
(Deuteronomy 7: 6–9).

By the latter books of the Old Testament, these ideas begin to be challenged.
When the prophet Elijah, for example, suggests that the God of the Israelites
(Yahweh) was the God for *all people*, he implied that all people—not just all
Israelites—were equal in the eyes of the Lord (1 Kings 19:1–18). Other prophets, such as Ezekiel, Amos, and Jeremiah, criticized the excesses of kings and
clergy and warned of catastrophe if the people did not correct their ways. These
radical teachers were the antecedents of Jesus and the apostles, whose teachings
stressed a universal message of equality and community to be achieved by a radical restructuring of the prevailing social order (Ezekiel 18:5, 9; 1 John 2:1, 29; 1
Peter 3:18).

Unity and equality are also prominent themes in the Qur'an, which—like
the redistributive principles expressed in both Old and New Testaments—
stresses the importance of reducing economic inequality as an aspect of justice.
The Qur'an declares that "wealth should not be allowed to circulate among the
rich only" (Qur'an 11:7). It also implies a prohibition against racial and ethnic
prejudice: "And among His signs are the creation of the Heavens and of the
Earth, and your variety of tongues and color. Herein truly are signs for all men"
(Qur'an 30:21). In fact, in his earliest work, Muhammed strived to include Jews
and Christians in his community. Not only did he acknowledge Moses and Jesus
as great teachers and prophets but he also gave each group the freedom to practice
its own religion and incorporated some of their traditions into his own teaching
(Huddleston, 1989). In most Islamic societies, this principle of religious tolerance
has persisted, despite periodic repression by fundamentalist groups.

Although Greek philosophers similarly emphasized the importance of
justice—Plato, for example, in *The Republic* (1974) equated justice with human
well-being and individual and societal harmony between reason, spirit, and
appetite—neither Plato nor Aristotle (1980) believed that justice implied universal equality. Because they believed people were fundamentally unequal, their
conception of justice required only that societal goods be distributed to each person based on his or her prescribed societal position in the existing hierarchical
social order. Their view of social justice, therefore, was designed to preserve the
Athenian status quo. It rationalized the coexistence of slavery with a democratic

community for the few (Campbell, 1989), an idea that had unfortunate echoes in the antebellum United States (Foner, 1998, 2015).

In ancient civilizations, despite the prevalence of goddess worship in many societies, one aspect of justice about which there was near universal agreement was the issue of gender inequality (Ruether, 2005). Some religions, however, took steps toward greater gender equality. Ancient Hindu texts note the "exalted position of women" and, like ancient Greek and Roman religions, include both gods and goddesses in their theology. Zoroastrianism implied full equality between men and women by stating that the Lord made no distinctions between the souls of men and those of women (Huddleston, 1989, p. 18). Anticipating the arguments of American secular proponents of social welfare policies 12 centuries later, the Qur'an states that women may need *more* protection through societal laws and customs than men. Although this statement reflects gender inequality and, perhaps, a patronizing attitude toward women, it arguably views that inequality as a step toward gender justice. This position was similar to that expressed by early 20th-century feminist social workers, who promoted a "maternalist" approach to social policy (Sklar, 1995). (See Chapter 3 for further discussion of this issue.)

This perspective on gender equality is also reflected in certain statements of Muhammed regarding equality for women in key areas such as property rights and the right to divorce (Badawi, 1995). Islamic principles require parents not only to support but also to show kindness and justice to their daughters. The Qur'an specifically states that justice is genderless in the application of punishment, financial matters, and the validity of testimony.

Despite the expression of justice principles in the Bhagavad Gita, Hinduism created an elaborate and rigidly defined caste system that still exists in India in some ways, particularly the persistent discrimination against the *Dalits* or so-called "untouchables." Buddhism, however, rejected this system of social stratification and substituted principles of unity, common humanity, and non-discrimination (Chew, 2004). Buddha argued that all people could achieve nirvana, regardless of wealth, rank, or privilege (Huddleston, 1989). He wrote that a good ruler "gives food to the poor" and ensures an equitable distribution of wealth in his kingdom. He advises that work conditions must be safe and just and that employers must respect their workers' rights to leisure and rest (Sigalaka Sutta, quoted in Walshe, 1995, as cited in Chew, 2004). For example, under King Asoka the Great (274–237 BC), who converted to Buddhism early in his reign, this emphasis on equality directly affected public policy. He created laws that reflected "the dignity of man, religious toleration and nonviolence" (Huddleston, 1989, p. 26). This legislation of religious toleration antedated similar Western efforts by nearly two millennia.

Justice and Freedom

Freedom has long been another important dimension of justice in both religious and secular writings. Often, it has been linked to the ideas of equality and tolerance of other faiths and cultures, or emancipation from slavery or oppression, particularly in the writings of prophets such as Isaiah, who implored the people to "let the oppressed go free and to break every yoke" (Isaiah 58:6). It was also linked in both Old and New Testaments with the goal of creating peace and promoting nonviolence (Isaiah 48:18, 60:17; Ephesians 2:14–17; 1 Corinthians).

Although biblical passages were used to rationalize the existence of slavery in the 18th- and 19th-century United States, the narrative of the persecution and liberation of the Hebrews in the Book of Exodus served as a powerful metaphor for enslaved African Americans during their decades-long freedom struggles. Activists incorporated the story into songs and folk tales, and it became an integral part of the African American freedom movement. It is also important to note that the concept of slavery in the Old Testament and throughout the ancient world was significantly different from the chattel slavery that existed in North America. Slaves possessed certain rights on which their masters could not infringe, and in Jubilee years, all slaves were required to be freed, debts and obligations to be forgiven, and land returned to its original owners. Slavery, therefore, while oppressive and reflective of social stratification, was not intended as a permanent condition. It implied an inferiority of *present status* rather than permanent inferiority of the person. For the first several centuries of its existence, Christianity, which preached a message of universal equality, was considered the religion of both common people and slaves.

Although the Qur'an did not abolish slavery, Muhammed's personal conduct indicates his opposition to slavery. He freed his own slaves and made public statements about the virtue of emancipation. He taught that slaves were equal to free men in Allah's eyes (Huddleston, 1989).

Because emancipation from oppression was a critical theme in many ancient religions, it is not surprising that justice was frequently equated with religious and cultural tolerance.[4] Particularly within powerful empires, the freedom to practice one's own faith was valued. The Persian Empire (~550–330 BC), for example, was noted for its tolerance of minority cultures within its borders, most famously its release of the Jewish people from their Babylonian captivity in the sixth-century BC and the subsequent assistance it provided in rebuilding the Jewish temple in Jerusalem (Huddleston, 1989).

---

4. In the 16th, 17th, and 18th centuries, this idea became the basis for many of the legal arguments, both secular and religious, on behalf of religious toleration—ideas that sought to end the religious wars that raged throughout Europe for decades.

During this period, Zoroastrianism was the most popular religion in the region. It emphasized the importance of kindness and good deeds, concern for others, and personal generosity (Huddleston, 1989). Six centuries later, early Christians prescribed tolerance by emphasizing the need to love all people because they are all children of God. This echoed the ideas of earlier Jewish prophets and was an important step toward the establishment of universal principles of justice (Leviticus 19:18; Galatians 5:13–14; 1 Corinthians 13:13–14).

Religious Justice and the Idea of Community

Nevertheless, many ancient and modern religions stress the special ties that exist among a community of believers and prescribe exclusive loyalty to community members. One of the oldest expressions of this concept was the idea of the children of Israel being "the chosen people." Most religions, however, have evolved to highlight the interdependence of all humankind and, in some form, convey respect for all peoples. The justifications for this interconnectedness vary, however. Buddhism, for example, is non-theistic and explains human interconnectedness by virtue of sharing a common natural or cosmic order (Chew, 2004). Similarly, Hindu concepts of justice—whether expressed as individual righteousness or duty to others—revolve around *dharma* or the preservation of cosmic and social order (Thakur, 1996). Religious beliefs also had significantly different effects on societies' views of justice. In part, this depended on whether they arose entirely from indigenous cultures, were imposed by conquerors, or emerged as a hybrid philosophy from the synthesis of indigenous beliefs and those spread by missionaries or the sword.

For example, Confucianism stressed the importance of caring for other individuals. This philosophy, known as "the Way of Jan" (humility/love), placed a strong emphasis on human interdependence. It stated "the truly virtuous man, desiring to be established himself, seeks to establish others; desiring success for himself, he strives to help others succeed" (as quoted in Huddleston, 1989, p. 29). Today, this idea is reflected in Chinese ideas about charity and the role that mutual aid associations in Chinese American communities—both Buddhist and Christian—have played since the 19th century (Lai, 2004; Lee, 2003).

On the other hand, contemporary Judaic, Christian, and Islamic writings tend to emphasize that we are all God's children. In modern secular discourse, these ideas evolved into the revolutionary notion of fraternity and laid the foundation for 20th-century beliefs in universal human rights (McWilliams, 1973; Wronka, 2008). Thus, although religious texts often prescribe punishments for individual sins and group culpability for wrongs, there is also a common principle that emphasizes "unconditional reverence for human life" (Pelton, 2005).

It is likely that this sense of connection to others and reverence for life produces the empathy, compassion, and sense of injustice that motivate many people who engage in social justice work today. Many activists often identify a religious justification for their work—one that focuses on common human origins, a shared environment, and, as US social worker Charlotte Towle (1945) termed them, "common human needs" (Daloz, 2004; Wallis, 2008).

As recent global events demonstrate, compassion alone is an insufficient incentive to motivate people to take action directed at social justice. In order to move beyond benevolent sentiment, people must also acknowledge a deeper connection to others based on mutual interdependence. This sentiment is captured in the following anecdote from Buddhism (cited in Epstein, 2007):

> A disciple once asked the Buddha, "Would it be true to say that a part of our training is for the development of love and compassion?" The Buddha replied, "No, it would not be true to say this. It would be true to say that the *whole* of our training is for the development of love and compassion." (p. 19)

In summary, universal concepts of justice first appeared between 1500 and 2500 years ago in the teachings of most of the world's great religions and in Western literature, such as the Greek tragedies of Sophocles and Aeschylus. During this period, monotheistic religions emerged, characterized by an all-powerful deity who enforced divine principles of justice to all humankind, either on Earth or in heaven. As these religions evolved, however, they acquired hierarchical institutional characteristics that were remarkably similar to the systems they replaced. At the same time, the development of state-sponsored official religions eroded the ideal of universal justice. It is not surprising that the re-emergence of social justice in the West only occurred after the ideals of religious tolerance, secular humanism, and rationalism took root during the 17th and 18th centuries (Gay, 1966; Israel, 2001).

Secular Views of Social Justice

Lorenz (2014) argues that the social upheavals produced by the industrial revolution and the political revolutions of the late 18th and 19th centuries inspired the development of modern Western concepts of social justice. This resulted from a synthesis of two different principles (Reisch, 2014a):

> The creation of laws and policies that affect the multiple dimensions of people's lives in a society and the construction and nurturance of the

social relationships required to properly care for the people that live within that society in a nondiscriminatory manner. (p. 10)

This synthesis, however, did not emerge overnight. The English philosopher Thomas Hobbes (1996), for example, argued that justice could only be assured by an all-powerful monarch, hardly a democratic conception of social justice. Unlike later revolutionaries, he regarded government not as the expression of the collective will of an instinctively just people but, rather, as a political necessity to control humans' antisocial, self-interested instincts—an idea that still resonates in the early 21st century.

By contrast, during the "age of revolution," political philosophers and activists such as Rousseau (1994) and their 19th-century successors constructed a series of meta-narratives that explained and attacked persistent injustices and proposed a revolutionary idea of justice. By explicitly and implicitly linking social justice to the interrelated principles of individual liberty (or freedom), political equality, and universal humanity (fraternity) in such documents as the American Declaration of Independence and the French Universal Declaration of the Rights of Man and Citizen, revolutionaries in North America and Europe revised and expanded Aristotle's notion of social justice by stating its goal was the "pursuit" or "the perfection of happiness" (Saint-Just, 1968). These ideas about social justice provided the intellectual basis for most modern Western institutions to the present, at least in theory (Roemer, 1996).

At the same time, conservative interpretations of social justice expressed alternative definitions of social justice itself as well as different perspectives on how it could (or should) be attained. According to Stoesz (2014), conservative ideas about social justice focused more on political and social stability than on social solidarity (Burke, 1790/2001). They also promoted individual liberty (freedom *from* coercion) and advocated for fewer government restrictions on the market economy. This concept of social justice was the basis of 19th- and early 20th-century European liberalism, which emphasized the primacy of individual liberty and free markets, a perspective quite different from mid- to late 20th-century US liberalism or contemporary neoliberalism (Berlin, 2002).

Western concepts of social justice, therefore, evolved both to inspire social and revolutionary transformation and to rationalize the preservation of existing societal arrangements, political institutions, and economic systems. During the past two centuries, ideas about social justice have ranged in their focus from an emphasis on individual freedom and the preservation of private property rights to the promulgation of universal human rights. They also varied considerably in defining to whom social justice applied. For the past 200 years, the conflict between these perspectives on social justice has inspired both reform movements and revolutions. These conflicts persist throughout the world today.

Probably the most prominent and influential secular critic of social injustice during the past two centuries was Karl Marx. He asserted that injustice was the inevitable consequence of economic and political systems based on subjugation, discrimination, exploitation, and privilege (Berlin, 1996). A truly just society would emerge, he argued, when its goods were distributed, in Marx's famous phrase, "from each according to his abilities to each according to his need" rather than by inherited social status (Marx, 1964). Marx's ideas continue to be influential today, particularly in developing nations (The impact of Marx's ideas in developing nations will be discussed later in this chapter.)

Although the idea of a social contract underlies both liberal and radical interpretations of social justice, they have differed sharply over whether that contract prioritized individual liberty, particularly property rights, or social equality (Berlin, 1978; Nozick, 1974; Tomasi, 2001). At its core, the argument centers on how to determine what rights and goods people "deserve." This issue frames contemporary debates about how scarce resources should be distributed through public policy and even within human service organizations (George & Wilding, 1994; Held, 1984; Roemer, 1996; White, 2000).

In the United States, there have been six different ways of defining distributive justice (Reisch, 2002):

1. Equal political rights and equal opportunity to obtain social goods, such as property
2. Equal distribution to those of equal merit
3. Equal distribution to those of equal productivity
4. Unequal distribution based on an individual's needs or requirements
5. Unequal distribution based on an individual's status or position
6. Unequal distribution based on different "contractual" agreements

As stated in Chapter 1, during the late 20th century, the distinguished philosopher John Rawls challenged the prevailing view of social justice in the West on the basis that it had been used to rationalize the unequal distribution of resources and power. Justice, Rawls (1971/1999) argued, must be based "on how fundamental rights and duties are assigned and on the economic opportunities and social conditions in the various sectors of society" (p. 7; see also Rawls, 2001). In his classic work, *A Theory of Justice* (1971/1999), Rawls proposed two fundamental principles:

1. Each person has an equal right to the most extensive system of personal liberty compatible with a system of total liberty for all.
2. Social and economic inequality are to be arranged so that they are both (a) to the greatest benefit to the least advantaged in society and (b) attached to positions open to all under conditions of fair equality of opportunity.

Although these principles have been critiqued and expanded upon during the past two decades (Nussbaum, 2010; Sen, 2009) they remain largely consistent with social work's stated mission, values, and goals and with those of similarly minded religious groups such as the U.S. Conference of Catholic Bishops (1986).

As subsequent chapters discuss, three persistent problems create obstacles to the attainment of these ideas of social justice. One involves the challenge of implementing socially just principles within an institutional environment based, explicitly and implicitly, on the preservation of injustice (Smith, 2008). The second problem is the challenge of translating an idea of justice based largely on the expansion of individual rights and individual shares into the policies, programs, and practice interventions that recognize the injustices resulting from group membership (Caputo, 2000; Katz, 2001; Prigoff, 2000). The third problem concerns the intrinsic limits of most contemporary concepts of distributive justice. Sen (2009) and Nussbaum (2003), for example, point out that Rawls and his supporters fail to include nonmaterial resources in their allocation of societal goods and pay insufficient attention to the needs of particularly vulnerable populations, such as disabled persons. They expand on Rawls's ideas to incorporate into justice concepts the importance of human capabilities. In the decades ahead, social workers will have to resolve these problems if we are to achieve our stated social justice goals.

Social Movements and Social Justice

In the modern era, social and political justice movements in different societies throughout the world have expanded on these ideas and attempted to implement them in practice. A common theme in these struggles for justice is the desire of oppressed groups to rid themselves of the shackles of oppression imposed by slavery, racism, sexism, colonialism, imperialism, or neo-colonialism. Although many of these struggles were influenced by previous movements and, in turn, influenced those that followed, the idea of justice took different forms in different contexts and cultures.

The examples discussed next are presented roughly in chronological order; they are grouped in a manner designed to facilitate both connections among them and comparisons between them. The illustrations begin with the Haitian Revolution, which was, arguably, the first modern non-Western revolution whose leaders evoked justice concepts to rationalize their cause. It is followed by a brief discussion of the 19th-century antislavery movement in the United States and its Brazilian counterpart. The narrative then shifts to the 20th century, initially with a section on the anti-imperialist movement in India. This example was selected because it was a dominant social justice movement for much of the first half of the century and because of its lasting influence on justice movements throughout the developing world and, through the work of Martin Luther King, Jr., on the United States. Examples from modern Africa and Latin America conclude this section.

The Haitian Revolution: The First Modern Antislavery and Social Justice Movement

In the late 18th and early 19th centuries, the enslaved people of the French colony of Saint-Domingue, now the modern nation of Haiti, revolted against their colonial masters. This led to the temporary abolition of slavery in 1793 (when the first French Republic was established) and permanent emancipation and independence from France in 1804 (when Napoleon proclaimed himself Emperor). The ideas about social justice expressed by Haitian revolutionaries, particularly Toussaint L'Ouverture and Papaloi (High Priest) Boukman, combined themes of racial pride and native spirituality with Western ideas of freedom. This synthesis of indigenous and imposed cultural values recurs in other societies during the next two centuries.

In a 1791 ceremony that allegedly started the revolt, Boukman declared (as quoted in Karenga, 2007),

> The god who created the sun which gives us light, who rouses the waves and rules the storm . . . sees all that the White man does. . . . Our God who is good to us commands us to revenge our wrongs. He will direct our arms and aid us. Throw away the symbol of the god of the Whites . . . and listen to the voice of freedom which speaks in the hearts of us all. (p. A-9)

Although Toussaint similarly invoked traditional spiritual and religious values in support of his vision of liberty, equality, and justice, he also integrated European ideas into his writings and speeches, particularly statements from French revolutionary documents such as the Declaration of the Rights of Man and Citizen (James, 1963). Justice, in his view, required universal legal and political equality, in both theory and application: "When Blacks, men of color and Whites are under the same laws they must be equally protected and they must be equally repressed when they deviate from them" (as quoted in Tyson, 1973, p. 43; see also James, 1963). In a letter written in late 1789, he challenged the leaders of the French Revolution to live up to their universal ideals of liberty and justice and to demonstrate "that all men are born and remain free and equal in rights" (as quoted in Dubois & Garrigus, 2006, p. 69). Although he later tempered his revolutionary appeals, Toussaint continued to insist that despite the brutality of their past treatment, "the men of St. Domingue ... do not merit being classed apart from the rest of mankind, being confused with animals" (as quoted in Tyson, 1973, p. 37).

The US Antislavery Movement

The movement to abolish slavery in the United States reflected justice themes similar to the antislavery revolts in Haiti and (later) in Brazil, such as liberty, equality, and morality. A handbill for an abolitionist meeting illustrated these sentiments (Filler, 1960, Figure 24):

> Let the North awake! T. B. M'Cormick will discuss the immorality, illegality and unconstitutionality of American Slavery and the duty and power of the general government to abolish it.

Music and song, particularly hymns and spirituals, were important vehicles to express justice for slaves and abolitionists alike. Two antislavery songs, written by the Hutchinson family of New Hampshire, reflect the movement's spirit among Whites well (as quoted in Filler, 1960):

> *We're the friends of emancipation*
> *And we'll sing the proclamation*
> *Till it echoes through the nation*
> *From the Old Granite State*
> *That the tribe of Jesse*
> *Are the friends of equal rights. (p. 185)*

Similar messages were conveyed in popular African American spirituals (Foner, 2015) and in essays written on the subjects of equality and justice by African American activists such as Maria W. Stewart. She declared (as quoted in Gates & McKay, 1997), "The Whites have so long and so loudly proclaimed the theme of equal rights and privileges, that our souls have caught the flame also, ragged as we are. . . . We feel a common desire to rise above the condition of servants and drudges" (p. 205).[5] Slave narratives were also a critical medium to denounce slavery and raise awareness about the conditions under which many slaves lived. Works such as *Incidents in the Life of a Slave Girl* by Harriet

---

5. For a modern comparison, see Alice Walker's (2002), "The Right to Life: What Can the White Man Say to the Black Woman?"

Jacobs (1861/2010), *Narrative of William W. Brown, a Fugitive Slave* (Brown, 1847), and *Narrative of the Life of Frederick Douglass* (1845/2014) enabled slaves to share their experiences from enslavement to freedom with a broad audience (Foner, 2015).

To bolster their arguments on behalf of racial equality and justice, both slave narratives and abolitionist pamphlets frequently pointed out the discrepancy between Christian values and the existence of slavery in a "Christian nation." They also underscored the contradictions between the nation's cherished revolutionary ideas and the institution of chattel slavery. These dual themes—the immorality of slavery and the inconsistency between American ideals and the reality of slavery—were dominant themes before the Civil War (Foner, 1998; Zinn, 1980).

In his articles and speeches, William Lloyd Garrison, the editor of *The Liberator*, often referred to statements about equality and liberty in the nation's founding documents to demonstrate the hypocrisy of the US government's acquiescence to the continued existence of slavery and to the judiciary's sanctioning slavery through misguided interpretations of the Constitution. The following excerpt from "A Call to the New England Anti-Slavery Convention" illustrates the language, tone, and themes of abolitionist propaganda (Garrison, 1836):

> The spirit of usurpation and impiety—the spirit of slavery—is struggling for the ascendancy over us. The abettors of our republican despotism are setting themselves up above all righteousness, above the Constitution of our country, above the authority of God. Slavery and Liberty cannot longer dwell, at peace, within the same borders. One or the other must depart from us. (p. 83)

David Walker and Henry Highland Garnet were two of the more outspoken African American abolitionists—the former in his use of language, and the latter in the solutions he proposed. Walker's *Appeal* (1829/2000) blended religious and constitutional imagery effectively in its call for justice (as quoted in Gates & McKay, 1997):

> I appeal to Heaven for my motive in writing—who knows that my object is, if possible, to awaken in the breasts of my afflicted, degraded and slumbering brethren, a spirit of inquiry and investigation respecting our miseries and wretchedness in this Republican Land of Liberty!!!!! (p. 180)

He compared the plight of African Americans to other subjugated peoples throughout history; they were (as quoted in Gates & McKay, 1997) the *most wretched, degraded and abject* set of beings that ever lived since the world began. … White Americans have reduced us to the wretched state of slavery, treated us in that condition *more cruel* … than any heathen nation did any people whom it had reduced to our condition. (p. 183)

Fifteen years later, Garnet echoed similar themes in a speech at the Negro National Convention. He criticized slaveholders for their failure to uphold God's word and invoked biblical references to locate American slavery in a long history of oppression. He also accused the US government of hypocrisy. Writing about the nation's hallowed war of independence, he sarcastically proclaimed (as quoted in Gates & McKay, 1997),

When the power of government returned to [the colonists'] hands, did they emancipate the slaves? No; they rather added new links to our chains. Were they ignorant of the principles of Liberty? Certainly they were not. The sentiments of the revolutionary orators fell in burning eloquence upon their hearts, and with one voice they cried, "Liberty or Death"! Oh, what a sentence was that. It ran from soul to soul like electric fire, and nerved the arms of thousands to fight in the holy cause of Freedom. Among the diversity of opinions that are entertained in regard to physical resistance, there are but a few found to gainsay the stern declaration. We are among those who do not. (p. 281)

Perhaps the most eloquent champion of justice in the antislavery movement was Frederick Douglass, himself a freed slave. In his famous July 1852 speech, "What to the Slave Is the Fourth of July?" Douglass pointedly addressed the hypocrisy of the majority of the American people. In his view, the nation's most sacred holiday was (as quoted in Gates & McKay, 1997)

a day that reveals … more than all other days in the year, the gross injustice and cruelty to which he [the slave] is the constant victim. To him, your celebration is a sham; your boasted liberty, an unholy license; your national greatness, swelling vanity; your sounds of rejoicing are empty and heartless; your denunciations of tyrants, brass fronted impudence; your shouts of liberty and equality, hollow mockery; your prayers and hymns, your sermons and thanksgivings, with all your religious parade and solemnity, are, to him, mere bombast, fraud, deception, impiety, and hypocrisy—a thin veil to cover up crimes which would disgrace a nation of savages. *There is not a nation on the earth guilty of practice, more shocking or bloody, than are the people of these United States, at this very hour* [emphasis added]. (p. 388)

The Brazilian Antislavery Movement

Unlike the Haitian Revolution and the antislavery movement in the United States, justice movements in Brazil had much broader goals than the eradication of slavery. Throughout the 19th century, Brazilian reformers considered abolition merely a prelude to efforts that would address the nation's widespread social, economic, and political problems. Although Brazilian abolitionists regarded slavery as immoral—the *Gazeta de Tarde*, one of the leading abolitionist newspapers, described it as a "moribund and nefarious institution" and a "criminal injustice and a horrible violation of rights" (as quoted in Toplin, 1972, pp. 115–116)—their view of justice also focused on other issues, including equality of religion, more equitable political representation, improved labor conditions, and fair access to education. One of their leaders, Tavares Bastos, declared (as quoted in Conrad, 1972), "To emancipate and to instruct are two intimately linked tasks" (p. 158).[6] Another prominent leader, Joaquim Nabuco, asserted that abolition was not only about emancipation but also about ending the "demoralization, inertia, servility, and irresponsibility" of slavery (Nabuco, 1883, as quoted in Conrad, 1972, p. 157).

The Brazilian abolitionist movement employed three arguments in its struggle against slavery, which both previous and subsequent justice movements have also used. One approach emphasized its illegal nature. A second focused on its immorality, and a third argued that slavery was counterproductive to the nation's economic and moral progress (Toplin, 1972).

In asserting the illegality of slavery, reformers attempted to use the judicial system both to emancipate slaves and to demand punishment for slaveholders. Advocates such as Luiz Gama argued that, unlike the antebellum United States, Brazil's laws did not condone the practice of slavery (Graden, 2006). In language similar to that of Haitian revolutionaries and some American antislavery advocates, he implied that fundamental ideas about justice were embedded in the Brazilian constitution, legislative statutes, and judicial interpretations of these documents.

In their antislavery propaganda, reformers also condemned the immorality not only of slaveholders but also of *all* Brazilians for condoning the practice and for continuing to rely on slave labor. They sought to create a "new moral conscience for the Brazilian nation" (Toplin, 1972, p. 116), although unlike comparable movements in the United States, Great Britain, and the Caribbean, the Brazilian abolitionist movement was primarily secular. In fact, some churches owned slaves, and most failed to adopt a strong position on the issue (Baronov, 2000).

---

6. This dual emphasis on emancipation and education is also reflected in the writings of the influential Brazilian educator Paulo Freire, particularly his classic *Pedagogy of the Oppressed* (1970).

In addition, abolitionists such as Nabuco focused on the "developmental" problems that resulted from the widespread practice of slavery. For example, it prevented the expansion of the agricultural market and experimentation with new crops. The primary supporters of abolition—the White and mulatto urban middle classes, poor freed Blacks, and mulattos—also feared that the continued existence of slavery would slow the process of urbanization and produce a permanently stratified social structure consisting of a wealthy upper class, a huge lower class, and virtually no middle class (Bethell, 1991). Consequently, one of their most important justice-oriented demands was for greater property rights for small landholders, reflected in the slogan "the democratization of the soil" (Conrad, 1972, p. 162).

Finally, the goals of abolition in Brazil were intimately tied to the nation's reputation in the international community that had become increasingly important both economically and politically. Declaring slavery "an obstacle to national self-respect" that led to "censure from the civilized world," reformers in the Brazilian Anti-Slavery Society sought to make their nation more competitive in the emerging global market system and "elevate Brazil to the category of useful member in the human community" (Toplin, 1972, pp. 121, 127). Part of their argument linked the issue of slavery to patriotism. One example of these sentiments is found in the following poem by Castro Alves, the "poet of the slaves" (as quoted in Graden, 2006):

> *Wake up, mother country. Don't bow your head.*
> *The tropic sun will dry up all your tears.*
> *Look on the edge of the wide horizon:*
> *The dawn moon of better years.*
> *It won't take much. Shake off the chain*
> *that you call wealth. It mars what could be good.*
> *Don't stain the page of the nation's story*
> *with foul displays of slave's blood.*
> *If you'll be poor, so what? Be free,*
> *As noble as the condor of the high lands.*
> *Remove the weight off Atlas's shoulders.*
> *Lift the cross from God's hands. (p. 87)*

Twentieth-Century Anti-Imperialist Movements

Gandhi and Indian Independence

The leaders of 20th-century anti-imperialist movements each developed a distinct view of justice to provide the intellectual foundation for their struggle. Sometimes, different views of justice competed within the same movement. One of the most important examples of this phenomenon occurred in the Indian struggle for independence during the first half of the 20th century.

Although some Indian leaders, such as Subhash Chandra Bose (commonly known as Netaji), President of the Indian National Congress in 1938–1939 and later the head of the Indian National Army, emphasized the need for a socialist path to justice that would focus on the elimination of racial discrimination and economic inequality, the most famous and influential Indian leader, Mohandas Gandhi, argued that India's problems stemmed from Western modernization and urbanization, particularly British influence on Indian culture and its institutions (Ahluwalia & Ahluwalia, 1982). As early as 1917, Gandhi declared,

> It is not the British people who are ruling India, but it is modern civilization, through its railways, telegraph, telephone, and almost every invention which has been claimed to be a triumph of civilization. . . . India's salvation consists in *unlearning what she has learnt during the past fifty years* [emphasis added]. (pp. 84–86)

Gandhi believed that imperialism and Westernization themselves were antithetical to justice and, therefore, that independence from Britain was a requisite first step, but not the sole step, to achieve it (Chakrabarty, 2006).

Seeking to produce both a political and a spiritual revolution, Gandhi rejected the material world of possession and consumption, violence and oppression in favor of a life that brings balance and joy, healing and justice. He regarded the pursuit of justice as inseparable from the pursuit of both the emotional and the physical well-being of individuals and communities. Gandhi believed that the most critical manifestation of justice occurred in the fusion of ethics and economics and that this integration was impossible in a market-driven culture that sanctioned immoral practices and the accumulation of wealth at the expense of the needy. His ideas about social justice continue to influence activists and revolutionaries on every continent.

Gandhi rejected Western concepts of social justice because of their materialist foundation. Yet, unlike many of his socialist colleagues in the Congress Party, Gandhi's view of justice was inherently spiritual, not material. He regarded the pursuit of justice as inseparable from the pursuit of both the emotional and the physical well-being of individuals and communities. Although he was also anticapitalist, he opposed it on non-Marxist grounds. Gandhi asserted that Western market economies created materialism, consumerism, competition, and assertive urbanization, all of which were fundamentally incompatible with economic equity or justice.

He often used the United States as an example of what India should *not* become, asserting that "[America] is the most industrialized country in the

world, and yet, it has not banished poverty and degradation. This is because it ...
concentrates power in the hands of the few who amass fortunes at the expense of
the many" (as quoted in Kaushik, 2001, p. 83). Gandhi believed that the most critical manifestation of justice occurred in the fusion of ethics and economics and
that this integration was impossible in a market-driven culture that sanctioned
immoral practices and the accumulation of wealth at the expense of the needy. In
his view, "True economics stands for social justice" (as quoted in Kaushik, 2001,
p. 82; see also Prasant, 2014).

In developing a rationale for Indian independence, Gandhi and his supporters transformed some Western ideas about colonialism and national sovereignty
into uniquely Indian concepts, such as *swaraj*. Chakrabarty (2006) explains
that Gandhi never precisely defined this concept but indicated that it had four
facets: national independence and political, economic, and spiritual freedom.
Throughout the long struggle for independence, Gandhi made several references
to *swaraj* as a symbol of collective and individual justice, involving both democratic rule and a sense of spiritual control over one's personal destiny—somewhat
analogous to the modern concepts of community and individual empowerment.
Swaraj required "educating the masses to a sense of their capacity to regulate and
control authority ... [and raising] the consciousness in the average villager that
he is ... his own legislator (as quoted in Jack, 1961, pp. 134–135).

Gandhi's view of justice also included the establishment of certain concrete
Western-style rights, such as freedom of speech and the press, the right to decent
and safe employment, the right to an education, and racial equality. In this
regard, his principles of justice resembled those of his communist and socialist
allies. He dedicated most of his energy, however, to the elimination of economic
and caste inequalities.

Gandhi believed that poverty and economic inequalities were inherently
unjust and that wealth should exist only to meet basic human needs. This required
more than an abstract commitment to justice. He asserted (as quoted in Jack, 1961),

> The golden rule ... is ... to refuse to have what the millions can-
> not.... The first thing is to cultivate the mental attitude that we will not
> have possessions or facilities denied to millions, and the next immediate
> thing is to rearrange our lives as fast as possible in accordance with that
> mentality. (p. 53)

This represented a challenge not only to prevailing institutional structures but
also to people's basic ways of living.

Thus, unlike many of his allies, Gandhi argued that the eradication of injustice in India required more than independence; it required the elimination of the

caste system that produced unfair distinctions and substantial socioeconomic disparities. He wrote (as quoted in Kaushik, 2001),

> *Varna* [the original social division of Vedic people into four groups] reveals the law of one's being and thus the duty one has to perform it confers no right. [Indeed] the idea of superiority or inferiority is wholly repugnant to it. All *varnas* are equal, for the community depends no less on one than on another. . . . Gradations of high and low . . . [are] hideous travesties of the original [because] *varnashram* is not a vertical division. It is a horizontal one. Hence, there can be no question of untouchability. (p. 153; see also Chakrabarty, 2006, p. 156)

African Liberation Movements

Inspired by the example of the Indian independence movement and influenced by 20th-century socialism, during the half century after World War II the colonized peoples of Africa also broke the bonds of imperialism and established independent nations. Like the struggles in India, Haiti, and Brazil, their social justice movements reflected a broad range of ideologies and political strategies. Some borrowed heavily—with considerable adaptation—from Western philosophies such as Marxism or blended European and African concepts. Others emphasized the history and culture of indigenous populations. In the immediate post–World War II era, the Mau Mau rebellion in Kenya was, perhaps, the best known, although the writings of Kwame Nkrumah in Ghana were arguably the most influential on movements social justice in other African nations.

KENYAN IDEAS OF JUSTICE

Although they differed substantially in their views on the use of violence, the Mau Maus's ideas of justice bore some similarity to those expressed by advocates of nonviolence such as Gandhi. These included recovery of the land confiscated by the British; self-government; the destruction of the influence of Christianity; the restoration of ancient customs and traditions, wherever possible; the expulsion or subjugation of foreigners; and the growth of secular education (Arnold, 1974). These goals differed substantially, however, from those promoted by Jomo Kenyatta, the leader of the Kenya African National Union (KANU) who became the nation's first president.

In his writings and speeches, Kenyatta articulated both negative and positive forms of justice. He attacked the harsh and discriminatory treatment of native Africans by British imperialists and argued that the nature of British colonial rule made a just society impossible to achieve because it sustained the three major "enemies" of the Kenyan people: poverty, ignorance, and disease (Cullen, 1976). Kenyatta also fought for economic freedoms for all Africans, including equal pay for equal work, the right to grow and sell products of their choosing, and the right to own property. In addition, he spoke out against discrimination in access to education, health care, and other public services (Kenyatta, 1968).

Like Gandhi, Kenyatta believed that justice required both independence and the establishment of democratic political rights. Prophetically, he asserted, "Until . . . representation of Africans by Africans is justly settled, there can be no peace or prosperity in Africa" (Kenyatta, 1968, p. 36).

Also like Gandhi, he blended Western and African ideas in his concept of justice. For example, in his emphasis on "freedom, equality, and brotherhood," Kenyatta echoed the ideals of the French Revolution. He also promoted a socialist (or positive) conception of liberty: "Liberty [he argued] is not the mere absence of restraint. [It] also means the ability to fulfil [sic] the meaningful will of the people and to enjoy a certain area of personal freedom" (as quoted in Cullen, 1976, p. 22). Toward the end of his career, Kenyatta explicitly declared, "Only in a *free and liberal society* [emphasis added] can each individual develop fully to serve his fellow-citizens" (Kenyatta, 1968, p. 200).

A cofounder with Kwame Nkrumah of the Pan-African Federation in 1946, Kenyatta believed that these ideas about justice must transcend national boundaries. He stressed, however, that Kenyan national unity, particularly the eradication of racial and tribal discrimination, and the restoration of uniquely African traditions and intellect were necessary preconditions before the broader justice goals of African nationalism could be achieved. The paramount goal of national unity was expressed symbolically in the pre- and post-independence slogans of KANU—the shift from *"Uhuru"* ("freedom") to *"Harambee"* ("let us pull together"). These concepts reflected the link between Kenya's struggle for justice and the themes of African nationalism, working-class values, and unity across racial and tribal lines (Cullen, 1976). Kenyatta based his view of justice, therefore, on the ability of all Africans to "gain their rightful place" in the world. Like Senghor's conceptualization of *negritude* in the Senegalese fight for independence, justice and freedom in the Kenyan struggle were inseparable from the broader Pan-African unity movement.

KWAME NKRUMAH AND THE PAN-AFRICAN MOVEMENT

In response to the widespread oppression Africans faced under colonial and imperialist rule, leaders of newly emerging African nations began to meet in the 1950s to discuss the possibility of creating a united front. In 1958, Kwame Nkrumah, the first president of Ghana, organized a meeting of African leaders with the dual goals of improving the conditions of all African peoples and gaining respect in the international community. In their discourse, Nkrumah and other African leaders framed justice as the ability to pursue African unity and express their unique "African personality." This would liberate Africans "to act in [their] individual and collective interests at any particular time" (Nkrumah, 1961, p. 128).

In developing his concept of justice, Nkrumah drew upon ideas developed in the 20th-century Pan-African movement, from such diverse sources as W. E. B. Dubois, Henry Sylvester Williams, Edward Blyden, and Marcus Garvey.[7] He also relied heavily on the strategies of nonviolence and non-cooperation promoted by Gandhi. In fact, Nkrumah visited India frequently during his efforts to advance African independence (Nkrumah, 1963).

The Declaration of Principles developed by Nkrumah, W. V. S. Tubman of Liberia, and Sekou Touré of Guinea for the African National Union in 1959 embodied these principles of justice. It stressed "freedom, independence, unity, the African personality [and] African dignity" (Nkrumah, 1961, p. 177). These ideas would be spread through public education systems that emphasized knowledge of African history and culture. In the late 1960s, African American activists such as the Black Panthers adopted many of the same goals in the creation of freedom schools. Similar ideas undergird the more recent emphasis on Afrocentrism among some activists, intellectuals, and social workers in the United States (Austin, 2006; Schiele, 2000).

At the 1959 All-African People's Conference in Accra, Ghana, Nkrumah explained that "the African personality and the African community must have a free and fertile soil in which to flourish and blossom (Nkrumah, 1961, p. 187). His reference to the land in these remarks was not just a figure of speech. Part of the Ghanaian and Pan-African quest for independence and freedom involved both a physical and a metaphorical struggle to take back the land as a critical aspect of justice (Nkrumah, 1963). These themes reflect many of the ideas previously expressed by Kenyatta and Pan-Africanists since the early 20th century, including the existence of an inherent relationship between the African people and the land, the concepts of unity and partnership, and the notion that the struggles of the African people must return them to their natural place. Nkrumah (1961) declared, "*Only the African* can speak for the African and *only the African* can be the spokesman of this great continent" (p. 48). Leaders of other African liberation struggles in Senegal, Mozambique, and South Africa echoed similar themes.

---

7. The Pan-African movement began in the early 20th century among leading African and African American intellectuals and activists. In the words of one its founders, W. E. B. DuBois (1903/1999), it recognized the common bonds of African peoples throughout the world and accurately predicted that "the problem of the 20th century will be the problem of the color line." The movement sought to promote the liberation of all African peoples by coordinated efforts in the cultural and political arenas.

THE SENEGALESE ANTICOLONIAL STRUGGLE
AND THE CONCEPT OF NEGRITUDE

In the 1940s and 1950s, as anti-imperialist independence movements flourished in many former British colonies, the Senegalese anti-imperialist movement against France gained strength, drawing heavily on ideas that had been expressed there for two decades. During this period, the concept of justice, expressed through formal and informal means of resistance to French oppression, centered primarily on the notion of *negritude*, a term initially created by a group of African scholars, including Leopold Senghor (a well-known author and poet who became Senegal's first president) and Aime Cesaire.

According to some scholars (Skurnick, 1965), the concept of negritude reflected a rejection of market-driven capitalism and the Western tendency to separate cultural values and ethics from economics similar to the philosophy Gandhi espoused in India. Negritude was an attempt to replace the "invisible hand during the industrial revolution in Europe" with a "visible arm of government as an agent of social justice" (Skurnick, 1965, p. 354). Although they rejected Marxist determinism, leaders of the negritude movement thought that Marxism had some utility for Africans because of its humanistic focus (Le Baron, 1966, p. 273).

Senghor also asserted that French imperialism suffocated the people's ability to nurture their traditions, history, and cultural identity. Like Black nationalists in the United States, such as Malcolm X, Senghor argued that Senegal's cultural and psychological survival required independence (Senghor, 1965):

> There can be no unfolding of the personality of a people without freedom of development.... There can be no freedom in the *alienation* of self from self which constitutes the colonial condition. There can be no freedom in the stifling of one's being. There can be no independence in dependency. It is all this that justifies the struggle against colonialism. (p. 72)

Algerian psychiatrist Frantz Fanon discussed similar ideas in such influential works as *Black Skin, White Masks* (2008), *The Wretched of the Earth* (2004), and *Toward the African Revolution* (1967). Black power advocates in the United States, such as Stokely Carmichael (Aka Kwame Touré) and Charles Hamilton (1967), applied these ideas to American society.

Through poetry and other artistic forms, Senghor expressed his belief that negritude must be built on affirmation rather than negation to overcome the systematic degradation of African qualities by Europeans and White Americans (Irele, 1965; Senghor, 1965, p. 97). Senghor (1965) wrote that "negritude ... is part of Africanity. It is made of human warmth. It is democracy quickened by the sense of communion and brotherhood between men" (p. 97). Thus, like other advocates for social justice in developing nations, Senghor distinguished between the culture of the oppressed and that of their oppressor in their conceptualization of property, their attitude toward the environment, and their understanding of religion and ethics. Cultural respect, therefore, was an integral component of justice (Spleth, 1985, pp. 24–25).

Thus, in African liberation movements, negritude was not merely a cultural or political theory but also a revolutionary tool. It constituted "no mere request for social equality . . . but, somewhat ironically, [a demand] to be valued precisely because they are unique and so are in a position to make a unique contribution to mankind" (Le Baron, 1966, p. 268). That is why the leaders of anticolonialist uprisings in Africa believed that their struggle was somewhat similar to those of the European working class (Senghor, 1965). They identified one critical distinction, however, that still resonates powerfully in the 21st century, particularly in the West: Although both populations were oppressed as inferiors, the European working class was forced to depend on elites due to the political–economic structure of their societies. By contrast, the colonization of Africans (and the oppression of African Americans) was rationalized on the basis of racial superiority. By recognizing this difference, African people were able to create a uniquely indigenous form of resistance to imperialism, which drew heavily on diverse African and US cultural sources, including Langston Hughes, Claude MacKay, Jean-Price Mars, and René Maran (Spleth, 1985). While the ideology and strategies of African and African American justice movements borrowed from Western ideas such as Marxism, they also integrated cultural concepts that resonated uniquely among Africans and that served as a powerful tool to undermine decades of racist denigration by colonial and imperialist powers.

FRELIMO AND MOZAMBIQUE'S STRUGGLE FOR INDEPENDENCE

Like other anticolonial struggles in the 20th century, the expressions of justice in Mozambique's national liberation movement focused on more than independence from Portuguese domination. Political leaders such as Eduardo Mondlane (the founder of FRELIMO, the Mozambique Liberation Front, and the nation's president from 1962 to 1969) and Samora Machel (FRELIMO'S military commander and president from 1975 to 1986) addressed both the inhumane treatment of Africans by Portuguese imperialists and their visions for national well-being after independence. Like Senghor, they pointed out the complex and multidimensional nature of colonial subjugation, including its political, economic, cultural, and psychological components.

Mondlane repeatedly complained, "Everywhere references . . . are full of scorn or at least pity. . . . The implication is that the Portuguese are naturally superior to the people they have conquered, and that these can only claim any sort of equality by actually becoming 'Portuguese'" (Mondlane, 1969, p. 37). The colonial educational system and the imposition of Christianity assumed that Mozambicans would assimilate into Portuguese culture. Similar to the obstacles to political participation and socioeconomic integration African Americans confronted during much of the 20th and 21st centuries, Mozambicans had to demonstrate sufficient mastery of the Portuguese language, the ability to support one's family, and the necessary educational credentials to obtain legal rights—criteria that Whites were not required to meet (p. 48).

FRELIMO spokespersons developed their concept of justice directly from the experience of systematic racism in virtually every institution. They conceptualized justice as the acquisition of the social, economic, and political rights they had been denied as a consequence of "the experience of discrimination, exploitation, forced labor, and other such aspects of colonial rule" (Mondlane, 1969, p. 101). The following 1932 editorial (as quoted in Mondlane, 1969) reflects their initial resistance to oppression:

> We've had a mouthful of it.... We can no longer put up with the pernicious effects of your political and administrative decisions. From now on we refuse to make ever greater and ever more useless sacrifices.... We insist that you carry out your fundamental duties not with laws and decrees but with acts.... We want to be treated in the same way that you are. We do not aspire to the comforts you surround yourselves with, thanks to our strength. We do not aspire to your refined education.... Even less do we aspire to a life dominated by the ideas of robbing your brother.... We aspire to our "savage state" which, however, fills your mouths and your pockets. And we demand something ... we demand bread and light.... We repeat that we do not want hunger or thirst or poverty or a law of discrimination based on colour. (pp. 106–107)

Like many contemporaneous African liberation struggles, FRELIMO's ideas about justice combined socialist practice and nationalist ideals (Afro American Information Service (AIS); Mondlane, 1969). FRELIMO's definition of justice included equal treatment and the opportunity to pursue well-being; the existence of racial and regional unity; regulations that sufficiently protect the health and safety of workers; widespread education based on indigenous notions of formal and informal schooling (particularly regarding literacy campaigns); and accessible health care for all people. Unlike many African liberation struggles, however, FRELIMO paid particular attention to women's issues, both during and after the revolution, including the need for more comprehensive education and care for those women (and their children) whose husbands were at war. Justice also required that all workers be treated equally.

Like Senghor and Gandhi, Machel also conceived of justice in terms of economic self-sufficiency and self-determination, specifically the ability to produce food for oneself and one's country and to determine which crops to plant. In a just society, he wrote (as quoted in AIS, 1975),

> Labor is a liberating activity because the product of labor benefits the workers, serves the interests of the workers, i.e., it serves to liberate man from hunger and poverty. . . . We have abolished the exploitation of man by man, because what is produced is the property of the people. (p. 35)

The Chope people of southern Mozambique expressed similar sentiments about their historical suffering (as quoted in Mondlane, 1969):

> *We are still angry; it's always the same story.*
> *The oldest daughters must pay the tax.*
> *Natanele tells the white man to leave him alone.*
> *Natenele tells that white man to leave me be. (p. 103)*

THE SOUTH AFRICAN ANTI-APARTHEID STRUGGLE

The South African liberation movement similarly blended a combination of political ideologies and cultural tools to articulate its vision of justice. During their long struggle against imperialism and apartheid, Black South Africans also developed their own definition of justice. An examination of the letters and speeches of their most prominent leader, Nelson Mandela, the head of the African National Congress (ANC) and the first president after apartheid was dismantled, reveals a concept of justice centered on political rights and representation, the importance of Pan-African unity, the elimination of poverty, and the importance of universal human dignity. The anti-apartheid movement also borrowed ideas of justice from other regional independence movements and from Pan-African philosophy. Mandela drew upon the experiences of such diverse nations as Zimbabwe, Mozambique, Kenya, Uganda, and Zanzibar and often referenced Gandhi and Martin Luther King, Jr. (International Defense and Aid Fund for Southern Africa (IDAF), 1986, pp. 344–346).

Although Mandela often employed class-conscious language, he was careful (perhaps for political reasons) to distinguish between Marxism and the ideas of the ANC. He stated (IDAF, 1986),

Today I am attracted by the idea of a classless society, an attraction which springs in part from Marxist reading and, in part, from my admiration of the structure and organization of early African societies in this country. The land, then the main means of production, belonged to the tribe. There were no rich or poor and there was no exploitation.... Many leaders of the new independent states accept the need for some form of socialism to enable our people to catch up with the advanced countries of the world and to overcome their legacy of extreme poverty. But this does not mean we are Marxists. (pp. 175–176)

Because the existence of apartheid created a unique political and institutional situation in South Africa, Mandela repeatedly asserted that the most important rights for Black South Africans to obtain were the right to vote and the right to participate in the nation's electoral process. These rights, he argued, would foster equal political representation and give Blacks the ability to influence laws and policies. Without these rights, he argued, no other rights could be gained, no other forms of oppression could be eliminated, and the people's "disabilities will be permanent" (IDAF, 1986, p. 4). Thus, from the beginning of Mandela's political activism in the 1950s through his presidency in the 1990s, he defined justice primarily as the achievement of democratic rule based on the will of the people. In the Freedom Charter adopted by the National Action Council in 1955, political rights are listed first, and one of the major slogans of the anti-apartheid movement was "full democratic rights in South Africa now" (Asmal, Chidester, & James, 2003, p. 14). In April 1994, the dramatic images of Black South Africans waiting for hours to vote for the first time exemplified their widespread acceptance of this priority.

The anti-apartheid movement, however, did not focus solely on political rights. It also emphasized narrowing the gap between rich and poor and eliminating suffering due to poverty. Like Gandhi, Mandela repeatedly asserted that fair economic practices were essential to the attainment of a just society. These included the reallocation of land, the eradication of race-based land discrimination, state assistance to the poor, improved and regulated labor conditions, the right of workers to form unions, and the elimination of racial and gender-based bias in wages and employment. Linking political and economic rights, Mandela declared, "The complaint of Africans . . . is not only that they are poor and the whites are rich, but that the laws which are made by the whites are designed to preserve this situation" (IDAF, 1986, p. 178).

Like other African independence leaders, Mandela also consistently focused on the relationship between justice and human dignity. He asserted, "The lack of human dignity experienced by Africans is the direct result of the policy of white supremacy. White supremacy implies black inferiority" (IDAF, 1986, p. 179). At his historical presidential inauguration, using the clear biblical symbolism of a covenant, he stated (as quoted in Asmal et al., 2003),

> We enter into a covenant that we shall build the society in which all South Africans, both black and white, will be able to walk tall, without any fear in their hearts, assured of their inalienable right to human dignity—a rainbow nation at peace with itself and the world. (p. 69)

The importance of human dignity also shaped Mandela's ideas about the need to eradicate physical and emotional violence, eliminate obstacles to education, bar segregated living spaces, restore local traditions and customs, and outlaw widespread curfews and travel restrictions.

Finally, as early as his 1962 trial, Mandela declared that the restoration of human dignity required Pan-African unity despite the diversity of tribes, classes, and religions on the continent. In his moving statement to the court, Mandela (as quoted in Asmar et al., 2003) asserted,

> All people, irrespective of the color of their skins, all people whose home is South Africa and who believe in the principles of democracy and of equality of men, should be treated as Africans; that all South Africans are entitled to live a free life on the basis of fullest equality of the rights and opportunities in every field, of full democratic rights, with a direct say in the affairs of the government. (p. 21)

Although African nations have not fully realized these social justice goals, their underlying ideas continue to inspire activists, including social workers, throughout the continent.

Justice in Modern Latin America

Prior to the Spanish conquest, the major civilizations of pre-colonial Central and South America—such as the Olmecs, Toltecs, Aztecs, and Mayas in what is now Mexico and Guatemala—were all stratified societies with an elite ruling class, which consisted primarily of religious male elders and noble families. The overwhelming majority of the people were peasants who farmed the land, built sacred temples, and fought in wars. Although there are no specific studies of Central (or Meso) American ideas about social justice, inferences about indigenous justice concepts can be made. Given the social and political structure of the region, it is probable that for centuries elites defined social justice in a manner that rationalized oligarchical management and control of the population, the land, and its resources—in a manner similar to most Western societies (Acuña, 2007; Davies, 1980, 1987; Hammond, 1993).

In another similarity to Western culture, religion played a major part in justifying the Meso-American civic order, although, as in the West, it did so in diverse ways. The theology and religious rites of the Aztecs used violence as a means of social control (Davies, 1987). By contrast, the theology of the Toltecs, whose civilization preceded the Aztecs and the Mayans, stressed personal responsibility and active pursuit of wisdom through self-awareness. With striking similarities to Buddhism, the Toltecs believed that the keys to enlightenment were detachment from the lure of personal possessions; the abandonment of fears stemming from loss, greed, and narcissism; and the attainment of harmony with all living things. In the Toltec worldview, social injustice could only be eradicated by becoming aware of these injustices, through individual and collective envisioning of an alternative conception of society, and through actions taken toward that alternative. Because Toltecs believed that individual and collective "reality" is determined by conscious perception and interpretation (a belief that anticipated postmodernism by two millennia), their views of social justice were context dependent and would vary across peoples, cultures, regions, and nations (Nelson, 1997).

The Spanish Conquest and the Role of the Church in Social Justice Movements

The Spanish *conquistadores*, who arrived in Central America in the early 16th century, had a concept of "social justice" similar to that of indigenous elites— that the existence of a social hierarchy was a God-given right (Acuña, 2007). Although these elites often used religious beliefs to rationalize their highly hierarchical cultures (Davies, 1980, 1987), Spaniards and their Portuguese counterparts indoctrinated indigenous peoples into Christianity as part of a strategy to oppress and control them (Segal, 1995; Thomas, 1997). For example, the powerful emphasis in Christian (largely Catholic) thought and practice on an afterlife that promised salvation and redemption rationalized the existence of extensive material suffering and the unequal distribution of resources, power, and status on Earth. It also justified and even encouraged the passive acceptance of suffering and the unequal status quo (Acuña, 2007; Jones, 1984).

Paradoxically, the Church frequently presented itself as an ally of the poor, particularly at the parish level. This contrasted sharply with the close alignment of the Church hierarchy with ruling elites, who both profited handsomely from this relationship. These conflicting tendencies continue to be reflected in contemporary indigenous narratives and expressions of faith in mainstream Catholic and newly emerging evangelical Christian churches (Freston, 2004).

Consequently, most contemporary indigenous narratives in Latin America incorporate ideas gleaned from multiple belief systems. Christian values such as hope, forgiveness, and reciprocity continue to have a high priority among Catholics in Central America, and God's grace is a central theme in the struggles of the oppressed (Bravo, 1994). These communities and their clergy emphasize the love God has for the poor, His forgiveness and compassion for those who do harm, and His vision of solidarity for all humankind. Indigenous narratives, however, are more critical of the impact of colonialism on traditional cultures and people's economic well-being than that of the mainstream Church. As a result, activists motivated by such narratives are more likely to focus on such reforms as equal and complete protection under the law and access to natural, scientific, and financial resources as a means to achieve social justice (Bravo, 1994).

Latin American Christianity, therefore, has influenced regional ideas about social justice in four ways (Jones, 1984). First, the Catholic hierarchy has often been more concerned with maintaining traditional religious dogma and the salvation of individuals than with societal transformation. This is reflected in the celebratory rituals or *mandas* that the faithful complete before requesting a miracle from God. In such religious practices, there is no reference to social inequalities or any challenge to the status quo.

Second, since the establishment of Christianity in the region by the Spanish conquest, the Church made clear distinctions between the body and the soul (i.e., between physical or material and spiritual needs), politics and history, and heaven and Earth. These distinctions required followers to remove themselves from any earthly concerns and place their faith in God's grace and promise of a better afterlife. In this view, injustices will be rectified in heaven, not on Earth.

In the early 1960s, however, Vatican II transformed the Church into a more progressive institution and led to a third way in which it influenced Latin American ideas about justice through its cultural practices. Priests began to conduct the mass in native languages and to include music and rituals that incorporated elements of the congregation's indigenous culture. As a result, during the 1970s and 1980s, Church leaders became involved in political advocacy, particularly against oppressive regimes in El Salvador and Chile. During the former nation's bloody civil war, Archbishop Romero so antagonized ruling elites with his support of the revolutionary movement that he was assassinated. More recently, the Catholic Church in Mexico has criticized corrupt government practices that destabilize the democratic voting process (Bernard, 1995). Most Church leaders, however, have hesitated to analyze the structural forces that perpetuate oppression. Consequently, more radical Christian doctrines have acquired increasing popularity, especially in impoverished areas.

Beginning in the early 1950s, a fourth pattern of influence from Church doctrine began to appear. The "new church" has actively mobilized the community in nonviolent struggles against long-standing power structures and mechanisms of oppression, initially by focusing on issues such as poverty and class stratification (Jones, 1984). After a decade of organizing the poor around these themes, the emergence of liberation theology in the 1960s provided the ideological basis for a fusion of traditional Catholic doctrine and indigenous beliefs within a social justice and social action-oriented framework (Aguilar, 2007; Petrella, 2005).

Proponents of liberation theology argued that traditional Christianity overlooked the original social justice messages in Jesus's teachings. They sought to infuse these ideas again into Church doctrine by emphasizing the "economic and political liberation of the poor, the oppressed, and the weak in society" (Thakur, 1996), what the US Conference of Catholic Bishops (1986) referred to as the "preferential option for the poor." Unlike many evangelicals, they stressed that faith alone is insufficient; people must also engage in right action to address their material and spiritual needs.

Furthermore, in contrast to Protestant doctrine, proponents of liberation theology believe that sin is not a private or individual matter. Instead, it is a "domination of evil which prohibits the freedom of God's children" (Ellacuria, 1976, pp. 73–74). Therefore, sin is a social phenomenon that can only be corrected by social action. As Gutierrez (1973) explains,

> In ["the"] liberation approach . . . sin is regarded as a social, historical fact, the absence of brotherhood and love in the relationships of men, the breach of friendship with God and with other men, and therefore, an interior personal fracture. . . . *Sin is evident in oppressive structures, in the exploitation of man by man, in the domination and slavery of peoples, races, and social classes. Sin appears, therefore, as the fundamental alienation, the root of a situation of injustice and exploitation. . . . Sin demands a radical liberation which in turn necessarily implies a political liberation* [emphasis added]. (pp. 175–176)

During the past half century, liberation theology has inspired popular movements and community organizing efforts throughout Latin America, in which social workers have been frequently involved. In contrast to past divisions between secular and religious political forces, its proponents found common cause with secular activists. For example, by incorporating the pedagogical theories of Paulo Freire (1970), disenfranchised communities were empowered to interpret scripture in a manner that facilitated both a direct connection with God and the ability to take collective action against oppressive institutions (Burdick & Hewitt, 2000).

A particularly compelling feature of liberation theology was its encouragement of civic engagement by all persons in society, especially those elements of the population, such as women and *campesinos* (landless peasants), who had been denied access to critical political and economic decisions (Arceo, 1985; Bravo, 1994; Burdick & Hewitt, 2000). Like Gandhi, proponents of liberation theology asserted that the elimination of social injustice involved both a spiritual and a political experience. This was consistent with their call for more democratic and egalitarian political and social systems in nations with strong authoritarian traditions. A recent feature of liberation theology is its explicit recognition of the exploitative and racist tendencies embedded in market economics and neocolonial practices, including those emerging out of economic globalization such as the North American Free Trade Agreement (NAFTA). This issue has helped forge close alliances with secular reformers and revolutionary movements.

Although the Church continues to be a powerful force in organized change efforts in such countries as El Salvador, Mexico, and Guatemala, its influence has been curtailed by outright oppression (e.g., political assassination and terrorism), the denunciation of liberation theology by Popes John Paul II and Pope Benedict, and the growing influence of evangelical Protestantism in the region, perhaps inspired by the linkage between evangelical worldviews and the values underlying neoliberal economic globalization (Gill, 2004). There is also evidence in nations such as Ecuador that the practices of liberation theology have alienated some community members who did not identify with liberationist views (Burdick & Hewitt, 2000). It remains to be seen how Pope Francis will apply his statements about poverty to future social change efforts.

A recent justice-oriented addition to Catholic theology underscores the significance of the feminine influence in the Bible, religious rites, and public life. Linked closely to organized secular efforts to promote gender equality, this reinterpretation of traditional doctrine portrays Christ as someone who loved, respected, and gave equal treatment to his female followers. Building upon the long-standing Latin American adoration of the Virgin Mary as the bearer of truth or life, this perspective maintains that social transformation must incorporate the concerns of women and cannot be achieved without their equal participation (Arceo, 1985).

Since the 1990s, some justice-oriented priests and nuns have also played a critical role in the struggles of the Mexican people in regions as diverse as Chiapas and Chihuahua. Often, these clergy frame social justice as inseparable from the

Christian notion of the "common good," which must be attained through the development and implementation of a collective vision of justice (Gago Guerrero, n.d.). In Chihuahua, Catholic leaders have frequently condemned the corruption and destabilization of the democratic process by political elites and articulated a conception of social justice that focuses on the full and meaningful participation of all citizens (Bernard, 1995). In Chiapas, using language similar to that employed by Freire (1970) and Boal (2008) in Brazil, both the indigenous culture of the people and the teachings of the Church (as conveyed by sympathetic clergy) place God as a central actor in the struggle of the oppressed. Church teachings emphasize God's love for the poor, His forgiveness and compassion for those who do harm (including in a revolutionary cause), and His vision of solidarity for all humankind.

The indigenous narrative, however, goes somewhat further in its depiction of justice. It presents a more powerful critique of colonialism and the impact it continues to have on the theology, culture, and material well-being of indigenous peoples. This narrative is even critical of some of the Zapatistas in Chiapas for engaging in excessive destruction of property and violence. It includes a core element of forgiveness in combination with the assertion of certain rights and demands regarded as essential for the establishment of peace and social justice, such as the development of schools that reflect and respect the cultures of indigenous communities and their need for equal access to natural, scientific, and financial resources (Bravo, 1994). In many ways, these ideas about social justice are similar to those long articulated by Latin American Marxists and by leaders of African and Asian liberation struggles.

Marxism and Social Justice in Latin America

Marxist ideas about social justice were first introduced into Latin America between 1890 and 1920 during the height of their influence in Germany, France, and Russia. In the two decades after World War I, communist parties emerged in Argentina, Chile, and Cuba, and communist-inspired movements grew in Mexico and Brazil (Aguilar, 1978). At the height of the Cold War, similar movements throughout Latin America and the Caribbean were repressed by military governments, often with the backing of the United States. The success of the Cuban Revolution in 1959 and the persistence of widespread socioeconomic inequality and political repression, however, produced a resurgence of interest in Marxism throughout the region, which guided both revolutionary groups (such as in Bolivia and Peru) and reformist political parties (such as in Chile under Salvador Allende) and recent governments in Bolivia and Uruguay.

In each nation, the intersection of colonialism, imperialism, and capitalism created a context for the emergence of Marxist ideas and strategies that was quite different from those that appeared in industrialized societies with large working-class movements and parties or those in African or Asian nations. Where colonialism still existed, the struggle for social justice was equally inspired by nationalist ideas. In contrast to their European counterparts, Latin American Marxists viewed the fundamental contradictions in their societies in terms of class conflict and the dichotomies that existed between rural and urban populations and indigenous and foreign social systems, practices, and worldviews. Although US political leaders often spoke of a unified Latin American communist conspiracy, the anti-imperialist and anticapitalist struggles of the region each reflected a specific history and social context (Cabral, 1966).

One central theme, expressed in the writings of Cuban revolutionary leader Ernesto (Ché) Guevara, was that justice is not solely a method of redistribution. Instead, it represented a social system founded on moral reasoning in which the search for balance between economic and social well-being required ongoing struggle. On a practical level—particularly in the context of well-funded efforts to subvert justice movements—this required constant sacrifice (which, ironically, often produced a redistribution of poverty rather than affluence) and efforts to maintain optimism about the ultimate triumph of social justice in the face of persistent hardship (Lizarraga, 2006).

The survival of the Cuban Revolution, despite the US blockade and the political excesses of the Castro regime, and the recent electoral successes of left-wing candidates in Bolivia, Brazil, Chile, and Venezuela underscore the enduring appeal of such ideas throughout Latin America. Western criticisms of these social justice-oriented regimes often focus on their failure to adhere to international standards of human rights, particularly in the political arena. The response of contemporary Latin American governments—for example, in Bolivia, Brazil, and Venezuela—to these criticisms underscores ongoing divisions about the relationship between human rights and social justice in practice and the meaning of these concepts in the 21st century (Douzinas, 2000).

In summary, ideas about social justice in Latin America have reflected a unique blend of indigenous theology, Christianity, particularly liberation theology, and European Marxism that emerged as a response to centuries of colonization and exploitation by Western powers (Esteves, 2014). This synthesis builds on traditions that date back over a millennium while substantially revising long-standing ideas about justice. For example, the most recent interpretation of social justice in Latin America takes the form of efforts to promote a "solidarity economy," which eliminates the Western dichotomy of "public" and "private" spheres of life. It "reflects an approach to community that includes all living and inanimate beings and recognizes the emancipatory potential of the norms, social dynamics, and forms of organization of [marginalized] groups" (Esteves, 2014, p. 74). Although the idea of a solidarity economy reflects Western ideas of social justice that date back to the Enlightenment, it adds the dimension of solidarity whose purpose is to strengthen and broaden the concept of democracy.

The writings of a number of influential contemporary South American authors contain a strong criticism of the exploitation of poor citizens, especially indigenous peoples, and a denial of their rights on that continent. They have emphasize the role of the United States and multinational corporations in supporting repressive regimes. Among the most influential of these writers are Carlos Fuentes (1968, 1992) and Eduardo Galeano (1997, 2010).

Summary

As this chapter demonstrates, a society's definition of social justice is strongly influenced by the historical conditions in which it develops, the diverse cultural traditions that shape its belief systems, the relative importance of religious or secular ideas, and the existence of institutions to implement or thwart the attainment of social justice goals. In some circumstances, such as in the South African liberation struggle, the establishment of civil or political rights was regarded as a prerequisite for the attainment of social and economic justice. In other places, such as India, West Africa, and areas of Latin America, primacy was given to overcoming hegemonic cultural norms and values that had been imposed by colonial or imperial powers.

Context also plays a critical role in shaping how different societies articulate their conceptions of justice. For example, Latin American narratives, which are expressed most vividly through poetry and the visual arts, reflect a synthesis of indigenous myths and a hybrid form of Catholicism. In Africa, justice concepts have utilized a new vocabulary (negritude) and are frequently depicted through traditional language, songs, and stories. Asian conceptions of social justice borrow heavily from Hindu, Buddhist, and Confucian philosophy and are often expressed through the use of educational aphorisms.

In each region, movements for justice emerged for all of the reasons suggested previously: the growth of political discontent due to the intransigence of elite-dominated institutions; the influence of external events and foreign ideas; the interplay of various evolutionary change processes, such as industrialization and urbanization; and the response to long-standing conditions of oppression.

Similarly, the justice concepts on which these movements were based also reflected diverse ideological and political sources—religious and secular, indigenous and foreign—in often unexpected syntheses. These concepts emerged to give voice to people's struggles against oppression, to articulate specific grievances, to present a vision of an alternative society, to inspire people to take action, and to justify the use of certain tactics to achieve revolutionary goals. Some have rationalized the use of violence against repressive regimes, such as in South Africa; others have promoted nonviolent forms of resistance, such as in India and the US civil rights movement.

Cultural and contextual influences also shaped how societies expressed and implemented their justice concepts through the establishment of policy priorities, laws, and institutions and through the modification of long-established customs and traditions. One common theme, whether expressed through the Latin American conscientization movement or the African negritude movement, is the importance of education and re-education—of providing people not only with basic skills but also with new ways of thinking about themselves and their role in the world. Another is the need for people to regain control of the land, to determine the ways in which it will be used, and to develop economic self-sufficiency. A related theme is the goal of ending poverty and overcoming its consequences, particularly in the areas of health care, child welfare, housing, the environment, and labor rights. These themes continue to be of critical significance today as a consequence of economic globalization.

Most of the political and social struggles described in this chapter defined the beneficiaries of justice in group rather than individual terms, reflecting the collectivist orientation of the cultures in which they emerged. This contrasts sharply with the Western emphasis on individual rights. Ironically, although many non-Western justice movements have used the language of universal rights to promote their causes, they often reject the application of a universal human rights framework to their societies because it fails to acknowledge their unique cultural values and traditions and is regarded, therefore, as another means of imposing Western dominance. These differences have been most clearly expressed around such issues as the separation of church and state; the role of women; the structure of the economic system, especially regarding the concept of private property; and the means by which societies will resolve their differences or conflicting justice goals. Here, too, the imposition of Western notions of political democracy has been frequently resisted.

Chapter 3 discusses the evolution of social justice concepts in the social work profession, with a particular emphasis on the United States. The chapters in Part II apply these ideas to contemporary social work practice.

Discussion Questions

1. What are some common and different themes reflected in the alternate conceptions of social justice described in this chapter?
2. What conflicts may arise in contemporary US society and in international social work as a result of these differences?
3. What are the implications of these differences for social work practice in an increasingly diverse society?

3

Social Justice and the Social Work Profession

Introduction

Since the early 20th century, the pursuit of social justice has been a core value of the social work profession in the United States, providing an alternative to the concept of social welfare as charity (Hunter, 1904; Woods, 1905). For more than a century, the conflict between justice and charitable perspectives has influenced the evolution of social policy and social work practice through the creation of an awkward synthesis of individualistic and collectivist orientations to society and its problems (George & Wilding, 1994). This focus on social justice, which has been closely linked in social work practice through the concepts of self-determination and empowerment to the ideal of personal freedom, has provided the intellectual and ideological foundation for the major contributions that social workers have made in the United States and other nations in such areas as income support, civil rights, women's rights, public health and housing, labor and occupational safety, child welfare and juvenile justice, and international peace (Stern & Axinn, 2013).

As a "value-based profession," social work strives to promote individual and social change consistent with "principles of human rights and social justice" (Hare, 2004). The revised National Association of Social Workers' (NASW) *Code of Ethics* (2015) asserts that the pursuit of social justice and the eradication of injustice constitute one of the six "ethical imperatives" of the profession. The *Educational Policy and Accreditation Standards* of the Council on Social Work Education (2008, 2015) require programs to teach content on the mechanisms of oppression and how to advocate on behalf of economic and social justice.

However, the profession of social work has long struggled with translating its social justice concepts into policies, programs, and practice frameworks. The profession's pursuit of social justice has sometimes been compromised by its pursuit of professional status and contradicted by its complicity, intentional and unintentional, in mechanisms of social control. Since the 1990s, despite the rhetorical certainty of mainstream professional organizations that social justice is a fundamental social work value, the meaning of social justice has become increasingly ambiguous and contentious, both in the United States and internationally (Reisch, 2002).

Proponents of social justice within social work, like their counterparts in other fields, have often been vilified and marginalized, sometimes even by the profession itself (Reisch & Andrews, 2002). Modest victories for social justice have rarely been permanent; each generation must refight old battles, reframe old issues, and redefine the meaning of social justice to match the changing context. The need to re-examine how the idea of social justice can be applied to our increasingly complex and diverse society is more urgent and challenging than ever.

This chapter provides a brief history of the relationship between social justice and social work practice in the United States since its origins at the turn of the 20th century, with particular emphases on its contemporary implications.[1] The chapter traces the influence of religious and secular ideologies, the evolution of the profession's "vocabulary" of social justice, the emergence of diverse ways of expressing social justice concerns, and the impact of professionalism on the social justice mission of social work. The chapter contains a summary of recent critiques of the profession's current approach to social justice and some suggestions as to how its practice could reflect social justice principles in the context of 21st-century realities.

Social Justice and the Origins of US Social Work

Since the late 19th century, social workers in the United States have regarded the construction of a socially just system of social welfare through the provision of assistance to vulnerable individuals and families as a primary means to achieve the collective public good and to correct what the British scholar Richard Titmuss (1968) later referred to as the "diswelfares" of industrial society, such as unemployment. Because of the deeply entrenched value of self-reliance in American society, they sought to accomplish these goals through the provision of material assistance and nonmaterial support to vulnerable individuals and families. This produced a patchwork system of social welfare consisting of state and federal policies and private initiatives. Policies often used the provision of aid to

---

1. For more detailed histories, the reader should consult the following: Wenocur and Reisch (1989), Specht and Courtenay (1994), and Reisch and Andrews (2002).

reinforce cultural values about work through the stigmatization of dependency, and services were structured in a manner designed to maintain gender and racial hierarchies (Jansson, 2005; Katz, 2001; Patterson, 2001; Stern & Axinn, 2013). Social policies and social work practice have also been based on certain assumptions about the relationship of government to the economy; the causes of individual behavior; the goals of social welfare; and by persistent views about race, gender, sexual orientation, and ability status (Abramovitz, 1999; Baynton, 2001; Brown, 1999; Lieberman, 1998).

The emergence of social justice as an alternative to centuries-old ideas about charity first appeared in the social welfare field at the turn of the 20th century. The first formal reference to "social justice" as a goal of social work appeared during the Progressive Era (Wise, 1909). The concept of social justice replaced hierarchical principles of private benevolence with universal public standards of decency that would (eventually) be enforced through government policies and professional standards and rationalized by social scientific research (Abbott, 1924; Addams, 1902, 1912; Tucker, 1913; Wise, 1909). Initially promoted largely by secular and religious elites out of enlightened self-interest, this definition of social justice synthesized long-standing liberal ideas about individual rights, the emerging ideology of social democracy, and moral values derived from such diverse sources as the Social Gospel movement among White American Protestants; Quakerism; Catholic ideas about benevolence and good works; Jewish principles of justice; concepts of mutual aid rooted in African American, Latino, and Asian American communities; and the work of such diverse secular philosophers as Karl Marx, John Dewey, and William James (Reisch & Andrews, 2002). Social work leaders such as Jane Addams, Florence Kelley, Ellen Gates Starr, and Lillian Wald regarded the pursuit of social justice as a necessary response to growing economic inequality and the breakdown of community (Carson, 1990; Daniels, 1989; Elshtain, 2002; Sklar, 1995; Tucker, 1903). They allied with feminists, trade unionists, civil rights activists, and radicals outside of social work to promote more socially just child welfare, housing, public health, and juvenile justice policies (Davis, 1967; Fisher, 1994; Holder, 1922; Karger, 1988; Reisch & Andrews, 2002).

From the outset, however, because social work emerged during the most "thoroughly racialized . . . point in American history" (Foner, 1999, pp. 12–13), the pursuit of social justice among social workers was hampered by the exclusion or marginalization of a significant portion of the US population, based on their gender, race, ethnicity, and religion. This led to the denial of inclusive rights of citizenship to millions and the erection of structural barriers to equal opportunity. Even many settlement houses, including those that explicitly professed social justice goals, denied access to people of color and reflected traditional stereotypes about gender, class, and ethnicity in their programs and staffing patterns (Carson, 1990; Lasch-Quinn, 1993). The failure of White social workers to embrace inclusive ideas significantly hindered their ability to apply social justice concepts to their practice. To a considerable extent, the history of US social work reflects the struggle to overcome these barriers and apply social justice principles on a more universal basis (Katz, 2001; Reisch, 1998, 2008a).

Barred access to White-dominated institutions, people of color and religious minorities developed their own concepts of social justice that through the organizations they created combined elements of cultural pride (e.g., racial or ethnic uplift, sisterhood, or religious solidarity) and social assimilation. These group-specific ideas of social justice contrasted sharply with those professed by most social workers of the period, which stressed a mythical "general welfare" or the "common good" (Beito, 2001; Chan, 1991; Gerstle, 2001; Hernandez, 1983; Iglehart & Becerra, 2011; Morris & Freund, 1966; O'Grady, 1931; Rivera, 1987). Members of marginalized communities also used dramatic issues, such as lynching in the South or the exploitation of women and girls in Northern factories, to increase public awareness of persistent injustice (Gordon, 1991; Hammond, 1920; Hine, 1990; Salem, 1990).

By emphasizing self-help, mutual aid, and socioeconomic (not just political) equality, racial, ethnic, and religious minorities redefined the meaning of social justice in ways that would eventually have wider implications for other marginalized social groups, such as individuals with disabilities and the lesbian, gay, bisexual, transgendered, and queer (LGBTQ) population (Carlton-Laney, 2001; Carson, 1993; Hamilton & Hamilton, 1997; Reisch & Andrews, 2002). Ironically, although the development of these alternative views of social justice enabled disenfranchised groups to retain their cultural heritages and provided the philosophical foundation for efforts to improve the lives of their communities, they also made it more difficult for American social workers to develop a unified vision of what a socially just society would be (Reisch, 2007, 2008a).

Efforts by disenfranchised groups to forge alternative concepts of social justice and apply them to their needs *as they understood them* also underscored an often unacknowledged problem of mainstream social work—that, for the most part, it continued to ignore the structural and ideological sources of racism and sexism. Even sympathetic social workers failed to recognize that prevailing "universalist" ideas of social justice primarily emphasized *political* democracy and equality *before the law* rather than equality of resources, power, or status *through the law*. It overlooked the structural inequalities that were woven into the fabric of laws and policies, no matter how well-intentioned. Even social work leaders who were sensitive to issues of cultural diversity did not seriously consider the concept of cultural or social equality until the mid-1970s (Elshtain, 2002).

Jane Addams, often heralded as the leading example of social work values, had a strong identification with mainstream Protestant ideals of altruism, despite conservative attempts to label her as a a dangerous radical (Knight, 2005; Reisch & Andrews, 2002). However, a few radical social workers, such as Ellen Gates Starr (the cofounder of Hull House in Chicago) and Florence Kelley (the director of the influential National Consumers League for three decades), were influenced by socialist ideas—ideas that social workers in the Charities Organization Societies (COS) and public sector largely disdained. In fact, the practices of the COS and many public sector agencies—two primary sources for the development of the social work profession and social work education—often reflected repressive tendencies that mirrored dominant cultural perspectives on race, ethnicity, class, and gender (Day, 2013).

Although most efforts at social reform during this period focused primarily on the needs of White native-born men and, to a lesser extent, recent immigrants from Eastern and Southern Europe (Stern & Axinn, 2013), a few prominent social workers began to address the problems of African Americans and women (Addams, 1902; Elshtain, 2002; Lundblad, 1995; Sklar, 1998; Van Kleeck, 1915). Their work was also influenced by African American activists and scholars such as W. E. B. DuBois (1903/1999), George Edmund Haynes (1912), and Ida Wells-Barnett (1970).

Social Justice and the Creation of the Welfare State

The so-called Progressive Era, which began in approximately 1890, came to an abrupt end during World War I (1914–1918). Both during and after the war, social workers who promoted social justice endured political repression and social approbation for their support of pacifist causes, opposition to American militarism, and their alliances with radical groups. They were attacked by major newspapers, elected officials, and powerful conservative organizations and accused of subversive activities by state legislators and the courts (Reisch & Andrews, 2002). After the war, the repressive political climate of the 1920s discouraged social workers' pursuit of social justice. In response, the profession shifted its focus from policy advocacy and social change to the development of enhanced social services and psychiatric social work (Wenocur & Reisch, 1989). For more than a decade, social workers did not address rising inequality and unemployment and the intolerable working conditions in factories, mines, and mills during the "Roaring 20s" (Andrews, 1997; Reisch, 2009, 2015c; Van Kleeck, 1932, 1934).

The cause of social justice within social work, however, was not completely silenced during this period. Some social workers continued to promote civil rights and the establishment of "social security" for the elderly and unemployed (Chambers, 1963; Lubove, 1968). During the Great Depression of the 1930s, their efforts finally began to bear fruit. The policies of the Franklin Roosevelt administration, in which social workers such as Harry Hopkins and Frances Perkins played major roles, produced significant social reforms in such areas as labor rights, public assistance to the elderly and the jobless, and child welfare (Downey, 2010; McJimsey, 1987). By the mid-1930s, many social workers regarded the creation of the welfare state as the key to achieving social justice and reducing long-standing structural inequalities in American society (Katz, 2001). It would establish the ideas of social citizenship and social democracy as a right and substitute collective responsibility for individualistic values (Marshall, 1950).

Social workers' justice-oriented activism was not confined to the policy arena during these years. Social workers also made serious efforts to integrate social justice values into practice—for example, in the democratic principles underlying the emerging field of social group work (Wenocur & Reisch, 1989) and the services developed to assist immigrant families, the working poor, and members of newly formed unions, including those created by social workers (Reisch, 2009). The radical Rank and File Movement, which had more members in the mid-1930s than the American Association of Social Workers, not only advocated for racial and gender equality decades before these views were embraced by mainstream social work organizations but also developed "five simple principles" as the foundation for justice-centered practice (Fisher, 1980). Bertha Capen Reynolds (1963), a leader among the rank and filers, summarized these principles in her autobiography (as cited in Withorn, 1986, pp. 1–2):

1. The purpose of social work is to serve people in need. If social workers serve other classes who have other purposes, they become too dishonest to be capable of either theoretical or practical development.
2. Social work exists to help people help themselves and, therefore, social workers should not be alarmed when people do so by organized means.
3. Social work practice operates by communication, listening, and sharing experiences.
4. Social workers have to find their place among other movements for human betterment by forming and joining coalitions with clients, community groups, and like-minded colleagues from all disciplines.
5. Social workers cannot consider themselves superior to their clients, as if they do not have the same problems.

The rank and file movement disappeared during World War II, a consequence of internal factionalism, external attacks, and the promotion of wartime unity

(Fisher, 1980). Nevertheless, its ideas have been integrated into several contemporary models of social work practice, largely without acknowledgment of their origins (Spano, 1982).

During the 1930s, the number of social workers in the United States tripled and the profession's influence grew in both public and private sectors. Activist social workers exercised considerable influence in the following decade on US public opinion. They organized educational programs in factories and unions to "critically evaluate economic and social values from a national and international point of view" (Cohn, 1943, p. 6) and openly discussed the problems of women and African Americans. They supported Franklin Roosevelt's Second Bill of Rights, issued in 1944, which concisely articulated social justice goals in the areas of employment, wages, education, health care, housing, civil rights, and civil liberties (Sunstein, 2004). Through professional conference papers and their unions, social workers proposed antidiscrimination measures, promoted racial and gender equality, and supported efforts to improve interracial relations at the community level. Organizations such as the YWCA, which had been at the forefront of social justice advocacy within the social work profession since 1910, proposed antipoverty measures, the expansion of labor rights, and legislation that acknowledged the unique problems of women and people of color (Reisch & Andrews, 2002).

Although the expansion of US social welfare policies between the mid-1930s and the mid-1970s potentially provided the structure through which social workers could fulfill their social justice goals, for the most part these policies continued to reflect institutional racism and sexism (Hamilton & Hamilton, 1997; Patterson, 2001; Rose, 1994.) There are several possible reasons why the creation of the American welfare state fell considerably short of the expectations of social workers who aspired to establish a more socially just society.

One reason is that post–World War II prosperity masked persistent social divisions, particularly those based on race. As the demographic composition of Northern, Midwestern, and Western cities changed, the media continued to portray minority groups in unfavorable, stereotypical ways (Gerstle, 2001; Massey & Denton, 1993; Sugrue, 1995). Second, the existence or perception of external enemies, such as Nazism or communism, produced a façade of national unity and thwarted efforts to spotlight domestic social injustices.

This emphasis on national unity rationalized attacks on social critics, particularly those who promoted social justice goals. Advocates for civil rights, labor protections, disarmament, and fair housing, for example, were viewed as unpatriotic or subversive, as they had been during and after World War I (Reisch & Andrews, 2002). During the height of the "Red Scare" (~1940s to the early 1960s), many social workers lost their jobs in government and academia, were blacklisted by major agencies and universities, and could not publish in well-established journals (Schrecker, 1998). This political repression led social workers to pursue greater professional status and refrain from advocacy for social justice causes (Specht & Courtenay, 1994).

New Views of Social Justice

The diverse social movements of the 1960s, 1970s, and 1980s stimulated renewed interest in social justice among US social workers, particularly around issues of civil rights, welfare rights, and the condition of women. In response to pressure from activists inside and outside the profession, NASW took a forceful position against "institutional racism" in the late 1960s (Reisch & Andrews, 2002). During the 1970s–1990s, however, frequent conflicts erupted between radicals and reformers over the meaning of social justice and its application to practice. These debates "inspired new forms of scholarship, new models of social services, and new theoretical frameworks that considerably expanded and revised the meaning of social justice" (Reisch, 2007, p. 77). They also underscored the gap between the profession's social justice rhetoric and its growing emphasis on therapeutic interventions with individuals.

The *Working Statement on the Purpose of Social Work* (NASW, 1981) reflected these tensions and philosophical ambiguities. It emphasized consensus rather than conflict-oriented approaches to social change, focused more on expanding equality of opportunity than producing more equitable outcomes, and demonstrated a preference for programs that stressed individual adaptation and enhancement rather than systemic or structural change. NASW continued to articulate this view of social justice through the 1990s. In 1997, it stated that social work's goals were "individual well-being in a social context and the well-being of society" (NASW, 1998) while simultaneously revising the *Code of Ethics* (1998) to establish the pursuit of social justice as an ethical imperative. These statements implied that social justice can be achieved through a complementary ("win–win") relationship between persons and their environment rather than through political and social struggle as social workers had advocated during the Progressive Era, the New Deal, and the War on Poverty of the 1960s (Reisch & Jani, 2012). Recently, however, NASW has developed several broadly worded policy statements that address increasing socioeconomic inequality and the multiple consequences of globalization, deindustrialization, and racial inequities (Kelly & Clark, 2009; Polack, 2004).

The persistent gap between the profession's rhetoric about social justice and the realities of social injustice had several contradictory effects. It rationalized the development of new, identity-based social movements, inspired more inclusive social services, and created a receptive climate for innovative ideas derived from critical theory and postmodernism. These ideas transformed the meaning of social justice and have influenced the direction of social work theory and practice to the present (Gray, Agglias, & Davies, 2014; Hill Collins, 2000; Johnson, 2001; Kim & Sherraden, 2014; Leonard, 1997; Nussbaum, 1999; Young, 1990, 2008, 2011; Swenson, 1998; Wakefield, 1988a, 1988b).

For example, advocates of postmodernism critiqued long-standing conceptions of social justice in several fundamental ways. They challenged the presence of "meta-narratives," whatever their ideological basis, because these excluded the voices of marginalized groups (Leonard, 1995). They proposed an expansion of modern visions of social justice to include groups traditionally omitted from justice-oriented debates, an examination of justice/injustice in the sociocultural as well as the political–economic spheres of society, and a focus on societal processes as well as societal goals and outcomes (Witkin & Irving, 2014). Like feminists in the 1960s and 1970s, they defined social justice as both a process and an outcome and emphasized how dominant cultural institutions—including social service organizations—contributed to oppression and social exclusion and the unequal distribution of societal resources (Dominelli, 2010; Gibelman, 2000; Leonard, 1995; Mullaly, 2010). (See Part II.) By rejecting universal liberal ideals of social justice, however, postmodern critics increased the credibility of conservative attacks on social welfare and its underlying social justice goals (Mead, 1992; Murray, 1984).

Recently, some postmodernists have taken these arguments further, questioning whether social justice "exists" or even if it is possible or necessary to attain (Witkin & Irving, 2014). Rather than promoting, defending, or criticizing a particular interpretation of social justice, they explore why certain views of social justice gain ascendance and how the concept of social justice functions in different societies. Witkin and Irving, for example, assert that modern ideas about justice reflect a particular framing of the world that has acquired the quality of a universal truth. Similar to the arguments presented previously, they are particularly concerned with the widespread assumption of the linkage between social justice and human rights (discussed later). Instead, they attempt to shift the discourse to such questions as the following: What is a *right*? What does it mean to *have* a right? Who counts as *human*?

In addition, postmodernists posit that social justice goals will never be achieved until the current intellectual foundation of its liberal proponents, particularly its attachment to universal principles, is subverted (Bauman, 2000, 2001, 2004; Lyotard, 1984, 1985, 1988, 1992; Rorty, 1989, 1991, 1998). In their view, all forms of justice are context-specific. Although he supported the need to establish a "human rights culture," Richard Rorty (1998), a leading postmodernist philosopher, "reject[ed] the essentialist justifications for human rights and . . . the ahistorical conception of rationality on which contemporary ideas of social justice are based" (as quoted in Reisch, 2014b, p. 128). Ironically, his preference for linking social justice to group loyalty would produce a return to the group-exclusive principles that existed several millennia ago. (See Chapter 2.) In summary, postmodern critics believe that today's discourse on social justice and human rights could be improved if it was "freed from the straightjacket of modernist rationality . . . [and if justice was] considered . . . as a plural, [as] 'justices'" (Rorty as quoted in Reisch, 2014b, p. 128).

Other contemporary critics of traditional ideas about social justice similarly argue that the concept has not been sufficiently inclusive in its design or bold in its application. Fook (2014), for example, discusses the relationship between the articulation of social justice concepts and the means by which they are implemented in theory and practice. Within the social work field, these create what she regards as a "central problem for social work: the struggle to balance its dual focus on social action and individual change" (as quoted in Reisch, 2014b, p. 127). Fook argues that "this struggle has recently been complicated by a shift from the politics of redistribution to the politics of recognition" (p. 127). This conflict is difficult to resolve for three reasons: (1) persistent ambiguities and conflicts over the meaning of social justice; (2) the ever-changing contexts in which practitioners attempt to apply the concept consistently and coherently; and (3) "the absence of an analytical practice framework that addresses both individual and social well-being" (p. 127).

Unlike earlier feminist writers, some contemporary feminist authors focus on "social justice feminism" that promotes structural changes in society to address such women's issues as paid work, unpaid caregiving in the home, culture and identity, sexuality, domestic violence, and the provision of state welfare (Gray et al., 2014). One influential feminist theorist, Nancy Fraser (1989, 1997, 2000, 2008, 2009), emphasizes the importance of creating a political agenda of social justice to challenge what she terms "neoliberal reprivatization discourse." Its advocates are committed to public policies that improve the lives of women through a bottom-up, action-oriented approach that focuses on unmasking and dismantling the sociopolitical structures and ideologies that perpetuate all forms of oppression and distributive injustice. It also reflects an empowerment perspective that goes beyond the removal of injustices by enhancing personal and public awareness of privilege and inequity and how they are multiplied by the presence of multiple forms of oppression. Through action research and critical analysis, social justice feminists in social work strive to create more democratic relationships with service users to empower ordinary citizens and "to interpret their needs democratically, via political deliberation and contestation" (Fraser, 2009, p. 102).

The Politics of Social Justice

During the past several decades, dramatic shifts in the global economy and an unprecedented demographic and cultural transformation in the United States have challenged the assumption that economic, social, and cultural issues arise from distinct sources and can therefore, be addressed separately. As a result, the social justice goals underlying social work practice have come under increasing attack from all points on the political/ideological spectrum, and the implementation of these goals into practice has become more difficult.

Conservatives and neoliberals have challenged the principles of centralized state planning and regulation and the emphasis on collective or community-oriented goals. Both have attacked the existence of a so-called "dependency culture" produced by a combination of liberal social welfare policies and social work benevolence. Conservatives, in particular, have criticized government-funded assistance on the grounds that it undermines freedom, personal choice, individual responsibility, and motivation (Mead, 1992; Murray, 1984). They prefer a minimalist state that interferes infrequently with the operations of the market. Although they are often critical of public programs, neoliberals acknowledge that government has a role to play in the nation's social welfare system. They define this role, however, as "enabling" individuals to compete in the global market economy of the future (Gilbert, 1989; Reisch, 2013b).

At the same time, critics on the left have attacked contemporary social policies on the grounds that they compel cultural assimilation, normalization, and social control—goals that primarily serve corporate interests and that preserve the dominance of elites (Blau, 2014; Margolin, 1997; Piven & Cloward, 1995). Proponents of multiculturalism have criticized social welfare provisions and the social workers who implement them for defining personal well-being primarily in universal terms as the "common good," thereby ignoring the specific needs of gender, racial, ethnic, cultural, religious, and sexual minorities (Ewalt, Freeman, Kirk, & Poole, 1996; Hill Collins, 2000; Reisch, 2008a; Young, 1990, 2011).

Recent demographic and cultural changes have intensified these critiques. For example, the development of policies that expanded the rights of women and sexual minorities has sometimes conflicted with the cultural norms and values of new immigrant groups, African American religious congregations, and White evangelicals (Fellin, 2000). Since the terrorist attack on September 11, 2001, the government's response to the threat of terrorism has further complicated debates over the meaning of social justice (Greenwald, 2014).

From another angle, Caputo (2000) questions whether social justice can be achieved in a political–economic environment in which market forces are ascendant. He asserts that an emphasis on the caring function of social work can serve as the basis for more socially just social and political goals. However, this would require a return to universal approaches to social welfare, within which the unique needs of persons and groups could then be accommodated.

One of the most influential contemporary critiques of liberal ideas about social justice is the "capabilities approach," developed by the Nobel Prize economist Amartya Sen (2009) and the political philosopher Martha Nussbaum (2011). Expanding on the principles developed by John Rawls in *A Theory of Justice* (1971/1999), they focus on the omissions and oversights in his arguments. Many social workers have embraced this perspective because of its compatibility with the mission and goals of the profession (Kim & Sherraden, 2014; Morris, 2002).

Like postmodernists, Sen's critique of Rawls's distributional notion of "justice as fairness" focuses more on means rather than ends. He defines means as *functionings* that constitute "the various things that [a person] . . . manages to do or be in leading a life" and, in turn, that *capability* refers to "the alternative combination of functionings the person can achieve, and from which he or she can choose one collection" (Sen, 1992, p. 31). Thus, in Sen's framework, social work practice should emphasize a person's potential (capabilities) to make life choices rather than focusing solely on his or her current situation (Sen, 1999). In addition, whereas the liberal approach to social justice emphasizes a negative idea of freedom, Sen's capability approach emphasizes a "positive" concept of freedom— the freedom to do "what a person can choose to do or achieve [capabilities]" (Sen & Muellbauer, 1988, p. 272). This view of freedom and human agency is strikingly similar to the ideas expressed in Marx's early work (1844/1964), although it lacks Marx's critique of capitalism as a socioeconomic system.

Although she basically concurs with Sen and Rawls, Nussbaum (2003, 2011) argues that they both overlook the issue of unequal power relations. She asserts that vulnerable populations cannot achieve their capabilities without expanding their power at the cost of those who currently hold power and that unless a society guarantees these capabilities to all citizens, it cannot be considered just. She includes the following in her list of essential capabilities: life; bodily health; bodily integrity; the ability to use one's senses, intellect, and imagination; the ability to create and sustain emotional attachments; the ability to form a conception of good and to engage in critical reflection about the planning of one's life; the ability to live with others, to recognize and show concern for other human beings, to engage in various forms of social interaction, and to be treated as a dignified being whose worth is equal to that of others; the ability to live with concern for and in relation to animals, plants, and the world of nature; the ability to laugh, play, and enjoy recreational activities; and the ability to control one's political and economic environment (Nussbaum, 2003, pp. 41–42). Her ideas provide a framework that can help social workers identify whose rights and which capabilities should be prioritized and how social policies and programs can be used to promote these goals. Morris (2002) argues that the capabilities approach combines social work's historic emphasis on human dignity and self-determination with the redistributive principles articulated by Rawls. She asserts that this approach to practice would produce interventions that would enable all people to achieve their full human potential.

As these diverse perspectives reflect, today's complex environment obscures both the meaning and goals of social justice. New and persistent questions frame both philosophical and political debates. These include the following: Are the goals of social justice and multiculturalism compatible (Reisch, 2008a)? Through what means is justice to be achieved? How can we reconcile traditional ideas of social justice with the emerging interest in human rights? Are such rights individual or social? Can they all be legislated? Should they be (Reisch, 2013b)?

Social work scholars and practitioners continue to struggle with these difficult questions. They have tried to apply the profession's philosophical commitment to a variety of diverse issues, including peace and nuclear nonproliferation; opposition to US military intervention; support for marriage equality; defense of affirmative action; environmental justice; and concerns about structural racial inequalities, particularly in the areas of health, mental health, education, housing, and employment (Brawley & Martinez-Brawley, 1999; Dominelli, 2012; Gibelman, 2000; Van Soest, 1994; Verschelden, 1993; Witkin, 1999). These diverse and frequently ambiguous interpretations of social justice, however, have created considerable confusion within all branches of the profession (Reisch, Ife, & Weil, 2012; Wakefield, 2014).

Some social workers equate the profession's commitment to human rights with its commitment to social justice and question "whether social justice goals can be met without redistribution" (Beck & Eichler, 2000, p. 100). Others define social justice as the pursuit of social change that would specifically aid disadvantaged and vulnerable groups, particularly people living in poverty (Witkin, 1998, 1999, 2000), or as a form of compensation for past injustices (Gal, 2001). NASW has recently embraced the concept of "racial equity" as a means of applying a structural analysis to the challenges posed by institutional racism (NASW, 2013).

Van Soest (1994) argues that all three different justice theories—libertarianism, utilitarianism, and egalitarianism—could be used as the basis for reordering national priorities. Others focus on the roots of injustice in institutional discrimination (Gibelman, 2000), growing social inequality, and whether social work's dual goals of self-determination and social justice are mutually exclusive (Figueira-McDonough, 1993). Social workers who have adopted a communitarian perspective have proposed four possible definitions of social justice ranging from individual to community hegemony:

1. Social justice involves individual sacrifice to the common good.
2. Social justice requires an attempt to link individual rights with community rights.
3. Social justice is defined as policies that will benefit all individuals that the market cannot deliver.
4. "Social justice is sacrificing oneself to the common good" (McNutt, 1997, p. 50).

In summary, these diverse views—from pragmatic liberalism to neo-Marxism, postmodernism, and communitarianism—have further obscured the meaning of social justice and made its application to social work practice more challenging than ever. Currently, each of these approaches also lacks specificity and clarity, which limits their utility as guides for policy change. Although some social workers suggest that a human rights framework is a potential bridging concept (Reichert, 2011; Wronka, 2008), this approach has been criticized both in the United States and abroad because of its cultural biases and implications (Reisch, 2015c).

Human Rights and Social Justice

Although there had been periodic attempts for centuries to develop a "universal concept" of social justice in the West (e.g., medieval Christian doctrine; the work of 18th-century Enlightenment philosophers and political theorists in France, Great Britain, and the United States; the writings of German philosophers such as Kant and Hegel; and the numerous documents of revolutionary socialism and anarchism in the 19th and 20th centuries), until the mid-20th century there was no systematic attempt to codify social justice in a global way. This first occurred in the United Nations' *Universal Declaration of Human Rights* (1948).

Since its adoption, many civil society organizations and social movements have used the United Nations' *Declaration* as a framework to promote their social justice agendas, particularly in the West. For social workers, a human rights framework is appealing because it provides a "moral grounding for social work's more complex interpretations of social justice, equality, and empowerment" (Dewees & Roche, 2001, p. 137). Held (1984) and Gil (1998) maintain that the pursuit of social justice complements the pursuit of human rights because they are both products of social cooperation, trust, and mutuality. Consequently, during the past two decades, a number of social work scholars have proposed integrating a human rights framework into all areas of social work practice (Dominelli, 2007; George, 1999; Ife, 2001, 2007; Patterson, 2004; Reichert 2004, 2007, 2011; Wronka, 2008).

However, the use of a human rights framework as the foundation for social justice efforts is not without problems. The concept of universal human rights has a complex and contested history.[2] Much of the controversy regarding human rights is a product of its origins.

The 1948 *Declaration* was drafted in response to the horrors of World War II. It now contains three sets of rights. The first "generation of rights," sometimes referred to as "negative rights" (Ife, 2007), includes civic and political freedoms similar to those in the US Constitution that guarantee the right to due process; freedom of speech and religion; freedom of movement and assembly; and the right to be free from slavery, discrimination, and torture. The second generation of rights, also called "positive rights," emphasizes protections that ensure an adequate standard of living and the basic material amenities required to sustain oneself and one's family. These include education, food, clothing, medical care, and social services. The third and newest generation of rights refers to the collective rights among nations that promote intergovernmental cooperation in the pursuit of peace, economic and human development, and environmental protection. Two important underlying assumptions of a human rights frameworks are that the rights are universal (i.e., applicable to all people regardless of group membership) and indivisible or interdependent (i.e., all rights are equally important and certain rights are preconditions for the realization and enjoyment of others).

During the past half century, a serious schism—sometimes subtle, sometimes explicit—has emerged among both philosophers and activists, inside and outside social work, about the contradictions between social justice and human rights. Some proponents of social justice emphasize universal human rights, whereas others focus on the need for a redistribution of resources, power, privilege, status, and opportunities (Kallen, 2004; Kurasawa, 2007). The most common criticisms of the human rights framework relate to its Eurocentric bias (Ignatieff, 2001).

For example, the concept of social justice in many Islamic nations today reflects their colonial history, the cultural influence of Islam, and the long-term relationship of these societies to their European counterparts (Thompson, 2014). In many Asian societies, family and community are emphasized over individual rights, freedom, and democracy. Many Asians, therefore, regard human rights claims as an "alien, Western import not suited to local normative systems"

---

2. In the introduction to her book on social work and human rights, Reichert cites the NASW 2003 policy statement on the subject: "Social work . . . is the only profession imbued with social justice as its fundamental value and concern. But social justice is a fairness doctrine that provides civil and political leeway in deciding what is just and unjust. Human rights, on the other hand, encompass social justice, but transcend civil and political customs, in consideration of the basic life-sustaining needs of all human beings, without distinction" (Reichert, 2007, p. 4).

(Merry 2006, p. 38; see also Bauer & Bell, 1999). Akimoto (2014) questions whether Western concepts of social justice can be applied to a vastly different society such as Japan, even in an era of globalization. He argues that the Japanese people seldom refer to the concept of "justice" directly. Instead, they base norms of distribution on principles of social obligation and solidarity in evaluating the practices of other societies and in promoting human well-being.

A second source of criticism comes from within the West. These arguments are rooted in a number of traditions, including Marxist critiques of the rights of man [sic], anthropological critiques of imperialism, and postmodern arguments related to the "universalizing pretentions of Enlightenment thought" (Ignatieff, 2001, p. 105). These critics assert that the promotion of human rights furthers the goals of Western imperialism and that its underlying liberal values have meaning only in a small number of Western nations. From this perspective, the promotion of universal human rights principles is merely another mechanism to maintain Western cultural domination.

In her analysis of the meaning of social justice for the indigenous peoples of North America, Weaver (2014) makes similar arguments. Although she asserts that the oppression and injustices experienced by indigenous peoples are beyond dispute, she notes that the means of applying indigenous concepts of social justice to the goal of their liberation is somewhat ambiguous. She maintains that even well-intentioned "Band-Aid" efforts that merely seek to remediate contemporary and historical injustices will never fully be sufficient to heal the damages caused by centuries of cultural domination, exploitation, and genocide.

A related problem with equating a human rights perspective to social justice is that it primarily emphasizes individual rights. Merry and Levitt (2008) argue that rather than promoting collective responsibility, dominant perspectives on human rights subtly promote a "neoliberal capitalist" worldview that places the onus on individuals, often members of subordinated groups, to pursue remedies rather than communities, society, or government. A final challenge to the linkage between human rights and social justice stems from the conceptual and practical problems related to their enforcement, which has generally relied on voluntary compliance by governments. Many social justice advocates have noted that this assumption is naive; governments, including the US government, often violate human rights with impunity.

Although disputes persist between proponents of social justice and human rights, Wronka (2014) maintains that these concepts are complementary and that they both could serve as the foundation of efforts to create a more socially just world. He asserts that the establishment of human rights based on five principles—human dignity; nondiscrimination; civil and political rights; economic, social, and economic rights; and solidarity rights—would help clarify some of the ambiguities within contemporary definitions of justice and adds an ethical imperative to practical efforts to achieve social justice goals. He acknowledges, however, that these rights cannot be attained without ongoing struggle and serious discussions as to how they can be applied at the micro, mezzo, and macro levels of practice.

These critiques underscore how an uncritical adoption of a human rights framework may not advance the social justice mission of social work. Although the goals of human rights are consistent with social work's aim to improve the conditions of society's most vulnerable members, in contemporary practice it is difficult, if not impossible, to operationalize these principles in ways that do not reinforce and reproduce the dominant order. To respond effectively to 21st-century realities, a social justice orientation to social work practice would have to recognize how people's needs for economic assistance and non-economic supports (e.g., social services and information) are complementary. As postmodernists might argue, it would also challenge prevailing assumptions about the universal nature of human needs that frequently underlie current strategies to achieve more just societies. It might even question the fundamental assumption that a universal idea of social justice exists. It would pay closer attention to the effects of differential power and privilege. In summary, a social justice orientation to social work would require the development of an alternative vision of society—a vision that takes into account the implications of global interdependence and demographic and cultural diversity.

To forge this alternative vision, Ife (2007) proposes a model based on "human rights from below" that would preserve the profession's long-standing commitment to end exploitation and inequality while avoiding the unquestioned imposition of hegemonic Western standards and goals. He suggests using existing human rights doctrine as a starting point that can then be deconstructed and critiqued because "universalism need not mean uniformity" (p. 94). This vision of justice would reflect specific contexts, local sources of knowledge, and traditional cultural norms. Although the application of this vision to practice presents numerous complex challenges, it may be more suitable as a guide to "doing justice" in the rapidly changing and complex economic and demographic environment of the future (Table 3.1).

The Past Is in the Present

Two major social justice traditions have influenced the evolution of social welfare and the profession of social work. The liberal tradition, based on the concept of a social contract, has emphasized the preservation of individual liberty, particularly private property rights, whereas the social democratic tradition has focused on the goal of social equality (Tomasi, 2001). For much of the 20th

Table 3.1 Matrix of Human Rights

	Social Rights	Economic Rights	Civil/Political Rights	Cultural Rights	Environmental Rights	Spiritual Rights	Survival Rights
Examples of rights in each category (not exhaustive)	Family life, privacy, leisure, education, choice of partner, housing, lifestyle, sexuality	Basic living standard, earn a living, work, social security, savings, choice of spending	Free speech, free assembly, vote, fair trial, stand for office, join unions, strike	Cultural expression, cultural practices, clothing, religious expression, intellectual property, land rights	Pollution free, poison free, wilderness, beauty, sustainability, access to land	Choice of religious expression, rituals, experience nature, personal fulfillment, sacred land/objects	Life, food, water, shelter, clothing, health, safety

Source: Ife, J. (2010). *Human rights from below.* Reproduced with permission of Cambridge University Press.

century, a synthesis of these ideas produced a widely held consensus that a more equitable distribution of resources, political and social rights, and life's opportunities was a prerequisite of a socially just society. Based on the American value of self-reliance, this consensus also stressed the importance of an individual's past, present, or potential contributions to society in assessing what that person "deserved" (Held, 1995; Miller, 2001; Nussbaum, 1999).

This reflects the close association of the concepts of social justice and individual freedom in the United States and much of the West (Reisch, 2014c). This perspective has shaped our national identity and individual self-concepts (Foner, 2002). It is important to note that in the United States, the concept of freedom has primarily focused on freedom from interference, particularly by the government, and the sanctity of private property. Nevertheless, the American interpretation of freedom has evolved considerably since the *Declaration of Independence* proclaimed that "life, liberty, and the pursuit of happiness" were "inalienable rights" (Smith, 1997).

Prior to the Civil War, the concept of "freedom" in the United States coexisted with the reality of chattel slavery. Well into the 20th century, it was compatible with legal racial segregation; ethnocentric immigration policies; restrictive housing covenants that discriminated against Jews; antisodomy laws directed against the LGBTQ population; and laws that reinforced second-class citizenship, stratified employment, lower wages, and lesser social status for women. The consequences of this restrictive view of freedom persist in the 21st century (Alexander, 2010).

Beginning in the early 20th century, many Americans expanded their ideas about freedom and came to regard economic security for ordinary people as one of its essential components. A variety of social movements dramatized the importance of broadening the American concept of freedom to include greater political equality and social equity for oppressed, marginalized, and excluded populations. Influenced by European and Latin American ideas, this new view of freedom reframed ideas about social justice and changed the focus of the social work profession.

Relatively recently, conservatives (Mead, 1986, 1997; Nozick, 1974) have attempted in four important ways to revise the ideological consensus about justice that existed in the United States for most of the 20th century. First, they would assign rights solely to individuals and not to groups or classes of persons. This has significant implications for policies such as affirmative action (Sabbagh, 2011; Sterba, 2009). Second, they would limit these rights to the political sphere and exclude the redistribution of resources and social status. Third, they regard the protection of property rights as of equal or greater importance to the enhancement of socioeconomic rights (Hayek, 1976; Sunstein, 1997). Finally, they assert that social justice requires a balancing of rights with responsibilities or obligations (Gilbert, 1995; Mead, 1992; Schmidtz & Goodin 1998). The provisions of welfare reform legislation and the Affordable Care Act reflect these perspectives (Gorin & Moniz, 2014; Piven, 2002; Schram, Soss, & Fording, 2014).

Consequently, during the past three decades, with some notable exceptions (LGBTQ rights and the rights of persons with disabilities), the United States has retreated from this enhanced view of freedom with substantial policy implications. The dominant meaning of freedom once again centers on the elimination of restrictions on market activities, lower taxes, limited government, and a definition of democracy and individual rights that has produced greater elite influence in the electoral and policymaking arenas. At the same time, for complex reasons, social workers have lost considerable influence in policymaking circles (Reisch & Jani, 2012).

This cultural and political transformation has produced significant negative consequences for the populations with whom social workers are engaged: more widespread, chronic, and intensive poverty; a widening gap between rich and poor (Piketty, 2014; Stiglitz, 2013); a shrinking middle class (Reich, 2012); and persistent racial and ethnic inequities in the areas of health, housing, employment, education, child welfare, and criminal justice (Alexander, 2010; Braveman et al., 2011; Katiuzhinsky & Okech, 2014; Mays, Cochrane, & Barnes, 2007; Twill & Fisher, 2010). Our society not only has failed to respond adequately to these growing problems it has often failed to acknowledge the emergence of new issues, such as climate change, that have profound implications for "environmental justice" and the practice of social work (Dominelli, 2012; Klein, 2014; Shaw, 2013).

Thus, throughout US social work history there has been considerable tension between views of social justice that emphasize social inequalities and those that focus on individual rights. Several long-standing assumptions, whose validity has been challenged by recent events, have further complicated this debate, including the assumptions that Americans even share a common definition of social justice (Reisch, 2002, 2007, 2008a) and that religious and secular conceptions of social justice are complementary in principle and compatible in practice. Yet, as in ancient times, views of social justice continue to range from the universal to the group-specific (see Chapter 2). In our increasingly diverse and polarized society, Americans also do not agree on how to achieve social justice, however it is defined.

Several lessons can be derived from this dynamic history. First, concepts such as freedom and social justice are historically specific; they consciously serve specific social, economic, political, and cultural purposes. Second, people, particularly through collective action, can reinterpret these concepts and promote different ways of applying them to meet their ever-changing ideas about human needs and the ways in which these needs should be addressed. Third, many different groups have contributed to the transformation of the meaning of social justice in the United States, influenced by their struggles to address their particular needs and aspirations within a specific historical context. Fourth, these struggles influenced the social work profession to move beyond its initial ethnocentric emphasis on assimilation and cultural homogenization to its current emphasis on the values of diversity, cultural competence, and cultural humility. (See Part II.) Social work organizations are now strong supporters of affirmative action, comparable worth legislation, reasonable accommodations for individuals with disabilities, reproductive rights, marriage equality, and elimination of institutional racial inequities (Kelly & Clark, 2009).

Four distinct conflicts have influenced the evolving views of social justice within social work. One is the conflict between cultural and social homogeneity (celebrating our common needs) and heterogeneity (acknowledging and celebrating our differences). The competing metaphors of America as a "melting pot," a "mosaic," or a "cultural salad" symbolize these differences. In the 21st century, the question persists whether the United States is one nation or, in Walt Whitman's (1855) words, "a nation of nations." A related conflict is between coerced assimilation (even if benign in intention and subtle in its motives)—for example, the use of policies, programs, and services to compel diverse groups to adopt dominant cultural norms, values, and behaviors—and the realities of what Massey and Denton (1993) refer to as "American apartheid"—the maintenance of structural barriers to economic opportunity and political participation (Alexander, 2010; Marable, Steinberg, & Middlemass, 2007).

A third conflict involves finding the preferred balance between individual and group identity and group rights. Through the mid-1960s, social justice in the United States was largely equated with the application of "color-blind" meritocratic principles—in the words of Martin Luther King, Jr.'s "I Have a Dream" speech delivered in 1963, that individuals be judged "not by the color of their skin but by the content of their character." During the past several decades, however, the emergence of the concept of multiculturalism and the "identity politics" that spawned it have been, in part, a reaction against both the persistent realities of social injustice and oppression and the *ideal* of a color-blind society itself. According to this perspective, the affirmation of individual worth and identity requires the recognition of the existence of systematic discrimination on the basis of group identity and not on an individual-by-individual basis (Hill Collins, 2000; Johnson, 2001; Young, 1990, 2011). In recent years, the resolution of this issue has produced intense conflict along hardened partisan political, ideological, and racial lines.

A fourth theme, with particular implications for the field of social work, focuses on the connection between "Americanization" and the equal application of justice (Foner, 2002). As recent controversies over immigration demonstrate, answering the question, "Who is an American?" is closely tied to the questions, "Who deserves help?" and "Who must provide it?" (Gordon, 2002). This requires clarifying the meaning of citizenship, particularly eligibility for the legal rights and social protections it provides, and determining the desirable balance between the attainment of universal ideals of life and liberty and the preservation of cultural distinctions as to the meaning of the "pursuit of happiness" (Katz, 2001).

Through their use of different strategies to define and achieve social justice, subordinate groups in US society have redefined the nation's social justice goals. For example, they have applied a critical perspective to the concept of assimilation. More than a century ago, W. E. B. DuBois accurately forecast that "the problem of the 20th century [would be] the problem of the color line" (1901). Soon after, African American social work leaders, such as E. Franklin Frazier, George Edmund Haynes (1912), and Forrester Washington, drew attention to the deficiencies in mainstream social work's idea of social justice. At the 1920 National Conference on Social Work, Roosevelt Wright (1920) declared, "The Negro wants a democracy, not a whiteocracy" (p. 286). He asserted that a socially just "melting pot" was impossible in the absence of mutual respect, the abolition of oppressive laws and institutions, and the establishment of equal rights and responsibilities. The declarations of civil rights activists and social workers during the 1960s and 1970s echoed these sentiments (Young, 1965); recently, they have appeared in the writings of critical theorists inside and outside the social work profession (Fook, 2014).

However, for most of the 20th century, most social workers in the United States could not accept a view of social justice that embraced full social equality. Initially, part of this failure was due to their inability to distinguish between the problems of White European immigrants and those experienced by African Americans, indigenous persons, and immigrants of color from Latin America or Asia (Stern & Axinn, 2013). Certainly, racism and religious and class prejudice had a significant influence on the thinking of many social workers. However, in hindsight, the presence of these invidious distinctions provides only a partial explanation. A fundamental issue, still unresolved today, is whether the universal goals of social justice are compatible with a multicultural society that embraces diversity in all its forms (Reisch, 2013b).

Given this dilemma, what vision of social justice can social workers rely on to guide their work in the decades ahead? How can the profession forge a unified conception of social justice when different communities have fundamentally different ideas of social justice—ideas that often contradict each other? We argue that social workers must first overcome several outdated assumptions about the nature of social justice in a multicultural society.

First, we must recognize that the social divisions in US society no longer occur strictly along a "majority–minority" axis. They are serious tensions between different "minority" groups as well. Second, we must acknowledge that increased social welfare provision alone, whether through government programs, market mechanisms, the private sector, the nonprofit sector, or some combination thereof, will not be sufficient to eradicate long-standing inequities in the structure of US society (Bates & Swan, 2010; Stiglitz, 2013). As a consequence of globalization, national governments (to say nothing of state or local governments) lack the scope, speed of action, and institutional capacity to respond to economic, demographic, and social problems emanating from forces outside their span of control. This new reality undermines the foundational belief of the 20th-century welfare state that national governments could regulate the effects of national economies. Finally, we must reluctantly accept that there is little evidence that increased demographic and cultural diversity *alone* will eliminate social conflicts over such contentious issues as abortion, faith-based social services, gay marriage, stem cell research, child welfare laws, school vouchers, health care, welfare reform, and immigration (Reisch & Jani, 2012).

Summary: Social Work, Social Justice, and the Future

How, then, do we move beyond rhetorical calls for social justice and develop principles we can apply to our practice? The following are ideas that we elaborate on in Part II.

Our policies, programs, and services should prioritize the needs of the most vulnerable populations in the allocation of material and nonmaterial resources, particularly in periods of economic contraction or fiscal scarcity. These populations did not create the recent economic crisis, for example, but they have suffered disproportionally from its effects (Reich, 2012). Second, in our practice, we should emphasize the values of collective and mutual responsibility. This implies an embrace of our common humanity and common but not necessarily identical needs, even if these needs vary somewhat due to cultural norms and life circumstances.

Third, our programs should prioritize prevention over remediation, not merely for its long-term consequences and cost efficiencies but also for the structural, nonstigmatizing analysis of human needs it implies. Fourth, in order to receive help, people should not be required to adjust their problem definitions or preferences for assistance to models of intervention determined by others who do not share their values, history, or current circumstances. Finally, we should promote genuine civic participation of all stakeholders within democratic institutions and organizations. Unless people's agency is recognized and they have a meaningful decision-making role, efforts to promote nominal participation will only heighten widespread cynicism, apathy, and withdrawal (Marable et al., 2007; Young, 2011).

These suggestions imply that the pursuit of social justice in the 21st century is a political process in whatever field of practice and around whatever issues social workers engage (Reisch & Jani, 2012). A social justice perspective would also challenge prevailing assumptions about power, privilege, and various forms of oppression in the theories that underlie our practice (see Chapter 4). Finally, as many social workers have long argued, it would integrate an alternative model of social relationships into all social work interventions. These are discussed in Part II.

In addition, social work practice will not fully reflect social justice principles until our society prioritizes the protection of human rights over property rights. This is the implicit imperative within our *Code of Ethics*. As Reynolds (1951) remarked prophetically more than 60 years ago, "The philosophy of social work cannot be separated from the prevailing philosophy of a nation, as to how it values people and what importance it sets upon their welfare" (p. 174).

During the formative years of the profession, social workers heeded the call for social justice based on a combination of religious and secular values and, to a certain extent, the recognition of elite responsibility to address the needs and aspirations of those below them in the social hierarchy. In this era, social workers largely saw the means to achieve social justice as assimilation and the re-creation of a harmonious "organic community" (Bender, 1975). The "second generation" of social workers—from the late 1920s through the early 1950s—changed this perspective considerably (Andrews, 1993). They regarded the expansion of government provision and the social rights of citizenship as critical components of social justice and forged strategic alliances with unions, left-wing political parties, and, later, civil rights organizations to support universal social policies and government-sponsored labor protections. McCarthyism and the resultant emphasis on professional status enhancement instead of social change shifted social work's focus away from policy advocacy to individual adjustment (Reisch & Andrews, 2002). The gap between social work's rhetoric and practice this created has still not been bridged despite periodic revivals of social justice activism, such as the recent "Occupy" Black Lives Matter movements (Reisch, 2015b) and the social work response to racial inequalities in criminal justice.

Thus, the relationship between social work and social justice throughout its history appears to be influenced by several themes. One is the tension between activism and professionalism. The more social workers have sought occupational status, the more they have distanced themselves from their clients and constituents and widened the gap between the profession's rhetoric and practice realities. Another theme reflects the focus of the profession's policy advocacy. The articulation of social justice goals appears to be more consistent with practice realities when it focuses on universal rather than selective social policies. Finally, the "social justice gap" has narrowed when social workers expanded their concept of social justice to include excluded and marginalized populations, including immigrants (Reisch, 2009). The resolution of these conflicts may present the fundamental challenge facing social workers in the decades ahead.

Despite its persistent ambiguities, the social work profession's emphasis on social justice has inspired the development of innovative solutions to the nation's problems, important insights on the sources of these problems, and new ways of defining fundamental practice concepts. It has produced a broad social definition of health and recognition of the impact of the physical and social environment on the well-being of individuals, families, and communities (Gorin & Moniz, 2014; Reisch, 2012b). Inspired by social justice ideals, social workers have demonstrated how research can be used to illuminate the structural sources of people's problems and have disseminated information about these problems widely to policymakers and the general public. Social workers have also contributed to the expansion of the boundaries of citizenship in US society—from civil and political rights to social rights—and made it far more inclusive.

In the 21st century, social workers might include the following additional components in their social justice framework: a return to the structural analysis of US society and the root causes of its problems, with particular attention to the causes and consequences of inequality, oppression, marginalization, and exclusion; increased recognition of the significance of history, culture, and context in the development of people's problems and ways to resolve them; an understanding of the interconnectedness between individual problems and their structural sources and between domestic and international issues; integration of a critical perspective on the impact of race, gender, ethnicity, sexual orientation, and ability status on people's lives; an enhanced focus on the impact of the distribution of power, resources, rights, status, privilege, and opportunities in US society and their ideological justifications; a view of society and social change that emphasizes the basic humanity and equality of all people; and a goal of not simply ameliorating people's problems but of transforming society through the creation of alternative values, institutions, laws, and processes (Reisch, 2013b).

At its best, social work stands for the creation of a society in which people, individually and in community, can live decent lives and realize their full human potential. This requires us to advocate for the elimination of those policies that diminish people's sense of control over their lives and drain finite resources from basic human needs. Simultaneously, we need to work for the expansion of those programs that enable people to exercise personal freedom by removing the fear of economic and physical calamity from their lives and making them feel like integral and valued parts of society. These goals reflect a potential synthesis of the historic divisions between individual and collective well-being at the heart of debates over social justice and may provide the basis for its attainment in an increasingly diverse and conflict-ridden society.

The remainder of the book focuses on how contemporary social workers can apply social justice concepts to all forms of practice in an increasingly diverse society.

Discussion Questions

1. How does social work's emphasis on social justice differ from its original focus on charity? Why did it emerge?
2. What are the implications of the NASW *Code of Ethics* establishing social justice as one of the "ethical imperatives" for social workers?
3. How has the definition of social justice evolved within the social work profession? What factors influenced this evolution?
4. In what ways are social justice and human rights perspectives compatible? In what ways are they in conflict? What are the practice implications of applying a human rights perspective?

4

Theories and Concepts Underlying Socially Just Practice

Introduction

In this chapter, we introduce a framework for socially just practice that we expand upon in Part II of the book. Building on Chapters 1–3, this chapter begins with a discussion of how we view the variety of people and systems with which social workers are likely to interact in their practice. We then discuss our ideas about so-called generalist practice that reflect a somewhat different conception of such practice, particularly in terms of how social workers should understand their roles in the many situations they encounter. We then present our underlying assumptions regarding socially just practice, the principles derived from these assumptions, and the processes that emanate from these principles and assumptions. Through critical reflection, these processes may be revisited, often at a deeper and more complex manner. Finally, we outline the circular or cyclical (rather than linear) phases of socially just practice, which we believe unfolds in a reiterative manner as the practice situation evolves.

Practice Defined

To emphasize what we previously stated in Chapter 1, we present here our definition of practice based on concepts of social justice. Finn and Jacobson (2008) begin their discussion of "just practice" by considering what practice principles would emerge through the infusion of critical social and cultural theory. They state,

> The term "practice" in contemporary social theory does not have the same meaning as practice in the traditional social work sense of a series

of planned interventions. Rather practice refers more broadly to social action carried out in the context of unequal power relations. Also a post-modern and critical social work practice is primarily concerned with practicing in ways which further a society without domination, exploitation, and oppression. It should focus on how structures dominate and also on how people construct and are constructed by changing social structures and relations. (p. 8)

We agree with Finn and Jacobson and have sought to develop and expand upon these ideas in the chapters that follow.

Evidence-Based Practice

During the past two decades, following the lead of medicine, the social work profession has embraced the concept of "evidence-based practice" (EBP). A major goal of EBP is to apply evidence obtained about the outcomes of practice to future decisions about actions the worker intends to take (Wodarski & Feit, 2009). We agree that social work practice—in all its forms—should be based on evidence of its efficacy in achieving established goals and objectives. This includes gathering evidence about previous applications of a practice approach with service users in similar circumstances. However, there are a number of issues about the application of EBP that a socially just practitioner should consider including the following:

- To what extent have relevant stakeholders, especially service users, participated in the processes of defining evidence, determining how it would be obtained, examining the evidence collected, and assessing its implications?
- How were social justice issues considered in the practice that is being examined?
- Was the evidence obtained by utilizing research approaches that embody the criteria for socially just research? (See Chapter 10.)
- Were the views of the service users adequately represented throughout the research process? Were they representative of the total population of service users in terms of their race, ethnicity, gender, sexual orientation, and social class?

People and Systems Considered in Practice

We find it helpful to use some of the concepts developed four decades ago by Pincus and Minahan (1973) to discuss the various people and systems that are the foci of attention of practitioners and service users. They considered four systems: the *action system*—those individuals with whom the practitioner interacts; the *target system*—those entities that the practitioner and service users seek to change; the *client system*—those who have contracted for the services of the practitioner (voluntarily or involuntarily); and the *agency system*—the organizational location within which these interactions take place. To achieve the type of awareness that we assert provides the foundation of socially just practice, social workers must carefully assess the nature of these systems and the social justice issues present in each of them.

Thus, understanding the role of the social context in shaping both desired practice goals and the means used to achieve them is a central consideration of socially just practice. However, from a socially just perspective, we do not view the social context merely as an entity to be entered into a "practice equation." It is often the source of people's oppression, which places barriers to their attainment of life goals. In addition, environmental systems and structures frequently base this oppression on people's demographic or cultural characteristics such as their race, gender, and sexual orientation. Consequently, issues such as family violence or mental health conditions can be exacerbated or abated (or both) by agency and community conditions, as we discuss later.

Another important component of the social context involves the unequal distribution of power to maintain oppressive structures and their underlying values. In both explicit and subtle ways, this use of power has significant effects on any change effort and on the ability of those individuals or groups who seek to implement change, particularly if they are in a position of power disadvantage (Foucault, 1975/1995). Finally, the unequal distribution of power serves a larger political–economic function: It perpetuates the dominance of particular groups, whether in the market economy, the government, or the organizations that affect people's daily lives (Garvin & Tropman, 1998).

Becoming a socially just practitioner, therefore, involves more than the acquisition of sophisticated knowledge and skills. Practitioners must also understand the nature and extent of unjust social conditions and help those with whom they work to overcome the forces that act as barriers to their attainment of their life's goals. In summary, socially just practice is not simply effective social work practice. *Social justice practice refers more broadly to social action in the context of unequal power relations.*

This form of practice also involves helping those who use social work services develop their own vision of a more just society and work toward it. We do not believe it is feasible or realistic for one practitioner or even one agency or organization to engage with all the people, groups, organizations, and communities in such a way as to make this possible. Rather, we envision a practitioner who struggles to understand these many entities and to determine, in collaboration with service users or constituents, with which issues and entities to engage, given the purposes of the encounter, the resources available, and the political and fiscal realities of the situation. This may require service users and practitioners to take financial, legal, or employment risks, and these should be carefully considered prior to taking action. Through careful assessment, it is possible to anticipate some risks and develop a plan to mitigate them or respond to them should they arise.

An example of the need to assess potential risks carefully *in advance* is an action taken some years ago in which a group of social work students and mothers "sat in" a welfare office after closing hours. They were demonstrating in favor of providing special clothing allowances for children as they returned to school in the fall. The police arrested everyone. Although the social work students were proud of their stamina, no one had planned how the children of these mothers would be cared for during their detention—a problem that could have been foreseen. Later, one mother confided that she "would never trust a social work student again"—such a poor outcome for this presumably noble endeavor.

Our Approach to Practice

In summary, we believe that practice that concerns itself with the struggles of people to deal with the issues they face in their day-to-day lives must seriously incorporate attention to their broader social concerns. This is true whether these issues arise from their interpersonal relationships, including those in the families and the groups to which they belong; in the ways people attempt to use groups to effect changes in their communities and organizations; or in the manner communities and organizations strive to revise, create, and implement policies in the larger society. Thus, we assert that work at any level of the social order (individual, dyadic, family, group, organization, community, and larger society) must be informed by what is transpiring at other levels, especially as these developments relate to issues of justice and injustice.

Our Perspective on Generalist Practice

Our perspective on social work practice differs somewhat from what has been termed the generalist model of practice in which every practitioner is presumed to have the competence to engage many levels of the social system and to possess the legitimacy to do so (Miley, O'Melia, & DuBois, 2009). We believe there are limits to each practitioner's training, experience, and resources. Nevertheless, a social justice perspective should help a practitioner make every action—however small—reflect the social justice processes and outcomes we envision while he or she looks for opportunities to create coalitions and collaborations toward larger goals. In addition, the practitioner should continually analyze the unjust contextual forces that exist in the situation. In Part II, we seek to help the reader recognize the many levels of the social order that affect either the application of socially just processes or the attainment of socially just outcomes, even if the focus of practice may be on a limited set of levels.

Assumptions and Principles of Socially Just Practice

We have developed a set of assumptions and principles about socially just practice that we elaborate on in later chapters as they are applied to different practice levels (e.g., individual, group, and organizational). In the process of developing these assumptions and principles, we were concerned that this effort might be viewed by practitioners as a way of asserting our professional superiority over service users and other practitioners who may profess different principles. This is not our intent. We wish, therefore, to remind the reader to bear this in mind and to struggle against such a misuse of such "lists."

We are also concerned that any assumption or principles we include might contribute to dichotomous thinking, which Fook (2002) defines as "creating forced categories of choices, often opposed to each other, in which one member of the pair is usually privileged" (pp. 72–73). If this kind of thinking has crept in as we develop this set of ideas, we have sought to recognize this and to modify our views accordingly.

Assumptions

As stated in Chapter 1, we contend that all types of socially just practice at all levels are based on a similar set of assumptions. In this chapter and those in Part II, we comment on and give further examples of how these may be operationalized. These assumptions include the following:

1. *Social justice is central to practice, not an add-on.* We believe that social justice should be the core of social work practice. This does not mean that the practitioner forces the users of service to adopt goals that express social justice. Rather, we believe that ethical practice involves helping service users understand the ways that social justice-related forces impede, enhance, or redirect their goals and means of pursuing them. This relates to Schwartz's (1961) idea of the social worker as "lending a vision" with respect to the nature of a productive life in a just society. There are many skills, however, that we explore

in Part II as to how and when these ideas may be introduced in supportive, respectful, and empowering ways.

2. *Social justice practice is an "ongoing journey."* By this, we mean several things. One's vision of social justice expands with experience—that is, both workers and service users will develop a deepened understanding of social justice issues as they attempt to seek change in themselves and their circumstances. Injustice does not cease, however, when these original goals are attained; new forms of injustice are likely to arise as circumstances change. As steps are taken to attain change, resistance to change is likely to emerge within service users, practitioners, and the environment. Because conflicts and contestations often arise in the course of change efforts, service users and practitioners must and can learn to respond effectively to them.

3. *Socially just practice must attend to both goals and processes.* Practitioners and those with whom we work not only need to develop a vision of what social justice could look like (in a particular situation and more generally) and take strategic steps to achieve that vision but also must seek to remove long-standing sources of injustice, whether these are structural or in the nature of practice itself. Socially just processes and outcomes are thus inextricably linked (Gil, 1998). This requires us in our day-to-day work to employ those processes that challenge and reduce the mechanisms that sustain injustice and to revisit our goals regularly because our visions of what is possible expand through our experience.

4. *Positionalities and standpoints matter.* We all occupy multiple roles and social locations, sometimes called *positionalities*. The values and cognitions we have of these roles and locations are what we refer to as *standpoints*. Our sense of self and our identities emerge from some of these positions, but all are important in social justice work. Some of these positions bring us unearned privilege that can block our ability to see injustices. Some make us more likely to experience injustice. These positions intersect, and their salience changes in different contexts. Therefore, the practitioner should assess her or his own positionalities and standpoints with respect to multiple dimensions, including those such as nationality/citizenship that define "insider/outsider statuses," and should take these into account in all practitioner–service user interactions.

In addition, workers and collaborators, including service participants, should continuously reflect on the complex ways their positions and standpoints contribute to their privilege (e.g., unearned benefits and opportunities) as well as to their oppression. In this regard, the practitioner should continually examine her or his own assumptions and perspectives in order to understand alternative worldviews.

Because our multiple social locations interact, they often generate different worldviews, perspectives, unearned privileges (in different circumstances), and increased challenges. It is therefore important to consider one's multiple standpoints and to negotiate regularly with others across and within group boundaries. The practitioner should use skills to strengthen and maintain her or his own social support and self-care processes and look for joy and meaning in her or his practice. Working for social justice is a marathon, not a sprint.

5. *Context matters and is critical.* Terms that are used to refer to these contexts include the political, social, cultural, structural, organizational, community, family, and group circumstances surrounding practice. These contexts may serve either to enhance or to constrain the attainment of social justice goals. Ironically, both enhancing and constraining forces may be present in the same situation and operate in complex ways. We began this discussion of contexts in previous chapters, especially Chapter 1.

6. *Power is always relevant to practice, and power analyses must be recurrent.* Power is associated with structure, culture, and both interpersonal and intrapersonal processes. In Chapters 7 and 8, we discuss our concept of power and its importance to socially just practice and the ways in which power has been used to perpetuate social injustice.

7. *Socially just practice requires visioning how the achievement of the purposes of a specific service can make a contribution to a more just world.* Although in this book we portray many ideas of what a more socially just world would be, we do not have a single "one size fits all" vision; we believe that practitioners and all the participants in creating and implementing a service will already possess or be able to develop their own visions as part of the change process.

8. *Collectivism is a central feature of socially just practice.* Mullaly (2007) asserts that this concept—sometimes referred to as mutuality or interdependence— involves recognition "that people are social beings who depend on one another for the satisfaction of most of their primary and social needs" (p. 310). Because of this relationship, groups are a major resource for service users in their efforts to accomplish their immediate purposes and attain their longer term goals. An important related concept in this regard is that of mutual aid. There are important differences, however, in the ways in which people in different cultures view the individual's relationship to various groups and collectivities; this has major implications for how and when practitioners and service users seek to work through groups to attain socially just goals. (See Chapter 6 for further discussion.)

9. *Problem conception is a critical component of socially just practice.* Socially just practitioners recognize that the problems (or issues) that the practice situation

seeks to address are the result of a complex array of forces. Among the most significant of these forces are the structural circumstances surrounding the practice situation. Important questions to be explored in the identification of such forces include the following: Who benefits from the way the problem is currently defined? Who gains or loses if the problem is reduced or eliminated or if it is redefined? This analysis will be enhanced if we recognize that personal problems are reflections of structural conditions that, in turn, are reflected in people individually and collectively.

10. *The interests of service users are the primary consideration of practitioners* and not their professional interests or those of the service agency and other environmental entities.

Principles

We utilize Lewis's (1982) definition of a practice principle as one that "combines a propositional statement (based on knowledge and theory) and a commendation providing guidelines for appropriate action (which are derived from ethical imperatives). Principles structure programs and *justify* [emphasis added] a practice" (p. 43). Practice principles should also be derived from knowledge, whether based on empirical evidence, experience, or the collective wisdom of experienced individuals. This is a somewhat broader conception of the knowledge underlying social work practice than expressed by proponents of EBP. The following are the major features we believe underlie socially just practice.

Analyzing, Theorizing, and Contextualizing

The practitioner should engage in multiple kinds of theorizing and analyses alone and with others, throughout all phases of practice. This will increase the action alternatives available. The worker should include components of envisioning justice in the concepts and theories utilized; this will also help develop multiple, alternative approaches to achieving socially just outcomes.

Key Social Justice Goals and Issues

In assessing practice situations, the worker should consider various social levels because this will produce increased attention to complex social, political, historical, and cultural contexts that affect people's lives. The worker should consider interconnections that exist across and within social levels; this will help the practitioner produce desired outcomes by using one level to change another. For example, by helping an individual to change, the worker may increase the likelihood that the individual will work for changes in his or her group, organization, or community.

Using Multiple Frames for Analyzing and Theorizing

The worker will apply different analytical frames to help service users broaden their understanding of their current circumstances, revise their goals, and recognize the sources of oppression and privilege that either support or challenge the attainment of these aims. In so doing, the worker should examine the different dimensions of power that operate in these domains and how they interact in order to challenge them if they present barriers to the achievement of practice goals. In addition, the worker should identify potential sources of resistance to change and what sustains this resistance in each domain so that these may be ameliorated. Figure 4.1 reflects the importance of applying critical analyses in practice. It illustrates two key components of this aspect of socially just practice: (1) The processes of theorizing, reflection, and analysis are dynamic, iterative (ongoing), and interconnected; and (2) these processes continually examine the relationship among service users/constituents, practitioners, and the context (organization, community, and society) in which practice occurs.

Contextual Analysis at the Services Level

The worker should examine how issues (and problems) are defined, conceptualized, and framed by external bodies and the service organization and determine whether the definitions used advantage or disadvantage service users and are sources of oppression or empowerment. In some circumstances, the worker and service users will use this information to identify barriers to social justice; determine how various explicit or subtle aspects of social injustice oppress practitioners

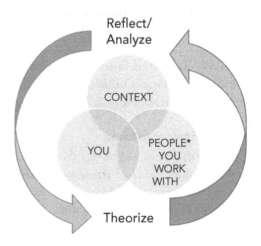

* People/organization/community you work with

FIGURE 4.1   Critical Analyses

and service users, hinder their attainment of goals, and affect the quality of their interactions with each other; and formulate an action plan to overcome them.

The Worker: Reflection/Praxis

As initially presented in Chapter 1, socially just practitioners should engage in praxis. This term signifies the "circular reflexive process" in which people reflect upon their actions in the light of their ideas and theories, reflect upon their ideas and theories in the light of their actions and the consequences of their actions, and subsequently create future actions and new or revised ideas (Freire, 1970).

The Practitioner: Use of Both Reflection and Reflexivity

Reflection refers to an ongoing review and critique of one's actions, interactions, processes, progress, and social contexts to learn and deepen one's understanding and sense of options. It is a precondition for praxis. Reflexivity requires us to view ourselves in relation to our practice, along with all our social roles and related identities, historical contexts, and assumptions. (See the previous discussion on positionalities and standpoints.) This involves a consideration of "who we are" and how our self-concept influences the situation and our understanding of it. Practitioners should engage in these processes regularly, as Figure 4.2 indicates. This figure adds the external dimension of action to the more internal processes of reflection, analysis, and theorizing illustrated in Figure 4.1.

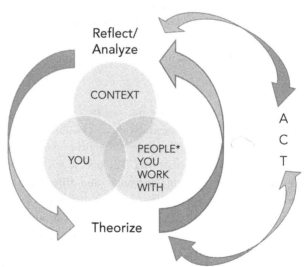

* People/organization/community with whom you work

FIGURE 4.2   Praxis and Critical Consciousness

Selection of a General Approach to Change (Intervention)

The intervention methods utilized by the practitioner should be determined by what will best achieve the social justice and personal goals of the service users rather than by the practitioner's preferences and experiences. This requires those who will be affected by planned interventions to participate in assessing the issue or problem, determining desired outcomes and goals, selecting change strategies, and identifying acceptable risks and consequences. This selection should be informed by an assessment of all available options and an analysis of the underlying assumptions of the approach to be used.

Developing Plans and Strategies

Those likely to be affected by work for change should, therefore, have input into planning and strategy development at all phases of the change process—not merely during the assessment and evaluation phases. Multiple frames and different types of knowledge should inform planning. Plans should incorporate social justice goals, clear action steps, and ways to ensure that the information gathering and implementation procedures utilize socially just processes.

Action Components and Steps

Practitioners should monitor the steps being taken toward established goals, and they should identify and address the unintended, negative, or unjust consequences of actions that emerge. Practitioners should regularly review how people are working together, how progress and problems are being framed, and how different manifestations of power occur. Practitioners should also examine, in cooperation with service users, constituents, or colleagues, how social locations are influencing perceptions and interactions at each phase of the intervention.

Working with Others

All social work practice, including research and program evaluation, involves work with others. These individuals and groups may be the targets of our actions, allies and collaborators (sometimes with different goals and approaches), or clients or constituents. The people with whom we work will share some of our social locations and values and differ on others. This means that practitioners should be conscious of these differences and their effects on practice and the achievement of social justice goals. Social justice practitioners must also accommodate to or build on the goals and approaches of many different service users and consider the power issues involved. To be effective in this regard, practitioners should challenge dichotomous ways of thinking because these often lead to unjust constructions of power and questionable definitions of who are our allies and enemies.

Addressing the Consequences of Oppression

When some form of help is needed (e.g., counseling) to deal with the intrapersonal and community effects of injustice, practitioners should reframe symptoms and struggles to recognize different types of coping and resilience. Practitioners should acknowledge and negotiate power differences between those seeking and those providing assistance, and the should recognize the knowledge, information, skills, and power that each brings to the transaction (Hasenfeld, 1987). Practitioners should also examine how other actors in the practice situation have incorporated information and whether their social positions have distorted their understanding of this information and their self-perceptions. Although everyone inevitably has somewhat different perceptions (and constructions) of reality, it is important to engage in dialogue in order for each party to obtain a picture of how others "see" the world.

Using and Challenging Power and Conflict

Practitioners should rename or interrogate the meaning of words and symbols used in the practice situation especially in relation to how these words and symbols define justice, injustice, and differences, as well as how they reflect subtle or hidden power dynamics. Practitioners should incorporate in their practice regular and continuous mechanisms for examining how power and conflict are being negotiated as well as the sources of domination and subordination in their practice (e.g., sexism, racism, ageism, and homophobia). Practitioners should also seek to help members of all constituencies challenge the negative consequences of unearned power and to develop and use the power they have earned toward social justice goals. Because all transformation will inevitably uncover or even intensify conflict, situations that generate conflict should be regarded as opportunities to learn about differences and justice and to work for change. Thus, practitioners should cultivate skills in identifying, valuing, and working with conflict. Constituencies should regularly leave time to recover and learn from conflict. They are likely to learn about power and sources of injustice by engaging in dialogue in conflict situations; determining how to act in the face of conflict; and learning how to resolve conflicts in ways that are peaceful, just, and that reduce or eliminate unequal uses of power. All constituencies should scrutinize the types of power involved in situations, the constructions of power that are at play, and the ways the actors in these situations maintain imbalances of power and seek to rectify them. (This issue is discussed in more detail in Part II.)

Monitoring, Evaluating, Learning, and Reducing Unintended Unjust Consequences

Practitioners should regularly work with others, including users of service, to determine whether social justice goals were identified initially and developed further over time and the extent to which progress has been made to their attainment. Practitioners and service users should also examine whether socially just methods and processes were employed throughout the change process. In addition, practitioners should determine whether multiple constituencies were able to develop and use their own sources of power to help them attain their goals. Finally in this regard, practitioners should ascertain whether conflicts were resolved in socially just ways and with appropriate regard for the rights and needs of relevant and multiple constituencies and attention to relevant conditions such as structures, language, and symbols.[1]

Practice Processes and Procedures

In the chapters in Part II in which we discuss socially just practice, we suggest processes and procedures related to the assumptions and principles outlined previously. This discussion should enable the reader to accomplish several things. First, by seeing how these processes and procedures occur at each level, the reader will gain a better understanding of them. For example, one procedure that is discussed at each level is how to enable people to *resolve conflicts* in socially just ways while working toward socially just ends. Conflicts are described when they occur between individuals in one-on-one encounters with practitioners; in family situations; in groups, organizations, and communities; and in large entities such as cities and entire societies. Conflicts are certainly evident today as we consider both national and global events.

Second, there are similarities in how social justice-oriented practitioners approach conflict, but there are also differences as such practitioners encounter new circumstances and complexities related to the societal levels with which they are engaged. Recognizing that the issues of conflict and conflict resolution are likely to occur at all levels will enable the social justice-oriented practitioner to have a deeper understanding of what issues to address when working at any level. The following is a general description of the processes and procedures that occur at all levels of practice.

Definition of Purpose

At each level of practice, the practitioner considers the potential purpose(s) of the work in order to select one or more "professional" purposes. The important issue in socially just practice involves determining how this purpose relates to achieving a socially just outcome or reducing a socially unjust situation. Of course,

---

1. A full discussion of research and evaluation issues is included in Chapter 10.

there may be professionally appropriate purposes that do not immediately relate to social justice or injustice. It behooves a social justice-oriented worker, however, to consider the relevance of social justice to this purpose.

It is our contention that as practitioners develop a deeper understanding of social justice, they will be more likely to perceive the relevance of social justice in many, if not most, practice situations. This can be the result of consciousness-raising on the part of the practitioner and other actors involved in the situation; we discuss this in more detail later. For example, an agency that employs the social worker may desire to develop new services but may not have considered achieving social justice for the populations it purports to serve as one of its priorities in the allocation of organizational resources. It may only have considered such issues as the size of demand, popularity with funders, and the organization's previous experience with meeting this need. The social justice issue may involve some aspect of oppression endured by the target population, such as a lack of access to vital services due to societal prejudice.

Starting a practice intervention with at least an initial determination of its purpose helps determine the choice of the *action system* and addresses two questions: Which action system will be most effective in accomplishing the purpose? Which should be the focus of a change strategy the worker and service user are likely to employ? We discuss these two issues separately.

The issue of effectiveness has to do with which action system has the power, resources, and legitimacy to accomplish the determined purpose. Although this is discussed in more detail in the chapters that follow, a few examples here should help the reader to follow this discussion in the succeeding chapters. For example, a worker might be working with a woman who experiences spousal abuse. In this case, the worker might involve such action systems as the police (an organization) and a program that works with male batterers (another organization)—after appropriate agreement of the woman involved. Not involving these action systems might limit the ability of the woman to secure both immediate and future physical safety.

Another illustration of the issue of effectiveness involves the efforts of a worker to support a tenants group that sought to obtain the help of a lawyer (an individual action system) in presenting its demands regarding building safety to a landlord (an individual target system). In order to be effective with the landlord, the tenants group required the technical assistance of an attorney who knew the legal recourses on which it could rely.

In both of these examples, the choice of action systems is determined by strategic considerations. An important issue, of course, is the likelihood that the action system will be effective in securing the changes desired. In the case of the abusive partner, the worker and the woman who is the victim of domestic violence might need to learn the past policies and practices of the police before approaching them. If the police have failed in the past to do what is required by law, a media campaign might need to be initiated or a public official might need to be approached to change their behavioral pattern. This would involve other action systems as part of an overall strategy.

In the case of the tenants, the worker might decide to help them understand how similar actions have been resolved in their community. This might involve consulting with various civil rights organizations in the community as other action systems. These two issues of effectiveness and strategy are referred to in the following chapters in relation to each of the systems and processes described.

Responding to Value and Ethical Issues

According to Reamer (2013), values are "generalized, emotionally charged conceptions of what is desirable; historically created and derived from experience; shared by a population or group within it; and they provide the means for organizing and structuring patterns of behavior" (p.14). "Ethics," which are guidelines for action derived from values, ensure that individuals behave in ways that are consistent with their values to achieve desirable ends. All of the practices described in Part II are related implicitly or explicitly to values and ethics. Whereas we seek to present a general discussion of values and ethics in relationship to social work practice in this chapter, each succeeding chapter will expand on this discussion with reference to the social justice issues being addressed in that chapter and the specific ethical and value issues that arise.

The National Association of Social Workers (NASW) in the United States, the International Federation of Social Workers, and social work organizations in other nations have each adopted codes of ethics. These are regularly revised based on changing ideologies and circumstances, the emergence of new issues or perspectives, and evolving insights into the nature of values and ethics in the social work field. Finn and Jacobson (2008) make the important point that valuing is a dialectical process. By this, they mean that whereas our actions are shaped by our values, our critical reflections on our actions and their results can and should lead to modifications in the ethics and values that have driven these actions.

In the 2008 revision of the NASW *Code of Ethics*, social justice was defined as one of the profession's six ethical imperatives. The *Code* further states (NASW, 2008, as quoted in Reamer, 2013),

> Social workers should promote the general welfare of society, from local to global levels, and the development of people, their communities, and their environments. Social workers should advocate for living conditions conducive to the fulfillment of basic human needs and should promote

social, economic, political, and cultural values and institutions that are compatible with the realization of social justice. Social workers should promote the conditions that encourage respect for cultural and social diversity within the United States and globally. Social workers should promote policies and practices that demonstrate respect for difference, support the expansion of cultural knowledge and resources, advocate for programs and institutions that demonstrate cultural competence, and promote policies that safeguard the rights of and confirm equity and social justice for all people.

Social workers should act to prevent and eliminate domination of, exploitation of, and discrimination against any person, group, or class on the basis of race, ethnicity, national origin, color, sex, sexual orientation, age, marital status, political belief, religion, or mental or physical disability. (p. 240)

These ethical and value considerations underlie all practice. Thus, all practitioners, and especially those operating from a social justice foundation, should be clear on how these values contribute to the consciousness required to engage in socially just practice.

Analyzing both Macro and Micro Conditions

All entities with which social workers interact are embedded in, interact with, or have embedded within them other systems. These various systems affect how socially just processes and outcomes can or do occur and how practitioners and other people work toward these outcomes.

Practitioners should know how to assess these influences and outcomes, at least in broad terms, even if their competence, job position, or strategy for change do not permit an active role with some of these systems. These kinds of issues are considered in more detail in Part II. Suffice it to say here that social work education and practice have created divisions between so-called "macro," "mezzo," and "micro" practice. These are reflected in students' choice of concentration, the ways schools' curricula are divided, and the ways courses are devised and grouped.

Although many faculty members present various arguments regarding the "unity" of the social work field, they are constrained by the current structure of social work education, the amount of material they are required to deliver, and their own knowledge.[2] We have no easy solutions to these problems, but we strongly believe that social justice practice in all methods and arenas requires a

---

2. For an extensive critique of social work education, see Stoesz, Karger, and Carrilio (2010).

focus on the connection between private troubles and public issues; the material we present on practice emphasizes this connection.

As stated previously, no social worker can competently assume all the practice roles required to engage effectively in the range of social systems, from individuals to entire societies, with whom we interact. Instead, we propose that all workers be able to envision this complex interplay of systems and to see what has to be changed in order for social justice goals to be attained while simultaneously limiting their efforts to aspects of practice for which they have both legitimacy and competence. At the same time, however, they must be able to reach out to other types of workers and work with other systems in relationship to a well-conceived strategy of change.

Selection of Levels for Practice

Work at any level in socially just practice requires the practitioner to be aware of and frequently interact with entities at other levels or to encourage those using their service to do so. For example, a practitioner working with a group of foster children who have been mistreated will consider how their foster families, families of origin, the foster care agency, the courts, their schools, and their communities can also help them attain just solutions to the difficulties they may be experiencing.

Similarly, a practitioner helping a community obtain the resources it needs to address a problem will consider how community leaders respond and the impact of the governmental systems that are involved in addressing this problem. When working with various task groups in the community, the practitioner will also consider whether members of these groups interact with each other in socially just ways built on principles of respect and equality.

Impact of Practice Setting

Another major consideration for socially just practice to occur is the impact of the practice setting. This is usually the entity that employs the practitioner, provides space and resources for work to occur, and legitimizes the work being done. This setting (e.g., a nonprofit agency or governmental unit) will have a strong influence on whether the practice is socially just. The organization may have policies that are either socially just or unjust, which are reflected in how it allocates scarce resources, to whom its services are offered, the ways in which its policies are implemented, and its overall organizational culture. All agencies reflect both just and unjust qualities as a result of their historical evolution and the current external environment. All of these conditions affect the practitioner's ability to provide service according to principles of social justice. Consequently, all social workers must consider the impact of their practice setting on the justice or injustice embodied in the service developed. (For further discussion of the impact of organizations on practice, see Chapter 7.)

Social Justice Practice Concepts Expanded

Each level or aspect of practice makes use of social justice practice concepts that are likely to have relevance for concepts used by practitioners at other levels as well. In addition, new concepts may be introduced and previous ones expanded due to conditions that exist at some levels/aspects and not at others. These conditions are often the result of structures and processes that arise due to complexities intrinsic to various levels of social organization. For example, organizations and communities may have formal structures such as committees with elected officers, whereas families and small groups are not likely to be organized in this way.

There are seven major practice dimensions, however, that are likely to occur in some form at all levels and types of socially just practice. The following presentation of these dimensions may imply that they occur in a linear manner. Although it is probable that some of these dimensions may be more pronounced at some times than others, we do not envision them in this way. For example, engagement processes may be emphasized when people first meet, although new people may undertake an engagement process at any time they join in the work. In addition, engagement may also become deeper as people work together. Celebrations might be emphasized when a service is ending but may also be created when any significant accomplishment is achieved or when the participants wish to experience joy to bolster their collective morale. Finally, each practice dimension has three components: a process, a goal-oriented activity, and the worker's self-reflection.

Practice Dimensions

With the previous caveats in mind, we now discuss our concept of practice dimensions in more detail, and they are illustrated in Figure 4.3. As this figure reflects, these dimensions are exploring, engaging, planning, implementing, monitoring/evaluating, and celebrating/terminating.

Exploring

Exploring typically occurs in the beginning of service as practitioners and service users consider how they will work together to accomplish mutually agreed upon purposes. This involves discussing the various perspectives of the service users

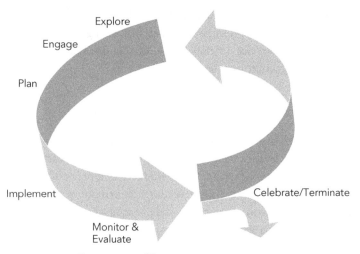

FIGURE 4.3   Dimensions of Practice

and practitioners. The exploration may be informal as people discuss what they intend to do as they utilize the service. Exploration may continue in an ongoing way as participants modify their original perceptions of each other and the service transaction as circumstances evolve. As a result of further exploration, practitioners and service users may decide to revise their original ideas about the use of the service or reaffirm them.

There are many social justice issues related to exploring, including the following:

- Has the practitioner or service agency used their power to impose limits on the service user's exploration of the possible outcomes of the service? Is there an assumption that the practitioner or other representatives of the agency or some other system in the environment is more capable, knowledgeable, or entitled to determine the goals of the service or the means by which these goals will be achieved? This is a subtle but persistent issue because practitioners may have knowledge that service users lack. However, it is often true that service users possess knowledge (often of a technical nature) that practitioners do not. In such circumstances, it is important to determine whether the development of a service is a unilateral process or an opportunity for practitioners and service users to learn from one another.
- Have the service users used their own power to develop their own ideas? To what extent has the practitioner attempted to learn what these ideas are? People develop a personal system for viewing their situation, and much can be learned by practitioners who are open to learning from service users.

- The process of exploration may occur in various ways in different cultures and contexts; for example, men may not engage in exploration in the same ways as women, and older people may explore differently from youth. To what extent does the practitioner recognize these differences and integrate them in the assessment of the situation? Does the practitioner value some forms of exploring more than others? This requires considerable reflection.
- The environmental context, such as the agency, may also exert considerable influence on the exploration process based on its priorities, purposes, and ideology and how it distributes its resources.

Engagement and the Role of Power

Engagement is the process that occurs as practitioners and service users interact with each other to plan what they will do together and why they have chosen (or are deciding to choose) to work together. The process involves practitioners and service users becoming better acquainted with each other; developing a degree of closeness, to the extent required by the purposes of the service; and establishing trust and mutual respect, a means of communication, and a set of clear role expectations. If the service users are multiple, such as in a group, engagement processes also must occur with reference to the group or larger system, such as the agency or community.

Several critical activities occur during the engagement phase of practice. Practitioners and service users learn about each other; this enables service users to determine whether they wish to be involved in an ongoing relationship with these specific practitioners. Practitioners and service users determine the purposes of the work they will do together. Practitioners and service users determine the rules and norms that will govern their work together in a manner that enables service users to trust that their needs and interests will be protected. Service users help determine which third parties will be involved in the service relationship (e.g., family members, group members, and resource persons) on the basis of whether these "compositional" factors also protect their needs and interests.

During the engagement process, service users and practitioners consider the goals that they seek to attain through the service offered. A social justice approach requires that the social contexts be considered in setting these goals. Often, the context (e.g., the agency, community, or social policy) pressures service users to accept goals that are oppressive and counter to their needs. It is also possible, of course, that the contexts may support the service users' attainment of their goals. What makes such situations complex is that both of these circumstances may occur at the same time. It is incumbent on all concerned to "unpack" this issue and act according to both their best interests and their aspirations.

Several types of activities are employed by service users and practitioners during the engagement process that can be either socially just or unjust. For example, dialogue is a socially just process in which all participants demonstrate their willingness to listen carefully to what others say, think about what has been said, and respond respectfully. (A more comprehensive discussion of dialogue is presented in Chapter 6.)

In summary, during the engagement phase of practice, practitioners should reflect on the following:

- Is the engagement forced on the service user by the practitioner(s) or other persons in the agency or larger environment because of the power they possess? Such pressure to engage may also come from the service user's family or other persons in his or her network. This is a particularly complex issue today because an increasing number of service users are involuntary (Rooney, 2009). The involuntary nature of many services may be the consequence of a decision by a legally mandated authority such as a judge or prison personnel. It may also come from family members or associates who threaten the service user with loss of a job or a divorce if he or she does not comply. In an organization, a member of a committee may be ordered by his or her superiors to participate in the committee in a certain way with consequences if he or she fails to do so. Rooney (2009) presents a full discussion of the ethical issues involved in involuntary engagement processes and asserts effectively that much work needs to be done to clarify what is socially just under such circumstances.
- To what degree are practitioners engaged in actual dialogue with service users? Are they "hearing" what service users think and feel about becoming engaged in this endeavor?
- Are practitioners misusing their power in soliciting the service users' engagement?
- Are the practitioners relying on stereotypes or other preconceptions of the service users based on preexisting beliefs that may oppress the service users, distort their needs for service, limit the development of their own power, and impose on the service users conditions that are not in their best interests?

These questions reflect the belief that from the outset, socially just practice requires practitioners to assist service users to develop their own power and become increasingly conscious of that power. (This is a major component of empowerment.) Practitioners also seek to raise service users' consciousness of the power exercised by relevant others that in intent or effect supports or diminishes service users' power. This involves deconstructing the language used to convey the possession of power as well as other, more subtle symbols of power, such as the pictures that adorn the walls of an organization, the symbols or cultural artifacts that are displayed, and whether the rights of service users are posted in some other way. For example, upon entering a medical office today, one is likely to see a posted statement of the rights of patients regarding privacy and the expression of grievances and with information about how a complaint should be filed if these rights are violated.

As consciousness of power develops, practitioners and service users should introduce new ways to express power that support the evolving power of service users. This might involve processes such as emphasizing that service users make their own decisions about their activities and agendas. This does not deny the practitioner's expertise or ability to offer ideas and suggestions. Nor does it imply that the legitimate interests of others (third parties) will be ignored or denied. However, there are likely to be conflicts of interest and points of view in such situations. Therefore, it is important that practitioners strive to resolve these conflicts by taking into consideration the needs and legitimate interests of all actors. The search of the agency for funding (another level of practice) to support practice goals may require other actions. Service users in this circumstance may decide to play an active role in the agency's search for funding rather than asserting that this is "none of their business." All of these contextual factors require practitioners to reflect on the various power dynamics involved as well as their own use of power or lack thereof in the situation. This requires practitioners to understand their sources of power, such as those derived from their personal characteristics (e.g., gender, race, and ethnicity), their position in the agency, their position in the actual service situation (e.g., group leader and mediator), the norms in the situation that grant them power, their ability to administer rewards or aversive consequences, and the power they acquire due to the service users' identification with the practitioner. Although these sources of power may always be present, the practitioner may or may not choose to draw upon them. In addition, both practitioners and service users may be aware of these sources of power; this has implications for how they act and interact with each other. Therefore, it behooves practitioners to consider the implications of this power dynamic for the service users' development and utilization of their own power.

Planning

During the planning phase, practitioners and service users determine the ends they seek and how they intend to reach them. These can be proximal ends such as a step that is required to achieve the ultimate purpose of the service. For example, a final end for a committee might be rewriting an agency policy. The proximal ends might involve obtaining copies of related policies from other agencies, determining statutory requirements, or surveying the staff for their views. In some approaches to practice, these proximal ends are referred to as "tasks."

In whatever social work context, planning includes the following activities:

- Obtaining resources needed to implement the plan (e.g., money and physical space)
- Acquiring the specific skills required for effective action (e.g., to create a brochure and to learn how to bargain with a key collaborator)
- Coping with conflicts that may arise
- Raising one's critical consciousness about the context of the action and helping to raise the consciousness of others in the situation
- Engaging in dialogue with the various individuals and groups with whom practitioners and service users will cooperate or collaborate in the planned action

All of the bases for an action have critical social justice components. Using the previous examples, we indicate in Table 4.1 some of these social justice components. The following are some social justice issues for practitioners with respect to planning:

- How are they using power during this phase of the process? Are they using it to enable others to participate fully or are they using their presumed expertise, position in the agency, or personal qualities to subtly influence the bases for action?

Table 4.1 Social Justice Components for Establishing a Basis for Action

Basis for Action	Social Justice Component
Obtaining resources	Are resources distributed equitably?
Learning skills	Are these skills "protected" by workers or others who assume that they "own" them and that use of power in this way is their "right"?
Learning how to cope with conflicts	Do service users have the opportunity to develop and use their power in this situation so that resolving conflict occurs on a "level playing field"?
Raising one's critical consciousness about the situation	Are service users assisted with the information, time, and skills required to develop this consciousness?

- What kinds of perspectives are being used to establish the bases for action? Are these "traditional" ones that have been used to steer actions in ways that benefit the dominant power sources in the agency or community? Or will the perspectives employed enable service users to achieve their objectives, overcome the barriers they will face, and become more empowered?

Implementing

The purpose of a social work service is to take action to change some condition. The condition may be internal to the individual or individuals who have sought service from the practitioner, as reflected in their beliefs, attitudes, ways of thinking, emotional responses, or characteristic behaviors. The condition may be the consequence of the interaction of two or more persons, such as partners in an intimate relationship, colleagues, friends, employer–employees, neighbors, peers, citizens, or members of a governmental or nongovernmental organization. The condition may also be the product of the structures, processes, or policies of a community, organization, or governmental body. As noted previously, however, we believe that all these conditions exist in a broader social context that contributes to the condition and that may be socially unjust and oppressive. Thus, all of these conditions may be related in whole or in part to social justice concerns. Table 4.2 provides examples.

Potential actions to address these conditions are discussed in detail in subsequent chapters. As we have stated throughout this book, the actions taken

Table 4.2 Possible Social Justice Issues and Conditions in Which
Change Is Sought

Condition	Possible Social Justice Issue
Internal to the person	Individual is angry at unjust treatment; individual's identity is denigrated; individual has failed to acquire skills because of prejudice and discrimination.
Interaction among or between persons	Two intimate partners are in a relationship in which one holds more power due to such attributes as gender; two individuals are in a relationship in which one holds power and wields it unjustly because of position, personal attribute, etc.
Structures and processes of the community, organization, or governmental body	Policies discriminate against classes of people; structure of system maintains power of some individuals based on their group identifications; individuals denied power in systems in which they are participants (service users, employees).

(i.e., the processes used) must be guided by principles of social justice as much as the outcomes that are sought. Engaging in actions should also be part of the processes of praxis in which theory helps to guide actions and reflection of the results of these actions contributes to the construction of enhanced theory.

ACTIONS TO CHANGE CONDITIONS INTERNAL TO THE SERVICE USER
In Part II, we discuss the following types of actions and the social justice implications of each type of action:

- *Changing thoughts, beliefs, and attitudes*: Service users (and practitioners) examine their cognitions and beliefs and determine to change them. This may also be the consequence of a problem-solving process. Another way this occurs is through feedback from others such as peers in a group.
- *Consciousness-raising*: All participants in the action examine their awareness and understanding of oppression.
- *Changing behavior*: Service users obtain different sources of reinforcement, choose new models, and assume new roles. This may also be the result of experiences in a group including feedback from peers. Through the use of reflexivity and praxis, practitioners modify their behavior in response to critical reflection about how the change process is unfolding.
- *Changing feelings*: Service users have an opportunity for catharsis or for relaxation and other means of tension reduction.

ACTIONS TO CHANGE CONDITIONS EXTERNAL TO
THE SERVICE USER
Interventions in this regard could address such issues and concerns as the following:

- *Avoidance*: Service users avoid contact with individuals and/or systems and withdraw from their social environment.
- *Alternate reactions*: Service users change their actions without demanding others to do the same.
- *Request*: Service users ask that the behavior of others change or that the physical situation be changed.
- *Interpretation*: Service users explain to others the consequences of others' behavior or their own.
- *Education*: Service users seek to add to their self-knowledge or that of others.
- *Evaluation*: Service users seek to change a situation by collecting data about the causes or consequences of a condition.
- *Use of influential others*: Service users seek to collaborate with others who possess the power to contribute to the desired change effort.

- *Bargaining*: Service users seek to do something in exchange for a commensurate change in others.
- *Confrontation*: Service users present to others the nature and consequences of their actions by means of any of the following: mass media, passive resistance, and active resistance.

In helping service users employ one or more of the previously discussed actions (or to use them on behalf of service users), there are many social justice issues for practitioners to consider. As discussed previously, one of the most important issues is how the practitioner uses power. For example, in a bargaining situation, it is important to ask whether the service user's power is brought into play or whether the practitioner intercedes with his or her own power. The use of some form of resistance as part of a change effort provides another example of a social justice issue. Occasionally, service users with limited power have been pressed to take risks while practitioners (who may have greater power) have sat safely on the sidelines.

Another issue for practitioners involves selecting a means of action based on the needs of the practitioner rather than those of the service user. For example, the previously presented set of actions to change conditions external to the service situation have been arranged in order from less conflict-ridden to more conflict-ridden approaches. Aside from the strategic issues involved, several other issues govern the choice of approaches. One is that the choice appears socially just to the various publics whom the service users regard as allies. Practitioners, however, may have their own needs, biases, and agendas in such situations (e.g., the desire to impose one's values, appear successful, use resources more efficiently, and satisfy their superiors), and it is important that practitioners be aware of how these subjective factors may influence their choice of approach. Finally, the issue of praxis is important here: Is the practitioner continuing to build theory and the relationship of theory to practice in the choice of approaches to change?

Monitoring/Evaluating

All participants in a socially just social work process should be interested in and informed about the outcomes of the process. By outcomes, we are referring both to the immediate outcomes of some action and to the long-term consequences when participants determine that their efforts to reach a goal have been completed. Thus, all relevant parties may be asked to present their assessment of outcomes at any one of several points during the practice relationship.

The most proximate moment for evaluation may occur during a session or group meeting when participants are asked how satisfied they are with a discussion that has occurred, a decision that has been made, or an activity that has been completed. They may also be asked similar questions at the end of a session or several sessions, at the end of a season, or when service is being terminated. Power issues are as important when an evaluation occurs as at the beginning of a service relationship. Individuals may be either encouraged or inhibited by the opinions of others who have the power to reward or punish them when their opinions are expressed.

Finally, an important part of the evaluation process is the practitioners' critical reflections on the events that have taken place and their role in these events. In the spirit of equalizing power between practitioners and service users, this information should be shared with the latter and, sometimes, with other stakeholders.

A critical social justice issue in the evaluation/monitoring phase concerns what is done with the evaluative information. If there is a conflict or a difference of opinion, what are the consequences? Do the views of less powerful participants have an impact on subsequent activities and events, including the role played by others, if their opinions differ from those of more powerful participants? For example, if some service users believe the practitioner or other forces in the agency were responsible for the lack of desired outcomes, are there consequences for the service user or the service itself?

In Chapter 10, we provide considerable detail regarding socially just evaluation. This chapter emphasizes that there are many different approaches to evaluation, and the ones selected should be appropriate to the type of activity that is being evaluated and the characteristics of the various persons who will provide information, receive results, and determine how these results will be used.

Celebrating/Terminating

Although the celebration concept is not typically part of the "list" in most social work texts, we include this type of activity here for several reasons. One is that work for social justice can and should be joyful. This does not deny that there can be moments of discouragement, pain, and frustration in this as in any kind of work. However, the underlying struggle for a more just society can and should be a source of personal fulfillment, a way of leading a useful and meaningful life, a means to benefit oneself as well as others, and a process that helps us draw closer to others who are engaged in similar struggles.

When victories, even small victories, are achieved, it is a cause for much elation. However, defeats can also provide opportunities to learn and grow stronger. A celebration can be an event that attests to both victories and setbacks in joyous and meaningful ways that can draw people even closer; make them feel more united; and provide them with the strength, hope, and persistence that comes from being part of something larger that oneself.

The elation such moments create was dramatically displayed when a large crowd gathered on Chicago's waterfront to celebrate the election of Barack Obama to his first term as president and in the faces of the million-plus individuals who attended his inauguration. At such times, people express their emotions differently—through laughter and tears, dancing and song.

As with any of the other processes discussed in this chapter, such events are typically jointly planned by all participants. However, this does not rule out the role of spontaneity or the possibility of an occasional surprise event planned by one group as a gift to another. Under either circumstance, such events replenish and nourish the practitioner as well as all others involved. The joy others receive from a victory is an important part of the many intangible gifts a practitioner obtains as a result of being engaged and committed to social justice work.

There are other aspects to the termination process in addition to evaluating and celebrating. When the experience with the practitioner has been an essentially positive one, service users will view the end of their work together as a loss. In addition, they are likely to have the same sense of loss when there are multiple service users or other people with whom they have worked in this process. Many social work texts deal extensively with the termination process (Hepworth, Rooney, & Larson, 2010; Seabury, Seabury, & Garvin, 2011); we will not repeat their major points. However, there are specific social justice issues to be considered in the termination process.

As a result of the termination process, will participants possess a new sense of their power that will enable them to plan subsequent change efforts with greater confidence and skill? Will participants possess and carry forth to future endeavors a deeper understanding of how social justice goals and processes can strengthen their future activities? Will participants be able to help others understand the goals and processes of social justice in order to create a broader unity of efforts that can achieve both their personal goals and a more just society? Often, as a result of socially just work, forces may be unleashed that are likely to bring negative consequences to bear on both participants and practitioners. Will the termination process prepare all of those involved in the work to recognize and resist such consequences?

Finally, Figure 4.4 demonstrates how the different components of social justice practice we have outlined come together. It illustrates how these multiple components—from the intellectual work involved in reflecting, analyzing, and theorizing about oneself, other participants in social justice work, and the context in which this work occurs to the often challenging and occasionally painful activities of praxis, self-reflection, and attention to power and privilege—are present in all phases of practice (in whatever mode or setting it occurs) and interact in a dynamic, dialectical, and ongoing manner.

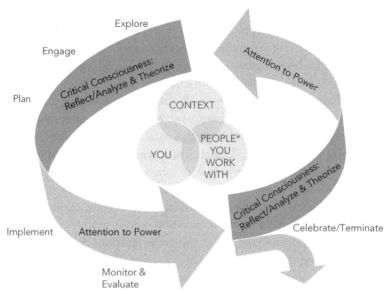

FIGURE 4.4   Dimensions of Practice—Praxis

Summary

In this chapter, we introduced a model of socially just practice that can be applied to all social work methods and in all fields of practice. We situated this practice in its environmental context and emphasized the importance of critical consciousness, awareness of one's positionality, and the use of praxis in its development and implementation. We incorporated into the model the various phases and dimensions of practice, and we discussed how social justice concepts could be infused in each of these phases and dimensions. Finally, we identified some ethical issues and practice challenges that might arise in attempting to apply this model to one's practice. Part II elaborates on this social justice model in greater detail and applies it to practice with individuals and families, groups, organizations, and communities and in the spheres of policy development and research.

Discussion Questions

1. Are some "action systems" (e.g., individual, family, group, and organization) more likely to lead to efforts to change socially unjust situations than others? If so, for what reasons?

2. Identify a practice situation in which you are involved. To what extent does the social context create injustice in that situation? What form does that injustice take?
3. Select a practice situation in which you are involved. How do your assumptions about socially just practice influence your response to this situation?

PART II

Doing Justice

This part of the book builds on the material we presented in previous chapters, including our definitions of social justice theories, concepts, and history and its relationship to social work. It also draws upon other relevant issues we have discussed, such as power and resistance and the processes of praxis, critical thinking, and the practitioner's use of self.

In Part I, we discussed theories and concepts that provide a foundation for social justice-oriented practice. In Part II, we provide a more detailed discussion of how to use these ideas in a variety of practice methods and practice situations. We believe that social justice goals and processes are not solely the province of organizations with explicit social justice missions; they can and should be integrated into all forms of practice. This requires those who work with individuals and families to think critically about the implications of the organizational, community, and societal context. Conversely, it requires social workers engaged in community, organizational, or policy practice to consider the implications of their work for the individuals and families it affects. This approach explicitly rejects the artificial dichotomy between "micro" and "macro" practice that we believe has impeded the social justice mission of the social work profession for decades.

In Chapter 4, we outlined our assumptions about socially just practice and the theories and practice principles derived from these assumptions. These skills are illustrated through critical discussion of the activities involved in goal setting, assessment, planning, implementation, and monitoring progress across multiple levels, settings, and domains of practice (see Figure II.1).

The first chapter in Part II (Chapter 5) applies our ideas about practice to work with individuals and families. This chapter is based on the assumption that all social workers interact professionally with individuals, albeit with different functions. We believe it is important in many instances to assess the situation of individuals in the context of their families while at the same time recognizing that families are made up of individuals with their own needs and goals.

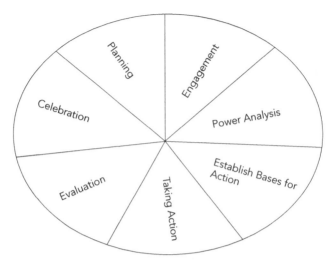

FIGURE II.I   Phases of Practice.

In Chapter 6, we discuss how these principles can be used in work with both task and therapeutic groups. Social justice principles and group work are a natural "fit" because this method emerged as a means to promote and expand democratic ideas. In this chapter, we consider the complexity of intragroup and intergroup relationships—for example, by acknowledging that some groups consist of individuals who seek help with individual concerns and other groups can only achieve their goals by interacting with the organizations, communities, and societal institutions that comprise their environmental context. Underlying this work is the need for social workers to understand the conditions that affect practice with all types of groups. As Mullender, Ward, and Fleming (2013) assert, a major part of what they call "self-directed group work" is asking the question "Why?" along with "What?" and "How?"

In Chapter 7, we address the challenges involved in creating and sustaining socially just organizations, both those that provide services to people and those with specific social justice missions. We describe the various attributes of a socially just organization, present the principles that underlie socially just administrative practice, and discuss some of the challenges of implementing these principles in a multicultural environment. We focus on such issues as how injustices can be embedded in organizational structures, concepts of leadership, and decision-making processes. As in other chapters, we examine the various manifestations of power and its consequences for socially just practice.

In Chapter 8, we discuss working with communities to promote social justice, such as transforming institutions, structures, and meso/mezzo systems to be more inclusive, democratic, redistributive, and de-centered. We regard community practice both as a means to promote social justice goals and in terms of its use of socially just processes. We distinguish between community work that is directed toward explicitly social justice-related goals and the use of socially just means in varieties of community work that are not directed toward explicit social justice goals.

Chapter 9 presents material on how social workers can create more socially just policies through various forms of analysis and advocacy. This chapter is divided into two parts. The first part clarifies what constitutes socially just policies (at the societal, community, and organizational levels) in terms of their goals, substance, and impact. The second part includes content on the development of social policies from a dual perspective. It explores how socially just policies can be promoted both from inside what are often socially unjust institutions and from the outside, through advocacy and other forms of community-based social action. As in other chapters, we provide examples of ways the policy-level practitioner can use his or her own critical consciousness throughout the policy development and implementation process.

The last chapter, Chapter 10, focuses on research. We do not view research as primarily a process to evaluate programs or determine how variables of interest affect one another. Rather, as Brown and Strega (2005) assert, we view socially just research as developed *with* stakeholders (e.g., the individuals served, group members, and agency personnel) in order to bring about change in socially unjust situations. This chapter is presented with the recognition that knowledge development plays a major role in the evolution of socially just practice. Therefore, this chapter reviews and critiques the methodologies utilized by social workers and the assumptions about epistemology; the purposes of knowledge development; the criteria for valid and useful knowledge; and the power issues that exist among researchers, practitioners, and those being "researched." An important component of this chapter is a critique of so-called "evidence-based practice" and the ways in which such practice does or does not advance the cause of socially just practice. We especially emphasize in this chapter research activities that have the potential for promoting social justice. Because research tools are used to evaluate practice, we also consider how research should be used in socially just approaches to evaluation.

In summary, these chapters comprise the core of the book. Each chapter contains brief, annotated case studies or exercises, drawn for the most part from the "real-world" experiences of the authors, and concludes with several discussion questions. Our goal in these chapters is to provide social workers with the concepts and skills needed to engage in socially just practice and, in so doing, contribute to the creation of a more socially just society.

5

Social Justice and Individual and Family Change

Charles D. Garvin and Edith Lewis

Introduction

In this chapter, we discuss how social justice issues inform and affect practice with individuals and families. The chapter begins with a discussion of the approaches currently in use that can contribute to a socially just practice. We then critique them with respect to their adequacy for socially just practice with individuals and families. Thus, this discussion considers both their shortcomings and their contributions to socially just practice.

Because a major feature of socially just practice is its attention to system change as well as individual and family change, we also discuss how individual and family practitioners can view and implement system change at the level of the family, group, organization, community, or society. In addition, we describe the roles of practitioners and service users in the change process. An important ingredient of practice with individuals and groups is the practitioners themselves, particularly the privileged positions practitioners may hold. We also consider how the practitioners' actions and characteristics may affect the change process and how practitioners can be aware of this possibility.

The chapter then considers the phases of practice conceptualized as beginnings, middles, and endings. We view these processes in a nonlinear manner so that some phases, in one form or another, are likely to reoccur during the other phases. For example, evaluation may occur in the beginning of a practice relationship as practitioners and service users define their purposes and goals, during the middle phase as they seek to assess movement, and at the end as the effectiveness of the service is assessed and the next steps are anticipated.

Approaches to Facilitating Individual Change

As practice with individuals evolved in social work, a number of approaches or models emerged, often based on the incorporation of one or more of the psychological or sociological theories prevalent at the time. In the early years of social work, however, the practices of the day, particularly in the charity organization societies (COS), were based on moral principles and frequently biased assumptions about racial and ethnic minority clients (Wenocur & Reisch, 1989). In her classic book, *Social Diagnosis* (1917), Mary Richmond sought to develop a model of practice that was "scientific" using concepts based on the experiences of COS workers and developing practice principles derived from these experiences. At the time, social work practice focused primarily on persons who were poor or immigrants to American society. As this form of practice, referred to as casework at the time, evolved, it was soon applied to work with people who were in hospitals, schools, and prisons and to individuals suffering from mental illness.

Richmond soon expanded on her work and developed the concept of "person in environment" (Richmond, 1922). In her view, an important component of practitioners' work with individuals involved finding and developing the environmental resources they needed. Early caseworkers, however, did not regard the environment as a source of oppression, nor did they examine the structural conditions that promote injustice.

As casework evolved as a method in the 1930s and 1940s, theorists sought to strengthen its scientific base by infusing ideas drawn from emerging psychological theories. Two schools of thought came to dominate the social work literature during this period: the "diagnostic" and "functional" schools (Kasius, 1950). The diagnostic school, whose principal champions were on the faculty of the New York School of Social Work (now Columbia University School of Social Work), was based on the writings of Sigmund Freud and his followers. It emphasized a psychodynamic model of practice. The functional school, centered at the University of Pennsylvania, based its practice model on the ideas of Otto Rank (1936, 1958). Although the former was the most widespread in social work practice and education, it was primarily devoted to understanding individual behavior in the context of the family and not on oppressive environmental forces.

The functional school had greater potential to address issues of injustice because its use of the word "functional" reflected its recognition of individual–agency–practitioner dynamics and the processes they set in play. Nevertheless, the diagnostic school dominated the social work field until the 1950s when Helen Harris Perlman challenged this psychological emphasis in her famous article, "Putting the Social Back in Social Case Work" (Perlman, 1971). Her critique led to a shift in casework's emphasis from a psychodynamic to a "psychosocial" model (Woods & Hollis, 2000) and, ultimately, the emergence of the "social ecological" model (Pardeck, 1996). Although this model paid attention to environmental–individual transactions, it did not intrinsically incorporate a critique of the social forces at play, the related power issues, the development of the practitioner's critical consciousness, the oppression of many groups (e.g., women, persons of color, LGBT persons, and disabled persons), or the empowerment of the users of social work services (Jani & Reisch, 2011). As these models evolved in the 1930s, a movement known as the Rank and File Movement emerged. It reflected a more radical perspective on practice and critiqued many of the underlying assumptions of the models' underlying assumptions (Spano, 1982). Many of the movement's ideas appeared in its journal, *Social Work Today*.

In response to these critiques, social work theorists developed new models of practice. One was the "structural" model developed by Wood and Middleman (1989). This model was subsequently given a stronger empowerment orientation including a critique of the oppressive nature of social institutions by Canadian authors such as Moreau (1979) and Mullaly (2007).

In recent years, a number of other models have emerged that have added a social justice perspective for practice at all levels (Table 5.1). The importance of these models lies in their focus on the need for practitioners to view individuals in terms of their social location and to understand people's social contexts in terms of their effects on individuals and other levels of social organization. Although they differ somewhat in emphasis, each of these models serves as a counterpoint to the conservative, individual responsibility-oriented philosophy that has dominated public discourse in recent decades. Also, although they support the expression of agency, particularly by individuals and groups from historically disempowered and disadvantaged populations, they recognize human interdependence and mutuality rather than autonomy. In addition, they acknowledge the different manifestations of human need and the impact of the external environment both on producing these needs and on shaping the forms of helping developed to address them (Stone, 2008).

One contemporary body of work is based on *feminist* ideas (DeChant, 1996; Gutierrez & Lewis, 1999; Reed & Garvin 1995), which have produced different and occasionally conflicting approaches to practice. Some feminist practice models primarily emphasize a critique of sexist conditions in most, if not all, social institutions. Liberal feminists focus on changing individual behavior, cultural attitudes, and discriminatory practices. At the other end of the spectrum, radical feminists argue that overcoming gender discrimination and the disempowerment of women is impossible without a reorganization of a society that is built on male dominance. These models are discussed in detail in Reed and Garvin (1995).

The following is an example of how feminist ideas are applied to practice: A practitioner was working with a woman who was depressed. The worker observed that the woman thought that her husband dominated her, made all

Table 5.1 Models of Individual and Family Change: Contributions and Limitations

Approach	Contributions to Socially Just Practice	Limitations with Respect to Socially Just Practice
Structural	Views service user in terms of social contexts Views such contexts in terms of issues such as the power and actual or potential oppression of social structures	May underestimate the role of the consciousness of the service users and how they construct their social realities For example, creates standardized roles for family members, irrespective of their ability to enact those roles
Feminist	Women as agents Focus on process as well as content of intervention styles and strategies Recognition of social, historical, and political contexts	Focus primarily on women, sometimes to the exclusion of their families Recognition of contexts narrowly defined so that it excludes ethnically diverse or extended family systems
Multicultural	Increased attention to ethnicity and race as factors influencing individual and family functioning	Inability to fully integrate ethnicity and race with other social group memberships reflective of actual individual and familial lives: gender identity and expression Has often confused race and social class in the analysis of individuals and families
Constructivist	Places human actors within the multiple contexts in which they serve as both agents of change and recipients of external forces of change	Continued impasse with regard to whose constructions are the most valid Even agency is legitimated by external forces
Narrative	Contributions, such as the Stone School model, placing the emphasis of the person-in-environment on the integration of environments and persons	Has had limited influence on individual and/or family practice because of its attention to issues of social justice influencing humans in their interactions with their environments "Whose reality?" is ultimately determined by the therapist

Table 5.1 Continued

Approach	Contributions to Socially Just Practice	Limitations with Respect to Socially Just Practice
	Development of nuanced, contextualized constructions of individuals and families	
Solution	Pragmatic approach aimed at resolving current individual/ familial problems	Decontextualized, particularly with regard to historical and political individual and family realities
Strengths	Focus on abilities rather than problems faced by individuals and families, with an emphasis on using those identified strengths as the building blocks of intervention	"Who determines what family strengths are?" This discussion of strengths has often led to the exclusion of strategies utilized by some groups, deeming them pathological.
Empowerment	Requires an analysis of current reality in its social, political, and historical contexts Focuses on the development of new skills through interactions or connections with others	Definition of presenting issue often the purview of the practitioner rather than those who will engage in the empowerment process Lack of recognition that one cannot empower someone else
Radical	Emphasis on changing existing systems of oppression, particularly those with structural and political bases View of social worker as active change agent in the wider society/ environment as well as at the individual/family levels	In United States, has been limited by its insistence on a Marxist perspective Emphasis on new forms of domination rather than constructions of new systems of cooperation (e.g., North American Free Trade Agreement)

major family decisions, and handled all the family finances. She was required to ask him for money each time she went food shopping. With the help of the worker, the woman was able to understand that she felt useless and demeaned as a result of this marital situation and that this situation led to her depression.

Other contemporary models have focused on practice with people of color or people from other countries than the United States. Although there are significant differences among these models, they all challenge the universalist assumption that all people have needs and patterns of help-seeking similar to those of middle-class, White, urban, heterosexual citizens of the United States (Anderson & Carter, 2003; Gutierrez & Lewis, 1999; Lum, 1999; Sue, 1981). These models draw heavily on ideas about empowerment, particularly the work of Solomon (1976) and Pinderhughes (1983), and the recognition that many ethnic groups, particularly people of color, suffered from the unequal distribution of power in American society.

The following is an illustration of how these concepts can be applied to practice: A practitioner was working with an African American man (Mr. H) who was employed as a regional manager by a large sales firm. This man frequently felt angry but was not sure where his anger came from. With the worker's help, he became aware that the other managers (who were all White) were given the more lucrative territories as their responsibility. Consequently, Mr. H. became determined to raise this issue with the management of the company.

Constructivist and constructionist approaches are also relevant to social justice practice because they place heavy emphasis on the perceptions and experiences of service users. As stated by Van Soest and Garcia (2003), the main thesis of these approaches is that reality is socially and psychologically constructed through interaction. These approaches "highlight the significance of the connection between individual and social influences" (p. 39). Although constructionism "places an emphasis on language, narrative, sociohistorical and cultural processes" and "constructivism highlights cognitive structures (schemas) and interactive feedback from the environment" (p. 39), these approaches may limit the attention of practitioners to what the service users think and perceive rather than to the actual structural conditions that may oppress them. Although the use of these models helps empower service users by legitimating and supporting their perspectives, they pay less attention to raising their consciousness of the injustices they may suffer. Less work has also been done in social work to examine the outcomes of practices derived from these approaches (Thyer, 2010).

An example of the application of these models occurred in the case of a practitioner who was working with an Asian man who believed that the United States was a fair country devoid of any racism. When he failed on several occasions to be promoted when it was clear he was the superior candidate, the man began to question his views on this issue.

Another approach often linked to the constructionist one is the narrative approach. According to Kelley (2011), narrative therapy has a "focus on social justice, viewing problems in cultural context, individualization of clients, and collaboration with and respect for them through hearing and honoring their views" (p. 315). According to Kelley,

> The goal of NT (narrative therapy) is first to help clients understand the stories around which they have organized their lives (deconstruction) and then to broaden and challenge them creating new realities (reconstruction). . . . In the process clients are encouraged to question familial and cultural stories that have restricted them. (p. 315)

An example of this is a gay client who told the story of how, because of his fears of rejection by his family, he denied his sexual orientation to his family and friends. Through the narrative approach, he created a future story in which he "came out" to these people and risked the consequences. In this story, he pictured himself as strong and resilient and able to deal with the consequences of his self-revelation. The worker helped him to embellish this future story and plan the details as to how he would put the story into practice.

Another similar approach is called solution-focused practice (Walsh, 2009). This model is essentially goal-oriented in that it asks the service users to create statements of what the future will be like if the problems that brought them to the social worker are resolved. This approach to practice is likely to be more acceptable to many clients than creating a traditional goal statement in the form of a concrete definition of behavior. The social justice implications of the solution-focused approach are that this scenario could incorporate elements of the situation such as the responses of others and changes in the social context. A problem arises, however, when the "solution" is narrowly defined and restricted to the individual's or family members' actions. A narrative in a socially just sense incorporates elements of the larger situation, especially more just ones than currently exist.

An example of this is a service user who sought help with her problematic interactions with fellow employees. Her initial "solution" involved her becoming more assertive when they scapegoated her. Through her discussions with the social worker, she realized that the scapegoating resulted from the efforts of the organization to blame her for productivity problems rather than to examine the ways that speed-up pressures and the sexist judgments of administrators played a role. In her revised "solution," her all-women's team resisted speed-up pressures and confronted the sexism of administrators.

The so-called "strengths-based" perspective has also contributed to the development of socially just practice (Saleeby, 2002). In this approach, the focus of the assessment is on the service user's competencies rather than deficits or medical disease labels. For example, a service user was diagnosed by a psychiatrist as having a generalized anxiety disorder. Instead of treating this disorder, the social worker focused on this person's strengths, such as intelligence, ability to carry out complex tasks, and use of yoga to relax. In another example, a family was initially defined in terms of "family pathologies," such as special alliances between father and daughter and the unlikelihood that members were listening to each other. Using the strengths-based approach, the social worker focused on the genuine caring that existed among family members, the willingness of the parents to make financial sacrifices for their children, and the supports they received and accepted from extended family.

The limitation of this approach is that strengths are too often defined in a manner that limits the environment's contribution to the family's situation. The definition of clients' strengths has often failed to recognize cultural variations in what these strengths are (e.g., how indigenous healers are used), how other non-family members contribute their strengths, and how cultural practices can be strengths rather than barriers to problem solving.

During the past three decades, the concept of empowerment has become a central focus of social work, although different authors have defined it in different ways (Gutierrez, Parsons, & Cox, 1998; Lee, 2001; Simon, 1994; Solomon, 1976). One difficulty with defining empowerment is that it is a complex concept that involves incorporating many phenomena, such as the individual's, family's, or group's sense of self-efficacy to bring about change in their social situations, satisfy their wants and needs as they define them, and master their own affairs. Thus, empowered individuals, singly or as collectivities, believe they have the right and can obtain the resources, skills, and allies required to achieve change. However, this is a process in which these concomitants of power will increase as a result of the process. This means that as individuals act in ways that give them a sense of power and their ability to influence social conditions, they are likely to take on new challenges that require new kinds and degrees of power. This enriches their repertoire of ways of creating change and their sense that they have the "power" to do this.

It is clear, however, that a social justice approach to practice must incorporate an understanding of all of these dimensions of empowerment practice and theory. There are problems and limitations in this work. One is that practitioners may believe that their commitment to the concept alone is sufficient to "empower" the users of service. This is important because empowerment ideas imply a critique of socially unjust conditions or the aspiration to work for a more socially just society. Many social workers do not introduce these concepts into their interactions with service users. A respect for client self-determination, itself not always found in practice, is not sufficient.

Radical Approaches

Approaches that have been described as "radical" or "progressive" have been employed in social work practice for many decades, although the meaning of these terms in social work has evolved over time. There are several common threads in these approaches. There is recognition that the larger political and economic systems contribute to a substantial degree to the oppression of people and produce many of the problems people face. This is due to the power and resources possessed by what Mills (1956) termed "the power elite," who use their power and resources to the detriment of people who are poor, of color, or oppressed because of other attributes.

A second theme is the emphasis on the importance of activism to transform human relations and structures in fundamental ways rather than merely on a superficial level. Another is a belief that professional action should be grounded in an analysis of all social, political, and economic structures that impede the fulfillment of basic human needs. In addition, radical practitioners use theories and constructs that are derived from political–economic and power analyses, an understanding of the dynamics of oppression and exploitation, human needs theory, social movement theories, and theories of social transformation (Turbett, 2014).

With regard to practice with individuals and families, many radical theorists have been influenced by the writings of Karl Marx and his analyses of class conflicts within the contemporary structures of societies. Other theorists assert that Marxian thinking pays insufficient attention to cooperative relations, coalitions, gradual transformation, and the importance of the ideas people have about their situations—although class consciousness and its lack thereof have figured prominently in Marxist literature. An important corrective to this is the works of Paulo Freire (1970), who considered in detail the kinds of consciousness and people's ideas that play a role in their commitments to social change.

Family Change

Historical Evolution of Family Therapy Models

According to Kaslow (2010), the field of family therapy as a distinct mode of practice began to develop in the 1950s. Its emergence was inspired by the observations of a number of theorists and practitioners that individual approaches to practice often produced slow therapeutic progress, that individual change had an impact on the family, and that the lack of participation of other family members in the therapeutic process might undermine changes in the member in treatment. Some of the concepts for family therapy came from family-oriented social work (casework); in fact, the original name of the major casework journal was

The Family. Another source of ideas was the child guidance movement, which first appeared in the 1920s. Its practitioners typically interviewed the child who had a problem separately from other family members. The child was seen by a psychiatrist and the family by a social worker. Psychoanalytic practice also played a role, especially when such practice examined interpersonal interactions.[1]

A number of people contributed to the evolution of family therapy. They were not fully aware of each other's existence until they began to attend professional conferences at which each other's papers were presented. Among the first of these conferences was the 1938 meeting of the National Conference on Family Relations in New York City. Participants discussed such practice issues as the lives of children, marriage, divorce, and the role of social welfare institutions in family life. Two years later, this organization published the first of three prominent journals, *The Journal of Marriage and the Family*, and helped support international scholarship on families.

An especially notable occasion was the 1955 meeting of the American Orthopsychiatric Association. At this meeting, Ackerman organized a session on family diagnosis during which many of this early generation of therapists discovered their common interests. Among these "grandparents" of family therapy were the following individuals:

- Gregory Bateson, John Weakland, and Jay Haley, who were especially interested in the impact of family communication patterns on individual and family problems (Bateson, Jackson, Haley, & Weakland, 1956)
- Paul Watzliwick, Virginia Satir, and Don Jackson, who became particularly interested in the impact of contradictory communications, especially the "double bind" in which one individual sends contradictory messages simultaneously—one often verbal and the other through the expression of affect (Jackson & Weakland, 1959)
- Murray Bowen at Georgetown Medical School, who was interested in mother–child dynamics and the impact of family of origin dynamics on the child's psyche
- Lyman Wynn (1984), who worked with families with a member who suffered from schizophrenia and defined the family dynamics existing in such families
- Nathan Ackerman at the Family Institute in New York (later named the Ackerman Institute), who emphasized the intrapsychic and interpersonal, the conscious and the unconscious, and the use of defense mechanisms while working with families as units (Ackerman, Beatman, & Sherman, 1961)

---

1. For an excellent yet brief summary of the evolution of family therapy, see Kaslow (2010).

- Carl Whitaker at the University of Wisconsin, who developed a model that challenged family members in new and sometimes provocative ways (Napier & Whitaker, 1978)
- James Framo and Ross Speck at the Eastern Pennsylvania Psychiatric Institute, who developed a "network therapy" that, according to Kaslow (2010), "used sociocultural and racial diversity and the natural networks within families with schizophrenic or drug addict members" (p. 54)
- Salvador Minuchin at the Philadelphia Child Guidance Clinic, who explored in depth family structure, including subgroups within the family, and discovered the relationship of these subgroups to many family problems (Minuchin, Montalvo, Guerney, Rosman, & Schumer, 1967)
- Jay Haley, also at the Philadelphia Child Guidance Clinic, who viewed individual problems as maintained by family processes and sought to change these processes in ways that were often confrontational (Haley, 1984). Although there is empirical evidence for the efficacy of what has come to be called "strategic family therapy" (Coatsworth, Santisteban, McBride, & Szapocznik, 2001), some practitioners have been leery of the strong role assigned to the workers regarding the ways that they intervene in the family's processes.
- Vosler (1996) and Waldegrave (1998), who have sought to develop models of family practice that incorporate social justice into their models. They emphasize the impact of oppressive social conditions on the family and help the family to find ways of working against forces that oppress the family as a unit as well as family members. Another set of authors who broadened the concepts used by family practitioners to consider environmental factors related to culture and ethnicity are McGoldrick, Giordano, and Garcia-Preto (2005). The latest edition of their book incorporated much more than previous editions on the special issues faced by families of color.

Kaslow (2010.) and others have developed typologies of contemporary models of family practice. An in-depth analysis of these is beyond the scope of the chapter. However, we do add a focus on social justice as a necessary construct for exploring the utility of contemporary models of family practice in social work. Kaslow's typology of the contemporary models of family therapy is as follows (pp. 58-59):[2]

I. Transgenerational models
   a. Psychodynamically informed (including object relations and attachment approaches)

---

2. In our experience, we have found that many family therapists use some combination of approaches drawn from more than one model, depending on the particular family issues. However, many theorize about the family from one or a limited number of perspectives.

b. Bowenian
c. Contextual/relational
d. Symbolic/experiential
e. Emotionally focused

II. Systems models
a. Communications
b. Strategic
c. Structural
d. Systemic
e. Brief and solution focused

III. Cognitive and behavioral models
a. Behavioral
b. Functional
c. Cognitive–behavioral

IV. Postmodern models
a. Narrative
b. Social constructionist (including linguistic approaches)

V. Miscellaneous
a. Psychoeducational
b. Integrative (including comprehensive and multimodal models)

To this list, we add

VI. Social justice models[3]

There has been increasing attention to social justice models that incorporate attention to cultural diversity, social class, and sources of oppression such as sexism, homophobia, and racism. A book edited by McGoldrick and Hardy (2008), for example, has sections devoted to theoretical perspectives, cultural legacies (e.g., Black genealogy, Polish, Arab Muslim, racial identity, and White privilege), the clinical implications of working with many kinds of families (e.g., LGBTQ, interracial couples, and homeless families), and training implications including a chapter titled "Visioning Social Justice: Narratives of Diversity, Social Location, and Personal Compassion." Another widely used text with a similar perspective is *Family Therapy with Ethnic Minorities* (Ho, Rasheed, & Rasheed, 2004).

---

3. Many newer models that in some way relate to social justice have emerged, and we allude to these with the single term "social justice models."

Family Therapy and Social Justice

We have developed a series of principles that we believe should guide a socially just family practice. We draw upon a modified version of the work of Bernard (2006) as cited in Finn and Jacobson (2008):

1. The family exists in a social environment that can be oppressive to the family. As Imber-Black (2011) states, "Like many in the so-called second generation of family therapy theorists and practitioners, I came to the field experienced in the civil rights and antiwar movements, and the struggles for women's rights. I was attracted to a field focused on systemic thought and action, and where appreciating context enabled a rich and deep obligation to families and communities in their own request for integrity and fairness. . . . These authors [she refers to authors in the journal issue in which her essay appears] keep us true to our legacy in their recognition that families exist in a larger ecology for which we bear responsibilities. Going forward, if our efforts remain only within the boundary of the family, when that larger ecology is marked by injustice, our efforts will be a derisive collusion. If rather, we glean from this paper a new set of requirements, we will ally ourselves with Dr. King's imperative, the arc of history that bends toward justice." (pp. 129–131).

2. The family is helped to understand not only transactions within the family but also external conditions that promote or maintain problems for which the family has sought help.

3. The family is helped to take some action in relationship to these external conditions or to join with others to do so. This process might help to avoid placing all the blame on a so-called "identified patient" (i.e., a family member who is viewed solely or largely as the source of family difficulties). Whether to do this is the family's decision.

4. The family is the final arbiter of the outcomes sought from family therapy.

5. Workers must explain their roles and what they expect of the family. This is problematic in the strategic therapies in which the worker provides directives for family behaviors in order to change family patterns because socially just therapy should emphasize empowerment and the equalization of power between worker and service users. Strategic therapy is justified by its proponents, of course, because the family presumably attains family goals more quickly than in other nonstrategic approaches. This is a dilemma about which practitioners should think seriously. We do not have a solution to this problem but are clear that workers need to explain the nature of strategic approaches and obtain permission from the family to use them even if this limits their

impact. After the intervention, feedback should be obtained from the family about the directive nature of the intervention.

6. The worker helps the family to enhance its capacity to support the growth and development of all family members.

7. Workers affirm and strengthen families' cultural, racial, and linguistic identities and enhance their ability to function in a multicultural society. They are helped to confront forces that undermine this (e.g., school systems that punish students who speak Spanish).

8. The worker advocates with families for services and systems that are fair, responsive, and accountable to the families served.

9. The worker strives to help the family have appropriate power distributed among the family members. Especially important is to challenge sexism exhibited among family members. Although we recognize that parents require more power than children to carry out their responsibilities, the children should be accorded power, appropriate to their ages, in decision making and actions that affect them.

System Change and Individual and Family Practice

As discussed throughout this book, all socially just practice is seen as occurring within a social context, some aspect of which is likely to be oppressive with reference to users of our services. We also remind the reader that the worker, as well as service users, may occupy some positions within the larger system that are privileged. This may be the result of such qualities as one's color, gender, age, and educational level. The question then must be raised as to actions that the service user can take if that person seeks to change an oppressive aspect of her of his situation. The following are some possibilities:

- The person/family member may seek to change a family condition. There are many ways, frequently mentioned in the family therapy literature, that this can occur. These include helping to bring about new roles in the family, facilitating a change in the roles of other family members, engaging in group processes such as problem solving that can lead to a change in family conditions, or changing one's way of reinforcing or extinguishing the behavior of other family members.

- The service user or family member may seek to change a condition existing in a primary group of which she or he is a member. Some of the same approaches to changing family conditions apply here. In addition, the individual may seek to enlist forces outside the group to change the group, such as an appeal to the worker, the agency, family members, or other groups. In family therapy, the other family members should be helped to support a family member who seeks system change.

- Individuals or family members may utilize a group of which they are a member by convincing the group to undertake change in some entity outside of the group, such as an agency policy, community condition, or social policy. In doing this, the group may seek to work in concert with other groups. In the same manner, an individual may involve the agency in utilizing its resources to obtain the sought-after change.
- The individual or family member acting alone may seek to promote change by such means as writing a letter or circulating a petition, contacting an influential person such as a member of a legislature or an administrator, or writing a letter to the editor of a newspaper.

Table 5.2 indicates some of the limits of various family therapy models in pursuing social justice and some ideas as to what they can contribute to socially just family practice.

Table 5.2 Models of Family Therapy and Their Relationship to Socially Just Family Practice

Model of Family Therapy	Limitations from Socially Just Family Perspective	Contributions to Socially Just Family Practice
Transgenerational models: These include many that have their basis in the intrapsychic life of family members, although this is related to family interactions and history of these interactions.	The impact of oppression from external systems, which may be experienced by the family as a whole as well as by family members individually, is not emphasized. The worker plays a central role in the interactions.	The oppression that may be imposed on some family members by others in the family is recognized and discussed. Literature is available from writers regarding these models and their application in families from diverse cultures that have assigned culturally specific roles to family members.

(continued)

Table 5.2 Continued

Model of Family Therapy	Limitations from Socially Just Family Perspective	Contributions to Socially Just Family Practice
Systems models: These focus on communications among family members and family structures. Strategic family therapy is usually included here as an approach to promoting structural and process changes.	These models are likely to focus more on intrafamily structures rather than the impact of an oppressive environment on the family.	These models move us beyond a focus on individuals as such to persons who are molded in interaction with other family members and the family's structured interactions. There are many articles on applications to people of varied ethnic and cultural backgrounds that can help us move to newer theoretical approaches that take issues of diversity into account.
Cognitive and behavioral models	These focus on specific individual behaviors, including interactions among family members, but do not intrinsically address the influence of oppressive social conditions on these behaviors or the cultural and social forces that mold these behaviors.	From a social justice perspective, it is important to correctly identify behaviors of family members as well as behaviors of others who interact with the family but to identify oppressive behaviors of individuals and institutions and to help families consider acting to change these, often in concert with other individuals and families outside the family who are or can become allies.

Table 5.2 Continued

Model of Family Therapy	Limitations from Socially Just Family Perspective	Contributions to Socially Just Family Practice
Postmodern models: These recognize that individuals construct their own realities based on their unique perceptions.	These models emphasize information as it is perceived and constructed by the individual, such as in the form of personal narratives. This overlooks the impact on one's cognitive and affective experiences of external forces, particularly oppressive ones.	These models can contribute to a social justice approach if family members are helped to view how they may distort events (especially oppressive ones such as false consciousness). If consciousness-raising activities are included, this may help the process of change as the individual(s) is helped to "correct" his or her views in the light of new information about the impact of external systems on them.
Miscellaneous (e.g., psychoeducational and integrative)	These are disparate models, but all lack the limitation of not specifically drawing attention to the external environment, especially when it is oppressive. Integrative models will have the same limitations because the models that are part of the integration have similar limitations.	Psychoeducational models can provide methods to help members acquire skills. These methods can be used in the service of social justice when a component is developing skills in recognizing and changing oppressive circumstances emanating from either oppressive family interactions or oppressive conditions stemming from other systems.

The Process of Social Justice Work with Individuals and Families

As stated previously, we believe that practice has beginnings, middles, and endings but that the processes between the worker and the individuals or families served have similarities as well as differences as time progresses. Some of these processes may predominate in some time frames compared to others; thus, we considered various practice processes to be best portrayed in a circular rather than linear manner, as shown in Figure 5.1. In the following sections, we discuss beginnings, middles, and endings as these relate to work with individuals and families.

Beginnings

Two of the processes in the beginning of service are exploration and engagement. These occur as service users and practitioner consider how they will work together and what their purposes and desired outcomes are and also to plan specifically what they will do together, at least in the short term. We consider these two processes together because as these parties explore the service users' situations, they become more engaged, and as they become more engaged, they are likely to be comfortable with deepening their exploration. By engagement, we mean the emergence of positive feelings and perceptions of each other to enable them to make at least an initial commitment to work together.

Many processes occur during the phases of exploration and engagement. These are covered in detail in texts by Schulman (1999), Hepworth, Rooney, and Larson (2010), and Seabury, Seabury, and Garvin (2011), and we do not present

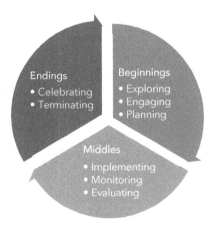

FIGURE 5.1   Beginnings, Middles, and Endings in Social Work Practice

them here. Our purpose is to add the specific social justice issues and processes to these established models.

We also note that all of the practice processes that take place do not occur only at specific phases of the work but, rather, reoccur throughout the process. For example, the practitioners and the individuals or families with whom they are working may become less engaged when conflicts arise between or among them. They may then have to work to restore their trust and confidence in one another. Similarly, as new issues are presented or their feeling of safety increases, these parties may engage in more exploration related to such issues. A number of social justice issues arise as these processes evolve during the initial process of engagement.

Power of the Agency and Social Justice Issues

With respect to the individuals and families whom it serves, the agency has a great deal of power that influences the process of engagement. The following questions reflect this power:

1. Does the agency hire, supervise, and dictate policy with respect to the practitioner(s)? The agency is likely to have policies with respect to a family that has members who have broken laws, been imprisoned, belong to a sexual minority, are undocumented, or do not live lives as prescribed by sectarian agencies. This may influence the perceptions of service users and workers. The practitioner should consider feelings and thoughts of both service users and other staff members of influence.
2. Does the agency provide resources (e.g., adequate space), thus demonstrating its commitment to supporting work with families, when many family members choose to attend a session?
3. What are agency policies with respect to how long a family may receive services and how is this affected by the family's access to insurance?
4. Can the agency provide competent couples or multifamily counseling if these are needed?
5. Does the agency provide or have access to the other services this family needs or may need? How does the décor of the agency affect the engagement process? For example, do the service users see pictures and other decorations that show that the agency is familiar with and welcoming of people like themselves?
6. When the service users enter the agency, are they greeted in a way that they view as showing respect for them? Examples of the opposite are receptionists who look suspiciously at them, make them wait while they talk on the phone or chat with other staff, ask their names in ways that demonstrate a lack of privacy, and instruct them to sit in the waiting room until called in a manner that treats them as supplicants rather than respected people who are seeking a service.

Power of the Worker and Social Justice Issues

Many actions of the worker quickly convey to service users the worker's respect for the latter's rights, identities, and status within the agency. These include how the service users like to be addressed. (They can be asked what they would like to be called and/or the worker can introduce herself or himself and invite the service users to do the same.) A choice of seating may be possible, and the worker can consider the meaning conveyed if she or he positions herself or himself behind a desk. If the worker asks how the service users wish to begin the session (including asking what they might like to know about the worker), this is a further means of responding to or even reducing the amount of power accruing to the worker.[4]

The worker should also be cognizant of how the culture of the service users influences their expectations of the beginning of relationships. In some cultures, first interactions should be used for the parties getting to know each other; in other cultures, getting quickly to the purposes of the encounter is expected. In some cultures, it is expected that the father of the family, if the entire family is present, is addressed first. In other cultures, this is not expected.

We have found that trust is promoted if the worker asks how the service user feels about seeing someone with the same race or gender (and sometimes apparent age group) of the practitioner. The age group may particularly matter when the practitioner looks much older or much younger than the service user. A more sensitive matter, but one that should not be ignored, is the sexual orientation of the practitioner, especially when straight practitioners are serving gay or lesbian service users. We do not mean that "coming out" of either practitioner or service user is automatic but that this issue needs to be handled with sensitivity and honesty. Another issue is when either the practitioner or service users have an evident disability. One of the writers of this chapter is deaf in one ear and seeks to place himself with his "good" ear toward the service users. Disclosure of this fact, however, precludes the service users immediately assuming he is not listening when he asks for them to repeat a comment. All of these issues, when handled with openness, respect, and sensitivity, help to reduce distance and power differentials between practitioners and service users.

Several issues related to social justice are likely to arise in the initial process of exploration. First, the service user is highly likely to see how the practitioners use their power. When the practitioners ask a series of questions in order to explore the user's situation and need for service, this may be viewed by the user as a use of "expert power." Practitioners should explain that both they and the service users

---

4. Although not a social work example, an instance of this occurred when one of the author's wives was seen by a doctor who never faced her but wrote what she said on a computer with his back to her.

should decide together what information is required in order to decide together how to proceed. Thus, service users should be asked what kind of exploration they think will be helpful in this endeavor.

If the practitioners think they need information beyond the initial agreement, they should explain the reasons for this to the users and obtain their permission to proceed.[5] A problem here is that agency policies may require the practitioner to obtain still additional information. This should be explained to the users who may decline to supply this information. We know of situations in which practitioners have protested to agency administrators policies of this sort that, in themselves, demonstrate the power of the agency; power used in this way may be severely disempowering to service users. Examples often found on agency forms are history of marriages and divorces, birth of children and marital status at the time, citizenship status, religion, national origin, sexual orientation, age of first sexual experience, and health history.

Within a social justice perspective, it is obviously important to explore social justice issues related to the reasons the users have come for service. In addition to the practitioner's own lack of knowledge of such issues, these issues may not be explored because of agency conditions, practitioner attitudes, or pressures from others in the practitioner's or users' network. The following are examples:

Agency conditions: The worker is employed by an agency that provides employee assistance services. The insurer, as a condition of reimbursement of the agency, insists that no contact be initiated with employers. A service user comes to this service and explains to the practitioner that because he is an African American, he was given less lucrative assignments. It became apparent to the practitioner that the user's issue is a consequence of racist practices at his place of employment, but the employment assistance agency forbids her to make contact with the employing agency. In this case, in addition to exploring this issue with him, she informed the user about community agencies that will advocate for him. In this instance, such an agency was an employment agency serving the local African American community.

Practitioner attitudes: In the previous example, it is possible that the worker might have held the view that it was the user's "fault" that the workplace situation arose and that it was a consequence of his level of expertise. If this occurred, she would seek to help him improve his level of expertise and focus all of her exploration on this.

---

5. This, of course, assumes a major new source of inquiry will be initiated. We recognize it would be unnecessarily cumbersome for the practitioner to ask permission to pose every question when the necessity of doing this is obvious to all concerned.

Pressure from others: In the preceding example, the user's wife did not want to "make any waves" and she discouraged him from taking any action that involved criticism of the agency. The practitioner explored with the user how he wished to deal with his wife's views and how he wanted to proceed in the face of them.

A major issue in the exploration of social justice issues is how a problem or concern is defined because this will guide what problem or concern is explored. Some agencies limit this exploration process by their policies and procedures. A school may direct the practitioner to focus on academic achievement or classroom disruption, prison authorities may dictate that the focus of practice with inmates be on previous wrongdoing, and a psychiatric facility may direct the focus to be on behaviors defined as deviant. In the school example, the user may want to focus on being bullied; in the prison illustration, the user may want to focus on getting a job after his release; and in the psychiatric facility, the user may want to focus on enrolling in school. In each of these instances, the users may experience themselves as oppressed by the imposition of topics by the agency instead of being able to define the purpose of practice themselves.

This is especially an issue with so-called *involuntary clients.* These are clients who are required to participate in "therapy" or to receive other social work services, frequently by courts but also by correctional or police authorities, officials in psychiatric institutions, or other adults who have control such as parents. Individuals may also be required to seek services by schools or their sources of employment in order to receive an education or retain a job.

A full discussion of this topic, including the ethical and justice issues involved, is provided by Rooney (2009). His material includes such matters as whether the service users have engaged in illegal behaviors (or are likely to do so) or whether they are likely to injure or kill themselves or others. He states that there are four guidelines with respect to determining whether it is legal and/or ethical to require behavioral change:

1. If the behavior is not illegal, the practitioner cannot require the client to change and should be guided by informed consent and self-determination.
2. The practitioner can act ethically to attempt persuasion. Rooney qualified this by stating that "persuasion means helping clients consider the possible consequences of their choices and exploring alternatives in terms of their own best interest. Persuasion is not the same as coercion when the influence attempt is open, does not resort to threats, and ultimately respects the client's power to decide."
3. The practitioner can offer an incentive to influence a client choice. Rooney qualifies this by stating that "this approach should not be used to barter for

basic necessities but rather as an *additional* benefit that the client can chose to accept or ignore."

4. The practitioner can advocate that the legal threshold for harm should be expanded. By this he means that the client's safety will be endangered but has not yet reached the legal threshold with respect to the definition of harm. (pp. 41–42)

With respect to social justice, Rooney asserts,

> Should practitioners ignore issues of prejudice and unfair conditions in the larger society, they run the risk of providing social control with a smiling face: using otherwise ethical means to pursue unethical goals. This is a very important issue as it is the way that practitioners are likely to transgress with involuntary clients with respect to their rights and the related social justice issues. (p. 349)

Examples of these issues include the following:

- A practitioner who sought to encourage a prison inmate's planning for eventual employment but disregarded the discrimination she would face because of her gender.
- A practitioner pressured a student to turn in assignments although she was fully aware that the teacher held a stereotypical view of the student because of her ethnicity and was unfair to her in grading.
- A practitioner in a psychiatric facility urged a gay client to attend a group therapy session even though the practitioner was aware that the group contained several members who were homophobic.

The Middle Phase of Intervention: Implementing, Monitoring, and Evaluating

The middle phase of social work practice has been the focus of much of our writing and conceptualization. Practitioners and students are eager to identify new ways of "doing practice," often without regard for the assumptions underlying the "doing." Previously, we discussed how social work theory has been formed within social, historical, and political contexts. Those contexts and their resultant theories have guided social work interventions. The extent to which socially just ways of implementing, monitoring, and evaluating practice are enacted within our interventions hinges on the recognition of these forces and their intersections.

Readers may recognize that the middle phase of socially just practice, as we have outlined it here, includes not only choosing a course of action and implementing it but also monitoring progress as changes within the individual, family, and environment occur. The process of monitoring often receives limited attention because of the myriad legal and ethical issues that accompany it. However, we argue that learning ways to negotiate the tension between external requirements and internal integrity of the process is important. The evaluation portion of this middle phase is also placed here with an understanding that there is a strong potential for using the information gained in monitoring the intervention to revisit and alter aspects of it. Constant re-evaluation is commonplace among numerous disciplines seeking to predict economic, social, political, and environmental behavior. As new variables affecting outcomes become apparent within political circles, for example, changes in strategies are made to accommodate them. The same method has utility for social justice practice, and the lack of attention to the forces influencing change within individuals and families can lead to erroneous perceptions about why a set of intervention strategies either worked or did not work.

When the focus is on developing socially just intervention strategies, the worker's and service user's preferences must be addressed, with conscious attention to the underlying theoretical assumptions of the strategies chosen. Workers seeking to engage in social justice practice with families will think about family members' ability to engage in strategic tasks as well as the environmental and political factors that may impede their performance of these tasks.

Furthermore, we suggest that families move through phases of growth as a family in a systematic way, and the practitioner should help the family obtain sufficient economic and environmental resources to secure the assistance it might need. The current phenomenon of adult offspring moving back into their parents' homes because of the lack of economic and employment opportunities cannot be addressed by the development or life span perspectives in work with families. These models are also problematic for understanding the increasing numbers of grandparents who care for their grandchildren due to the inability of their children to do so. Because these are not deviant families, our recognition of the forces that influence life decisions at the individual and family levels are critical to engaging in effective social justice practice.

Moving to a later and more inclusive model such as empowerment theory without attention to the issues raised previously in this chapter has the potential to be equally problematic for attempting system change. The worker may adhere to an empowerment perspective, but without the service user's articulation of the external issues influencing his or her internal problems, this approach does not truly empower the service user. The worker should draw upon the *service user's worldview* (i.e., the individuals in the family or the individual receiving service) rather than only his or her own.

Socially just practice requires more transparency on the part of the worker than is usually the case, thus reducing the "mystique" of social work practice as something only professional practitioners can achieve. It is typical of analytically oriented practitioners to ask the service users why they ask such questions as the worker's age, marital status, and so on. A socially just practice will not be as circumspect, although practitioners will still remain judicious about what they share. It is not unusual for a gay service user to ask about the practitioner's sexual orientation, a woman to ask a male worker about his professional experience with women, or an African American to inquire about the practitioner's experience with African Americans.

This does not mean that implementation of a strategy is limited to those who can engage in verbal interaction. Even individuals with developmental disabilities have methods of negotiating their environments. Our task as workers is to learn to access those negotiation strategies and incorporate them into interventions.

One illustration of this is the rapid expansion of strength-based programs for autistic children that simultaneously recognize the unique ways in which the children negotiate their environments, the ways some parents have learned to communicate with their children, the educational policies in states such as Iowa to support the ability of children to remain in their homes without placing sole burden for their special needs on their parents, and the passage and refinement of federal policies such as the Americans with Disabilities Act.

For more than 40 years, programs such as Systems Unlimited in Iowa City, Iowa, have continued to generate practice-based theory and have altered the opportunities available to developmentally disabled children and adults to live productive lives. This has much in common with the social justice perspectives discussed in this chapter. In fact, the social justice practice perspectives of one of the authors were shaped by her work as Director of Social Services for this organization in the late 1970s. The program has been influential in modeling comprehensive services for other agencies and states throughout the country. It has effectively linked with local, county, and statewide educational institutions to engage in systematic monitoring. It has helped design programs for social work students interested in developmental disabilities.

Lobbying efforts started by Systems Unlimited have resulted in state law changes so that unrelated individuals can share a single family dwelling, thus allowing adults needing minimal supervision to live and work within their communities. The founders of Systems Unlimited, including its first executive director, Barry Leonard, designed the program with an emphasis on what would be socially just practice enabling children with developmental disabilities to reach their highest potential. As new research has yielded information, the program has expanded to utilize this new knowledge to develop its services. These services, in turn, are monitored by service users, workers, and families. Those monitoring efforts become the basis of evaluation methods, in many cases done quarterly, so that there is detailed information about the impact of the intervention on the family, community, city, and state, as well as the individual.

Monitoring is done by all parties who will be affected by the change—even those individuals who may be nonverbal, because an inability to speak does not necessarily imply an inability to provide feedback. The worker(s) in this agency, in turn, collects, integrates, and feeds back knowledge to those who have been engaged in the intervention and perform the formal evaluation tasks. The evaluations are then used to help regional and statewide partners understand the environmental changes required for fully serving all of the residents of the state. Clients are also empowered to choose services that meet their needs as they define them.

The middle phase of socially just practice requires the constant monitoring gained by power analyses. This may initially be met with resistance by agencies and workers who have competing demands (Rooney, 2009). In order to incorporate a social justice practice framework effectively, staff must be able to engage in the same middle phase issues of implementation, monitoring, and evaluation that are being done in conjunction with service users.

If the beginning phases of socially just interventions focus on clearing the soil that will impede the successful planting of crops, then the middle phase can be likened to tending those crops. They must be weeded to remove those plants that may interfere with the growth of the desired crops, serendipitous beneficial plants that are linked to the main crops need to be supported, and the growers need to be kept healthy so that they can engage in the growing enterprise.

The Ending Phase of Intervention

For those utilizing a social justice framework in social work practice, endings are not considered terminations. Instead, they are steps in a process that continues beyond the service user/worker relationship. Within our social justice framework, we remember that the origins of practice in the United Kingdom and the United States were designed initially to reduce the need for interventions by formal social welfare institutions. Newer, more culturally congruent practices form the foundation for social justice and social change within individuals and families. Those, in turn, alter relationships in communities, the wider society, and the world.

As discussed previously, enacting socially just practice at the individual or family level is an iterative process. As individuals become more aware of the micro, mezzo, and macro intersections of their lives, they can help to create interventions to address one or more of these elements. For example, a woman with meager resources who is in need of child care lest her children lose their Medicaid funding might address the issue across levels. At the individual level, the stress of working at a low-wage job can lead to physical and psychological discomfort, and part of socially just practice is geared toward addressing the stressors. At the same time, balancing the woman's needs with those of her family must be considered.

The use of narratives may help the mother to pinpoint the areas to be addressed that are peculiar to her situation. As these narratives are developed, the mother is encouraged to address directly the link normally absent from most social work interventions but desired by some service users, namely spirituality and/or religiosity. The inner strength derived from having a spiritual practice or network is a potential source of power for those who learn to use insights and ideas gained from it to address their everyday lives (Walsh, 2009). Ignoring this level has led to incomplete interventions by omitting the benefits and challenges people face during their relationships with corporate or individual worship practices. Incorporating this level of intervention into social justice practice, as was popular during the civil rights movement in the 1950s, 1960s, and 1970s, allows people to utilize existing social networks in their natural environment rather than create new ones dependent on an external worker as the change agent.

The mother described previously could link with other mothers in similar circumstances via multiple family groups in which an emphasis has been placed on maximizing group cohesion through a priori attention to group composition by group facilitators. These mezzo level groups can reshape an old practice common within families of color—child lending. In this situation, women identify their familial needs and how these must be balanced with external expectations examined as they created their narratives. The women, in turn, plan and engage in sharing the care of their children so that all can meet the requirements of their employment. Child care schedules are developed, and the children are raised in a community as family. Within low-income communities in the United States, older relatives have been utilized to provide child care, allowing them greater access to the younger generation as well as some income for doing so. The community child lending practices are used in other ways throughout the world. In Germany, some women and men share jobs and live in multiple family dwellings, allowing the children to be supervised by several adults. In the United States and The Netherlands, people who live in co-housing have done the same. Research on child lending practices in Ghana has determined that those children who have had multiple family members engaged in their primary education years are less likely to have trouble with authorities and more likely to have adult involvement in their education (Imoh, 2012).

As individuals and families recognize and begin to share the similarities of their circumstances, macro interventions may be developed to systemically change their common concerns. These may take the form of building new skill sets such as learning to lobby their local, regional, state, and national governments.

One powerful example of this joint social justice action aimed at the macro level occurred within an organization founded by a small group of women who had married non-German men during the 1970s only to find that neither they nor their children had rights to German citizenship. As one of the founders, Rosi Wolf-Almanesreh, began to tell her story, other women throughout the country added theirs until there was a national movement of women successfully lobbying for a change in the country's laws. This social change did not occur without conflict, and many members' lives were threatened. Recognizing the common links with the women's struggle, other nongovernmental organizations (NGOs) that were engaged in social justice work joined with and provided protection for members of this organization as they traveled throughout the country for meetings and social action. Having met their initial goal for legal parity for all women who marry, the group now focuses its efforts on the racial segregation and abuse of ethnic groups within Germany.

In all of the previously mentioned examples, professionals were involved to some extent. Sustaining the changes, however, was a result of the evolution of persons' careful analyses of their situations, attaining skills to address their needs, engaging others in the process of change, and enacting empowered interactions with their environments.

Findings from a social justice framework shift the focus of general social work practice from "I–I" to "we–we," as is illustrated in Figure 5.2. In Figure 5.2A, two individuals with different backgrounds and norms find a mutual interest at some level and build on it. This is common in social work practice in which the change is focused at only one level of interaction. At best, these arrows are drawn in a parallel manner, signifying egalitarianism in the relationship between the bodies represented. At its lowest, social work could also be enacted with the two arrows drawn hierarchically, recognizing the subordination of one group and dominance of the other. The dominant group would have the agency to direct the change toward the targeted subordinate group.

In Figure 5.2B, varied interests are inherent in sets of people with some similarities and a variety of differences. In the "we–we" paradigm, individuals recognize their mutual interests and then build linkages among them. The example of an organization's connection with labor and health NGOs given previously demonstrates how possible exponential growth to effect change on multiple levels can result from working with individuals and families from a social justice perspective.

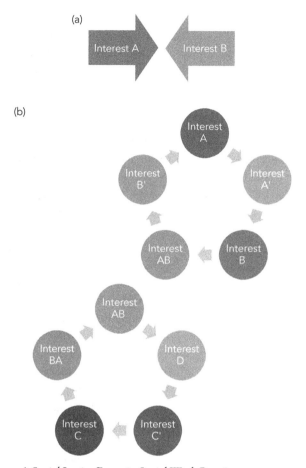

FIGURE 5.2   A Social Justice Focus in Social Work Practice

As services to individuals and families come to an end, the following processes take place that have social justice implications:

• Practitioners and service users cope with their feelings about ending.
• Practitioners and service users evaluate/assess what changes in themselves and their environments have taken place during the course of service.
• Service users plan for activities and services they will draw upon to continue to pursue changes in themselves and their environments.
• Service users plan ways of maintaining changes that have been made in themselves and their environments.
• Service users consider ways to utilize changes in an expanding set of circumstances.
• Service users and practitioners celebrate achievements.

Coping with Feelings

The work that practitioners and service users have done together is likely to have engendered warm feelings of each party to the other, and there may be sadness at parting. These feelings have a variety of practice implications. It may be appropriate for service users to occasionally contact the practitioner either verbally or through e-mail messages or other forms of written communication. The practitioner should always consider what is best for the service users in making any such arrangement, which may also include the practitioner occasionally contacting service users to find out how they are doing.[6] These types of contacts may reinforce the existence of the genuine concern of practitioners for those they serve. Sometimes there are negative or ambivalent feelings that trouble both parties and that may continue to trouble them; these contacts may lead to the resolution of these issues.

In addition, the ending of service may have implications for other parts of the service users' social network that affect their feelings and have social justice implications. For example, service users may be anxious about using other members of their social network for support for fear that this will negatively affect their relationships. Thus, with proper consultation and agreement with the service user, the practitioner might involve significant others in the termination process, and this may help the service user to continue to move forward.

In the situation of involuntary service users, the entities that have mandated the service may be critical or even angry if the outcome of the service reflected the legitimate desire of the service user but not of the agency. An example of this potential development can be found in work with a person on parole who resolved a family dispute with the help of the practitioner. Although this was a legitimate concern, the court wanted the service to focus on the client's accepting full responsibility for the crime. The judge explicitly stated this and was likely to criticize the practitioner and service user if this did not occur. This underscores the importance of taking into account not only the service user's and practitioner's feelings but also the expectations of others in the social network, including third parties, groups, and institutions. The practitioner, however, must continue to prioritize the outcomes desired by service users.

Evaluation and Assessment

Most approaches to evaluation and assessment as the service concludes stress changes in the user of service. Because social justice practice stresses the importance of changes in the political and social environment, socially just evaluations

---

6. This has been a recognized procedure in practice in the nature of follow up to determine if changes have been maintained over time.

also examine changes in those systems. The following are examples of how this might be done:

- A student who had been having problems in the classroom discovered that some of these problems were due to stereotypes the teacher had of her. She and her mother had conversations with the teacher about this issue, and the teacher recognized she had been evaluating the student based on these stereotypes. Part of the evaluation process, therefore, consisted of assessing whether the teacher had become more supportive of the student.
- The same student also became aware of the fact that school administrators and counselors had been "tracking" students based on their ethnicity. Her parents raised this issue at a parents' meeting, and all the parents agreed to raise this issue at the next meeting of the Board of Education Part of the evaluation, therefore, consisted of finding out whether this issue had been raised at the board meeting and what the board had done about it.
- In the same situation, one of the parents decided to run for election to the board of education. Again, the evaluation included finding out whether this had happened and whether the student and her family had done anything with respect to this election. During this ending phase, the practitioner and the student discussed what the student and her family thought about these actions with respect to the teacher, administrators, and the board of education and what they had learned from this experience.

Activities to Continue to Pursue Changes

Although the interactions between the practitioner and the service user are discontinuing, the family and/or individuals should discuss what they will do in the future to maintain changes or to seek new changes. We do not discuss all these activities here because they are well covered elsewhere (Seabury et al., 2011). From a social justice perspective, these activities will often include activities that either work against injustices experienced by service users or ways in which various systems can become more just. The following are examples of these activities:

- An individual who was using the service to help him "come out" as gay planned ways he will continue to have discussions with his mother and father to obtain their understanding and support.
- The same individual had located a "coming out" group as part of his work with the social worker. He discussed how he will use this group to find ways of combating the homophobia he experiences at his college.
- The individual will ask his friends to help him form a GLBT group at his college because there already are such support and advocacy groups for African

Americans, Latinos/as, Jews, and people with disabilities. The college environment, he believes, will be enriched by the presence of all these groups as they serve as models for students who seek an environment that is supportive of their identities.

This approach to change as an ongoing process reflects the assumption that change may occur in cycles in which there are periods of active change, followed by periods of rest and consolidation/integration, followed by more active change efforts.

Ways of Maintaining Changes

Seabury et al. (2011) note that changes in the service users and their environments cannot be assumed to be lasting unless actions are taken to make this more likely to occur. These authors indicate a set of circumstances that help to maintain change. Several factors, related to social justice, are relevant here. First, various individuals and institutions in the environment may have an investment in undermining these changes. Family members may seek to reverse changes in the family member in question in order to advance their own interests. For example, a sibling of a service user wished to monopolize family resources to achieve his own goals, although the parents viewed this as an unjust allocation of family resources. The practitioner urged the parents to hold family meetings to instill a sense of justice in the allocation of such resources.

Another example involves some actions of the board of education referred to previously. The board voted to hire an educational consulting firm to work with the school to identify and change practices that were detrimental to such groups as GLBT students and students of color. The board, however, set limits on this effort by setting an unreasonably short time limit in which the process would occur and by providing an inadequate budget for the work. The practitioner suggested that the parents with whom she was working suggest to the parents' organization that it continue to monitor the board's use of resources and advocate for more adequate appropriations.

Consideration of Utilizing Change in an Expanding Set of Circumstances

The service user has typically considered making changes and seeking changes in others under a limited (sometimes only one) set of circumstances. A user who sought ways of being assertive with his employers may generalize these skills by using them with other powerful figures in the community such as school administrators or political figures. From a social justice standpoint, it may be warranted to use these skills across cultural, political, economic, and social boundaries that were previously kept at a distance.

Celebrate Achievements

It is a maxim of social justice practice that the activity to achieve a more just set of circumstances should have joyous elements, and their attainment should be a particularly joyous occasion. There are various ways that individuals or families can engage in celebration. The individual may create a ceremonial event with the practitioner (e.g., congratulate one another, reflect on what one has learned, or share refreshments). The family may similarly plan a party, engage in a round of congratulations, or sing a song that is a family favorite. This has not appeared in family or individual change literature but is often described in group work literature, which may have suggestions that can be used with individuals or families.

Summary

This chapter explored the issues involved in socially just practice with individuals and families. It traced the historical development of individual and family practice and family therapy in the United States, identified past and contemporary models of these methods of practice in social work, and critiqued these models from a social justice perspective. The chapter also provided specific examples of socially just practice with individuals and families, with a focus on their application to the beginning, middle, and ending phases of the intervention process. It is our belief that social work practitioners who pay attention to these layers of intervention will increase the probability of successful outcomes not only for the people with whom they work but also for the profession of social work as a whole.

Discussion Questions

1. What approach or model of individual or family practice are you most likely to use in your practice? From a social justice standpoint, what are the strengths or limitations of this model?
2. This chapter presented several approaches to socially just practice with individuals and families. Which approaches do you favor? What are your reasons for preferring them?
3. What types of social justice issues may arise in social work with families? How might a practitioner respond to these issues?

6

Socially Just Group Work Practice

Charles D. Garvin and Robert M. Ortega

Introduction

In this chapter, we discuss social work practice in groups from a social justice perspective. As indicated in Chapter 1, we view the following as core principles of social justice: a more equal distribution of power among the groups in society; the elimination of the oppression of some individuals and groups by other individuals and groups, as reflected in both their goals and processes; an equitable distribution of resources; and the resolution of unjust power differentials. In groups, we seek to pursue social justice goals by asking the following guiding questions: "Do the group's purpose and goals accommodate issues of diversity and social justice that are relevant to its members both inside and outside the group?" "Does the group experience take into account the individual member differences, including their various positionalities and standpoints?" "Do the group's dynamics that emerge within the group shape or influence group participation in socially just ways?" "Does the group's leadership respect each member's unique background, perspective, and contributions?" "Do the group's processes contain built-in responses that identify and address its power dynamics and potentially counterproductive actions, appropriately manage conflict, and prevent undesirable outcomes?" Finally, "In what ways do core group work practices support socially just group work practice?"

In general, a group organizes itself to accomplish its purpose and goals. Group purpose represents the reason the group was formed. Group goals are the desired outcomes of the group's activities and are related to group purpose. In this chapter, we argue that social work with groups is concerned with furthering social justice; reducing injustice; and guarding against unintentionally contributing to mechanisms that support privilege, marginalization, and oppression. For example, the process of determining group goals requires participants to be critically conscious about the various "inputs" and "outputs" that sustain injustice and unearned privilege. Hence, from the establishment of the group's purpose and goals, social justice knowledge and principles should be made explicit.

The group's purpose is likely to be influenced by the knowledge and perspectives that group members obtain from the larger environment. Group members will bring to group tasks assumptions about social justice that are influenced by societal values and approaches to justice. These may include definitions of human well-being, values about the human condition, rights and responsibilities, and assumptions about conflict and community (Reed, Ortega, & Garvin, 2010). Similarly, societal beliefs and values, key symbols, rituals, and ideals influence what members value and define as acceptable and also how they understand and draw meaning from their lives and interactions.

An individual's unique background and perspective are composed of all the beliefs, attitudes, values, skills, and knowledge that are brought into group member relationships and interactions from the larger environment (Cohen, 2009; Crenshaw, 1995). Intersectional social identities (i.e., the way the various identities of individuals are activated based on cultural differences and the social consequences of these differences) emerge and guide social interactions. In the group, individual thoughts, feelings, and corresponding actions shape its patterns of communication and interaction, the sense of belonging or cohesion that members feel, the group's mechanisms of social control, and the group's overall culture and climate. A social justice perspective draws attention to dynamics operating within the group that, if left unchecked, re-create the multiple, often unrecognized microinequities that maintain status differences and that marginalize certain thoughts, feelings, and behaviors. Group processes are also influenced by societal socialization practices and assumptions about everyday interactions, including the multiple ways in which people monitor themselves and each other to maintain order and ensure that behaviors and thoughts fall within acceptable limits.

To emphasize the themes underlying our guiding questions, we suggest that the success of social work practice in groups from a social justice perspective be guided by the following important practice principles:

- The group's goals and purposes must be consistent with the social justice goals related to the context in which these goals are developed, (i.e., with the external environment in which the group and its members act).
- The unique intersectional social identities, needs, and experiences of each of its members both within and outside the group must be recognized, appreciated, and valued.

- The group's dynamics must support socially just participation.
- The group's leadership must facilitate reflection (including self-reflection), shared responsibility, and each member's contributions.
- Group processes must be mindful of how issues are conceptualized and understood, how language is being used, and the ways people interact and support each other. Also, power, authority, and conflict resolution must promote member participation.
- Practice dimensions, as a whole, must consistently demonstrate and adhere to socially just knowledge and skills.

We use these practice principles in this chapter. We consider the explicit purposes for which the group was formed, its goals and desired outcomes, and the overt agenda a group is assigned or elects to accomplish. In our focus on the issue of relevance, we consider what all members bring to the group as products of their social experiences. In our incorporation of the group's dynamics, we remain vigilant to the implicit and explicit influences operating within the group to which members respond. Group leadership is not restricted to practitioners. Our interest is in the way leadership operates as inclusive or exclusive of other members and also in the criteria used to weigh leadership qualities and characteristics.

A social justice lens requires us to consider group changes from moment to moment and over longer periods. The criteria to assess the accomplishments of the group should include a social justice evaluation lens, including whether or not there are equitable benefits for all the members (Barusch, 2006).

The Group's Purpose

We use a typology here originally developed by Garvin (1997) but modified to incorporate the social justice emphasis of this book. This is an "ideal type" typology in that it is based on dimensions that in actual groups are combined in various ways rather than representing a "pure" type. The intent of this typology is to help practitioners and members become conscious of the way they view the group's purposes. This typology originally conceptualized purposes as either socialization or resocialization. Socialization involves choosing goals that incorporate new skills for the members. Resocialization incorporates goals that represent relinquishing previous skills and behaviors and developing a contrasting set of skills and behaviors. Socialization skills, for example, would be reflected in a group member wishing to develop new skills in seeking out relationships, assuming a new role (e.g., the secretary of an organization), or preparing to enter college. Resocialization, for example, would be relinquishing dysfunctional ways of resolving conflict in the family or workplace and substituting them with ways more likely to achieve desired goals.

Social justice should be a strong component of these purposes. The new skills should be those that incorporate resistance to injustice or promote a more justice-oriented family, group, community, and society. Resocialization should involve relinquishing actions that oppress others or fail to resist the acts of an unjust society. An example of this is the relatively recent murder of an African American young man by a White police officer who claimed to be protecting himself although videos taken by bystanders raised serious doubts about his claim. Groups of people in the community initially protested in ways that had destructive elements. These groups began to change their tactics and engaged in social actions more likely to lead to changes in police behavior and to secure the support of other community members.

We have found it useful to subdivide the categories of socialization and resocialization. Socialization consists of "identity development" and "skill attainment." Identity development consists of purposes to help members work on the identities they seek, such as becoming a compassionate male, an assertive woman, or a self-accepting gay, lesbian, bisexual, transgender, intersex (GLBTI) person. The social justice components of these categories are to achieve identities that help members stand up for their rights and to combat unjust challenges to their aspirations. Skill attainment involves learning to behave in ways that accomplish one's purposes, such as attaining academic skills or skills in engaging in effective social action.

We view resocialization as "responding to social control" or "seeking rehabilitation." The former recognizes that in many settings, such as the criminal justice system or educational and psychiatric institutions, the organizational structure imposes its purpose onto the group (e.g., behavioral demands in involuntary settings). Our social justice framework requires that the worker be "up front" about these demands and help the members resist those they regard as unjust. This entails a great deal of work for the members and the workers as they decide how to react and how to interact with the agency that imposes such unjust demands.

We regard rehabilitation as a purpose of a group to help members relinquish former behaviors (e.g., criminal behaviors, socially intrusive responses, and acceding to illicit drugs) and replace them with behaviors that are acceptable in their social situations (e.g., law-abiding behaviors, listening carefully to others and responding in ways appropriate to the situation, and diminished use of illicit substances). From a social justice perspective, this requires members to develop ways of resisting forces that maintain dysfunctional behaviors, especially when these are socially unjust. An example of this is a group of former offenders who worked to educate various institutions of the validity of hiring former offenders who were previously discriminated against in employment practices.

Member Relevance

From a social justice perspective, members enter the group in possession of their own standpoints, positionalities, and epistemic privilege. This brings to the fore the notion that we are more than a social identity; we are multiple social identities that may differentiate us in terms of our positionalities, privilege, or oppressed status depending on the social context in which a particular identity has significance (Maher & Tetreault, 1993; Takacs, 1993). From a social justice perspective, positionality refers to one's social positions in relation to others with whom one is in contact and also the extent to which these positions influence aspects of the relations or perceptions about the others. Those who occupy different positionalities develop different knowledge and worldviews (standpoints) informed by their social locations. Recognizing and harnessing these different views and sources of knowledge are critical for incorporating social justice values and approaches into small groups because those with different standpoints will recognize different forces as the sources of existing inequities. We elaborate more on this point later in the chapter.

Narayan (1999) reminds us that differences are reflected not only in physical appearance or cognitions but also in an individual's affect or emotional resonance. Narayan's use of the phrase *epistemic privilege* focuses on the more immediate, subtle, and critical knowledge of one's oppression and the affective experience of this oppression outside the awareness of non-oppressed members. Matters of social status, power, privilege, and authority (undergirding standpoints and positionalities) are highly individualized, corresponding to one's epistemic privilege. From a social justice perspective, the practice challenge this involves is in knowing how to validate rather than ignore each member's experiences of oppression (and associated thoughts and feelings) while at the same time taking them into account as relevant to the group's work.

Case Example: Amira

Amira came into the group with serious trepidation. She believed her experiences were unparalleled compared to those of the other members of the social integration group, whose purpose was to help new community members adjust to the environment in which they recently immigrated. Amira felt like an outsider; she was both embarrassed and ashamed to admit that she needed help. This was especially the case when she thought about the long-awaited journey (and the journey itself) that allowed her to sit in this group. She had to do everything on her own, although her actions were consistent with expectations in her culture that promoted resilience in the face of constant danger. Her journey, however, was wrought with barriers and obstacles (physical, language, financial, "red tape," etc.) every step of the way. She looked at the other members and there was silence;

she wondered if it was due to language, distrust, or social anxiety—all of which she believed were operating within her to explain her own silence. Her perspiration, hypervigilance, and self-consciousness all weighed heavily on the powerlessness she felt as the group prepared to begin.

Group members bring their attitudes, experiences, ways of thinking, and behaviors into their group interactions, which are sustained by the individual and collective feelings, thoughts, and actions of members. Members enact patterns from the larger society, and it may take considerable effort to sort out individual factors affecting group members' behavior from those reflecting larger forces in the current situation. Personal change, then, occurs within an understanding of the societal and cultural contexts. Also, the experiences of members should be examined for both their individual components that are established historically and also those that reflect larger cultural patterns.

A social justice perspective challenges us to pursue member relevance in several different ways. We are challenged to engage in *critical consciousness*, which we define as a continuous examination of our own positionalities in order to recognize our own standpoints and continue to learn about the ways in which our life experiences are shaped by the forces of difference and constructed statuses (Suarez, Newman, & Reed, 2008). Included in this awareness is an appreciation of microinequities or microaggressions—the brief, covert or overt slights or condescending social exchanges that over time wear away at self-esteem and contribute to maintaining structural hierarchies and marginalizing dynamics (Rowe, 1990).

In the context of the group, critical consciousness enables us to acknowledge that other group members have different experiences and standpoints based on their unique backgrounds. In this regard, we expand our understanding of difference and the social consequences of difference as they continuously define us (based on our own perception), are used by us to define others, or are used by others to define us.

A social justice perspective in our work with groups helps us recognize our areas of privilege that if not attuned to can block our ability to see marginalization or oppression or to work with others who are different from us. Group members can learn about various types of microinequities and create ways to assess within the group whether and how these are occurring and develop ways to identify and stop them as they recur. Remaining conscious of our experiences of privilege and oppression related to our position on various status dimensions can help us to recognize and empathize with people or groups that experience disadvantages related to their social positions on that dimension or, by association, on another dimension (e.g., race).

By recognizing the importance of social contexts and the ways in which our identities may change over time, we are able to consider concepts such as multiple positionalities or standpoints together with their intersectionality. The intersectionality of our multiple social identities raises our complexity to a level that may seem difficult to understand, thereby privileging particular influences on our self definitions or else ignoring important differences about others that might be perceived as seemingly irrelevant but essential to their own self-definition (Collins, 2000; Crenshaw, 1995; Pyke & Johnson, 2003).

In our perspectives and responses to differences, we may unjustly rely on stereotypes, biases, and other aggregate means of identifying ourselves and others, essentially masking critical differences of ourselves and others. A social justice perspective moves us beyond binary comparisons (e.g., Black vs. White) and promotes engagement with our whole selves together with the wholeness of others in our practice (Reed et al., 2010). We argue that it also requires legitimizing differences and consciously elevating the uniqueness of individuals within their larger group and societal contexts. A growing literature discusses steps and processes for surfacing and "decentering" underlying paradigms and assumptions (Mann & Huffman, 2005; Narayan & Harding, 2000; Singleton & Linton, 2006). This includes examining phenomena and options through the eyes of those from different standpoints, especially from those in socially marginalized positions, and systematically considering the implications of different points of view. Through this decentering process, the practitioner takes individual interests, goals, and lifestyles into account in seeking to understand the ways in which people's multiple group memberships and statuses shape who they are and who they behave in their daily lives.

In addition, we emphasize a *cultural humility* perspective to encourage a less deterministic and less authoritative approach to understanding diversity and social justice issues and their impact on group membership and participation. Such a perspective places more value on the members' own contributions (Ortega & Faller, 2011; Tervalon & Murray-Garcia, 1998). Group membership from a cultural humility perspective encourages all participants to relinquish the role of expert in order to maximize the potential of each member while eliciting expertise from them that will most likely facilitate the group's movement toward its established purpose. Membership thus values both expert and learner roles in ways that support each member's potential to become a capable, contributing partner to the group's development and productivity. To do so in practice requires skills of *praxis*. According to Freire (1973), praxis requires (1) a willingness to deepen one's own knowledge of oneself as both a target and an agent for change; (2) an ability to act alone and with others; (3) the development of knowledge and skills for theorizing (critical personal, interpersonal, structural, and cultural analyses); and (4) engaging in strategies to recognize and promote change in situations that unjustly advantage or disadvantage social differences.

Group Dynamics

Case Example: Sergio

Sergio recently joined a men's group and had difficulty arriving at the group meeting on time. John, one of the members, reminded him of the group's agreement that it starts on time and told him to try harder to get there on time. He then added, "Remember, this ain't MP time." After some of the laughter by the other members subsided, one of the members asked what the MP stood for. As Sergio sat there half laughing, a member blurted out, "It means Mexican people time!" Sergio could see he did not have much in common with the other members and felt the proverbial wedge between him and other members based on racial or ethnic identity and stereotypes. His only response was to agree to arrive on time. He also realized something else wrong about the comment: He was not Mexican, he was Spanish, although he knew he had an ally in Octavio, who did acknowledge his Mexican ancestry and together they were the only Latinos in the group.

Becoming aware of and building on group members' multiple positionalities and standpoints is especially important at the interpersonal level. These work together and create opportunities for learning but may present barriers to social justice if not recognized. As indicated previously, this includes recognizing how dimensions of power, privilege, marginalization, oppression, and differences associated with positionalities influence peoples' perceptions, decisions, and actions.

Considerable knowledge now exists about different ways of knowing and learning and how people respond to novel social contexts depending on their backgrounds and cultural styles (Goodman, 2001). Opportunities to share relevant histories and experiences can help members learn to interpret each other's behaviors and support each other. To do so, unearned privilege must be recognized and challenged. In the previous example, it requires bringing to the fore stereotypes about the importance of time and assumptions about ethnic groups being monolithic. It means challenging the deeper meaning of stereotypes and potential for discrimination and the resulting marginalization and other harms that stereotypes engender. Group members who have experienced marginality and historical trauma may be distrustful or impatient for change. Professional wisdom consistently asserts the importance of assisting everyone to examine how they have internalized oppression and to learn skills for individual and group empowerment, consciousness-raising, increasing group connections and relationship building across differences, and taking action through advocacy with others (Burnes & Ross, 2010; Ratts, Anthony, & Santos 2010; Smith & Shin, 2008).

If they are to be effective, all groups must develop ways to negotiate and build on differences among members, who can then make decisions and work together. Even in situations in which variety and diverse perspectives are sought and valued, groups must develop ways to identify and use those differences. A group can make badly informed and reasoned decisions under these conditions, sometimes with major negative consequences. Soliciting differences, surfacing and embracing conflict as a positive force, and other strategies have emerged from the literature as a way to prevent groupthink and to build on the strengths that differences potentially provide (Curseu, Schruijer, & Boros, 2007; Ivey & Collins, 2003; Roysircar, 2008).

Conflict can be a positive, negative, or neutral force in small groups, but all types of conflict are important within and between groups, especially in working with groups to reach desired social justice goals. Conflict is an important component in the knowledge and theory of practice in groups in at least three ways: as a component in group development and maintenance, as a necessary element when negotiating and building on differences among members, and as a consequence of coming together across organizational interfaces or group boundaries. The most difficult conflicts to negotiate are those that occur around the "fault lines" in which differences are polarized and associated with patterns of distrust and power and/or when multiple types of differences coincide. Fault lines occur when subgroup categorizations or emerging power and status differentials influence or disrupt group processes such as decision-making that uses criteria other than the best knowledge and skills about how best to proceed (Homan, van Knippenberg, Van Kleef, & De Dreu, 2007).

For example, fault lines may undermine member trust and willingness to cooperate with others when certain privileges or priorities are assigned to some members because of their gender, age, or other social identities without acceptable rationale or justification. This increases tensions and conflict among group members, and it reduces communication among them. Especially when groups form, group members must determine how they will work together to accomplish their goals, discover and build on the talents and perspectives of group members, and negotiate members' different goals and ambitions. Conflict, from the group's initial development, has been described as the unavoidable, necessary, and important phase during which norms, procedures, and member roles and rankings are established (Forsythe, 2010). In an ongoing group, many of these issues will resurface and need to be renegotiated when a group's membership, goals, or environment changes or when it must transition to different sets of challenges and tasks. These are critical periods in which many aspects of groups can be re-examined and renegotiated.

The goal for this period of group development is frequently to negotiate, learn, or work together across differences. Intergroup relations units on many college campuses are an example of this type of conflict negotiation (Nagda, 2006; Nagda, Kim, & Truelove, 2004). In one model, half of a group's members represent people with lower status on a particular social category, and the other half have access to unearned advantage based on that category (e.g., African Americans and Caucasians, women and men, and those with disabilities and the able-bodied). The goal is to share experiences, learn from each other about how privilege and oppression work, and join together to identify and work toward some common goals. Ideally, members will discuss how their other social categories are also relevant (e.g., how gender affects one's experience of race). Other models are emerging that educate across multiple differences simultaneously or sequentially (Dessel, Rogger, & Garlington, 2006; Nagda, 2006).

At a more macro level, the use of a group may be to negotiate conflicts, disputes, and different interests in an organization or the larger society. For instance, such groups are used among unions and employers, gangs, nations, religious groups, or ethnic subgroups. International summits, for instance, frequently occur in small groups, with carefully developed protocols and skilled negotiators.

Within these groups, a facilitator needs to attend to emotional, cognitive, and behavioral issues and triggers so that people can develop more positive feelings and thoughts about others who represent other social categories and also skills for communicating and working together across differences (Stephan, 2008). For intergroup negotiations, members and negotiators must help the protagonists to articulate their issues and views, explore the sources of these views, and search for common ground or exchanges that can be made (Alexander & Levin, 1998).

Working with Connections and Conflict

Different types and severities of conflict may require different approaches. Conflict, for instance, may reflect an incompatibility or variance, a clash or divergence of opinions or interests, or a contention, battle, or struggle for mastery, including a hostile encounter. These suggest different levels or intensity of conflicts, which may be related to different types and sources of differences. Working with and building on differences requires that we recognize and consciously work with conflicts—that we not avoid the tensions and disputes that often accompany differences but, rather, view them as opportunities to learn from, build on, and negotiate differences. This is also essential if groups are to avoid marginalizing and exploiting some categories of members.

In some instances, one can include in the group members to represent particular types of diversity, including people who can create bridges and mediate between extremes. Whether or not a group's composition can be chosen to maximize desired diversity, every group can develop group norms and procedures that solicit, value, and systematically take into account the different approaches, knowledge and skill sets, and worldviews of its members. We can value, work with, and build on differences, agree to disagree in some instances, compromise, or continue to work toward negotiating alternatives when people cannot agree. When factions are polarized with great distrust, many strategies are possible for finding common ground (e.g., developing overarching goals) or at least reducing some of the worst negative consequences of dynamics associated with conflict and connection that create iniquities (Fisher et al., 2000).

Cohesion

Cohesion is a critical aspect when conceptualizing a group's dynamics because it can only occur when a group exists. It has been defined as all forces acting on members to remain in the group (Festinger, 1950) or why members are attracted to a group. Cohesiveness is essential for building and sustaining a viable group. The degree of cohesion has implications for sustained membership and improved performance. As groups form and cohesiveness develops, members become committed to the group and develop preferences for ideas, practices, and people associated with their group (Forsythe, 2010).

Whereas early research relied primarily on outcome studies that indicated membership and performance were highly subjective and relied heavily on member similarities, recent studies challenge this notion. Van Knippenberg, Haslam, and Platow (2007), for example, draw upon group (social) identification theory and propose that sometimes diversity rather than homogeneity fosters greater group identification. Their research suggests that successful group performance relies on member perceptions about the value of diversity and that group performance may be enhanced "precisely because of their diversity" (p. 208). Beyond performance, group studies in the organizational literature that examine the impact of diversity on organizational climate and culture underscore the fact that when diversity is perceived to increase group performance, it is likely to be embraced rather than viewed as aversive, especially when group members believe that there is greater value in diversity than homogeneity (Van Knippenberg et al., 2007).

Group diversity focuses on the ways in which group membership differs along specific dimensions. Research suggests that different types of diversity have different effects on the group's ability to achieve goals and complete tasks and on the ability of members to work together in an effective manner (Curseu et al., 2007). Group outcomes benefit from diversity to the extent that group performance is able to build on diversity dimensions most relevant to the group's achievement of its goals (Curseu et al., 2007; Harrison & Klein, 2007).

Thus, although diversity can stimulate or undermine group performance, decreased performance is most likely when dimensions of diversity converge to create diversity fault lines through subgroup social categorization processes. According to Homan and colleagues (2007), the group dynamics and processes that lead to positive outcomes in diverse groups, in terms of group performance, can also result in disadvantage and exclusion when diversity encourages separation and fails to address power and status disparities.

Group Structure

Group structure refers to how a group is organized, including such factors as group composition; group roles and its division of labor and resources; the group's formal procedures and rules, including decision-making processes; power and status hierarchies; communication and affectional patterns; and internal divisions, such as subgroups. These structures may either enhance working for social justice or impede it.

Previous sections of this chapter on dimensions of diversity have shown that the group's composition may involve such diversity. Group composition is defined as the pattern that exists in the group related to the personal characteristics of the members or its degree of homogeneity or heterogeneity. Groups can be composed of people who are similar on a dimension of concern (e.g., all women, all African Americans, and all gays or lesbians), who are selected to represent different characteristics (e.g., a group composed of women and men in equal numbers), or who randomly represent differences on some characteristic. Each of these types of composition will present opportunities and challenges with regard to promoting diversity and social justice. Here, we focus primarily on social categories associated with differential statuses in society.

A growing body of literature documents the consistent but complex effects of gender composition on a wide array of group conditions: dominance (Ridgeway & Diekema, 1989), legitimacy and status (Ridgeway, Diekema, & Johnson, 1995), communication patterns/interruptions (Karakowsky, McBey, & Willer, 2004; Smith-Lovin & Brody, 1989), and approaches to tasks. The salience of the social category is important (Randel, 2002), as is diversity in values (Rodriguez, 1998). These effects also depend on the nature of the task, environmental conditions, and a variety of other factors. In general, men appear to be more likely to exhibit dominance behaviors than women, whether they are in the minority or the majority, although this is influenced by the gender composition of the group and the nature of its task (Smith-Lovin & Brody, 1989).

In studies focusing on race and cross-race interactions, race-related expectations shape emotional responses (Butz & Plant, 2006) and participation (Li, Karakowsky, & Siegel, 1999), and some studies find different patterns than those one might expect if one were generalizing from studies that focus primarily on gender (Craig & Rand, 1998). These studies suggest that the intersection of race and gender requires additional thought and attention to social justice matters in small groups.

Some group theories stress status structures and their development—that is, stable differences in the patterns of power and influence among group members. The group is also affected by status characteristics outside the group that influence how people are perceived within the group, as well as power and influence structures within the group. Group members should be prepared to challenge those power and status dynamics that re-create gender-, race-, or other social identity-based inequities as well as other patterns of societal injustice that emerge within the group.

Gender, race, ethnicity, and other diversity factors are strong determinants of the structure of every group (e.g., when men sit with men and women with women) and influence subgroup and communication patterns. Previously, we noted that power structure consists of the degree to which members can influence the behavior of others by virtue of their position in the group, their ability to reward or punish others, their expertise, or their degree of attractiveness to others. A subset of members will likely attain or possess more power than other members by virtue of ascribed status (e.g., gender, social class, or ethnicity) and external roles. These power hierarchies can marginalize members with important knowledge and skills and create patterns of injustice in the group. Ideally, all members should be assisted to attain the power required for them to accomplish tasks they undertake and to utilize the expertise they develop through group experience.

Case Example: Reggie

Reggie was the storyteller in the task group. The members made it clear that his storytelling added nothing to the group's ability to accomplish its assignment and were clear in their expressions of annoyance each time he launched into another story. He would hear member groans and comments whenever he began a story. The members would immediately say, "Not now, Reggie!" or "Reggie that's

not helping!" Meanwhile, the group went about its business but with clear difficulty coordinating each member's contributions. Tension and conflict seemed to
define the group's climate, reflecting the members' frustrations with their lack of
direction. Reggie finally broke into a moment of group silence and stated, "You
guys are what my coach called a chump team." A group member immediately
responded by asking, "What in the world does that mean?" Reggie described
how his basketball coach would say that the championship team was the one in
which members looked to each other to help out—to pass, set screens so others
could get by—and they never worried about who scored because it was the team
effort that mattered. He continued, "I'm lookin' at you all and you're doin' your
own thing. No one is listening to anybody; no one is letting others take the lead.
It's like you're all smart except no one cares. My coach would say when we don't
act like a team we're playin' like chumps and not champs. What I see is a chump
team!" And with that insight, the team members looked at each other and knew
Reggie was right. Reggie rose to a socioemotional leadership role.

The *division of labor* in groups refers to the task-focused patterns of action
undertaken by members. Ideally, members assume tasks for the group based on
their ability and interests rather than status. The group's division of labor should
also encourage and support task assignments that open new opportunities for
members who have been oppressed or denied opportunities to contribute to the
group's progress.

Group task, which group workers often refer to as its *program*, consists of the
activities that members engage in together. Important issues to consider here
include the following: Is the group attending to the ways that some tasks are
preferred or rejected by people from different cultural groups or genders? Do
members of various groups bring different assumptions and working styles to
the tasks?

Internal *boundaries* define the degree to which membership in and access to
subgroups is easy or difficult to attain. Permeable boundaries allow members to
build social connections within new subgroups or reconstitute subgroups based
on individual and group need. When permeable boundaries exist, communications are open among all subgroups. With rigid boundaries, members are "locked
in" to existing subgroups, and communications are limited among subgroups.
Such boundary patterns often ensue from issues of power and privilege, and they
place barriers on the fulfillment of member and group needs.

Structural boundaries can also create insiders and outsiders: Those within a
subgroup derive support and status from other members, and those not included
can be marginalized and acquire less power and satisfaction. Hierarchies that

develop and their potential to replicate external power structures can lead to patterns of exploitation and exclusion in the group.

This discussion emphasizes the importance of assessing both visible or explicit and informal or subtle structures within the group and its environment, especially in relation to how power is created and manifested and whether these patterns of intragroup power distribution replicate external power structures. This can include evaluating formal policies and procedures that affect the group's work, as well as those that evolve in the group, in terms of how well the members address issues of social justice (how power and authority are defined, who is included or excluded, the relevance of the group's actions toward purposes and goals, and so on). Assessment should also include important boundaries that must be negotiated outside and within the group.

One way to identify structural sources of injustice is to engage in *critical structural analyses* to illuminate how societal forces are manifested and reinforced in small groups. Previously, we described the importance of decentering and becoming aware of and challenging microinequities at the interpersonal level. All these involve being skeptical about taken-for-granted features and working with others who have different standpoints and types of knowledge to recognize and name usually less visible forces. Once they are visible, it is easier to challenge and change them. We also previously alluded to the importance of addressing conflict, a factor that is important across all of the group components noted previously.

Group Culture

Culture is defined as the shared beliefs and traditions that exist among the members of the group and the ways in which group members create meaning within the group. Some aspects of a group culture may be very conscious, overt, and obvious to group members—for instance, its explicit rituals or rules for behavior—whereas others are more subtle. For example, participation may emerge in a group that replicates stereotyped participation outside the group based on gender, socioeconomic class, age, and so on. Cultural elements can also include the theories or intervention models being employed in a group.

Key cultural elements include norms, symbols, rituals, and taken-for granted assumptions that explain key group phenomena and the words used to signify them. Norms in groups refer to the expectations members have as to how other members should behave or refrain from behaving. These norms are shaped by societal assumptions (Ridgeway, 1991, 2001) in which beliefs about societal status create a network of expectations that then shape people's behaviors. Members are frequently rewarded or punished if they follow or violate shared expectations, sometimes overtly by being expelled from a group or explicitly sanctioned. Often, however, not "fitting in" leads to a gradual loss of influence and social connections in a group.

Unjust or inflexible norms can contribute to scapegoating and marginalizing, and they can leave some members more central than others in terms of power and status. This may be related to gender, ethnicity, age, social class, and other demographic characteristics as well as related behavioral expectations. One way of avoiding these norms is to actually discuss the concept of norms with the group and ask members to examine what kinds of unacknowledged norms exist in the group.

Many of these meaning-making processes can be very subtle—what Martin (2004) calls *luminal*—meaning beyond the awareness of most participants. One might also call them *tacit*, meaning not articulated or recognized, and maintained in the day-to-day interactions and thoughts that are taken for granted. Often, these processes become difficult to change, especially when left unattended. Status-creating behaviors, for instance, are frequently legitimated by members' assumptions about group members' competency that are associated with their conceptual schemas about social categories (Ridgeway, 2006). Often not recognized, they are very resistant to change, and they shape behaviors in many ways that may not be obvious to group members, except by the most marginalized group members who may be more aware of group forces because of their standpoints. Frequently, however, the group dynamics are not visible to the members, and those who end up being marginalized often attribute their experiences in a group to personal deficits (Ridgeway & Johnson, 1990).

What creates legitimacy also has cultural elements. Johnson, Dowd, and Ridgeway (2006) describe how legitimacy is shaped by beliefs and then, in turn, secures compliance with the existing social order. This order is embedded in shared and accepted (or at least not questioned) beliefs, norms, and values. These authors describe some ways to disrupt these shared assumptions. One of these is that group members can critique the knowledge, values, research, theories, and practice methods/actions being used in the group in terms of underlying paradigms and the assumptions they represent, illuminate, or obscure.

Exploring phenomena often viewed in terms of dichotomies is especially important. These dichotomies can create false distinctions and obscure the presence of other options, such as between the individual and the group, the group's outcome and processes, men and women, Whites and people of color, and right and wrong. Decentering the meanings of words, group symbols, norms, and values can identify dominant assumptions and ideologies that may marginalize some group members and increase the influence of others. This requires taking the time to clarify how different people understand and interpret various group features. For example, May (2007) discusses articles that distort concepts of race.

Group Leadership

We define *leadership* as an individual acting in ways that increase the effectiveness of a small group, while working toward social justice. Although many groups have a designated leader or leadership team, either appointed by some external authority or emerging from the group, every group member can exert leadership by contributing to the evolution and accomplishments of a group. A social worker will contribute leadership in many ways, not only when in formal leadership roles (e.g., chair, president, and facilitator).

A review of articles focused specifically on social justice in groups identified common themes regarding leadership that are considered central to social justice work (Singh & Salazar, 2010). Core among these themes are the leaders' willingness and ability to expand their understanding and appreciation of diversity and cultural differences and openness to different expressions of language.

A second core theme emphasizes the importance of attending to, planning, and mobilizing members' skills and abilities to address identified social injustices and misuses of power and privilege within and outside the group and also the importance of facilitating member empowerment. Collaborating to increase knowledge and skills that challenge the unequal access of goods and services and that teach self-advocacy and community-level advocacy is also emphasized. Specific social justice goals are to address underrepresented populations and issues (e.g., returning veterans, an increased aging population with health care challenges, individuals who are ability-challenged, LGBTQ youth and young adults, and homeless persons). Leaders are challenged to utilize social justice skills that expand beyond identity differences such as working across race or ethnicity, gender, or social class and working to address injustices that often discriminate across multiple differences.

A third core theme focuses on how group work practice, in general, addresses general human behavior with less of an emphasis on how privilege, marginalization, and oppression are reflected in the group's dynamics and processes. Concern focuses on the importance of the leaders' ability to examine carefully and openly how their own privilege may impede their ability to experience members' concerns in ways that reveal their origins in marginalization and oppression. Leaders are called upon to "unpack" their invisible knapsack of power and privilege (McIntosh, 1988) and reflect on how this content may lead to positionalities and standpoints that create barriers to experiencing members' concerns and challenges to effective practice as these aspects are expressed by members at different times in the group. From a social justice perspective, leaders are urged to develop practice skills that ensure attention to members' experiences and needs and expand their own learning about themselves beyond what occurs within the group itself.

The fourth core theme focuses on leaders' consciousness-raising and the actions that ensue from this process. As group members increase their awareness, develop a clearer sense of the interplay of power, privilege, marginalization, and oppression as systemic problems, and feel empowered (along with the urge to "do something"), a leader's abilities should assist members in ways that enable them to advocate for themselves. As members emerge from the group with social justice visions, leaders will ideally teach them strategies to promote effective change. Group leaders will be more successful when deficit-oriented perspectives are transformed into more meaningful and hopeful perspectives accompanied by the knowledge and skills to make and sustain change toward social justice causes.

Power and Leadership

Power is often defined as having the influence and resources needed to accomplish desired goals. Harnessing power is necessary to create change and work for social justice. Feminist scholars and activists, especially, have urged those concerned about creating change for social justice to strive to use collaborative forms of power—having power *with* others by working together—versus using power to dominate or control others (Townsend, Zapata, Rowlands, Alberti, & Mercado, 1999). At the individual level, French and Raven (1960) defined power in five ways: in terms of expertise (*expert*), control of resources (*reward*) or punishments (*coercive*), or related to a person's structural position or role in a social system (*legitimate*). *Referent* power refers to power gained because people admire someone and aspire to be like her or him.

Many studies have examined the types of leadership that are useful for different types of group purposes and goals, but it is beyond the scope of this chapter to summarize this literature. Needless to say, working for social justice, challenging the forces that sustain systemic inequalities and valuing and building on the diversity of group members require consistent leadership of all types.

The literature documents that leaders who occupy higher and lower power social status categories are perceived and reacted to differently by group members. Gender expectations continue to shape what is possible for women in leadership roles, although they do so less than they did in the past. In many studies, women are now perceived to be as competent as men, although they elicit considerably more negative affect than do men (Brower, Garvin, Hobson, Reed, & Reed, 1987; Carli & Eagly, 2001; Eagly, 2007; Koch, 2005). The situation for leaders in different racial categories is considerably less clear, with some studies suggesting they are perceived as less competent and others finding they are rated more favorably than Whites in leadership (Brower et al., 1987; Ellis, Ilgen, & Hollenbeck, 2006; Kelsey, 1998; Pyke & Johnson, 2003).

Another factor that is important to consider is that leadership is manifested in members who represent all social categories. Just because one has experienced oppression does not automatically prepare one to have skills in working for justice. The literature is just beginning to address strategies useful for people of color who assume leadership positions and yet are disparaged and discouraged from promoting social justice through their leadership (Marbley, 2004).

Disrupting and becoming aware of these forms of power is difficult and requires regular and ongoing collective reflection that members oriented only to outcomes often resist. It is also very difficult to repeatedly attend to these issues. Research suggests it is important to assess whose views and values are represented in the group's activities and decisions and to identify some of the ways that group members may be re-creating power differences among themselves. Attending to the entire group network is important in group work because everyone is involved in sustaining these forms of power. Even when some members are the primary protagonists, bystanders can play important roles in maintaining or challenging these dynamics (Ridgeway & Diekema, 1989). Many other forms of power derive from social structures and how groups and organizations work, and we describe some of these later. (For additional discussions about power, see Chapters 7 and 8.)

There is increasing knowledge about how different types and sources of power combine to contribute to the creation and maintenance of privilege and oppression. These are barriers to social justice that lead to unearned advantages and multiple types of disadvantages including threats to survival if they are not repeatedly challenged and reduced. Especially relevant here are concepts of earned and ascribed status.

The term *status* indicates differences in the power and influence among group members due to positions within and outside of the group. Some positions of status are earned (e.g., educational degrees and promotions in the workplace), but other types of status are associated with the social categories one occupies. Social categories that are commonly associated with different forms of ascribed status include ability, age, class, culture, ethnicity, family structure, gender (including gender identity and gender expression), marital status, national origin, geographic location (e.g., rural, suburban, and urban), race, religion or spirituality, and sexual orientation.

Having higher ascribed status usually makes it more likely that a person will be able to acquire greater earned status. In social justice work, the consequences of having more or less ascribed power are frequently described as having privilege or experiencing oppression. People bring these experiences with them into a group and re-create them within groups in ways that are often not recognized.

Privilege is defined as unearned advantages that are associated with social categories that have higher status in society (e.g., whiteness, masculinity, higher economic class, heterosexuality, and membership in a dominant religion) (Johnson, 2001). McIntosh (1988) defines at least two types of privilege: those that are desired states that should be accorded to everyone and those that create disadvantage for others that we work to eliminate. Those with privilege frequently are unaware of the disparities between their sources of power and those of others (Goodman, 2001).

Oppression refers to the ways that people experience barriers to participation in society, such as exercising their rights and taking advantage of opportunities. Mechanisms that create and sustain oppression are multiple, and they are often not recognized even by those affected by them. Young (1990) classifies five types of oppression: powerlessness, marginalization, exploitation, cultural hegemony, and violence. We describe ways that these can occur within small groups. People can have multiple responses to their own experiences with oppression (Mullaly, 2007). Some internalize their oppression and experience lower self-esteem and efficacy as a result. Others actively resist oppressive forces, often in concert with others.

Multiple theories are now focusing on these types of interactions and activities as ways in which power is manifested and through which societal structures and ideologies are sustained and reinforced or challenged and changed. For example, Ridgeway and colleagues (Ridgeway, 2006; Ridgeway, Boyle, Kuipers, & Robinson, 1998; Ridgeway & Erickson, 2000) articulate how status is evident in member transactions, often in unrecognized ways. Of particular importance are those transactions that support status hierarchies, dominant norms, and values and that suppress member differences.

Foucault (1975/1995) articulated how being observed and monitored by others (experiencing and participating in surveillance) led people to constrain their own behaviors and to constrain the behavior of others. Although groups need routines and procedures to accomplish their tasks, these can quickly constrain innovation and lead to censoring as they become more embedded in group traditions and procedural mechanisms.

Group Development and Process

Group process refers to how the group changes from moment to moment or over longer periods through member interactions, including enactment of procedures and tasks in the group. These interactions include group members' communications, affects, and conflicts and the patterns among these as the group begins and, over time, seeks to accomplish its goals and objectives. This latter process is referred to as "group development." Processes such as how decisions are made or the unfolding of a conversation among several people are also strongly affected by group members' culture, gender, and other status issues. For instance, men and women communicate differently in every culture (Tannen, 1990). People with higher status often talk more, express themselves differently, and interrupt others more than do those with less status, and there are also marked differences across cultures (Karakowsky et al., 2004; Smith-Lovin & Brody, 1989).

Communication patterns, affectational factors, and conflict are especially important in group dynamics. The pattern of positive and negative emotions that members direct at others in the group helps to shape subgroups and the overall climate of the group. Research suggests that over time, negative emotions are suppressed in groups and positive ones enhanced, which increases cohesiveness but may lead to the suppression of important differences (Ridgeway & Johnson, 1990). These differences are usually accompanied by varying degrees of negative emotions. As discussed later, engaging with conflict and disagreements is an important practice element in socially just groups that requires regular and special attention to maintain.

Practice Dimensions

In examining practice dimensions, we were strongly influenced by the work of Mullender, Ward, and Fleming (2013), particularly their model of "self-directed group work." They present many useful ways in which group members can work together to change oppressive conditions. They assert that this process is facilitated by attention to the following questions: What are the concerns of group members regarding the sources of their oppression? Why do these sources of oppression exist? What strategies will the group undertake to change these oppressive conditions? Although we agree with their assumption that members often will themselves change in the process of engaging in social change activities, we add that, at times, group members may wish to focus on their personal issues.

As stated in Chapter 4, we view all practice as consisting of the following dimensions:

1. Exploring
2. Engaging
3. Planning

4. Implementing
5. Monitoring/evaluating
6. Celebrating/terminating

We reiterate that we do not view these phases as sequential but, rather, as tasks that are engaged in as determined by the logic of the situation. Thus, a group may engage in exploration, as we shall define this further, when the members first come together, but it may also do so when new members join, previous members leave, or external circumstances change. Members may utilize processes of engagement in the first few meetings but may need to repeat this process when new members join or when internal or external events disrupt the relationships that have been evolving.

Exploring

When members first come together with the group worker, they are likely to "sound each other out" as they decide whether they will work together, what purposes and goals they will choose to work on, what methods they will use in the group, what norms they will decide to follow, and to whom in the group they will feel closest. Social justice issues will be apparent during all these exploration processes. Group members are likely to quickly size up what kinds of power and powerlessness are present in the situation. It is important whether the group worker begins by eliciting feelings and ideas from the group or by telling the members what is expected from them. The obvious or subtle experiences of the power of the agency are demonstrated by how the members were greeted when they first entered the agency, whether they thought that they were expected, or whether they initially perceived that they were regarded as intruders.

One of the first topics of discussion in the group is usually the purpose of the group. Ideally, this has already been discussed with the members on a one-to-one basis before the first meeting is held. The function, then, is to determine whether the members and the group worker think the same way about its purpose once they have the experience of seeing and interacting with each other. A key social justice issue here is how much power members perceive they have in determining the purpose of the group. If the group's purpose is imposed on them, they are likely to experience the group as not being relevant to their concerns and to resist participating in many ways.

An example of this is a group in a high school setting conducted by the school social worker. The principal has told the worker that the purpose of the group is to make the students compliant with school rules and to induce them to complete their class assignments on time. The students in this situation wished to complain about school rules that they purchase school supplies they could not afford. They also experienced one of their teachers as prejudiced against their ethnic group. The worker has a social justice orientation. She tells the members what the principal expects, but she also indicates that the group members can ask to speak with the principal if they disagree with his expectations. She also informs the group that she will accompany them and support them in expressing their opinions. In addition, she plans to tell the principal that the students want to discuss his expectations with him. She recognizes that he might be critical of her for bringing this matter to his attention, but she believes that her social work ethics and values, especially those associated with social justice, require her to act in this way. The social worker also tells the students that she will help them to find a way to express their concerns about the teacher's presumed prejudice, but they will have to discuss this together to determine the best way to approach this issue.

An important issue in the exploration phase is to convey to the members that they have knowledge that they can share to benefit each other. The worker does not have the same knowledge as the members have about their life circumstances. The worker's knowledge is primarily how to help the members *help each other* because they have found reasons to respect and care for each other. An example of this is a group of probationers facilitated by a social work student. The members approached the student in a challenging manner in which many questioned what she knew about their lives and their experiences in the larger system.[1] The worker responded that it was true that she had limited knowledge about them but that she was in the group to help them to help each other and to care what happens to each other. She also hoped to learn from them as much as they were willing to share with her about their lives and what has happened to them.

Members have many different ways of sharing information based on their age, ethnicity, educational experiences, and culture. The worker should respect these different ways of sharing. Examples are older folks who may wish to reminisce, children who may draw pictures about their lives, and Spanish-speaking people who may find it easier to communicate in Spanish and may require an interpreter (or interpret for each other).

Engaging

This process is one in which members deal with a commitment to interact with each other and with the worker. The way in which they do this indicates their

---

1. These, of course, were not their words, which were put much more colloquially.

willingness to engage, the depth of this engagement, and their level of commitment to remaining in the group. In this process, members decide how open they will be with each other and with the worker. This does not imply that they immediately make this commitment but, rather, that gradually their commitment will become "deeper" and that over time members will say more about themselves and reveal more about their experiences and feelings. This requires that group members develop increasing trust among themselves and toward the group worker as they experience others in the group as supportive and empathic rather than harmful. This trust is often enhanced as members see that the worker and other members understand their social justice issues, although they may express these concerns without explicitly using the term. An example is a group of abused women whose worker was aware that they had not experienced any help from the police when they called for help.

An important process during engagement (which also exists during all other activities) is that of dialogue. Dialogue is not the same as discussion; it exists when all group members, as well as the worker, apply the following principles:

1. Members share their own perceptions of the situation.
2. Members offer their own opinions and ideas.
3. Members listen closely to the perceptions, ideas, and opinions of others without seeking to debate or contradict these.
4. Only after establishing that they have understood the perceptions, ideas, and opinions of others as completely as possible do members then offer their own views. This is done in the spirit of seeking understanding of others and communicating one's own ideas with the expectation that these will be listened to in a reciprocal manner. This essentially means *honoring difference*.

As Finn and Jacobson (2008) state, also drawing from Freire (1973),

Dialogue requires empathy, identification with, and the inclusion of other people. Paulo Freire was convinced, based on his years of work with oppressed peoples, that only humble and loving dialogue can surmount the barrier of mistrust built from years of paternalism and the rampant subjugation of the knowledge and wisdom of the oppressed. "Founding itself upon love, humility, and faith, dialogue becomes a horizontal relationship of which mutual trust among dialoguers is the logical consequence." (pp. 79–80)

A caring community is a community that confirms otherness, in part by giving each person and group a ground of their own, and affirming this ground through encounters that are egalitarian and dedicated to healing and empowerment. (p. 241)

An example of this is a group member in a group of men who have abused their partners. He first told of how stressful his house was, especially when the children were ill and how he had run out of his house in frustration. The other members listened carefully and indicated that they understood how stressful this was. He later said that his wife drove him to shout at her when she told him to help with the children and he yelled that this was her job. The other members had previously discussed the ideas of dialogue. They did not confront this member, and they asked the member in question to say more about why he felt so driven. At a later session, he indicated that this was what his father had told his mother. Even later, he admitted that he expected that his shouting would stop his wife from making demands on him, and he was beginning to think this was unfair of him. The growing awareness of this man was enhanced by his perception that the other men were not judging him but were trying to understand him and "to walk in his shoes."

Another major social justice issue in engagement processes is whether the group is voluntary or involuntary. Many groups are involuntary, such as those in correctional settings. However, many other types of groups may be involuntary, such as students required to be in a therapeutic group as a condition of staying in school, employees required to attend a group as a condition of continued employment, or male batterers ordered by a court to attend a group as a condition of not being jailed. It can be assumed that these coercive individuals or systems expect that the individual will engage with other members and participate in the processes of the group. Such a situation can be expected to produce, at the most, a pretense of engagement.

It is incumbent on the group worker to discuss fully this issue with the members and seek to help them resolve it. They may decide willingly to accept the agency's purpose. On the other hand, they may wish to pursue their own purposes. The worker then acts as a mediator between the members and the agency, and a number of solutions are possible. Agency administrative personnel may choose to be present to interact personally with members. A resolution may be that one "side" accepts the proposition of the other, a compromise is reached, or a new set of purposes are devised. We suggest, however, that members' reluctant capitulation to the wishes of the agency is unjust and will result in a group process that accomplishes little in the direction desired by either the agency or the members.

On the other hand, some resolution in the direction of the members' wishes can be empowering, help the members to see how they can take charge of their own destinies, and help the "authorities" see the members in a new light as people who are learning to cope with the larger forces in their world.

These points about the engagement process are related to the issue of *power*. A social justice approach to group work recognizes that power issues arise throughout the group process but are first raised during the engagement process. The following are some of the ways this is done:

1. The workers can indicate that they are not the "experts" on the members' lives and experiences and that the group members know these best. The expertise of the workers lies in their ways of helping the members to help one another. Workers may also have knowledge regarding the stated concerns of the members, such as knowledge of substance abuse, mental illness, and grief/loss, but the workers explicitly acknowledge that group members also possess such knowledge and can share it with one another.
2. The group "belongs" to the members, not the worker or the agency. This means that the members have the final say on their rules and activities. The worker has the responsibility, however, to ensure that no member is harmed in the group in any way. This includes indicating that the group does not have the power to admit or expel members. Group members typically will be asked their thoughts and feelings, in general, about admission of new members. They also will be involved in decisions regarding any rules that may exclude a member, such as failing to attend sessions or harming another member. The major issue here is to help the members make the group a safe place.
3. A variety of other power issues arise that affect the group members, and they can be helped to recognize them in order to change the power dynamic within the group. These include the following:
   a. The gender, race, culture, or wealth of workers or members may be a source of power.
   b. The agency may provide sources of power to the worker, such as control of some agency resource (e.g., supplies, equipment, and use of space) or ready access to powerful agency staff or board members.
   c. A worker may be asked to provide information about the actions of a member to outsiders, such as school, correctional, or employment personnel. The worker acknowledges this with the member and that the member may choose to withhold information because of this. A social justice approach requires that the member be informed of the content of such reports.

Planning

To achieve the ultimate ends agreed to by the members and worker, the group usually chooses some proximal ends, often in the form of tasks to be performed. For example, in a group to help members with substance abuse problems, some proximal ends might be to keep a record of when and where substances were used, to involve family members in the process, or to affiliate with an Alcoholics

Anonymous (AA) group. A social justice approach requires that these activities be planned with the members and that social barriers hindering their attainment be identified and confronted.

Another planning activity is for the members to acquire the skills to carry out the types of tasks to which we have just referred. From a social justice perspective, this should also involve the members' increased sense of power. Members' new skills should be recognized. Whenever possible, they can also learn from one another so that the worker is less frequently viewed as the "expert." It is also possible that members may have skills not possessed by the worker, and these skills are less likely to be recognized if the worker maintains control of which skill-building exercises are utilized. In the previous example of the substance abuse group, a member was apprehensive about attending an AA meeting. With some prompting from the worker, a member who already attended AA volunteered to describe what a meeting was like, helped the member in question to decide how to introduce herself, and offered to accompany her to a meeting.

An additional planning issue is for the members to develop their ability to deal with conflicts that arise in the course of carrying out planning tasks. In the previous example of a substance abuse group, the member who wished to attend an AA group feared that her husband would oppose her doing this and in other ways also sought to dominate her. The members gave her ideas on how to stand up to him, and several members offered to role play these scenarios with her. She also indicated that she did not anticipate that he would use physical or verbal force to intimidate her.

Implementing

In group work practice, implementing (actions to produce change) may involve an individual member, the group as a whole, the agency, the community, or the larger society. The following are examples from a group of high school students who were having difficulties with interpersonal relationships:

- A Latino member practices with the other group members means of making friends. She also considers whether her ethnic background has caused some classmates to withdraw from her.
- Two members, one male and one female, discuss a conflict they had been having with each other. The young woman tells the young man that she believes he is seeking to dominate her.
- A young woman tells the others in the group that she thinks the men in the group interrupt the young women members and do not seem to listen to them when they speak.

- The entire group participates in an exercise that involves identifying whether members are listening to each other and promotes efforts to ensure all members listen when others speak.
- The members plan how to approach the school principal regarding discriminatory practices in the school and list the specific ways this discrimination is manifested.
- The members attend a meeting of the board of education to ask for a change in policies that arbitrarily steer African American students into vocational rather than college preparatory courses.
- The group joins other groups in collecting signatures on a letter to their member of Congress urging her to vote for the President's jobs bill.

In summary, implementing plans empowers members to enhance their understanding and consciousness of group and group–environment dynamics.

Monitoring/Evaluating

In the interest of facilitating the empowerment of members, the group worker will help the members to evaluate each session of the group as well as the outcomes they have experienced when the group ends for some or all of the members. An example of an instrument that can be used after each session is that developed by Sheldon Rose (1984). The following are some of the items in Rose's instrument:

1. How useful was today's session for you?
2. How important to you were the problems or situations you discussed (or others discussed) in the group today?
3. How satisfied were you with today's session.

It is sometimes beneficial to assess the members' satisfaction with one of the elements of the session. For example, it is helpful to ask if the members found an exercise useful or if they felt satisfied with the outcome of a problem-solving or decision-making discussion. It is likely that all members may not agree about an outcome or have different degrees of satisfaction with it. What should be done in such circumstances depends to some degree on what is termed the *decision rule.* Has the group established that it will be "governed" by majority rule or through consensus?[2] This should be discussed early in any group that is likely to make

---

2. The value on consensus is strongly held by Quaker groups, and these groups recognize that this is a time-consuming process. Whether this is feasible in social work groups, as far as we know, has not been adequately studied. It is also difficult to determine whether consensus has been reached because some members may be withholding, for a variety of reasons, their true opinions on an issue.

decisions. Unless there is complete consensus, the worker considers the basis of the dissension. Because such evaluations are usually completed anonymously, the logical action is to discuss this with the group. The worker may also make some inferences from her or his knowledge of the group and its members. Power issues are also important to consider in this regard because members may have apprehensions about the negative consequences for themselves if they are critical of the group as a whole or the worker.

An example of this is a group of abusive men who were court-mandated to be in the group. They may fear that if the court hears of their negative evaluation of the group or the worker, they may be forced into a situation they regard as more aversive. The worker may also feel inhibited from sharing this evaluation with systems outside of the group because of negative consequences for him- or herself and/or the members.

Workers are likely to have their own evaluations of the outcomes for each member as well as for what they consider to be the success, or lack thereof, of the group. A social justice approach requires that these opinions be shared with the group members. An even more complex issue is how this information is shared with the agency, referring agencies, or other organizations. Workers must consider the impact of this sharing on the members and on themselves, especially if the unequal power factors involved have negative consequences for members.

Sometimes, workers (in consultation with members) might choose to use standardized instruments to assess changes in the members of the group or the group's processes. Workers taking a social justice approach would acquaint members with the nature of such instruments and why they have been chosen. They would also share the results with members. If the integrity of the measure is threatened by this disclosure, the members' surrogates should be asked to approve the instrument. These may be peers, family members, or other trusted persons.

In such circumstances, aside from the usual concerns about the validity and reliability of the instruments, it is also important to assess whether the instruments are appropriate for the ethnicity, age, culture, or level of education of the members.[3] The creators of an instrument, or other users, should provide information on this, or the worker should plan appropriate pretesting and modification of the instrument to ensure its validity in this respect.

---

3. There may also be other characteristics to be considered in addition to those named here.

Celebrating/Terminating

As stated in Chapter 4, social justice work can be joyful, although in many instances there can be sorrow mixed with the joy related to the reasons members have utilized the services of group workers. In the case of task groups, the joy may be unmitigated because a task has been accomplished, such as a policy defined, a project completed, or a social action carried out. In a treatment group of members who are coping with loss, the celebration may be because members have learned to care for each other and to support one another. The termination of the group does not mean the members no longer feel sorrow; rather, they may wish to express satisfaction for what they have accomplished together.

For example, a group of high school students learning leadership skills to act as peer leaders of groups to reduce school intergroup conflicts completed a full semester of work on these skills. At the end of the semester, they planned a pizza party to celebrate the end of their work. The adult facilitators also distributed certificates of completion that were signed by the facilitators and by school administrators such as the principal. The facilitators thought the students could include these certificates with their college applications.

Prior to the celebration, the group spent part of several sessions in a termination process. This included several components:

- Members discussed and reviewed their accomplishments. This included reviewing what they had learned during their sessions, such as how to value their own identities as well as those of others, how their identity issues related to the larger picture of intergroup relations in the United States, how the school sometimes supported and sometimes undermined some of their identities, and how they had learned to work together on these issues.
- The members recalled some of the goals they had failed to accomplish as a group. One of the members had felt hurt by the group's lack of response to her suggestions. She thought this was due to her gender and that the group had failed to pick up on this. The group had also held a meeting with the principal to discuss some of its concerns but only a small number of members attended the meeting, thus defeating its purpose. The members, however, discussed this afterwards and vowed that they would take such commitments more seriously in the future.
- The members felt most positive about the discussions they had engaged in about the concept of social justice. They thought they had a better understanding of how this related to their relations with each other, with the group during sessions, with the way their worker responded to them, and with what they viewed as injustices in their school.

- The members noted that some of their teachers were opposed to what they sought to accomplish in the group, and these teachers showed this disapproval in the ways in which they responded to group members in the classroom.

- The members discussed how much they had come to value each other and the caring they had experienced from the group worker. They discussed how this caring took many sessions to develop because of their initial distrust that they would be valued and the power of each member would be recognized.

Summary

A major theme throughout this chapter is that the very elements that can make living and working in groups such a positive force within society may also create conditions that disempower members, lead to inequities, and promote injustice. We assert that this is likely to occur unless group members and leaders are constantly vigilant about unintended consequences or else are willing to confront intentional acts that unjustifiably privilege differences among participants.

Definitions that focus on the struggle for justice describe a deep commitment to an ongoing engagement with and understanding of the dynamics and forms of privilege and oppression. Skills also include working with people with diverse experiences, social locations, and perspectives toward socially just relationships, procedures, decision-making processes, and environments.

Barriers to justice exist in mechanisms for privilege and oppression that must be understood and challenged, as goals in themselves and as recurring processes in all social environments and systems. These barriers may be expressed in both the structures found in the group and in the interactions between the group and the larger society. All are associated with social categories/positions with and without power and influence and are maintained and can be challenged and changed through work in small groups.

We have integrated issues related to justice and injustice into a presentation of many basic concepts important for a general knowledge about small groups and the many important purposes they serve. We have stressed recognizing and engaging with multiple sources of power and all the types of conflict that are inevitable in the pursuit of social justice. This knowledge of groups and social justice is growing rapidly, and we hope that the reader will challenge her- or himself to continue to learn from some of the resources listed and by seeking out additional literature as it becomes available.

Discussion Questions

1. Choose a group with which you are familiar. How might the group's purposes relate to social justice issues?
2. Think of your own positionalities. How might these affect your view of social justice issues in the group?
3. Choose a group with which you are familiar. What types of conflict might occur in this group? How might these conflicts relate to social justice issues?
4. Choose a practice dimension that is evident in a group with which you are familiar. In what ways might social justice issues influence this dimension of practice?

7

Socially Just Organizational Practice

Introduction

Social work practice, whatever population it serves or issues it addresses, largely occurs in and through organizations. Although the relationships that a social worker develops with clients or constituents are a critical component of all practice, the agency in which the social worker is employed is a key partner in service delivery, advocacy, and social change. Through a range of social interactions— with clients, the community, funding sources, political supporters, policymakers, and the general public—the organization *sets the parameters* of all social work practice. Therefore, understanding how organizations operate and the distinctive qualities of socially just organizations is critical to enhancing the effectiveness and efficiency of our practice.

Organizations play a central role in the design, delivery, and evaluation of social services, as well as in the development and implementation of social change efforts. They engage in conscious processes of need definition and assessment; resource development, allocation, and management; issue prioritization; strategic planning to achieve organizational goals; program development and evaluation; and the establishment and maintenance of relationships with clients, constituents, collaborators, colleagues, and community sponsors.

Drawing upon the literature of diverse disciplines and professions, this chapter describes the various attributes of a socially just organization, presents principles that underlie socially just administrative practice, and discusses some of the challenges of implementing these principles in a multicultural environment. The chapter pays particular attention to the role of power and leadership and the distinctions among different types of organization structures, particularly as they relate to their definition of social justice and strategies of implementation. Where relevant, we apply the phases of practice described previously.

We focus mostly on issues that are particularly salient to the creation of socially just organizations:

- Organizational mission and goals
- Organization structure and decision-making processes
- The role of power and politics
- Socially just leadership
- Organizational climate and culture
- Dealing with intra- and interorganizational conflict and organizational change
- Socially just ethical decision-making
- Using technology in socially just ways

What Distinguishes Socially Just Organizations?

Many practitioners assume that the ideals of social justice are only reflected in an organization's mission statement and goals. In fact, every aspect of an organization reflects the extent of its commitment to social justice. It is ironic, therefore, that even among organizations with explicit social justice missions and goals, there is frequently a gap between the principles they espouse and their day-to-day practice. This occurs in two, strikingly different ways.

Some organizations with social justice missions, even some schools of social work, have a hierarchical structure and unjust organizational culture. In their practice, they reflect little awareness of or sensitivity toward issues of diversity. Critical decisions are made by a single person or a small group; resources, responsibilities, and workloads are allocated inequitably; and the specific needs and contributions of diverse clients, constituents, and staff are ignored. New social workers and social work students are often frustrated and confused by these contradictions between organizational rhetoric and organizational practice.

Conversely, although they appear to be philosophically compatible with the social justice values many social workers and social work students share, organizations with consciously egalitarian structures and decision-making processes or that deliberately reject structure, such as those spawned by the recent "Occupy" movement, can also be frustrating places in which to work. The absence of clearly articulated goals and objectives, the lack of procedures for making and implementing decisions, and the resistance to establishing formal leadership, even if collectively defined, can stymie the best efforts on behalf of social justice.

The contradiction between rhetoric and reality affects both types of organizations in several ways: (1) It undermines the attainment of their programmatic goals and social change strategies (including the manner by which these programs and strategies are designed, implemented, and evaluated) by diminishing trust among clients, constituents, and staff; (2) it has a negative impact on staff–client, staff–constituent, and intrastaff interactions, often reproducing social hierarchies within the organization, factional disputes, and the emergence of values that the organization officially opposes; (3) it damages the relationships between the organization and the communities it purports to serve; and (4) it shapes how the organization makes decisions, allocates resources, and treats the people who work or volunteer at the organization and those who seek services. Consequently, many organizations fall short of their social justice goals in their actual practice and often inadvertently perpetuate oppressive and privileged ways of thinking and acting.

As Figure 7.1 reflects, organizations do not exist in isolation. Just as clinical social workers assess clients through a person-in-environment framework, it is useful to view organizations as dynamic actors who interact regularly with a variety of internal and external environmental forces through porous boundaries. Because this "environmental set" is constantly changing, it is important to "scan" the environment continuously in order to respond effectively to these changes and maintain a social justice focus. For example, new political or fiscal circumstances, new leaders, changing community demographics, and different organizational life cycles may influence the composition of coalitions created to effect a specific change.

All organizations have to engage in the following activities:

- Establish goals and create structures of leadership and decision-making
- Translate these goals into the design and implementation of programs
- Create systems of intra- and interorganizational communication and relationships
- Develop means to acquire and distribute resources
- Recruit, train, supervise, and evaluate staff
- Interact with the external environment (funders, clients, constituents, and policymakers)

What, then, distinguishes a socially just organization from the thousands of other organizations that exist, including those that may proclaim socially just goals but not reflect these goals in their ongoing practice? Simply stated, these organizations have a different approach to their purpose and to people. In the memorable phrase of C. Wright Mills (1959), they transform "private troubles into public issues" through services, advocacy, and political action.

Many organizations, however, proclaim similar goals. The difference between a socially just organization and an organization that merely espouses a social

FIGURE 7.1 Organization-in-Environment

Source: Adapted from E.A. Mulroy (2004), Theoretical perspectives on the social environment to guide management and community practice: An organization-in-environment approach. *Administration in Social Work* 28(1), 77–96.

justice mission is how it treats people. Socially just organizations emphasize the importance of building and sustaining relationships—with clients, constituents, and colleagues—based on principles of mutuality and collaboration rather than status hierarchy. They focus on mobilizing individuals and groups to define their own needs, suggest more effective ways of helping, and formulate action strategies. They are facilitative, rather than directive, in their intraorganizational processes. What Greenberg (2007) termed "positive organizational justice" integrates a commitment to equality, fairness, transparency, and mutual communication in their practice. These values appear in all aspects of their work, not merely in their mission statements.

Socially just organizations also demonstrate value consistency through their horizontal and vertical relationships. Their organizational "set," therefore, depends on the quality of their horizontal or vertical relationships in the community and the broader societal context in which they exist. A critical determinant of the quality of these relationships is the presence or absence of what social scientists refer to as "bonding" (horizontal) and "bridging" (vertical) social capital (Portes, 2000; Szreter & Woolcock, 2004). The former refers to the relationships of individuals and organizations within a community that work on similar issues and of community subsystems to each other. These relationships primarily focus on informal processes and are characterized by informal linkages and ad hoc collaborations. In today's conflict-ridden and increasingly competitive environment, these relationships are often shaped by political sponsors and funders.

Vertical relationships are those that community-based organizations maintain with external entities that often possess power, resources, status, and influence that community-based organizations lack and need. These more formal, rule-governed relationships with government agencies, philanthropic foundations, and corporations require "bridging social capital" to be successful (Reisch & Guyet, 2007). For social justice organizations, these relationships are frequently adversarial because of their different ideological orientation and goals (Young, 1999). Therefore, it is more challenging for social justice organizations to build, sustain, and "cash in" social capital to benefit their clients and constituents (Chaskin & Joseph, 2010).

One way to address this challenge is by recognizing the relationship between an organization's internal features and the nature of its external environment. For example, a community organization that is staffed primarily by volunteers and has an informal leadership and decision-making structure relies more on the strength of its interpersonal relationships (bonding social capital) both inside the organization and between the organization and community residents. More formal organizations—for example, those with paid staff, an annual budget, and more clearly defined roles—generally depend more on financial and political support from sources outside the community. This requires their leaders to cultivate bridging social capital with these external sources of support. Many social justice organizations, however, particularly in low-income and low-power communities, have difficulty developing "vertical" relationships without compromising their original values and goals (Schneider, 2009).

Exploration: Creating Socially Just Organizational Structures, Goals, and Decision-Making Processes

The goals and structure of an organization reflect its overall vision of social justice and how it translates this vision into programs that assist individuals, families, groups, and communities. Within socially just organizations, this vision is also reflected in its patterns of decision-making, particularly how the organization involves clients, constituents, and staff in decision-making processes in meaningful (i.e., not merely nominal) ways. Just as definitions of social justice vary considerably, even within the same community (see Chapters 2 and 3), the ways in which an organization applies social justice principles in its daily practice vary depending on the ideological orientation of the agency, its client population, the type of services it provides, and its overall context. The organization's views of social justice are also reflected in its staffing pattern and role distribution and also in the character of its intrastaff and client/constituent–staff relationships. The latter is particularly important in diverse communities and organizations.

In order to create a socially just organization, therefore, it is insufficient to craft a mission statement and goals that include social justice rhetoric.

However lofty and high-minded its goals, an organization that fails to replicate its social justice rhetoric in its daily practice will often succumb to the persistent fiscal, political, and cultural pressures of the external environment and become a social justice organization in name only. To help avoid this inevitable problem, we have identified seven essential features of a socially just organization:

1. The structure and goals of the organization are compatible in substance (not merely in rhetoric) with the organization's stated mission and vision.
2. The organization maintains genuinely democratic decision-making processes that involve staff, clients, and constituents at all levels. This is particularly important in decisions about resource allocation and the overall strategic direction of the organization.
3. The allocation of scarce resources prioritizes the needs of the least advantaged.
4. The organization engages in ongoing efforts to develop the *critical consciousness* of its staff, clients, and constituents. This requires ongoing dialogue to enhance the breadth and depth of their awareness of the relationship between the organization and the political–economic and cultural environment in which it operates.
5. Intra- and interorganizational relationships reflect mutual respect and cultural humility.
6. The organization's culture and climate reflect social justice principles in its language, means of communications, and methods of dealing with conflict.
7. The organization uses technology as a means to enhance social justice rather than to sustain existing hierarchies and inequalities (Poole, Ferguson, DiNitto, & Schwab, 2002).

The importance of prioritizing social justice concepts in the formulation of organizational models cannot be understated. As Dover (2009) argues, an emphasis on social justice reflects awareness of both our common humanity and the range of human needs. As US society becomes increasingly diverse, it also provides a critical lens to "[examine] the interplay between race and service provision" and address the need to redistribute power and resources through both activism and service delivery (Alston, Harley, & Middleton, 2006, p. 129). A focus on social justice, which emphasizes the social, economic, and political roots of most contemporary problems, can also inspire the creation of alternatives to entrenched structural and institutional patterns and practices (Bell & Desai, 2011; Goddard & Myers, 2013).

Organizational Models

The most common organizational form, which predominates even among social justice-oriented organizations, is a hierarchical model that reflects the bureaucratic principles first described by Weber (2009). Such organizations are characterized by a strict division of labor, clearly established lines of authority, high specialization of function, formally recognized leaders, rule-driven behavior, highly routinized procedures, and top-down patterns of goal-setting and decision-making. Although some of these qualities are frequently necessitated by the size, complexity, geographic scope, and range of the organization's interests and activities, they also reflect the difficulty of escaping from the values of the dominant culture into which we are all socialized from birth. The contradiction this creates between an organization's espoused social justice values and the ways in which it operates on a daily basis is acutely felt over time. It can lead to high staff turnover and disillusionment with the organization's mission, contentious relationships between staff and administration and among staff, diminished standing in the public's eye, and a general decline in the organization's ability to achieve its stated goals.

Three potential risks are especially worth noting for social justice organizations. One is the danger of "founder's syndrome"—that is, the organization increasingly becomes defined by the leader or leaders who established it. This creates a quasi "cult of personality" in which the organization's mission, goals, and strategies are overidentified with the ambitions and personal qualities of its leadership. Their issues and conflicts with rivals or opponents often become the organization's issues; this distorts the organization's focus, strategic planning, external relationships, and public image. Thus, although the presence of a strong, long-standing leader provides stability, it may also restrict the participation of other staff in organizational decision-making and strategy development (English & Peters, 2011).

A related risk within hierarchically structured organizations is best expressed by Michels's (1915) "iron law of oligarchy": A small group of staff leaders or on the organization's board of directors dominates all decision-making. This oligarchy often develops over time, based on personal relationships, access to power and resources, and/or ideological compatibility. It excludes most staff and all clients and constituents from the process of establishing organizational goals and evaluating the organization's work. Ironically, organizations in which this occurs replicate the very qualities and values that their missions profess to oppose.

Third, there is the danger that even well-intentioned social justice-oriented organizations will engage in practices that contradict their goals because of their failure to integrate service users or constituents into their decision-making processes. Bowes and Sim (2006) note, for example, that advocacy for social justice is itself a contested concept and that service providers who advocate on behalf of marginalized groups rarely integrate the ideas of service users about advocacy into their practice. This problem has been reinforced by the impact of neoliberal values, which emphasize individual uplift rather than communal responsibility, on the structure, goals, funding, and personnel practices of nonprofit and public-sector organizations (Goode, 2006; Lacey & Ilcan, 2006). As a result, in many organizations, "collective interactions and understandings have been replaced by hierarchical ascriptions of differential worth, largely based on criteria of race, class, and gender" (Goode, 2006, p. 203).

Strolovitch (2006) found that despite their commitment to social justice, many organizations "are substantially less active when it comes to issues affecting disadvantaged subgroups than they are when it comes to issues affecting more advantaged subgroups" because these organizations frame the problems of excluded groups as "narrow and particularistic ... while framing issues affecting advantaged subgroups as if they ... have a broad and generalized impact" (p. 894). However, without efforts to produce "structural changes in organizations and greater participation of people of color [and other marginalized groups] in the governance of the agency, efforts toward change can be mostly symbolic and marginal" (Gutierrez, Nagda, Raffoul, & McNeece, 1996, p. 203).

A variety of social justice organizations have attempted to address these problems through the use of alternative organizational models. These holistic models focus on the transformative role of social justice practice by building responsive infrastructures; making their organizations more culturally accessible; and emphasizing the expansion of community members' voice, agency, and role in educating practitioners (National Gender and Equity Campaign, 2009). One alternative model that some social justice organizations have adopted emphasizes the values of collegiality and mutuality. Its most common form is the cooperative. In such organizations, there is little or no hierarchy, and there are either no formally recognized leaders or a rotation of leadership responsibilities. Work tasks are shared or work roles are constantly changed, and decisions are made collectively or by consensus. This model tends to work better in smaller, more homogeneous organizations that focus on a single issue or service, such as a babysitting or food co-op, a self-help group, or a mutual aid society. The model becomes more difficult to sustain in its original, pristine form as the organization takes on new, more complex programs and adds new members, particularly if these new members come from diverse backgrounds and may not share the same goals as those of the organization's founders.

Two examples of this phenomenon are the Mondragon cooperatives in the Basque region of Spain and the *mutualistas* established by Latinos in the southwestern United States during the 19th and 20th centuries (Hernandez, 1983; Kasmir, 1996; Rivera, 1987). Although both were originally small-scale organizations, they soon added new activities that made it more difficult to sustain a pure cooperative model. Consequently, they took on the characteristics of a "hybrid" organization, which included some bureaucratic qualities. Some individuals were given the authority to manage the organization's funds and its membership, and increased specialization or differentiation of function emerged. They balanced this trend toward hierarchy, however, by establishing and maintaining multiple centers of power, a dispersed authority structure, and a greater degree of staff discretion over their activities.

Another model, the "pancake" model or collective structure, carries the principles of a cooperative even further. Such organizations disdain any hierarchy in their structure or decision-making processes. There are no formally recognized leaders, and all decisions are made by consensus. (They may differ, however, in how "consensus" is defined. In some organizations, consensus is equated with unanimity; others establish different rules for determining agreement.) Like many cooperatives, in such organizations work roles rotate and no division of labor exists. This model is often associated with "feminist process" and, in fact, emerged from the feminist movement during the 1960s and 1970s. It was later adopted in whole or in part by environmental justice and peace organizations, and anti-nuclear groups (Dominelli, 2012). One advantage of this model is that it empowers staff and members through its collective conception of leadership. It tends to be more effective in smaller organizations and within organizations that possess a high degree of demographic and ideological homogeneity. It also requires extensive and ongoing intragroup communication, which may be more difficult in diverse organizations.

Even within the most democratically designed and egalitarian organizations, however, there are times when decisions need to be made quickly, when it is impossible to consult with all stakeholders, or when a consensus model of decision-making is not possible because of intractable conflicts within the organization. To acknowledge this possibility, an organization should establish—in advance—a process of determining who has the authority to resolve such conflicts and act on behalf of the organization when such situations arise.

Socially Just Leadership

Similar to traditional models of organizational structure, traditional views of organizational leadership, even in many organizations with social justice goals, are often "top-down" and exclusionary. Particularly in organizations with long-serving leaders, leadership ability is often equated with a person's charisma or vision of the organization's purpose. Despite the best of intentions, this creates a formal and informal division within the organization and between the organization and the people it purports to serve.

The literature on organizational development implicitly accepts this dichotomy. It tends to focus on such questions as Who becomes a leader and what are appropriate leadership styles? It tends to ascribe change to the actions of individuals (the so-called "great man/woman" theory of history) and ignores the relationships between context and culture and the emergence of leaders in a community or organization. Consequently, this perspective reproduces elite views of leadership and maintains hierarchical organizational structures and decision-making processes.

An alternate view of leadership recognizes that different leadership styles and roles emerge and are best suited for the different situations that arise within organizations and communities. One leadership style, directive–authoritative, most closely conforms to traditional views of leadership (Mann, 1959). This type of leader regulates activities, distributes resources, resolves conflicts, determines rules, and decides who is in/out of key positions. Ideally, these leaders also possess such characteristics as honesty and integrity, self-confidence, cognitive ability, and knowledge of the field (Kirkpatrick & Locke, 1991).

Another type of leader gives aid, protection, information, attention, affection, guidance, and support to staff. This type of leadership is generally more informal; it is frequently based on experience and expertise. Such leaders play a mentoring role to other staff or constituents and encourage an organizational culture that reflects an open exchange of ideas and opinions, cultural humility, and a learning environment. These "transformational leaders" try to inspire and stimulate their colleagues and people in the community with whom they work.

A third type of leader also plays a more social and empowering role. These leaders encourage innovation and creativity among their colleagues; defer to their knowledge and experience; and promote the integration of diverse ideas into the organization's goals, objectives, strategic direction, and programs. These leaders possess qualities such as determination, sociability, humility, and will (Johnson, 2005). Dierendonck (2011) argues that such leaders "combine their motivation to lead with a need to serve." This "servant leadership is demonstrated by empowering and developing people, by expressing humility, authenticity, interpersonal acceptance, and stewardship, and by providing direction" (p. 1228).

The implications of this revised view of leadership are important for the creation and maintenance of socially just organizations. It assumes that in a given situation, anyone can become a leader and that in different cultures leadership takes different forms. This recognition is critical if organizations are to resist the temptation to succumb to dominant cultural conceptions of leadership that reproduce hierarchical structures and processes and maintain a status quo that excludes many people from assuming leadership positions.

In addition, this view of leadership defines it not as an inborn attribute but, rather, as a behavior—in other words, as a relationship between a person and a specific situation. Such relationships can change over time; therefore, the assessment of a given situation is critical in determining who might be the best leader under a particular set of circumstances. This leads to a dynamic and adaptive rather than a fixed view of leadership (Thomas, Fann Thomas, & Schaubhut, 2008).

It is particularly important to pay attention to leadership development in organizations that ascribe to social justice goals because, as discussed previously, these high-minded goals often mask socially unjust or incompetent management practices. Braxton (2010) states,

> When organizations do not attend to social justice issues in a meaning-ful way, a pattern of covert practices and behavior distorts the concern for fairness, equity and inclusion to one of indifference, power and control. Ineffective leadership results in wounded staff and organizational dysfunction. Social justice in organizational life is a function of how well leaders and managers master six domains that influence and sustain institutional balance and self-regulation: safety and trust; boundaries and differences; accountability; communication; hierarchical power; and task and role clarity. Ultimately, leaders must do their own inner work by taking responsibility for their part in institutionalizing oppression in their organizations, as well as the outer work of creating processes and structures that implement solutions to social justice issues within their organizations. (p. 89)

As in all forms of social work practice, effective leadership in socially just organizations requires attention to *praxis*—that is, to a dynamic synthesis of reflection and action—and the capacity to engage in both concurrently. It also involves a multidimensional conception of leadership that includes personal qualities; interpersonal skills; and communal, systemic, and ecological perspectives (Furman, 2012). This type of transformative leadership "critiques inequitable practices, and addresses both individual and public good" (Shields, 2010, p. 558).

Particularly in today's rapidly changing social and cultural environment, socially just leadership also implies multicultural competence (Arredondo & Perez, 2003), "a commitment to acknowledge and embrace difference" (Pazey & Cole, 2013, p. 243), and a conscious linkage of one's professional work with advocacy and social and political action (Jean-Marie, 2006; Mosley, 2013; Simon,

2006). Socially just leaders "make issues of race, class, gender, disability, sexual orientation, and other historically marginalizing factors central to their advocacy, leadership practice, and vision" (Theoharis, 2007, p. 221). They strive to create strong relationships both within their organizations and across boundaries with other groups, focusing on interdependence and democratic participation (Foldy & Ospina, 2010).

Socially just organizations also recognize that leadership attributes are not restricted to a certain demographic or personality type. Instead, their practices reflect the belief that leaders can be developed through training, work, and experience; that leadership skills combine interpersonal, political, analytical, and motivational qualities; and that there is a clear distinction between an individual leader and individual or collective leadership behavior (Alban-Metcalfe & Alimo-Metcalfe, 2009). This situational view of leadership emphasizes the importance of context and history.

Embracing these alternative views of leadership is particularly important in the social work field because of the unique gender demographics of the profession. Researchers have found that women, who dominate the social work profession but not necessarily its leadership positions, tend to be more transformational and engage in more contingent reward behaviors (Eagly & Carli, 2003), teamwork, and consensus-building (Cheung & Halpern, 2010). They are more likely to use democratic decision-making and consultative styles and to possess relationship-oriented skills. Their effectiveness as leaders often depends on the domain; they have greater ability to adapt their personal qualities and values to the needs of the organization. As discussed previously, all of these qualities are critical attributes of socially just leadership.

Another reason to adopt a revised conception of leadership is to promote greater involvement of youth in social justice work. Many social justice organizations do not pay sufficient attention to cultivating the next generation of social justice leaders (Kim, 2006). Those that do, such as the Youth Leadership Institute, combine "inside" and "outside" approaches "to educate, inform, and partner" with existing systems and community groups in order to "build an infrastructure that supports inclusive youth participation and leadership and create tools for them to make the process work" (Libby, Sedonaen, & Bliss, 2006, p. 13).

A more socially just conception of organizational leadership is also required as social work practice in the United States adopts an increased international focus. Although a relatively recent study (House, Hanges, Javidan, Dorfman, & Gupta, 2008) identified six types of leadership behaviors worldwide, only half of them—team-oriented leadership, participative leadership, and humane-oriented leadership—are compatible with social justice principles. Other desirable leadership traits reflected both traditional and modern concepts, including trustworthiness, fairness, and honesty; optimism; dynamism; confidence; foresight; motivation; dependability; intelligence; decisiveness; and skills in communication, administration, planning, team-building, problem-solving, and coordination.

In addition, leadership in socially just organizations is defined as the ability to create positive change in the absence of a crisis that is consistent with organizational values and vision. Socially just organizations believe that, depending on the context and with proper training, every person can become a leader. Leaders, therefore, emerge out of a particular context; they respond to and stimulate dissatisfaction with an unjust status quo and point the organization on a new path. They generate excitement, speak "truth to power," contribute to the strategic direction of the organization, emphasize the strengths of people with whom they work, and acknowledge the contributions of others freely and generously. Finally, socially just organizations believe that "leadership" is a collective as well as an individual attribute and establish decision-making structures that are genuinely democratic, egalitarian, and participatory.

How, then, can social workers become effective leaders or work effectively with their organization's leaders to promote social justice? The following are some "prescriptions for leadership":

1. Know yourself and know the situation, both the broader context of the organization and its mission and the specific, immediate circumstances in which you are engaged.
2. Particularly in contentious situations, be aware of what people say and do not say. Notice who listens when someone speaks and where people sit.
3. Distinguish facts and the subjective feelings that they produce. In conflict-driven situations, be aware of how and when things were said, by whom, and what was said.
4. Know the position of leaders in a particular setting—assess how their behavior reflects or does not reflect the organization's values.
5. Select the setting in which you engage with others carefully. Make it comfortable (for allies and constituents) or uncomfortable (for opponents), depending on circumstances.
6. Be aware of your personal biases—not merely about major issues such as racism but also about moral issues and questions of lifestyle, dress, formality/informality, and personal appearance. Make a conscious effort to acknowledge and address your prejudices.
7. Set realistic objectives for yourself and your organization or project, and derive satisfaction from limited accomplishments.

8. In conflict-ridden situations or disputes, focus on concrete, specific issues, not on abstractions. People can understand the meaning of social justice when the concept is clearly connected to their daily lives and experiences.

9. Speak language that is natural and understandable, particularly in situations in which you are working with diverse individuals and groups. Tailor your message but not your personal style to the group. In other words, always be yourself.

Engagement: Creating a Socially Just Organizational Culture

Socially just organizations are characterized not merely by their goals, decision-making structure, and patterns of leadership but also by the subtle features that comprise the three layers of their overall culture (Schein, 2010). Like communities and societies, these organizations develop cultural norms and patterns that evolve over time that both reflect and reinforce the values, beliefs, assumptions, and expectations of staff and board members and shape organizational behavior in diverse ways.

The surface layer consists of a wide range of organizational artifacts that are visible to most observers but may not always be decipherable. These include the organization's printed and web-based materials, the configuration of its physical space, and the distribution of staff roles. The middle layer consists of the organization's stated and unstated values; recognizing these values requires a greater level of awareness. Analyzing the organization's mission statement and philosophy and its established priorities in the distribution of scarce resources can provide some insights into these underlying values. The deepest layer of the organization's culture is composed of its basic assumptions, its precepts, which are invisible, rarely stated, and taken for granted, particularly by long-term staff. It is difficult for new staff and especially for service users or outside observers to unearth or understand this layer of an organization's culture.

Whether explicit or implied, an organization's culture is a powerful force in determining its general direction, program priorities, and the nature of the services it provides. An organization's culture can be a strong and empowering foundation for its social justice work, or it can be a negative force—an obstacle to its stated goals. In times of crisis, an organization's culture can be in conflict. For example, external stresses (funding cuts, political attacks, and a decline in public support) or internal strains (factional disputes, difficult leadership transitions, and competition among staff or programs) can produce serious disagreements about the mission and goals of an organization or how these goals are translated into practice. Examples of this effect include schisms within the HIV/AIDS and homelessness service networks and disputes within the feminist, LGBTQ, and civil rights movements.

Short-term changes in the external environment—for example, temporary funding cuts or the emergence of new issues among organizational constituents—will not necessarily alter the culture of an organization. Nor will internal shifts in the organizational climate, such as leadership changes, significantly affect its culture. In most circumstances, the organizational culture will, in the short term, interpret and accommodate to these changes in a manner consistent with its long-standing values and norms. If, however, these new circumstances become permanent, or if new, acute problems become chronic, they can effect lasting transformation in an organization's culture.

An organization's culture is therefore, a self-perpetuating phenomenon. Its permanence and all-pervasive nature give it power. It demonstrates this power in the preselection and hiring of staff; the socialization of new members (e.g., staff orientation); its sanctioned patterns of behavior, along with justifications for that behavior (e.g., through staff development and training); the removal of deviants (staff evaluation), sometimes through the use of direct and indirect intimidation rituals; and the reinforcement of cultural norms through its communication style, symbolic actions, and reward systems (Schein, 1981).

In their cultures, socially just organizations reflect organizational pluralism; that is, they are organizations in which staff with distinct differences work side by side as equals. They are willing to affirm each other's dignity, benefit from each other's experience, and acknowledge each other's contributions to common goals. Such organizations also tend to reflect a closer demographic and cultural "match" between their clients and constituents and paid or volunteer staff. They are often more innovative than homogeneous organizations; encourage diverse perspectives; create more opportunities for staff to grow, learn, and be more productive; and respond to the needs of different stakeholders. To move an established organization in this direction, it is useful to conduct periodic "cultural audits"—through the use of focus groups, attitude surveys, and one-on-one interviews with staff, clients, and constituents—that identify policies and practices that are discriminatory or dysfunctional, as well as those that contradict the organization's stated mission and goals. This also requires organizations to initiate a regular review of printed and online materials to ensure they are cultural sensitive and appropriate.

Although not all diverse organizations are socially just, we believe that diversity is an essential component of a socially just organization. In such organizations, the leadership—whether individual or collective—actively promotes the value of diversity. It creates a work environment that respects and values all members of the organization and makes a deliberate effort to correct biased or culturally inappropriate behaviors. The organization recruits, retains, and promotes "nontraditional" employees and ensures that all staff become cultural competent. The organization provides all employees, regardless of race, gender, age, disability, or sexual orientation, with opportunities to advance; consciously strives to tap their creative potential; and actively values teamwork and collaboration. Although few organizations have accomplished each of these objectives, they provide a model toward which social workers can strive.

The Racial Equity Institute has identified four levels of diversity awareness in organizations:

- Level 1: Token employment opportunity organization—In such organizations, there is limited racial or gender diversity, and women and persons of color are often hired and "showcased" solely to enhance the organization's public image.
- Level 2: Affirmative action organization—These organizations are more diverse primarily because they have instituted personnel policies that comply with federal affirmative action guidelines. However, they do not necessarily have more women or minorities of color in key leadership positions or recognize the distinct contributions and perspectives these individuals can make to the organization.
- Level 3: Self-renewing organization—In this type of organization, the value of diversity has been sufficiently embedded in its culture that it no longer has to depend on affirmative action guidelines in its hiring, retention, or promotion policies.
- Level 4: Pluralistic organization—A pluralistic organization goes beyond the previous level by thoroughly integrating not merely diverse individuals but also diverse perspectives into its mission, goals, and day-to-day functioning. An example of this is the model that the National Association of Social Workers proposed to move its organization and the entire social work profession closer to racial equity.

The transformation from a level 1 to a level 4 organization often occurs in three stages that can simplified as (1) "Talking the talk," (2) "Thinking the talk," and (3) "Walking the talk." It includes conscious efforts to overcome the consequences of privilege within the organization and the development of strategies for dealing with intra- and interorganizational conflict, including training in how to use conflict constructively (Goode, 2006).

In the first stage, the organization's leaders embrace the goals of diversity, express a willingness to change the organization's policies and procedures, and commit necessary resources to initiate these changes. In the second stage, they make a conscious effort to connect these goals to the social justice mission and vision of the organization and to its culture, policies, and procedures. They conduct "cultural audits," establish a set of organizational priorities toward this goal, and develop critical consciousness-raising educational and training programs for all staff. In the final stage, the leaders implement changes suggested by the cultural audit, maintain an ongoing dialogue with all stakeholders as the change process unfolds, and with full staff participation develop plans for ongoing monitoring and improvement of the organization.

Even individuals who are not in leadership positions can make important contributions to such efforts. They can respect the opinions of all coworkers, clients, and constituents regardless of their background, particularly those with which they differ. They cooperate willingly with diverse individuals and groups. This requires that all staff become aware that each member is a product of his or her background and that there is no single "right" way to accomplish an organization's goals and objectives. Ongoing training, cultural awareness programs, and the promotion of intraorganizational dialogue are useful tools to achieve these goals.

Communication

An obvious way in which an organization's commitment to social justice is expressed is in its communication patterns. As organizations become more diverse, reconciling cultural differences in communication becomes both more important and more difficult. The following list presents ways in which communication differences are expressed and how socially just organizations might respond:

> *Conventions for interpersonal interaction*: These include how people express intense emotions, including anger, frustration, and dissatisfaction. An important example is in the phasing of conversations—that is, determining when certain topics may be discussed and ensuring that no one dominates discussions. Some cultures, particularly in the West, get right down to "business," whereas others require some prior informal social interaction, such as asking about a colleague's health or family. The key here is to pose the right questions and listen carefully to coworkers and service users in order to understand the underlying cultural values behind what they are communicating and how. Socially just organizations should offer options to service users and staff to avoid prescribing a "one-size-fits-all" model of communication. They also establish "rules" at meetings to ensure more equitable participation.

Sequencing of ideas: At meetings, for example, some people present their ideas in a linear manner (A to B to C), whereas others express themselves with interjections that, to a linear thinker, can appear tangential. A socially just organization is sensitive to these different styles; it educates staff to respect diverse ways of thinking and expression and to not interrupt colleagues.

Objectivity and specificity: Some cultures value precision in speech; that is, a person states his or her ideas with specific examples. Others place greater value on ambiguity and state ideas more generally, sometimes in order to demonstrate deference to superiors or to avoid confrontation. Conversely, some cultures prefer argumentation that is impersonal ("fact-driven" or "rational"), which focuses on the substance of issues; others are more "emotional;" they focus on the underlying values of issues, and place greater emphasis on presentation style. The latter may communicate ideas through personal narratives or symbol-laden stories. In recognition of these differences, socially just organizations should promote cultural humility among staff in all aspects of their interpersonal practice.

Assertiveness and candor: Similarly, there are significant differences between cultures that place high value on such qualities as inquisitiveness, outspokenness, and candor and those that value silence, courtesy, and deference to authority. It is important to note that both patterns of communication are honest but express meaning, opinions, and disagreement in different ways.

Use of technology: The growing use of digital technology has the potential to exacerbate the cultural divide between cultures that value intimate, personal contact and those that are more tolerant of distant, impersonal contact. Even the latter group recognizes the potential problems created by technology in such mundane matters as using or interpreting gestures and vocal expressions and expressing or reading people's emotions. As discussed later, the key here is to use media strategically, to recognize that different media have different effects on the substance and interpretation of communication, and to develop safeguards to ensure confidentiality.

Use of criticism: This is a particularly sensitive topic for socially just organizations, which aspire to cultural diversity and cultural competence but want to maintain both service quality and a safe, supportive environment. Sometimes, well-intentioned organizations create environments in which staff are so fearful of offending colleagues of different cultures, even through constructive criticism (e.g., in performance evaluations), that they forego such critical processes or convert them into token rituals. The lack of constructive evaluations, however, can lead to the literal or figurative withdrawal of workers from the organization by failing to address ongoing staff issues. It uses the rationale of cultural sensitivity to cover up the organization's reluctance to address problems with staff behavior and may become a form of the biases it opposes. Ironically, this often exacerbates intraorganizational tensions along cultural lines.

In summary, effective cross-cultural communication in organizations involves the establishment and enforcement of both prescriptive and proscriptive behaviors. Socially just organizations make conscious efforts to expand their formal and informal networks to include representatives from different cultures. They actively promote—through staff training and ongoing dialogue—respect for different communication styles, and they teach staff positive ways to communicate with and influence people different from themselves, whether colleagues, constituents, or clients. On the other hand, they avoid using language in both formal and informal communication that reinforces stereotypes or generalizes individual behaviors, attitudes, or beliefs to an entire group. In such organizations, all staff members, particularly supervisors, exhibit zero tolerance for derogatory comments or behaviors.

Planning: Power and Empowerment in Socially Just Organizations

The acquisition and effective use of power is a principal goal of social justice organizations, whether to produce structural and policy changes, obtain additional resources, or create more culturally responsive services. An organization's power often reflects the quantity and intensity of support it receives from both inside

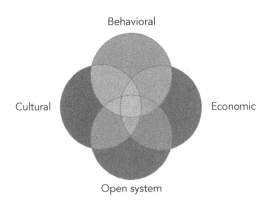

FIGURE 7.2   Organizational Functioning Theoretical Perspectives

and outside the organization (Figure 7.2). Its structure and culture are critical determinants of the nature and degree of power it possesses (Mondros & Wilson, 1994).

Power can "provide the social energy that transforms the insights of individuals and groups into the institutions of an organization" (Dyck, Kleysen, Lawrence, & Mauws, 2005, p. 180). This transformation is a consequence of specific learning processes within the organization. Understanding the different forms of power that exist within organizations can provide insights into why some changes become institutionalized and others do not. Power also determines the ability of organizations to innovate—a critical quality particularly in tumultuous times. Conversely, imbalances of power within organizations can lead to what Dover and Lawrence (2012) call "four innovation pathologies": "nothing happens," "nothing changes," "nothing scales" (expands beyond a pilot), or "nothing adapts" (p. 991).

At the structural level, power dynamics influence both intraorganizational processes and an organization's external relationships. A socially just organization recognizes the role of power inequities in creating personal and social problems and in limiting the opportunity to address them. It also acknowledges the subjective impact of power—the distinction between having power and being empowered, or believing in one's ability to effect personal or social change.

Because empowerment is an oft-used and oft-misused term in social work literature, it is useful to clarify how we are employing the concept here. We regard empowerment as "the process of increasing personal, interpersonal, or political power so that individuals, families, and communities can take action to improve their situations" (Gutierrez, GlenMaye, & DeLois, 1995, p. 249). It occurs on both personal and collective levels and synthesizes political–economic and psychosocial factors (Solomon, 1976). It is important to recognize, however, that social workers cannot give people power. They can, through respectful dialogue (Freire, 1970) and recognition of the mutuality between workers and clients, facilitate "a process capable of being initiated and sustained only by the agent or subject who seeks power or self-determination" (Simon, 1994, p. 4).

For example, socially just organizations can provide clients and constituents with information, skills, and support. They can involve them in all phases of problem definition, strategic planning, and evaluation. This includes recognizing that clients and constituents "own" their issues, using a problem or question-posing approach, and involving people in analyzing issues and making programmatic or policy recommendations to address them. Organizations can promote such activities by formally sanctioning decentralized problem-solving, promoting collaborative community-based action research, and including service users and community members in critical decision-making as more than symbolic tokens.

Several factors affect the ability of organizations to obtain power or use it for social justice purposes. External factors include the demands and expectations of funders or policymakers, the characteristics of the populations the organization serves or represents, the type of services it provides or the nature of the issues around which it advocates, and the community's attitudes toward the organization's values and goals. Internal factors include the organization's decision-making structure and culture, the nature of tasks assigned to staff and the degree of worker autonomy, the quality of supervisory relationships (the extent of encouragement and support), the quantity and quality of the organization's resources, and the organization's commitment to its workers as reflected in its personnel policies and practices.

Cohen and Austin (1997) maintain that empowering staff requires that worker participation in decision-making be built into the organizational structure, formally sanctioned by the organization's leaders and culture, and integrated into each worker's role as part of his or her job description. Leaders can contribute to such processes by promoting a hopeful climate within the organization that acknowledges people's common interests and common risk taking, by developing and recognizing (formally and informally) the strengths of staff, and by mentoring and modeling the attitudes and behaviors that reflect organizational values and goals.

Implementation: Addressing Conflict in Social Justice Organizations

Conflict is an ever-present feature of organizational life, particularly in times of resource scarcity and heightened tensions as communities and society become increasingly diverse (Jackson, 2006). Organizations frequently mirror the conflicts that occur in their external environments (Allyn, 2011). Staff members often believe that they are victims of distributive injustices comparable to those experienced by their clients or constituents, leading to increased turnover and intraorganizational turmoil (Soltis, Agneessens, Sasovova, & Labianca, 2013). Ironically, many social workers and social work students are uncomfortable with conflict. In part, this reflects the influence of a systems model of practice, which emphasizes the importance of balance and continuity. It may also be due to discomfort addressing the implications of racial, class, gender, or sexual privilege (Nenga, 2014).

In systems theory, conflict involves a disruption of the social equilibrium (dynamic homeostasis) and needs to be prevented or controlled. It is largely viewed in negative terms; it is considered a disruptive force within or between organizations, or even a threat to the social order (Coser, 1956). A modified version of this perspective—referred to as the ecological approach to practice (Pardeck, 1996)—regards organizational conflict as the consequence of competition among multiple stakeholders for resources, status, and influence. Within this pluralistic environment, conflict is resolved through compromise in which each side sacrifices some of what it desires.

A conflict perspective on practice, however, is more consistent with a social justice approach to practice because it regards the status quo as reflecting one group's dominance over others. From this perspective, conflict is regarded as a natural, recurring, dynamic, and inevitable phenomenon. It is the foundation of social relations and a condition to be accepted, even encouraged, not eliminated or suppressed, in order to initiate change. Within and between organizations, conflict frequently results from the presence of dominant and subdominant unequal entities in constant competition for finite resources and power. Social justice organizations, however, consistently challenge and seek to alter such inequalities.

Conflict theorists (Alinsky, 1971; Coser, 1956) identify two different types of conflict. *Conventional* or *normative conflict* is handled within established and generally accepted rules and procedures. Examples include elections and athletic events. This type of conflict is controlled and produces incremental change, such as a shift in which political party controls a legislative body or the White House. Within organizations, such conflict may result in the selection of new officers for the board of directors. Although this type of competition may arouse strong emotions and occasionally be boisterous, its overall effect is to channel discontent and rivalries within well-established boundaries and maintain the status quo.

By contrast, *rancorous conflict* occurs outside accepted behavioral norms and is disruptive of the status quo. It takes many forms; the most extreme and rarest versions include violence. Nonviolent conflict, however, has enormous potential value in social work practice, particularly when used strategically. It can increase the energy level of a group and add depth and passion to staff discussions. It can encourage people to challenge long-standing ideas and assumptions, and it can produce deeper understanding of issues, more creative solutions to persistent problems, and more effective collaboration. It can provide an outlet for frustrations and prevent more serious future conflicts from erupting. In summary, conflict is sometimes a necessary tool to pursue social justice goals, both inside and outside the organization.

Nevertheless, there are risks involved if conflict is not properly employed. Without effective, strategic leadership, conflict can polarize existing relations within or between organizations. It can produce more rigid group divisions, even factions, in a program or organization, particularly those with potential splits along racial, gender, class, or religious lines (Marbley, Bonner, Wimberly, Stevens, & Tatem, 2006). The strategic use of conflict, however, can facilitate the emergence of new leaders, promote more sustainable mobilization (especially in interorganizational work), and lead to more effective intra- and interorganizational communication. It can also help overcome the barriers to creating antiracist responses within organizations (Blitz & Kohl, 2012). Such efforts need to be tailored to the organization's specific history and context (Chen, 2014).

Using Conflict as a Problem-Solving Tool

Effective communication is critical to the use of conflict as a tool to solve organizational problems. In group situations, practitioners should state their views in clear, nonjudgmental language that does not personalize issues or attack those with different views. If emotions run out, call a brief "time out." As in clinical practice, it is important to listen carefully to each person's views and try to assess his or her underlying assumptions, interests, and motivations and create the possibility of a "win–win" situation (Boyd, Gupta, & Kuzmits, 2011; Gupta, Boyd, & Kuzmits, 2011). This is another example of the importance of reflexive practice (Keevers, Sykes, & Treleaven, 2006).

Intergroup dialogue (see Chapter 6) can be an effective bridging mechanism that enables conflict-ridden situations to be transformed into opportunities to pursue social justice goals (Dessel, Rogger, & Garlington, 2006). Through periodic clarification, identify areas of agreement and disagreement and be flexible when possible. It is possible to preserve one's principles without getting "locked into" a position. The goal is to establish and expand the "common ground" among competing groups, in some cases by emphasizing their mutual commitment to social justice and the organization's goals (Olkkonen & Lipponen, 2006), not merely to enhance staff's multicultural competence (Parker, 2008; Speight & Vera, 2003).

Socially Just Resource Allocation

A persistent problem within organizations often involves how to distribute scarce resources, both tangible and intangible, effectively, ethically, and consistent with social justice principles. These dilemmas appear in three forms: At the personal level, they involve the just use of self; the role conflicts experienced by many staff, particularly those in high-intensity, low-resource social justice-oriented organizations; and the need to avoid burnout through self-care. At the organizational level, they involve decisions regarding the allocation of resources to different programs or initiatives, the distribution of staff workloads, and the structure of personnel benefits and organizational rewards. At the societal level, they require social justice organizations to address the political, economic, and ideological factors that produce inequalities and injustice, including but not limited to those

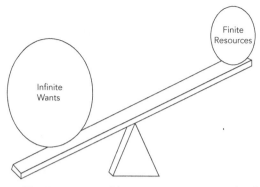

FIGURE 7.3   The Economic Problem: Finite Resources and Infinite Wants

that affect their clients and constituents. Even in optimum circumstances, these dilemmas will persist for the reasons shown in Figure 7.3—resources are always finite and needs are potentially infinite.

At each level, there are a variety of ways to distribute resources equitably, including the following:

- Providing equal shares and creating equal access to such "goods"
- Distributing resources on the basis of compensation for past or current "wrongs" or on the basis of past, current, or potential future contributions to society
- Distributing resources on the basis of ability to pay or merit, however defined, or on the basis of one's ability to take advantage of the service or benefit
- Distributing resources based on principles of equity or fairness

Each approach reflects a different definition of social justice and presents different challenges for organizational decision-making (Reisch, 2002).

Dealing with Organizational Change

Another challenge that all organizations must address is how to deal with purposive (i.e., intentional) change, whether it is change resulting from voluntary internal initiatives or external compulsion. These changes could include program innovations, such as the creation of a new service or the revision of an existing service that reflects the introduction of new ideas about problem causation or problem resolution. They could also emerge from a desire to revise the organization's structure or major policies or to alter the organization's culture (its values, attitudes, expectations, behaviors, or rituals) based on ideas proposed by clients, constituents, or new staff. The integration of new technology is itself a form of change that, in turn, can produce other major changes, both positive and negative, on the nature of the organization's work, the skills required to do this work effectively, and the organization's fundamental values.

Purposive change efforts can also reflect a response to changing social conditions or a new form of need among clients or constituents. They could be a consequence of external factors, such as changes in the organization's funding sources or client population, the general political climate, or the public's perception of the organization's effectiveness or efficiency. Regardless of the source, significant organizational change disrupts the organization's culture and often produces increased stress and resistance because it represents a discontinuity from the status quo (Lewin, 1948). Through the use of the qualities outlined previously, leaders of social justice organizations must prepare carefully for the implementation of planned change and demonstrate consistent energy and commitment, both to the change and to its relevance to the social justice values of the organization, in order for the change to be implemented successfully and become part of the organization's institutional fabric. To do so, leaders need to find a way to balance the rational/analytic and political/emotional components of the change process.

The following are some of the issues that organizational leaders need to consider:

- Is the change incremental or does it require a qualitative transformation of the organization?
- How much new learning is required of staff?
- Does the change affect the entire organization or only part of the organization?
- Is the change immediate or long term?
- Who are the targets of change?
- Who will be the change agents, leaders, and supporters? What will be their roles?
- What are the costs of change, in both material (dollars) and nonmaterial terms (e.g., social capital, political influence, and status)?
- What is the organization's history regarding the implementation of change?
- From where is the pressure for change coming?
- What changes are already underway? Will an additional change produce unbearable strain on the organization?
- Should change be stimulated or accelerated?
- What values should guide the change process?
- What are the risks/rewards of change and the use of particular change strategies?

- For whom are the changes beneficial?
- For whom are the changes detrimental?

Barriers to change frequently include management's excessive focus on the fiscal costs to the organization rather than the social costs to clients, constituents, or staff. Staff often fail to perceive the benefits of change due to a fear of uncertainty or loss (of power, role, status, or comfortable routine) or principled opposition to the imposition of top-down change. The use of socially just processes can be critical in overcoming this resistance. Organizational leaders play a crucial role throughout the change process, not merely at the outset. They should identify the need for change before the change process is initiated or even planned. They should anticipate the types of resistance that might arise and develop a plan to address or prevent it in whatever form it may take. One way to reduce resistance is to design the implementation of change in small increments and engage all stakeholders in ongoing assessment of the change process. Clear and consistent communication is also critical if democratic changes are to be implemented. In addition, whatever the external pressure, organizational innovations should reflect organizational needs and not merely respond to the latest trend.

Using Technology in a Socially Just Way

There is growing awareness that the current distribution and use of technology are major factors in sustaining or eradicating unjust social structures and institutions (Ottinger, 2011). Technology, however, is neutral; it can both inhibit and facilitate justice-oriented change. Digital communication and social media, for example, have become increasingly important elements of the practice of social justice organizations throughout the world during the 21st century. They have altered the internal dynamics of existing organizations, the ways in which established organizations relate to each other and to emerging networks and social formations, and changed the nature of social justice activities (Bennett & Segerberg, 2012). In a period of resource scarcity, they have also enhanced the ability of social justice organizations to deliver services to marginalized populations and to engage in more effective dialogue with constituents, such as urban youth, who have previously been left out of decision-making processes (Briones, Jin, Kuch, & Liu, 2011; Cabral et al., 2012; Kvasny, Ortiz, & Tapia, 2011). Internet-based technologies have also enabled organizations to strengthen accountability mechanisms in an era in which the demand for accountability has significantly increased (Guo & Saxton, 2011; Keevers, Treleaven, Sykes, & Darcy, 2012).

In addition, research has demonstrated that technological innovations can enhance the quality of an organization's services, assist in its resource development efforts, and enhance an organization's image and relationships with stakeholders and the public (Jaskyte, 2012). However, most nonprofit social justice organizations have failed thus far to tap the potential of technology, reflecting what Kamal (2014) refers to as an "organizational digital divide." Many nonprofits use technological innovation primarily for educational or administrative purposes (Jones & Waters, 2011; Singh, 2014) and do not exploit the opportunities provided by mobile technology (Kim, Mankoff, & Paulos, 2014).

It is beyond the scope of this chapter (or the capacity of its authors) to suggest all the ways in which social justice organizations could use technology more effectively. Digital technology is also changing so rapidly that whatever is included in this text may be obsolete by the time it is read. Instead, we suggest some principles to serve as a guide to its usage in a manner consistent with socially just organizational goals and values.

First, it is important for organizations to recognize the importance of equity and equality in the internal distribution of technology and its effects on clients and constituents. Technology not only has the potential to widen existing social and educational gaps, it can also dehumanize services and thereby diminish one of the unique aspects of social work practice. This possibility can be forestalled by conscious efforts to humanize the application of technology through democratic participation in its development and application. Organizations need to promote greater interactivity among all stakeholders and their active participation in planning how technology will be used to achieve the organization's people-centered goals. They also need to ensure that the rights and responsibilities of all technology users are protected. Finally, organizations must struggle with the question of how they can continue to engage in "political" work in an increasingly digital, virtual world in a manner compatible with the humanistic values on which they were established.

Resolving Ethical Dilemmas

Like intra- and interorganizational conflict and the challenges of resource scarcity and organizational change, the resolution of ethical dilemmas is a constant feature of organizational practice. Many ethical issues that emerge in practice with individuals, families, and groups exist in macro contexts as well, particularly for organizational leaders (Eisenbeiss, 2012; Reamer, 2013). Both forms of practice involve relationships between people or among groups, necessitate the application of critical consciousness to analyze the sources of people's problems, and regard the context and culture in which people's problems emerge as critical factors.

It is essential, therefore, for social workers in social justice organizations to develop the ability to resolve a variety of recurring ethical dilemmas in order to align their goals and practices with the needs of the people with whom they are working and to regard people as social beings rather than mere statistics (Banks, 2011). As a result of recent environmental changes, skills in ethical decision-making have become even more important because these changes have often involved the imposition of values that are at odds with the social justice mission of the social work profession (Lonne, Fox, & McDonald, 2004). There is increased risk, however, that organizations will overlook the effects of these external pressures and overestimate the degree of organizational consensus around social justice concerns (Flynn & Wiltermuth, 2010).

There are important distinctions between "macro" and "micro" practice that influence the nature of ethical dilemmas encountered by social work organizations. For example, in community practice, a staff member may be a resident of the community that the organization serves. This places boundary issues—an important ethical concern in clinical social work practice (Reamer, 2013)—in a different context. In addition, community or social change, not individual change, is often the primary goal of social justice organizations. Finally, the distinction between the clients of a socially just service agency and the constituents of a socially just advocacy organization creates different types of ethical dilemmas. Figure 7.4 demonstrates the conflicting demands that shape ethical decision-making in organizations.

The most common ethical conflicts within social justice organizations include the following:

1. The right of persons to autonomy and self-determination versus their right to assistance that will protect their well-being and increase their ability or life chances in the future

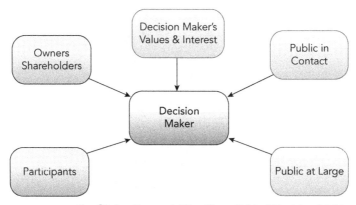

FIGURE 7.4 Conflicting Demands That Shape Ethical Decision-Making

2. Promoting peoples' interests as they define them versus "doing good" (e.g., through advocacy) to protect them. This involves reflection on the meaning of such concepts as "benevolence" and "paternalism."
3. Goals and strategies that focus solely on an individual's own good versus balancing the individual interests with those of the community or society

Other ethical issues that may arise in social justice organizations include the following:

- Informed consent (especially regarding the risks involved in activities)
- Legal liability: For example, can community practitioners be guilty of malpractice?
- The relationship between means and ends (e.g., regarding the design of programs or tactics). Do socially just ends justify the use of any means?
- The allocation of scarce resources
- Truth-telling versus organizational and constituent self-interest
- Compliance with unjust laws
- Whistleblowing (on corrupt or incompetent colleagues) versus organizational loyalty

As shown in Figure 7.5, there are three components to the resolution of an ethical dilemma: the facts, the theories used to interpret the facts, and the means by which to decide an ethical course of action. There are four basic approaches to resolving the ethical dilemmas that arise in organizational settings, each of which generates its own problems. One is to prioritize the interests of clients or constituents. As discussed previously, Sen (2009) and Nussbaum (2011) have emphasized the enhancement of a person's capabilities (interests). The challenge

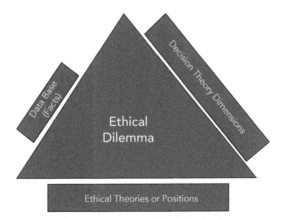

FIGURE 7.5 Analyzing an Ethical Dilemma

here is to determine what those interests are and to reconcile the often competing or conflicting interests of diverse individuals and groups. Ongoing and open communication with stakeholders and the primacy of a "community-driven" agenda are critical in this regard, particularly where the need to overcome racial or class divides is paramount (Minkler, 2004).

A second approach is to use what ethicists term a "prime directive"—that is, to impose a set of externally determined values (as in a religious organization). This approach, however, appears to contradict the democratic and egalitarian values of social justice organizations.

A third approach, which appears superficially similar to the second approach, is for the organization to create its own hierarchical (or lexical) ordering of values and apply them to all ethical dilemmas. This approach, which ethicists term a "deontological" approach (after the Greek word for "first principles"), can only be reconciled with social justice principles under three conditions: (1) The entire organizational community develops this hierarchy through some type of consensus process, (2) the hierarchy of values is periodically reassessed through a participatory process, and (3) the manner in which decisions are implemented is also socially just.

A fourth approach avoids—to some extent—the need for a hierarchical set of values by weighing the consequences of the various options that exist to resolve an ethical dilemma. Utilitarianism, the most widely used version of what ethicists refer to as a consequentialist or teleological approach (again, from the Greek word for "the end"), assesses these options by calculating which would produce "the greatest net balance of satisfaction"—that is, the greatest surplus of "good" over "bad" results. The challenges here for socially just organizations are to define what constitutes a "good," how to measure the impact of different goods on different persons or groups, how to assess the differences between the short-term and long-term consequences of decisions, and how to determine the effects of these decisions on third parties (Rawls, 1971/1999). In discussing the conflict between means and ends, Alinsky (1971) proposed a version of this approach that factors in the context in which the dilemma emerged and needs to be resolved.

Combining elements of each of these approaches, Reisch and Lowe (2000) developed the following seven-step method to help practitioners resolve recurrent ethical dilemmas:

1. Identify the ethical principles that apply to the situation.
2. Collect additional information needed to examine the ethical dilemma in question.
3. Identify the relevant ethical values and/or rules that apply to the ethical problem.

4. Identify any potential conflicts of interest and those likely to benefit from such conflicts.
5. Rank order the appropriate ethical rules in terms of importance in the situation.
6. Determine the consequences of applying different ethical rules or ranking these rules differently.
7. Determine who needs to resolve the dilemma.

Summary

This chapter applied a social justice perspective to some of the major aspects of organizational practice: organizational structure and decision-making processes, leadership and leadership styles, patterns of resource allocation, the role of organizational culture, the meaning of power within organizations, the use of technology, and the ethical dilemmas that organizations confront and how to address them in a socially just manner. It discussed the specific problems that social justice organizations face today as a consequence of changes in the political–economic environment, the demographic composition of the communities in which they work, and the transformation of the cultural and ideological context of practice. It suggested ways that organizational practitioners could respond effectively to these changes without sacrificing the social justice principles on which they were established. The next two chapters apply a similar lens to community practice and to what is commonly referred to as "policy practice."

Discussion Questions

1. In what ways is the organization in which you work a socially just organization? In what ways does it fall short of this goal?
2. How are issues of power reflected in the organization?
3. What model of leadership and decision-making exists in this organization? To what extent does it reflect social justice concepts?
4. To what extent does your organization respond to issues of diversity and conflict in a socially just manner? In what ways could it improve?
5. Identify an ethical dilemma that has emerged in your organization. How could this dilemma be resolved in a socially just manner?

Working with Communities to Promote Social Justice

Introduction

This chapter focuses on working with communities in a socially just manner to help them create strategies to transform existing institutions and organizations by making them more inclusive, democratic, redistributive, and decentered and also to forge new ways of addressing people's problems. Some community groups work explicitly toward social justice goals, whereas others use socially just means that are not specifically justice-oriented. Even within community organizations committed to social justice goals, however, the processes they employ to achieve their goals are not always socially just. Therefore, as elsewhere in this book, this chapter emphasizes the importance of linking socially just processes and goals for reasons of philosophical consistency, professional integrity, and practice efficacy.

Social justice work takes place within various types of communities, including those defined by geography, such as neighborhoods; those based on demographic or cultural identities, such as the African American or LGBTQ community; and those that are organized around shared interests or issues, such as military veterans and their families or individuals suffering from chronic mental illness. All communities have fluid boundaries, structures, and internal dynamics. They interact with, influence, and are influenced by both internal systems and the wider social, political, and economic environment. Thus, the community provides a critical context for practice and the context for critical practice, just as the societal and historical context shapes the nature of communities (Butcher et al., 2007). As societies become increasingly multicultural and the world becomes increasingly multipolar, it is critical that social justice work combine a respect for difference with recognition of our common humanity if we are to go beyond tolerance and "cultural competence" to embrace a universal, reciprocal obligation to all communities (Appiah, 2006).

This chapter also critically examines contemporary theories and practice models for work with communities. It explores how a worker's multiple and intersecting identities influence his or her work within a community, whose members also have multiple and intersecting identities, particularly in an increasingly diverse and globalized world. This chapter also pays particular attention to the impact of power differentials and structural inequities. Although many communities are affected by a multitude of social problems, no community lacks resources or assets, no matter how depleted it may appear to outsiders. Thus, in all forms of community practice (e.g., community development, planning, social action, and advocacy) and in each phase of practice (e.g., assessment, planning, entry to a community, engagement, mobilization, and evaluation), it is critical to build on a community's strength. It is equally critical, however, to address the structural inequities that reinforce the marginalization of certain communities while privileging others (Emejulu, 2011).

Specific topics covered in the chapter include the following:

- Concepts of community, community practice, and community change
- The goals of community practice: Issue-based and identity-based organizing
- Theories underlying community practice
- Models and phases of community practice
- Power, privilege, and community practice
- Leadership and leadership development
- Promoting community participation
- Interorganizational practice
- Ethical dilemmas

Concepts of Community, Community Practice, and Social/Community Change

The Meaning of Community

Some years ago while hiking in the high country at Yosemite National Park, one of the authors came across the following quotation on a plaque at Parsons Memorial Lodge:

> What is community? Not just where you were born or where you lay your head down to sleep. Community is a mix of history, experience, stories, and imagination: Possibility. The man who went away 20 years ago can still be very much a part of a community—as can, I believe, a woman who

has not yet been there, who will not cross paths with a given community for another 20 years.

Rick Bass, "Round River," *Orion*, Summer 1997

This quote reflects the breadth and complexity of the meaning of community. A community exists when a group of people form a social unit based on common location, interest, identification, culture, and/or activities (Garvin & Tropman, 1998). Communities, therefore, can be a geographic place (where people live); people with common interests, identity, and/or social concerns; and a set of common social relations or unit of organization or solution in society. Each individual's "personal community" is a combination of his or her location, identity, and interests (Etzioni, 1993).

All communities serve five major functions: production, distribution, and consumption of goods and services; socialization; social control; social participation; and mutual support/mutual aid. Communities that achieve these goals effectively are often labeled "competent communities." They collaborate effectively in identifying problems and needs, achieve consensus on goals and priorities, agree on how to implement goals, collaborate effectively in various actions, and work together to evaluate results (Warren, 1970).

Many communities, however, are less able to satisfy these functions because of structural and historical inequities reflected, for example, in persistent health disparities (Wallerstein, Yen, & Syme, 2011). At the community level, these inequities also create people's absence of social capital (relationships), an uneven distribution of power, demographic disparities, a lack of local neighborhood control, little or no history of community cooperation, conflicts between individuals or groups, and social or physical isolation (Harding & Simmons, 2010). Consequently, there are often considerable differences among community members about what their needs are and how these needs can be or should be addressed.

These different needs can be categorized as follows: *normative*—standards established by custom, authority, and consensus; *perceived*—what people think and feel their needs are; *expressed*—a need that is already being met or a demand for a need to be met; and *relative*—a gap between the level of existing services in one area and those in another area. As Figure 8.1 shows, the use of evidence-based practice is one way to determine what a community's needs are and how best to meet them. It involves "integrating practice experience and lessons learned with the best available external evidence from systematic research, while at the same time considering client values and expectations when making practice decisions" (Ohmer, 2008, p. 519).

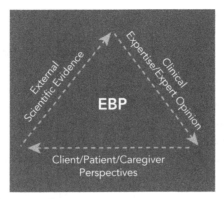

FIGURE 8.1   Evidence-Based Practice

To summarize, healthy contemporary communities embody a sense of wholeness that incorporates all forms of diversity. They strive to identify shared values and norms, and they use these common principles to promote greater community cohesion. They establish effective and diverse forms of internal communication that attempt to avoid the construction of "we/they" barriers in how people acquire and interpret information and express their views. They foster the development of trust, caring, and teamwork through a collective "ownership" of the community and a sense of mutual responsibility, in which the good of the community and individual well-being are considered complementary.

Exercise: Identifying Your Understanding of Community

1. List the communities to which you belong.
2. How do you know or demonstrate that you are a member of these communities?
3. How did you become part of these communities?
4. What are the notable features of these communities?
5. What are the requirements of membership?
6. How do your various community memberships complement or conflict with each other?
7. How would you apply the concept of community competence to these communities?

Not all community practice has the same philosophical perspective, goals, or methods. Thomas, O'Connor, and Netting (2011) identify three strands: traditional, collaborative, and radical. Social justice practice in communities has multiple roots within the radical branch of community practice. These include self-help/mutual aid organizations that were organized by virtually every marginalized community in US history; labor unions and other associations of working-class people; radical political organizations across the ideological spectrum; social movements on behalf of people of color, women, immigrants, the LGBTQ population, the elderly, and individuals with disabilities; and ideas acquired from other nations. Its evolution also has been shaped by rapid socioeconomic and political change; the different histories, cultures, and contexts of communities that organized; the increased heterogeneity of US society; the emergence of specific crises (e.g., HIV/AIDS); the impact of external events (e.g., war); and the influence of secular and religious ideologies from socialism to the Social Gospel (Reisch, 2012a).

From a social justice perspective, community practice involves developing greater cohesion among community groups, helping people improve their capacities for performing various community roles, mobilizing people and resources to improve social conditions and services, promoting the interests of disadvantaged groups within the community, and promoting community change (Evans et al., 2011). It emphasizes the same values as social justice practice with individuals, families, and groups: the right of all humans to be treated with dignity, the recognition of each person's ability to determine her or his own destiny, and the belief that individual and collective goals complement rather than conflict with each other. Like practice with individuals, families, and groups, it focuses on how context shapes both human needs and the means available to address them (Lewis, 2011), on the importance of power, and on the centrality of human relationships (Burghardt, 2013). Within a social justice framework, therefore, the oft-repeated distinctions between "direct" and "indirect" practice reflect a false dichotomy.

Community practice has served as a counternarrative in social work since the profession first emerged at the turn of the 20th century. Community practitioners challenged the prevailing conception of social welfare, based on a hierarchical charitable model, and proposed an alternative mission founded on principles of justice. They promoted environmental rather than individualistically oriented explanations for human need and a more democratic conceptualization of the service relationship (Reisch & Andrews, 2002). Although this counternarrative continues to be expressed in the rhetoric of the profession—for example, in the National Association of Social Workers' (NASW) *Code of Ethics* (1998, 2008) and the Council on Social Work Education's *Educational Policy and Accreditation Standards* (2008, 2015)—it has been frequently superseded by a master narrative that defined the mission of social work in terms consonant with the emerging structure of the US political–economy, the social roles it generated, and a positivist paradigm for the creation and organization of the knowledge needed to sustain it (Reisch & Jani, 2012d).

As a counternarrative of resistance, community-based social justice practice plays a significant role in reorienting social work's goals toward the elimination of oppression and the creation of a more egalitarian society by challenging prevailing practice assumptions; developing alternative frameworks and theories of explanation and change; posing different research questions; clarifying the meaning of ambiguous concepts, such as social justice and empowerment; forging new alliances; creating new social work roles; and building new partnerships in the pursuit of justice goals. Resistance at the intellectual and practice levels is an essential component of the processes that help people survive, find meaning in their lives, become aware of injustice, and work for justice. It includes the subversive ways in which people who are oppressed exert dignity and agency in the presence of dehumanizing circumstances.

Community practice involves collective efforts to transform "private troubles" into "public issues" (Mills, 1959) in order to enhance human well-being (Gamble, 2012) by increasing investments in health, education, and social supports (Hernandez, Montana, & Clarke, 2010); promoting greater social inclusion; eliminating all forms of violence in society (Van Soest, 1997); and protecting the physical environment (Hilmers, Hilmers, & Dave, 2012). "Troubles" occur within the character of the individual and within the range of his or her immediate relations with others. "Issues" have to do with matters that transcend these local environments of the individual and the range of his or her inner life. Community practitioners redefined each of these problems as a public issue: unemployment and poverty; child abuse and domestic violence; homelessness; substance abuse and mental illness; epidemic diseases from tuberculosis to HIV/AIDS; racial profiling (Shippen, Patterson, Green, & Smitherman, 2012); discrimination versus LGBTQ persons; and the needs of undocumented youth.

Community practitioners attempt to achieve these goals and objectives through both short-term and long-term steps. In the short term, they help communities identify and promote *their* interests as they perceive them, promote resistance at both intellectual and practical levels, and help oppressed communities exercise dignity and agency. Over the long term, they strive to forge "a new social discourse" that goes beyond replacing one set of rhetorical principles with another and to reframe the way we think, plan, and take action.

Community interventions are often needed to produce broader "structural changes" because many problems either are not or cannot be solved by individually focused solutions alone. As society becomes more complex and communities become more interdependent, the need for change in systems and institutions increases if social justice goals are to be achieved. In cooperation with community members, practitioners help produce these structural changes by replacing critical actors; redistributing and redefining social roles; and changing society's goals and reward structure and its distribution of rights, opportunities, status, and obligations. Community practitioners use a variety of strategies to achieve these objectives, including direct change in communities, empowering people by creating new or improved services, and organizing services specifically with structural change in mind.

These efforts are complicated by how social problems are defined or constructed. Think about it: Most things we accept as "givens" are neither "natural" nor inevitable. Examples include our economic system (e.g., capitalism), our educational system (how we learn), our major social institutions (e.g., marriage and family), our political system (e.g., representative democracy), and our social divisions (e.g., race, ethnicity, gender, religion, age, and sexual orientation). Who defines what constitutes a problem in our society or in a social service agency? Who determines why these problems exist? Who decides which problems get attention and what type of attention they need or deserve? In summary, who defines "need" and "helping"? (Gordon, 2002; Green, 1999).

Other challenges facing both community members and practitioners today are the consequences of attacks on social welfare as an institution and government as a problem-solving vehicle (Flynn, 2011); the impact of economic globalization; the privatization of politics and social life; a general decline in civic and political participation; the devolution of political authority/power from the federal government to states and localities; the industrialization and "marketization" of social services (Gronbjerg & Salamon, 2002); the persistence of a variety of forms of invidious discrimination, such as racism, sexism, and homophobia in such areas as health, employment, education, and housing; and value conflicts emerging from diversity itself. On the plus side, there has recently been increased awareness of the impact of socioeconomic inequality and the emergence of new social movements around such issues as immigration reform and racism in the criminal justice system.

Theories Underlying Community Practice

Traditional approaches to community practice are primarily based on social systems theory. This theory, which emerged after World War II, is based on a biological model. It views society as a system of interrelated parts consisting of such elements as individuals, families, organizations, communities, and economic and political systems. One advantage of this theory is its emphasis on the interdependent nature of communities, societies, and organizations. According to systems theory (Bertalanffy, 1969), no entity exists in isolation; all parties in a system are constantly seeking balance in order to survive and thrive. The ecological model of social work practice is a recent application of systems theory (Pardeck, 1996).

A disadvantage of systems theory, however, is that it assumes that conflict, individual and social, is not healthy—that conflict, in whatever form, is inevitably contrary to the interests of the organism or system; it needs to be stopped or controlled. According to systems theory, although periods of imbalance or disruption may occur within a system, all systems inevitably try to restore balance or quiescence. This has often produced community practice that failed to address the root causes of social problems out of fear of generating controversy, losing the support of influential power brokers or funders, or diminishing the status of social workers because their practice has become "politicized." Another problem with this approach is that it assumes that all parties within a system have equal power or the ability to determine alternative outcomes. As Finn and Jacobson (2008) note, however, practitioners who adopt an approach to practice grounded in critical social theory (e.g., critical race theory, structural analysis, and feminist theory) emphasize the relationship between knowledge and power, who defines the "reality" of a particular context and what constitutes "realistic" and acceptable means of change. According to Bottomore (1991) power is the ability to determine such alternatives.

To counteract this tendency, Stephens and Gillies (2012) propose that community-based researchers and practitioners revise their focus to encompass the multiple components of the socioeconomic and political environment. Based on Bourdieu's (2003) assertion that social and material inequalities are inextricably intertwined, and that power influences all aspects of practice, Stephens and Gillies assert that "many current interventions to improve material and social conditions within disadvantaged communities ignore the damaging effects of social inequalities between social groups" (p. 145) and thereby overlook the subtle ways that individuals and groups with privilege seek to retain their place in the social hierarchy. This occurs by determining what constitutes a problem worthy of attention, what impact on which segments of the population matters, and what solutions are politically feasible and socially desirable. To work toward socially just ends, community practitioners need to understand "the nature of power struggles in daily life . . . [to] . . . address the damaging effects of inequalities" (p. 145).

By contrast, socially just community practice assumes that conflict is a natural, ongoing, and even healthy part of life. Conflict theorists assume that inequality is a given; it arises in different forms because of the competition for scarce resources, whether this competition occurs within a family, a community, a society, or among nations (Alinsky, 1971; Coser, 1956). This inequality generates oppositional interests and power differentials that appear in both macro and micro systems. Constructive conflict, in this view, can be the foundation of meaningful social relations and social progress and a means to reduce or eliminate these inequalities. Community practitioners who operate from a conflict perspective assume that the notion that community or social change can be achieved without conflict is false, even naïve.

Another form of conflict can be labeled "rancorous" or "extrainstitutional." It includes both nonviolent activities that attempt to disrupt the status quo, such as demonstrations, strikes, and boycotts, and violent activities ranging from vandalism and sabotage to terrorism and armed revolution. Although the former activities may be risky, they are neither illegal nor unethical. In fact, in some circumstances, they may be necessary to raise public awareness of issues long ignored or to compel those with power and influence to adopt changes they have long resisted. Throughout the profession's history, social workers have participated in such activities through their involvement in social movements that addressed issues of racism and sexism, workers' and immigrants' rights, and global matters such as war and militarism (Van Soest, 1992).

In summary, conflict can often have positive functions in a community. Sometimes, consensus approaches to resolving persistent issues are not feasible (Eichler, 2007). Hibbing and Theiss-Morse (2005) pointedly assert, "The problem is that reinforcing the message that consensus and harmony are good whereas conflict and disagreements are bad undermines what democracy is all about" (p. 237). Conflict can also serve to strengthen solidarity among diverse community groups by directing people's energies toward an external "enemy." In addition, healthy conflict provides an outlet for people's frustrations and a catalyst for community and policy change. The demonstrations in Ferguson, Missouri, in the aftermath of the shooting of a young African American man by a police officer are an example. Protests during the civil rights movement and the early days of the HIV/AIDS epidemic aroused the public from its apathy toward issues of deadly seriousness. They changed the way many people understood long-standing social problems and generated greater support for reform measures and institutional change.

Community Change

Community change involves the modification of attitudes, policies, or practices in the community to reduce or eliminate problems or produce general improvement in how needs are met through policies, programs, and services that involve the redistribution of resources and power. The process of community change is challenging, whatever the nature of the community or the issues being addressed. It involves a series of steps that reflect both justice-oriented goals (e.g., the more equitable distribution of resources and power) and justice-oriented processes (e.g., a democratic conceptualization of leadership and decision-making). It requires the application of both research-generated evidence and practice wisdom. From a social justice perspective, promoting community change involves developing cohesion among community groups; helping people improve their capacities for performing various community roles, including leadership positions; encouraging greater participation in community activities and mobilizing people and resources to improve social conditions, social services, and power relationships; and prioritizing the interests of disadvantaged groups within the community.

Community change also requires the development of critical consciousness among its members; the ability to confront issues of racism, sexism, classism, and homophobia (Bettez & Hytten, 2013; McKay, 2010); and the practical knowledge and skills necessary to imagine and implement social justice-oriented change goals and strategies (Bieler, 2012; Edmonds-Cady & Sosulski, 2012). This often involves providing opportunities for community members to create their own identity-based narratives, engage in a critical dialogue with others (Farnsworth, 2010), and play a greater role in defining their own needs and helping interventions (Weaver, 2011). Facilitating greater participation in all aspects of the change process is another major component of community change efforts in such organizations as the Center for Participatory Change (CPC) and the Community Capacitation Center (Castelloe, Watson, & White, 2002; Wiggins et al., 2013). CPC focuses on community-based education through collective action. It has a dual goal (Wiggins et al., 2013):

> (1) To work with people to create alternative structures . . . through which groups of marginalized people can come together to articulate and meet their own needs, on their own terms, over the long haul; and (2) to work hand-in-hand with groups of marginalized people as they gain the collective power needed to shape existing systems to become more inclusive, responsive, accountable, and participatory. (p. 186)

Community-based participatory research from a social justice perspective can link social work's fundamental values with the increased demands of political and fiscal sponsors to provide credible outcome measures of effectiveness within community development and community change initiatives (Branom, 2012; Sander, 2012). This is a particularly important component of community change because there is little evidence that many interventions with a social justice focus, such as advocacy campaigns, are effective or cost-efficient (McNutt, 2011). During the past two decades, different kinds of organizations—major corporations, cooperatives, and neighborhood-based nonprofit organizations—have used participatory action research to address community problems (Greenwood, Foote Whyte, & Harkavy, 1993).

Community change efforts take different forms depending on environmental conditions, the community's history, and the specific context of the issues. Most efforts, however, involve the following components to some extent at some time:

- Grassroots mobilization of large numbers of people around issues that affect them
- Greater participation of the community in planning policies and developing programs
- Advocacy to effect policy change and a more equitable distribution of resources
- Efforts to empower people and create more responsive services
- The development of powerful community organizations to achieve these goals
- Popular education to raise critical consciousness (see Chapters 7 and 9)

The various components of an evidence-driven change process are shown in Figure 8.1 above.

Exercise: Planning a 10-Step Community Change Process

1. Select an issue that affects the community in which you live or work. Through discussions with community members, how would you frame the specific issue or issues around which you would organize? How would you express social justice values explicitly or implicitly?
2. What are the overall goals of the change effort?
3. Who/what would be the target(s) of the change effort you would propose?
4. What are the possible obstacles that could impede attainment of these goals?
5. What groups might have the power to facilitate the change(s) you desire?
6. Who might be your potential allies in a change effort toward this goal? What assets might they contribute to your change effort?
7. What overall strategic approach would the community prefer? For example, would you try to produce change through consensus,

persuasion or education (campaign), or conflict? What are your reasons for selecting this approach? (See Chapter 9)

8. What tactic(s) would you adopt as part of the selected strategy? What specific actions would be taken to implement it? How are the tactics selected related to the overall strategy and to the goals of the change effort? How do they reflect the underlying values of social justice?

9. Based on social justice values, what criteria should be used to assess the merit of the tactics selected? What made you choose these criteria? Which tactics do/do not meet these criteria?

10. What ethical issues might arise in the implementation of the strategy and tactics selected?

Think about:

1. How did the way you framed the issue influence your choice of strategies and tactics?

2. To what extent did your personal experiences with communities and community change and your personal values influence your choice of strategies and tactics?

3. In what ways did the definition of community being used (geographic or community of identity) shape your choice of strategy and tactics?

Exploring: Establishing the Goals of Community Practice

Although all forms of community practice share common goals, regardless of their conceptual or ideological foundation, when viewed from a social justice perspective the goals of community practice are somewhat distinct. They include (1) analyzing the root causes of inequality and injustice and not merely focusing on their symptoms and (2) emphasizing the power dynamics within a community, among different communities, and between a community and the external structures that possess economic and political resources that the community needs. In community work, social justice-oriented practitioners draw contrasts between the goals of a market economy and those of a more equitable society. They critique how dominant cultural values and norms perpetuate the marginalization and disempowerment of certain communities. They promote structural change, not mere participation within existing systems, and they work with community members to create alternative institutions and community-driven solutions to problems.

Because of this different orientation and the challenges involved in empowering disenfranchised communities, it is important to integrate an educational component into all aspects of community work. In addition to teaching community members the skills required to produce community and social change, while learning from them in turn, this educational aspect of community practice helps develop people's critical consciousness and enables their integration into mainstream political discourse and contests. This educational component of practice is particularly important if social workers are to address such issues as environmental sustainability, social inclusion, civic participation, and community engagement in a manner that will lead to greater social equality. Tools of popular education, for example, as developed in Latin America by such scholars/activists as Paulo Freire (1970) can enhance people's ability to understand their individual experiences and use that understanding to develop transformative strategies that address the larger, structural causes of individual oppression (Mullaly, 2010).

In an increasingly complex and conflict-ridden environment, community practitioners need to acquire the requisite skills to expand the scope and revise the focus of activities beyond traditional practice norms. Because community membership is more fluid and multifaceted today, we must now organize within and across established community boundaries and blend issue- and identity-based approaches to community engagement and mobilization. In order to expand community participation, we need to create diverse means for people to participate that reflect the ways people organize their lives and the increasing importance of social media for interpersonal communication. If we are to facilitate community empowerment, we must take the risks involved in surfacing and addressing issues of power and their underlying conflicts. Finally, to be effective in an increasingly diverse society, we need to be clear about the impact of our own social position and be open to ideas emerging from different cultures and countries.

All communities have their resources and their limitations, some of which are more obvious than others. Until recently, social workers tended to focus on a community's problems or deficits instead of its assets and potential. However, like an individual's personal problems, the presence of problems or challenges in a community also provides an opportunity for growth and change. In order for this to occur, a community must believe in its ability to change and must take responsibility for its actions or inactions. The role of a social worker in this regard is not to instigate the change or determine its direction but, rather, to assist the community in acquiring the capacity to define its own destiny and to develop the strategy to fulfill it. The purpose of community empowerment, therefore, is to enhance a community's ability to define and solve its own problems, develop independent community support systems, and educate itself about the issues that affect the lives of its members. The formation of broad-based community organizations is a necessary step in this direction. Such organizations, if structured democratically and directed toward socially just ends, are the vehicles through which communities determine their goals, their decision-making processes, and the strategies and tactics (means) they will use to achieve their desired ends.

From a social justice perspective, an important step in community empowerment and change is to identify a community's assets (McKnight & Kretzmann, 2008). Through a process called "assets mapping," practitioners and members locate and make an inventory of the various resources and capacities that individuals, groups, associations, and local institutions possess. These varied assets can include the skills and energy of youth, the knowledge and experience of community elders, and the talents of artists and other cultural workers (Sakamoto, 2014).

Most communities, even if they are impoverished and marginalized, have schools and libraries, parks and recreational or cultural facilities, social service and health care agencies, police and fire stations, churches, social clubs, and community associations. The latter can be a great help in defining community problems, deciding how to solve the problems (often based on past successes and failures), and organizing community members to implement solutions. There are a number of ways in which these associations or groups can be found: Many publish newsletters or newspapers, usually monthly or quarterly, and some have websites or blogs. Often, citywide magazines publish the names and addresses of these groups, or their contact information is posted in libraries and other community facilities. Sometimes the best way to identify community associations is to speak directly with community residents or read the notices placed on lampposts or the bulletin boards in neighborhood markets.

The goal here is to try to create an "associational community"—an informal network of groups of people working together to create and maintain the core of civil society. These associations can promote community participation in several ways. They provide networks of care and mutual aid that enable people to negotiate the struggles they encounter in their daily lives. They can respond rapidly to problems and provide an organizational context in which more rapid and unique solutions can be developed. Finally, they provide people, particularly those who lack power or perceive they lack power, with experience in taking responsibility for their community and for society as a whole. By building relationships among local assets for mutual gain, these community associations become a tool to empower the entire community and enhance a community's competence (McKnight & Kretzmann, 2008).

Community practitioners can play a critical role in this regard by helping communities strengthen their "bonding" social capital (Reisch & Guyet, 2007); encouraging marginalized people or groups within a community to regard themselves as part of a larger collective entity; helping a community forge relationships with external individuals and institutions such as foundations, corporations, political leaders, church groups, wealthy individuals, and universities (Harkavy & Puckett, 1994)—that is, by creating "bridging" social capital and leveraging outside resources; providing technical expertise to local associations; developing the means to share information within a community; and recruiting and training indigenous leaders. To initiate this asset-building process, community practitioners address the following questions:

- Who are the community's formal and informal leaders?
- What are the most effective means of communicating within the community?
- How might current places of information sharing—for example, beauty parlors, barber shops, clubs, radio, churches, cable access TV, taverns, local newspapers, schools, and street corners—be validated, strengthened, and expanded?

To craft a vision and a plan for the community, it is important to begin with the assets that are currently available and not to romanticize or exaggerate a community's strengths. In addition, to build viable and socially just community organizations, all community members must be regarded as potential community assets. This requires the recruitment of participants to any change effort beyond "the usual suspects"—those who are already recognized as leaders. The ideal planning team includes a mixture of community residents, service providers, and formal and informal leaders. Its initial work should combine longer term strategy development with attempts to solve short-term problems. This is because people in communities that have few resources and limited power need to see small but significant victories to increase their capacity and their confidence. A role of the community practitioner is to assist the group members in recognizing and understanding the need for change.

Baldwin (2010) emphasizes that in order for social workers to move beyond resource management to collective action and political advocacy, community practitioners have to help expose the flaws in society's current decision-making processes and underlying assumptions. The latter includes assumptions about what types of knowledge are considered "valid" and used to inform policy and practice, the balance between public responsibility and private risk, and the sources of people's problems. To forge a "social work of resistance" (Baldwin, 2010), community practitioners need to create alliances with service users and focus on collective needs. They also need to use theory to explain the roots of poverty, oppression, and marginalization rather than accepting the traditional focus on human error and pathology.

Engagement: Entering a Community

There are three critical elements to entering a community: (1) educating oneself about the community's culture, history, issues, and institutions; (2) identifying issues around which organizing is possible; and (3) making initial contacts through meetings and door knocking. There are two basic sources of these initial contacts: "cold contacts" (e.g., a phone directory or the membership lists of local organizations) and "warm contacts," such as a reference from an established community leader or a person who can serve as a liaison to an influential contact.

The key components of your initial contact are to establish your personal presence in order to build trust and confidence; to focus on the content of the discussion; and to recognize that the meeting is the beginning of a longer process, not an end in itself. In effect, the interview becomes a metaphor for a broader dialogue you want to encourage. It is best to hold the meeting in a place that is familiar and comfortable to community residents and to be constantly aware of how race, gender, class, culture, and age differences might influence the formality/informality of the meeting, including the use of certain courtesies or rituals.

If you begin from the position of metaphor, the dialogue in which you engage should have limited and focused expectations. Be aware of the physical, social, and cultural context of the situation and how it might affect the approach you employ. Listen carefully to what is said and not said, how it is said, in what sequence issues are raised, and—in a group meeting—who listens to whom. Try to distinguish between statements of "objective" facts and subjective feelings or opinions. Try to discern the underlying values of the individual or group and what prejudices or biases are expressed, not merely about broad issues such as racism but also about moral questions and lifestyle matters. Be clear about your specific objectives, and use your own style; do not try to imitate others. Being genuine is much more effective than being "cool."

To summarize, in preparing for an initial contact, make sure you address the following: (1) the content of what you will say and the questions you will ask, (2) the answers you will provide to questions you are likely to be asked, (3) the overall sequence of contacts you will try to establish (and your reasons), and (4) your frame of mind before you start. The following are some "do's" and "don'ts":

Always	Never
• Be yourself	• Threaten
• Project confidence	• Get "seduced" or
• Try to understand the others' context	sidetracked by issues
• Speak clearly and simply	different from your goals
• Be polite and nonthreatening	• Apologize for being there
but assertive	• Overpromise

- Use humor carefully
- Ask questions—Come to learn, not to teach
- Listen and pay attention to nonverbal cues
- Try to find some common ground or mutual experience
- Be aware of the contact's role in the community
- Make sure you get the information you were seeking
- Get a commitment before you leave

- Exaggerate your role
- Be afraid to say "no" to unreasonable or unfeasible requests
- Preach or proselytize
- Assume you "totally understand" another person's situation
- Stay too long

Exercise: Identifying Issues Around Which to Organize

Introduction

The class is divided into small groups. Each group focuses on one scenario and has 20 minutes to answer the questions that follow and prepare a brief report for the class.

Scenarios

1. You are social workers in a community-based mental health agency. The county has announced a proposed cut in funding due to budget short-falls. The director of your agency reports to the head of the city's Health Department. She, in turn, reports to the city's Health Commission, which recommends a budget to the city council. You have been asked by the director to organize an emergency meeting of the agency's staff, board, clients, and community advisory committee.

2. You work in a medium-sized family services agency in a middle-income sub-urb. The new executive director of the agency—with the support of the new chairperson of the board of directors—has recently imposed salary freezes, workload increases, and changes in agency procedures that have greatly upset all the staff. You have been asked by your colleagues to organize a meeting of staff, contract professionals, and concerned community allies.

3. You work at a large senior services center in a medium-sized, politically conservative city. The city manager has recently ruled that nonpartisan voter registration may not be conducted at the center. The center's senior action committee has called an all-center meeting and asked your advice in framing the issues for impending action.

4. You are social workers in a large Head Start program. Parents of children in the program are concerned because of recent conflicts between parents and staff regarding children who have tested positive for the HIV virus. Parents want to do something to demonstrate their concerns. You have been asked for advice on how to frame the issues before a citywide parents' meeting called to address this problem.

5. You are on the staff of the state Department of Human Resources. Some of the staff have been attending meetings of a local welfare rights organization to advise them as to how to advocate on behalf of TANF recipients. The director of the agency has recently distributed a memorandum forbidding staff to meet with representatives of this organization during working hours and strongly discouraging staff from assisting this organization in any way. You have been selected as an ad hoc committee charged with preparing a response to the director's memorandum.

6. You are on the staff of a community-based mental health agency that is working in cooperation with the county to implement its 10-year plan to eliminate homelessness in the county. You have been asked to identify ways in which the initiative's issue might be framed in various communities.

Questions

1. How would you recommend framing the issue around which to organize?
2. What factors led you to frame the issue in this way?
3. What are your goals in framing the issue in this way?
4. How will framing the issue as you recommended facilitate organizing efforts?
5. How will framing the issue this way be linked to your long-term strategy?
6. What questions/problems arose in your small group in discussing this situation?

Power and Empowerment in Community Practice

If community practitioners in social work are required by the NASW *Code of Ethics* (1998) to eradicate injustice and oppression, they must understand the phenomena that caused the inequitable distribution of resources, power, status, and opportunities (Mullaly, 2010). Community members experience oppression not in the abstract but, rather, in day-to-day exploitation, marginalization, and social exclusion. They often feel powerless about their life circumstances, are frequent victims of physical and psychological violence, and are led to believe that their persons and their cultures are inferior. Given the chronic nature of this systematic structural oppression, it is not surprising that oppressed people incorporate this imposed inferior status into their self-concepts. This is reflected in a variety of ways, including psychological and social withdrawal, in-group hostility, identity dilemmas, magical thinking, self-destructive behavior, individual and social resilience, and different forms of resistance (Mullaly, 2010; Payne, 2014). Throughout social work history, strategies to overcome oppression have ranged from assimilation to the promotion of difference.

The African American abolitionist Frederick Douglass (1847) stated, "Power yields nothing without a demand." In a similar vein, Homan (2016, p. 202) asserts that change is impossible without the use of power, which he defines as "the ability to realize one's values in the world" or "the ability to prevent other people from doing something they want to do" (Kirst-Ashman & Hull, 2015, p. 286) All human relationships are essentially political. In Goldberg and Elliott's (1980) pungent words, "As long as society is differentiated along ethnic, sex and social class lines, politics pervades all of social life. You are involved in politics and so is your mother" (p. 478).

As discussed in previous chapters, traditional forms of power include the power to bestow or withhold rewards or resources; the power of force or coercion to punish (ranging from physically to psychologically); the legitimate power that emanates from law or other institutional sources; referent power—the power that flows out of social/political relationships or access to hierarchies; and the power associated with expertise or the possession of critical information, organizational affiliation, charisma, and social or political connections.

In community practice, the exercise of power also occurs more subtly through what the Italian philosopher and activist, Antonio Gramsci (2007), termed "cultural hegemony." Jan Fook (2002), a leading critical theorist in social work, argues that practice issues

> are also questions of power—whose knowledge counts as legitimate, and whether practical knowledge is implicitly devalued ... I would argue that we need to recognize different forms of knowledge, and different ways of creating that knowledge, if we are to begin to gain a better representation of our own experiences, and that of many different groups with whom we work. (p. 129)

Alternative ways of conceptualizing power include regarding power as a commodity whose quantity, quality, or value can increase or decrease depending on circumstances. Another way of viewing power is as something people do, not something people possess, and that it is often based on relationship rather than other external factors. Patricia Hill Collins (2000) refers to the different "domains of power"; that is, the power of individuals or communities varies depending on the context. Some communities regard power as coming from within, such as spiritual power. Sources of "relational power" include knowledge, numbers, group discipline, vision, diversity, creativity, persistence, humor, courage, and the ability to take risks. Finally, it is particularly important for social justice-oriented practitioners to distinguish between exercising power *over* someone and exercising power *with* someone.

In community practice, a critical issue is the community's perceptions about what constitutes resources and who controls them. In a community, there are numerous sources of power, some of them more obvious than others. They include tangible things such as money, goods, services, status, and personal qualities (e.g., charisma) and intangibles such as information, energy, networks (social capital), and historical memory. This power is exercised in a variety ways—in the distribution of "rewards" and "punishments," in the application of expertise, in the presentation and withholding of information, in connecting people to others who have power, and in terms of an individual's or group's relationship to legitimate authorities. The analysis and effective application of power is critical to heighten community awareness of issues, organize and mobilize supporters, and ultimately overcome one's opponents.

Perception of one's power or powerlessness is a critical dimension of empowerment, an oft-used term that can be defined as a process that "strengthen[s] the basic *life skills* and capacities of individuals, but also [alters] . . . [the] underlying social and economic conditions and physical environments which [affect people's lives]" (Nutbeam & Kickbush, 1998, p. 354). Empowerment enables people and communities to develop a more positive and potent sense of self, construct a more critical comprehension of one's environment, and cultivate functional competence to attain their personal and collective goals (Simon, 1994). Theories of empowerment assume that empowerment is a value that infuses action on personal and collective levels, that it is a mutual process that requires respectful dialogue to occur, and that it involves the synthesis of political–economic and psychosocial factors to be effective. From a social justice perspective, social workers cannot "empower" people, give people power, or transfer the power they possess to others. At best, social workers can facilitate a community's process of empowerment (Hardina, 2005; Lee, 2001).

One way to overcome people's deeply entrenched powerlessness and despair is to help them create multicultural coalitions and alliances. Another is to engage the community in participatory action research. A third is to develop ongoing support mechanisms within the community, often linked to the provision of services the community has determined it needs.

Unfortunately, many social workers and social work students think of power only in terms of its negative connotation (e.g., "power corrupts"). This is particularly ironic given the profession's emphasis on individual and group empowerment. In most definitions, power is associated with force, influence, control, and domination. From this perspective, power arises from the gap between two primary elements—need (a service, knowledge, and material resources) and means (money, authority, knowledge, and raw material). In power-dependency theory, the relationship between a need and a means to satisfy this need transforms these two elements into equal and opposite forces known as dependence and influence. This produces the most easily recognized form of power—"active power." According to this theory, it is possible to determine the degree of power by measuring either the influence or the dependence of different individuals or groups. Feminists argue that this view of power reflects the influence of patriarchy. Through a feminist lens, an alternative view of power might be "the capacity to produce a change" (Miller, 1982, p. 3). Instead of viewing power as "power over," it could be conceptualized in a collaborative, more egalitarian manner as "power with." Identifying a community's power resources is generally the first step in identifying the "targets" for its change efforts.

Critical race theorists such as Derrick Bell (2004) regard structural and systemic racism as the primary mode of oppression in US society. From this perspective, the power of racially dominant individuals, organizations, and institutions is reflected in all aspects of social life. Community issues, therefore, must be analyzed and defined in terms of their racial dimensions if they are to reflect accurately the realities of 21st-century communities. Although few social workers have consciously integrated critical race theory into their practice frameworks, organizations such as the Center for Third World Organizing based in Oakland, California, have used a racial and multicultural lens to frame their organizing and training (Sen, 2012), in addition to incorporating an international perspective into their work. Other grassroots organizations emphasize the revitalization of indigenous cultures and values, particularly in their work within immigrant communities, and capacity-building among youth (Delgado, 1994; Weaver, 2014). They maintain a healthy skepticism about electoral-based reform or traditional organizing approaches and are open to the possibility of collaboration with progressive White organizations if people of color are represented "in the mix" (Sen, 2012).

This perspective on power is reflected in the different organizational configurations that have emerged in communities of color during the past two decades. These include single-issue and monoracial organizations, multiracial organizations, organizations that focus exclusively on immigrant rights, community-based workplace initiatives, local economic development efforts, and advocacy organizations that resemble professionalized groups (Delgado, 1994).

Two key questions underlie the analysis of power in community practice. The first is "Power for what?" That is, how is power currently being used and how might it be used to promote community change? The second question is "How do different conceptions of power influence our perspectives on the concept of empowerment and our ability to help empower "communities"?

Sources of Power in a Community

Source	Application
Knowledge	Technical or professional expertise
Resources	Raw materials, money, person power
Social pressure	Cliques, clubs, gangs, committees
Authority	Policies, elected officials, organization position
Law	Civil and criminal codes, legislation, courts
Norms, values, traditions	Religious beliefs, habits, customs, mores
Personal style	Charisma
Coercion	Strikes, riots, insurrections

This view of power—as an important component of analysis and as a tool to produce change—requires community practitioners to acknowledge the "political" nature of their work, the negative consequences of apolitical professionalism, and the way in which the "master narrative" underlying social work in the United States often serves to obscure the social control features of social work practice and the privilege and power that social workers possess, and to rationalize a form of political neutrality that contradicts the profession's ethical imperative to pursue social justice (Haynes & Mickelson, 2010; Reisch & Jani, 2012; Swalwell, 2013). Mondros and Wilson (1994) emphasize that activist organizations focus on acquiring power to achieve their goals even in the face of powerful resistance. They also distinguish between actual power and the feeling of being powerful—a critical distinction for practitioners who are concerned about community empowerment because empowerment is both a political and a psychological state (Solomon, 1976). In summary, it is just as important for community members and community organization to possess a sense of competence, control, and entitlement to rights, resources, status, and opportunities as it is for them to possess the means to obtain these desired ends.

Exercise: Power in Community Practice

Introduction (Students will be divided into small groups.)

You are working—as part of a group of social work students—with one of the following populations on a community effort whose goals include public education, group empowerment, and the enhancement of services:

- Homeless individuals in your community
- Women who have experienced domestic violence
- TANF recipients
- Elderly residents of nursing homes
- Incarcerated youth or formerly incarcerated adults
- Unemployed industrial workers*

Think about your role in working with this population and in working with the other students in your group—*NOT* about the specific strategies/tactics that might be employed in this particular social/political action effort.

Questions
- In what ways would you anticipate issues of power and privilege might emerge
  —with members of the particular population with whom you are working?
  —within your group (of students)?
- How might these issues affect intragroup and intergroup dynamics?
- What could you do to reduce the negative effects of imbalances of power and privilege?

* This list can be revised as appropriate.

Relationships and Communication Styles in Community Practice

Two common ways in which power is expressed in community practice are through the pattern of relationships that develop between social workers and community residents and in the different communication styles that exist when individuals and groups from different cultures interact. It is important for community practitioners to be aware of how social roles, status, and a person's history affect relationships and communication patterns. Community practitioners from the dominant culture, for example, are seldom aware of how their styles of communication are culturally specific. Each culture has largely unspoken rules about such things as conventions of courtesy, the sequencing of conversations, the use of gestures and body language, the degree and types of emotion that are acceptable, and the interpretation of different tones of voice.

There are also significant differences in the physical distances that are deemed culturally appropriate in different contexts and how these distances affect such features of communication as touching, formality of language, and the use of gestures or physical expressions (Kochman, 1981; Thomas, 1991). Practitioners should also be aware of other important forms of communication in a community, such as music, poetry, song, dance, and art, including graffiti. Developing sensitivity to others' communication styles can facilitate participation within diverse communities and provide members with heightened self-esteem, a sense of control over their lives, and the ability to sustain their involvement in change efforts (Seebohm et al., 2013).

Leadership and Socially Just Decision-Making

Traditional views of leaders and leadership reflect the so-called "great man [sic] theory of history" (see Chapter 7). They focus on individual charisma and create a dichotomous view of relationships within a community, organization, and society, such as between community practitioners/organizers and community residents, paid staff and volunteers, or management and staff. This perspective ascribes the success or failure of change efforts primarily to individuals and ignores the relationship between context and the emergence of leaders. When applied to community (or organizational) practice, this perspective reproduces elite views of leadership and maintains hierarchical forms and processes that perpetuate the social and political status quo.

An alternative view of leadership recognizes that who becomes a leader and what forms of leadership are most desirable are contingent upon the context. In some circumstances, a leader must be directive or authoritative. She or he regulates activities, distributes resources, resolves conflicts, determines rules, and decides who's in/out of a group. In other situations, a leader's role is more protective or education. She or he gives assistance, information, attention, or affection to group members and protects them from harm. In other circumstances, the leader is instrumental in forging and sustaining relationships (Wasonga, 2009).

The implications of this alternative view of leadership are important for socially just community practice. One implication is that in a given situation, *anyone* can be a leader. Another is that in different cultures, leaders and leadership take different forms requiring different preferred qualities or different styles of decision-making, including collective. This means that leadership is not an attribute but, rather, a behavior or set of behaviors and a relationship between a person and a specific situation that can change over time. It implies that leaders are not born but, rather, can be created through training, work, and experience and also that effective leadership requires interpersonal, political, analytical, and motivational skills (Alban-Metcalfe & Alimo-Metcalfe, 2009).

Traditional views of leadership frequently created obstacles to the democratization of organizations. They tended to emphasize such traits as intelligence, masculinity, adjustment, dominance, extraversion, and conservatism (Mann, 1959). More recent versions of this ideal leadership model focused on a desire to lead, honesty and integrity, self-confidence, cognitive ability, and knowledge of the field (Kirkpatrick & Locke, 1991, as cited in Northouse, 2007).

By contrast, alternative views of leadership stress a person's determination, sociability, humility, and will and his or her ability to inspire, transform, and stimulate others to action. Other desirable traits include trustworthiness, fairness, honesty, optimism, dynamism, confidence, foresight, motivation, dependability, intelligence, and decisiveness (Johnson, 2005). Transformational leaders must possess skills in communication, administration, planning, team-building, problem-solving, and coordination. In community practice, they must be able to stimulate community members' dissatisfaction with current conditions and their enthusiasm for seeking alternatives (Shields, 2010). They generate excitement, provide strategic direction, speak truth to power, use humor in a culturally sensitive manner to provide perspective and reduce people's fears, and emphasize the strengths of a community and the individuals who comprise it. Organizations that adopt this model of leadership reject deficit-based views of people and create collaborative structures and partnerships (Cooper, Riehl, & Hasan, 2010).

Community Participation and Mobilization

Researchers have found that neighborhood organizations are one of the most effective means of stimulating and sustaining community participation and mobilizing communities, particularly disadvantaged and marginalized communities, both urban and rural, to take action (Berry & Portney, 1997; Bradley, Werth, Hastings, & Pierce, 2012). One of the major challenges in community practice, particularly within communities that have long been oppressed and marginalized, is to overcome community members' apathy and encourage greater participation in decision-making and action. Mobilizing civic capacity almost always involves a major dislocation of the status quo, and this process involves considerable risk, which may intimidate many community members. An initial step in this complex process is to identify the beliefs, attitudes, misinformation, erroneous assumptions, and false imagery that often underlie the status quo and prevent communities from participating and mobilizing on their own behalf. In cooperation with indigenous community leaders, practitioners must then strive to neutralize and counter these ideas and replace them with viable alternatives, often through the use of consciousness-raising activities.

People have a wide range of motives and incentives when they risk participating in community change efforts. These motivations can be divided roughly into three categories: reactive, proactive, and compulsory. Reactive motives include a persistent sense of grievance or violation, a recent loss or fear of loss, and the existence of a threat or perceived threat to community well-being. Proactive motives include the prospects for gain or advancement, the desire to build or strengthen a sense of community, and the goal of preventing a problem from occurring or from getting worse. Compulsory motives for community participation include responding to a catastrophic event, the need to adapt to technological or political change, and the imperative to reduce community violence in order to survive as a community (Beck, 2012a).

Whatever the initial motives, as stated previously, the goals underlying the desire for greater community participation also vary considerably. They include both tangible goals, such as the redistribution of resources and power, the acquisition of expertise, and policy or program change, and intangibles such as heightened awareness or altered consciousness, changed attitudes, behaviors, and relationships, and individual and group empowerment. One of the challenges involved in stimulating and sustaining community participation, particularly in diverse environments, is finding a way to balance competing interests.

Environmental factors also play an important role in determining the extent to which a group will mobilize for collective action. Charles Tilly (1978), a renowned scholar of social movements, found that the likelihood of a group's collective action is a function of the following factors: (1) the extent of its shared interests, (2) the intensity of its organization, (3) the degree it is mobilized, (4) the degree of repression in the environment, (5) the amount of power the group possesses, and (6) the existence of an opportunity and/or a threat.

To engage communities effectively, practitioners must overcome their ignorance of a community's history and culture through active listening (Bettez, 2011). They must spend time discovering the underlying assumptions within the community and reflecting on their own. They must avoid thinking that not only should people do the right thing but also they should do it for the right reasons (i.e., the same reasons the practitioner would). This may require practitioners to acknowledge that religious rather than secular motives inspire people to take action on behalf of social justice (Todd & Allen, 2011; Torres-Harding, Carollo, Schamberger, & Clifton-Soderstrom, 2013; Turner, 2010). The Industrial Areas Foundation, originally established by community organizing pioneer Saul Alinsky (Horwitt, 1989), often bases its work in faith communities and fuses religious traditions and power politics in cities such as Baltimore and Detroit.

Practitioners must also help community residents identify the intended targets of change efforts, what strategies and tactics will be employed and how they will be linked, and facilitate the cooperation of often disparate community groups that may not have a history of cooperation for mutual benefit. A persistent challenge is how to mobilize community residents around a large enough sphere of activities to stimulate their interest and make a difference in their lives without making the scope and range of activities so large that it produces a series of impossible tasks and discourages the very participation one is trying to produce.

Participatory change efforts, therefore, combine elements of all models of community practice (discussed below), including grassroots organizing in geographic or functional communities, popular education, and strategic planning. Whatever combination of approaches is used, in order to promote sustained community involvement, the change effort must allow community members to gain from their experience, to engage in dialogue with each other, and to "drive" the change process. The long-term purpose is to create alternative structures through which people articulate and meet their needs and gain collective power to shape existing systems for the better.

Socially just community practice regards such participation as both a goal and a means. It stresses socially just decision-making, building individual and community capacity, prioritizing the needs of the least advantaged, analyzing community problems in their historical and contemporary context, and building sustainable organizations and movements. It is a project designed for the long haul, not the quick fix. Its underlying values reflect a genuine belief in people and a respect for their wisdom; a recognition that community practitioners need to ask questions, listen, and learn; and awareness that beyond the acquisition of concrete tools and techniques, sustainable community participation requires increased confidence, lasting interpersonal and intergroup relationships, and the creation of a culture of mutual learning (Bolland, 2002; Scanlan, 2013; Stokamer, 2013).

Sustained community participation requires the creation of a common purpose, which emerges through dialogue and the formation of new interorganizational relationships. The process consists of three overlapping phases: discovery, decision, and drive. The discovery phase focuses on building a case for change among community members. Practitioners need to consider both the array of competing interests in a community and the complexity of the environment. They use a variety of methods to frame current and future challenges and to assess the possibilities for change, including cultural tools such as hip-hop to involve youth and provide them with an understanding of how broader social justice issues affect their lives (Turner, Hayes, & Way, 2013). Working with both established leaders and "laypersons," they create a database of allies and bridge builders. A short-term objective is to break from traditional patterns to determine people's real needs and discover real supporters.

In the decision phase, community groups make critical choices about their goals and the strategies and tactics they will employ to achieve them. They define the scope of decisions that will need to be made and the process by which they will make them. They attempt to articulate a few breakthrough choices and to sketch out a story of change. They define simple rules or principles that can transform the complexity of interests into common purpose.

Finally, in the drive phase, community groups mobilize their members, allies, and supporters in action to produce the changes they desire. This may involve the creation and mobilization of new networking vehicles and the development of new community leaders. A community's ability to engage in and sustain a high level of participation throughout this complex process is influenced by the extent to which it is able to identify common values and norms; create a variety of means of democratic participation; define the purposes of that participation clearly and adapt these goals and objectives to changing circumstances; strengthen internal long-standing social ties (referred to as "bonding" social capital) and build new connections outside the community (referred to as "bridging" social capital).

Community practitioners play multiple roles in the process of promoting and sustaining community participation. They animate communities by stimulating people's critical awareness. They create a process of inquiry and encourage community members to construct their own narratives through which their history is connected to future action. Practitioners can assist community members in developing organizational structures that promote greater cohesion and group solidarity; they can facilitate a group's efforts to engage in specific actions and transfer their technical expertise. They can serve as intermediaries to the "outside world"; establish external contacts for community groups; introduce people to unfamiliar processes; and help forge alliances, networks, and coalitions (LeRoux, 2007).

Exercise: Overcoming Resistance to Community Participation

10 Reasons People May Resist Participating in their Communities and How You Might Respond

1. I am too busy/can't do much to help/going to school/already belong to another organization.
   - *Are you in support of what we are doing? We encourage everyone who supports us to show it by joining in some way. We encourage people to contribute whatever they can in terms of time, but the first step is to join. That way, you will be kept better informed and can become more active at any point in the future. OR Our organization/effort can only show our strength through our numbers. The more members we have, the better our chances of winning.*

2. I am too old and getting ready to retire.
   - *Not everything we are working on is going to be accomplished in our lifetimes, but we have to look at the future for our children, grandchildren, other working people, etc.*
3. I can't afford to pay the membership dues (where applicable).
   - *Dues can be paid in monthly installments. OR When would you be able to pay the dues? OR The dues only amount to ___/month. That is not much for what we do.*
4. I am thinking about changing jobs/just lost my job/afraid of losing my job.
   - *The work we are doing will affect all working people in the community.*
5. I am afraid my boss/company/neighbors/family will find out.
   - *They do not need to know. We do not identify the organization if we call you at work and we don't need to call you at work at all. What you choose to tell others is entirely your business.*
6. I have children/dependent care problems.
   - *Our organization can make some arrangements to furnish you with care, schedules meetings well in advance, or could work on the issue of providing such care to all families.*
7. My spouse/partner/parent doesn't like me to join organizations. I need to talk to him/her.
   - *Wouldn't _____ like you to solve the problem we are working on?*
8. How will this organization help me?
   - *The organization will help you in the following ways (be as specific as possible).*
9. I already have a friend who keeps me informed about your issues.
   - *Then you must know enough about us to show your support by joining.*
10. I am not a _____ (radical, socialist, feminist, activist, etc.).
    - *Not all of our members are _____.* (Unless your organization claims to be.) Repeat #8.

Planning: Models of Socially Just Community Practice

In the 1960s, Jack Rothman developed an ideal tripartite typology of community organization that has influenced the discourse on community practice in the United States for much of the past half century (Rothman, 1986). Some of the original assumptions in this typology have been criticized by feminist community practice scholars, such as Cheryl Hyde (1996), and those who are concerned about the importance of multicultural awareness, such as Lorraine

Gutierrez (2001). Rothman (1996) modified his original framework in response to some of these critiques. Other scholars (Weil, Gamble, & Ohmer, 2012) have expanded on Rothman's model and identified eight different varieties of community practice. For purposes of simplicity, however, the following discussion is based primarily on Rothman's model.

From a social justice perspective, Rothman's underlying assumption that the organizer or the organizing unit should determine the appropriate approach to community intervention pays insufficient attention to the importance of the community defining its own problems and goals. Another concern is the absence of a clear ideological or value foundation for community practice in the framework. Although methodological flexibility is critical for effective practice, it does not require the adoption of an apolitical or non-ideological perspective. Although social workers need to be flexible in their choice of strategies and tactics, a commitment to basic values is critical in all forms of community practice. Finally, Rothman's assertion that social action is incompatible with other forms of practice is contradicted by the numerous examples of their successful combination that have occurred throughout US history, such as the recent work of advocates for marriage equality and immigration reform.

Community and Social Development

This model regards the focus of community practice as the creation, expansion, or revision of services that people need and as *they* define these needs propose solutions to them. It has been particularly influential in Central and South America, South Africa, and India (Sekhon, 2006). In the United States, community practitioners in the so-called "voluntary sector" have played a critical role in this area as far back as the 18th century. Social work examples include the activities of settlement house workers during the Progressive Era (~1890–1917) and the interactionist approach developed by Mary Parker Follett and Eduard Lindeman in the 1920s.

In recent years, the popular education approach of Paulo Freire has been particularly influential in shaping community practice in Latin America and throughout the world. This approach emphasizes helping people redefine their place in the social structure and modify norms, role expectations, and community self-identification. It also utilizes a mutual aid philosophy that assumes not only the construction of new or renovation of old structures but also a reformulation of traditional professional roles. It assumes the existence of actual or potential common bonds among people and the need to establish mutual interdependence. This approach is consistent with social work's emphases on a strengths perspective and empowerment approach (Saleeby, 2002; Simon, 1994).

It has also been used by labor unions, faith-based organizations, and numerous self-help organizations and cooperatives (Kasmir, 1996).

From a social justice perspective, community or social development has three main characteristics: (1) an interest in community-building though the process of education and communication, (2) a process-oriented focus that emphasizes group and intergroup activities, and (3) a focus on self-help and leadership development. From a social justice perspective, the role of a community practitioner goes beyond program and staff development, volunteer recruitment and training, and service coordination. It also integrates a clear educational and ideological linkage of services or programs to organizational goals and values—what Lewis (2004) referred to as the "cause *in* function." Newer models combine strategies of economic development with long-standing approaches to community social development. Examples include the Grameen Bank and other forms of microenterprise development in South Asia and US cities, the Brotherhood of St. Lawrence Project in Australia, and the Mondragon Cooperatives in the Basque region of Spain (Alperovitz, 2011; Kasmir, 1996; Smyth, Reddel, & Jones, 2005; Yunus, 2007).

One of the most important features of this model of community practice is its emphasis on popular education and "reflexive learning" as a means of expanding the consciousness of community members (Bentley-Williams & Morgan, 2013). Often inspired by the work of the Brazilian educator/activist Paulo Freire, this emphasis on pedagogy as a strategy of social and community change has been applied globally to a wide range of issues, including health literacy in indigenous Pilipino communities (Estacio, 2013), matters of urban survival among new migrants to China's burgeoning cities (Dai, 2011), special needs education in Northern Ireland (Barr & Smith, 2009), sustainable development in Mauritius (Rambaree, 2013), and work with Aboriginal clients in Australia (Harms et al., 2011). Recently, community development strategies have been linked with rights-based approaches to achieve greater justice for villagers in northern China (Haijing, 2013), workers in Argentina and Venezuela affected by the forces of economic globalization (Larrabure, Vieta, & Schugurensky, 2011), and children at risk in widely varying environments throughout the world (Young, McKenzie, Schjelderup, & Omre, 2012).

Ongoing external political and social challenges for practitioners adopting this approach have influenced its core principles (Baumann, Domenech Rodriguez, & Parra-Cardona, 2011). These challenges include the constraints of a global economy and a hierarchical political–economic system on the possibility of creating change at a local level, the balance between community participation and meeting people's concrete needs, and the tension between the potentially divisive assertion of cultural identity for empowerment purposes and the importance of forging multicultural coalitions to produce sustainable change. Community development is based on an underlying, although unstated assumption: Communities are relatively simple entities, with many of the qualities of a person and with shared values. This assumption can lead practitioners to experience difficulties dealing with the emerging realities of class, racial, and gender stratification that are often masked by the superficial appearance of homogeneity.

The community development model, therefore, contains certain problems for a social worker who wishes to engage in socially just practice: Should the worker remain neutral or should she or he attempt to influence (or manipulate) the community to pursue certain goals or to follow a particular strategy? How should she or he pass on the role of leadership? What should the worker do when the community chooses a course of action that contradicts her or his values—for example, when it wishes to exclude certain community members from participation or distribute its resources inequitably? How can community development efforts sustain their commitment to social justice, radical democracy, and mutuality, particularly for excluded and marginalized populations, and not succumb to the tendency to replicate hierarchical patterns of authority and decision-making?

Despite these potential problems, features of the community development approach—its emphasis on democratic, community-wide collaboration, empowerment, public/private partnerships, the coordination of interrelated systems, and a community's strengths or assets—make it an attractive and accessible means to promote social and community change (Bryan & Henry, 2012). According to Rogge (1997), successful community change efforts also balance vision and action and take a pragmatic approach to community problem-solving. Through the application of a social justice agenda, popular education, and community outreach, it has overcome even physically dangerous and intentionally intimidating challenges from neo-Nazi hate groups in the western United States (Canfield-Davis, Gardiner, & Joki, 2009).

In recent years, several conceptual and practice innovations have revitalized the community development approach within social work. Some communities have actively engaged with Freire's (1970) theories of conscientization through the use of collective dialogue to challenge the systemic oppression that community members experience, raise their critical consciousness, and motivate them to take political action (Kline, Dolgon, & Dresser, 2000). The use of small groups in which participants discuss their ideas about social justice and sociopolitical identity and the issues that affect their lives, an approach that social justice-oriented social workers have used since the 1930s (Reisch, 2008b), has been particularly effective in empowering residents and raising their consciousness (Hays, Arredondo, Gladding, & Toporek, 2010). Other neighborhood groups have used Edward Soja's notion of "spatial justice" to transform interpersonal relationships and expand community activities through education about the nature of social inclusion and exclusion and collaboration to achieve a "fair and equitable distribution . . . of socially valued resources and the opportunities to use them" (Armstrong, 2012, p. 609). The Los Angeles County Community Disaster Resilience Project applies the core principles of community resilience theory, particularly in its integration of equity and social justice concepts into program planning and development (Plough et al., 2013). Other groups have introduced the concept of "restorative justice" to reduce high levels of community violence (Beck, 2012b).

Some groups have helped communities—through schools, religious congregations, and block associations—to overcome the demoralizing and stigmatizing effects of the dominant culture's "master narrative" by encouraging them to develop counter-storytelling practice (Johnson & Rosario-Ramos, 2012; Luttrell, 2013). Others have used photo-voice—a technique that draws upon community members' creativity and perceptive insights—to raise public awareness and demonstrate how relationship-building and problem-posing can enhance a community's power (Peabody, 2013). Neighborhood-based "community lawyering clinics" and groups employing restorative justice strategies have been successful in providing services with a social justice focus and using popular education methods to promote residents' empowerment and community transformation (Beck, 2012a; Brodie, 2009). Some groups have published guides to help community residents initiate face-to-face conversations, strengthen the "local commons" of community institutions, support local resources (community spaces and cultural institutions), and transform people's private problems into concerted social action (Forum Organizing Project, 2009).

Social or Community Planning

Although the roots of social or community planning are in top-down social provision or social engineering, recent innovations have created the opportunity to use planning as a tool of democratization and community empowerment. To a considerable extent, the nature of social or community planning depends on whether it focuses on means or ends, emphasizes participatory consensus or empirically driven rationality, and stresses incremental or institutional change. Planning focuses on the modification, elimination, or creation of policies, services, programs, or resources in service systems through the alteration of the processes of resource allocation, service delivery, and program development. A challenge for contemporary planners is how to integrate the model's three key traits—an emphasis on problem-solving around a concrete problem or specific issue, the use of technical expertise to achieve goals, and a task (as opposed to a process) orientation (Lauffer, 1978). To understand social planning, it is important to examine the linkages between systems and their consumers and the additions, revisions, or extensions of services that are desired. This is particularly important in today's hyperpartisan environment when working in marginalized communities that experience a high level of material deprivation and a lack of political power and influence (Hammond, 2013).

Traditional planning methods assumed that one or more of the following deficiencies exist within a community: (1) a lack of resources (quantitative or qualitative), (2) ineffective or inappropriate services/programs, (3) inappropriate structuring of services or distribution of resources, and (4) lack of responsiveness to community needs. A more socially just orientation to social planning places increased emphasis on the involvement of community residents in all phases of the planning process. In order to develop more community-based (i.e., relatively decentralized) planning processes, service users and constituents must be involved early and throughout the process in defining needs, determining outcome goals, developing measures of outcomes, and establishing criteria for program effectiveness (Green, 1999). They should also focus on community leadership development, technical assistance, and training.

Awareness of the range of actual or potential political actors and agendas is also critical. This will help communities avoid the unsuccessful experience of projects such as the Model Cities programs of the 1960s War on Poverty (Bailey & Danziger, 2013) and, recently, empowerment zones whose benefits largely accrue to businesses outside of the communities the projects were purported to help. Another critical step is the application of a broader definition of relevant evidence to include the use of qualitative data obtained from community residents. The data used to inform planning efforts must also constantly be reassessed. A social justice approach to planning, which emphasizes "equity praxis," also assumes that community members know the solutions to the problems they confront even if they occasionally have difficulty articulating them in typical planning language (Ruiz & Valverde, 2012). The application of this approach in an environment that increasingly stresses results-based accountability (RBA) is particularly crucial if local social justice organizations are to resist the introduction of regimes such as RBA that reflect antithetical values and vastly different goals (Keevers et al., 2012).

In addition, social justice-oriented planning requires the ongoing education of community participants to ensure their continuing involvement in the planning process. This requires staff, volunteers, and community representatives to revise their roles in order to maintain the mechanisms for ongoing dialogue. Part of this shift is the promotion of greater awareness of the planning process by a wide range of community groups. This assumes that the process of community change—from needs assessment and the creation of an assets inventory to the development of strategic solutions and the evaluation of the effectiveness of these solutions—is an ongoing, dynamic process and not a linear, time-limited one.

An example of an effective social justice-focused planning effort is the participatory budgeting process that has been used for years in Port Alegre, Brazil, and that has recently been implemented in New York City. Another example is a program in Toledo, Ohio, called "Second Chances," which combats the effects of trafficking through combining the individual-level services, program development, and advocacy of the faith-based community and social work organizations (Perdue, Prior, Williamson, & Sherman, 2012). In Brazil, planning theory has been used to address the chronic problem of spatially segregated, vastly unequal urban areas in cities such as Rio de Janeiro. A federal law passed in 2001 recognizes people's "right to the city" and requires the participation of community members in local planning processes (Friendly, 2013). In a similar vein, the promotion of "accountable democracy" in post-dictatorship Chile emphasizes the role of public opinion in shaping just policy outcomes (not merely just processes) by creating links between people's expression of their views and governmental policymaking bodies (Paley, 2001).

At the organizational level, a feminist planning model is an example of the application of social justice principles to the planning process. This model involves a different mode of analysis and a broader concept of what constitutes "truth," revised ways of approaching life and politics, asking questions and searching for answers, and different methods of formulating choices. One of its primary purposes is to demystify the planning process by making its underlying values and goals explicit and rejecting frameworks that reflect the inherent biases of dominant systems of thought and behavior. Its value base incorporates principles of egalitarianism, a reduction of status and power differentials, cooperation and collaboration, nurturance and support, sharing of resources and an expanded definition of what constitutes a "resource," divergent thinking, and the establishment of responsibility to self and others.

In addition to addressing such problems as false assumptions about women as analysts and planners, it challenges prevailing ideas about power and the persistence of dichotomies between experts and laypersons, particularly with regard to what is considered knowledge and evidence (Fawcett, Featherstone, Fook, & Rossiter, 2000). In summary, feminist planning replaces a binary concept of planning with a holistic, synergistic approach. It also involves a redefinition of power from "zero sum" to infinite (the basis of empowerment) and a redefinition of planning from "expert" to cooperative.

In order to develop and sustain a feminist planning model, social justice practitioners need to cultivate an approach to practice that emphasizes process as much as outcomes, encourages divergent thinking, values community members' ideas throughout the change process, makes underlying assumptions and values explicit, applies a collective model of leadership, and uses multiple forms of data in their analyses. They would develop services that focus on eradicating bias, promote individual and community empowerment, use both process and outcome evaluation, and reflect a commitment to self-determination and human dignity.

Social or Political Action

Social or political action is the approach to community practice that is most often associated with social justice. However, the social action model employed by practitioners is not monolithic. Traditional models, often based on the ideas of Saul Alinsky (1971), have three key features: They are conflict focused, they target sources of power for specific community needs and to establish the community's right to self-determination, and they are both process and task oriented. Many social action efforts are difficult to sustain due to the attempt to combine both means and ends in an effective and ethical manner. A major difference between community development and social action involves the distinction between self-help and self-determination.

The social reform approach, which combines elements of social planning and social action, is the path taken by many community social workers and social work organizations. Its features include the use of coalitions; an emphasis on task orientation; a view of community residents as victims or potential consumers; and the adoption of a pragmatic approach to social change that focuses on changing unjust policies, laws, and resource distribution patterns. Examples of this approach include efforts to end destructive mining practices in Appalachia and the Interior West, organizing Gulf Coast residents who are recovering from the impact of Hurricane Katrina, and working to promote fair trade practices that save community jobs (Oxfam, 2006). Unfortunately, this approach, although well-intended, sometimes involves doing good *for* people while maintaining a hierarchical, fundamentally unjust model of practice.

The most radical approach to social action, grassroots organizing or direct action, combines several strategies. With roots in a variety of indigenous and imported social movements, this type of community practice flowered in the 1930s and 1960s as a response to the severity of social and/or economic crises, the lack of more than symbolic successes obtained by other social action efforts, and the implications of changes in the demographic and political environment (Boyte, 1980). Recently, direct action strategies have been used by the Occupy movement to underscore the problem of growing economic inequality; by youth promoting more open immigration policies and greater equity in education and employment (Goddard & Myers, 2013), such as ColorLines; and by the "Black Lives Matter" protests against the treatment of racial minorities by the police and the criminal justice system (Alexander, 2010).

The focus of direct action organizing is to put pressure on elites and elite institutions to compel policy or institutional change. Some social action efforts focus on a single issue; others are multi-issue. They range in scope from neighborhood-based to national or even international.

Direct action strategies apply social justice principles to the basic approaches of social work intervention. They emphasize the development and utilization of people's strengths to the point at which they are empowered and can help themselves. They confront the root causes of social and economic problems and the current and historical contexts from which they emerged. They focus on cultivating people's strengths and attacking the points of contradiction within society and its institutions so that the ensuing crises will hasten the creation of solutions. Social action strategies also include the replacement of elites and attempts to bypass elites through the development of alternative institutions. In this manner, they combine elements of social action with those at the heart of social or community development, including the expansion of service provision to community members. Examples include cooperative movements, mutual aid societies, and self-help organizations.

Implementing: Developing Strategies and Tactics

All models of community practice include the following components:

1. Examining and analyzing the "big picture": This involves identifying the goals of the action effort and its underlying vision and mission, understanding what "success" would be, distinguishing between short-term objectives and long-term goals, and clarifying the role of ideology and values in the change process.
2. Addressing the structural factors that are necessary for effective social action to occur: These include the role of the organization, the range of strategies and tactics available and feasible, the locus of the group's actions, the source of the organization's funding and staff, and the other resources the organization would require.
3. Defining the roles of group members: This includes determining who should be included or excluded from participation; what are the preferred qualities and skills of participants; what are the preferred roles for practitioners, paid staff, and volunteers; and what are the preferred forms of leadership and decision-making.
4. Clarifying how the organization will function on a day-to-day basis: For example, will it emphasize task completion or process? What types of intragroup and intergroup relationships will it seek to create? How will the organization address the issue of power and power differentials? Will it make decisions by

consensus, majority rule, or some other means? How will the organization tap into the nonrational components of community practice, such as people's emotions, rituals, customs, and spiritual needs?

The following chart compares the use of consensus and conflict approaches to community practice and change:

Consensus Versus Conflict Strategies to Promote Community and Social Change	
Consensus Strategy	Conflict Strategy
1. General orientation	
a. Search for things that unite people by focusing on the commonalties all people experience and know.	a. Search for things that divide. Find structural cleavages that enable people to see their real interests.
b. Faith in the power and reality of ideas and values that people can discover if they will allow truth to emerge in a free and open encounter.	b. Faith in the power and reality of interests and that can motivate people to organize and act.
c. Truth is the correspondence of a statement with a state of affairs.	c. Truth is loyalty to group interests.
2. Organization	
a. Collaborate.	a. Fight.
b. Organize across interests.	b. Organize around structural interests.
c. Bring together various assortments of people to work on "real" problems that transcend divisions.	c. Bring together people in like situations. Make their interests manifest.
d. "Anti-ideological." Should be concerned with truth. Organize people by helping them create a common definition of a problem and a common solution through a collaborative process.	d. Develop an ideology that supports your interests in conflict with other groups.

3. Communication
   a. A means of sharing used to clarify need, problems, and goals of all parties.

   a. A weapon to be used to obtain strategic advantage, to describe your interests in the best light, and to disadvantage opponents.

   b. Stress openness and honesty. Attempt to achieve clarity about oneself and others and to check perceptions by communicating openly and freely. Share real needs and problems. Collaborate to achieve mutual goals.

   b. Make strategic use of information. Understand your own needs and interests but do not reveal them to the opposition. Make the enemy think you are stronger than you are.

   c. Use communication to develop trust and attraction between persons and groups.

   c. Establish a strong negotiating base. Keep the situation ambiguous and uncertain for the opposition.

   d. Be flexible and responsive. Keep all parties informed about what is going on.

   d. Catch the opposition off guard. Create anxiety and confusion for opponents, but keep your own group well informed.

4. Approach to opponents
   a. Opponents are to be brought into the dialogue so that a wider circle of relationship can be fashioned.

   a. Opponents are the enemy. Polarize the relationship to your advantage.

   b. Try to understand the opposition as much as possible and help them understand your group as well.

   b. Attack the opposition. Question their competence; impugn their motives; stereotype and exaggerate their positions.

5. Dealing with conflict
   a. Attempt to distinguish real from unreal conflict. Get at the real source of the problem.

   a. The real source is in interest cleavages. Use real and unreal conflict to improve your group's advantage.

   b. Ventilate hostility. Humanize opponents.

   b. Direct hostility toward the opposition.

   c. Seek to resolve ill feelings.

   c. Seek to achieve a better platform for negotiation.

d. Contain conflict by attempting to institutionalize it into existing arrangements or differentiate those arrangements so as to be able to deal with it.

e. Minimize distortion in the conflict and polarization.

d. Use conflict but do not allow it to be institutionalized or channeled by established procedures, when those procedures are created by the structures you are seeking to change.

e. Use distortion and polarization. Disrupt established procedures for handling conflict.

6. Alliances

a. Work with all those who are involved in a situation. Build alliances with those who think as you do or who will enter a process of working with you.

a. Build alliances with those who have the same interests.

b. Build alliances across interest cleavages.

b. Build alliances across interest cleavages only on a temporary basis and only on specific issues where there is a convergence of interests.

7. Attitude toward the system and vehicles of social change

a. Keep the system open.

a. Change the system.

b. Existing institutions within the system are the vehicles of change. They are capable of responding or adapting to deal with new problems and needs.

b. Oppressed groups—when organized—are the vehicles of change.

8. Criteria for use of each strategy

Use the consensus model when:

a. Power is shared so that equals are dealing with equals.

Use the conflict model when:

a. Power disparities exist; one group dominates the other.

b. Goals are distributable—that is, both sides can get what they need and want. Common ground exists. (Win/Win)

b. Goals are not distributable—that is, the situation is a "zero sum game." (Win/Lose)

c. People share values, interests, and goals, or at least it is possible to create consensus on them.

c. Sharp cleavages of values and interests exist.

Source: From Tex S. Sample (2001). Consensus v. conflict strategies. In J. Rothman, J. Erlich, & J. Tropman (Eds.), *Strategies of community intervention*, 7th ed. Itasca, IL: Peacock.

Recently, social workers have become increasingly involved in global activism. In both the Global North and Global South, they have responded to the effects of climate change and natural disasters and linked the environmental domain to issues of poverty and gender equality, based on ecological and ecofeminist theories (Alston, 2013). In places as diverse as Australia and the Middle East, social workers have become increasingly identified as human rights workers (Calma & Priday, 2011; Moshe Grodofsky, 2012). Despite the risks involved, they are now integral parts of social movements promoting women's participation in electoral politics in rural India (Sekhon, 2006) and anti-deportation movements in the United Kingdom (Grayson, 2011).

Glasius and Pleyers (2013) assert that recent activist efforts throughout the world possess three common tendencies:

> A common infrastructure of networks and meetings that facilitate rapid diffusion; a generational background shaped both by the [danger] of paid work and by exposure to and participation in global information streams; and, most fundamentally, a shared articulation of demands and practice. (p. 547)

They also share the common goals of democracy, social justice, and human dignity, and they reflect in their actions "a mistrust of institutional power and a determination to [avoid] becom[ing] corrupted by power" (p. 547).

Beyond the legal, political, and physical risks involved, there are several potential problems with using the social action approach in community practice. Once the goal of a direct action effort is attained, then what? How will the participation and cooperation of community members be sustained? How will the community avoid replicating the patterns of injustice they organized to correct? If, on the other hand, the effort encounters persistent obstacles or fails to achieve its objectives, there is a strong possibility that community members will become dispirited and retreat to frustration, cynicism, and apathy.

The focus on obtaining concrete ends through whatever means has the potential of draining resources from other community practice efforts and runs the risk of creating ethical dilemmas for practitioners (discussed later). Unless fundamental structural changes are made, what good is accomplished by achieving a few specific ends or changing a community's leaders? Even developing alternative institutions contains risks: Their creation may encourage a focus on survival rather than growth or change. In short, there is the danger of sacrificing long-term social justice goals to short-term pragmatic considerations.

Community practitioners can avoid some of these problems by keeping several points in mind. First, when it is impossible to build cross-cutting alliances, due to past or present community divisions or a hostile political environment, try to find or create issues that promote common ground. Second, try to maintain a focus on the community's agenda by avoiding distractions, including those that emerge from personality clashes within the organization or are foisted on the organization by external opponents. Help community members agree either to disagree or to remain silent on divisive issues that can never be resolved and that drain energy, time, and resources from your purpose. Third, emphasize the development of multiple leaders, a collective leadership style, and participatory decision-making. This avoids the emergence of top-down organizations even within groups founded on principles of social justice and equality. It also diminishes the risks to the organization and prevents the organization's goals from being too closely identified with a few individuals. Fourth, be aware of the power of language and the importance of how issues are framed and reframed. Fifth, strive to maintain the independence of the organizations with which you work. It is important for them to establish their own space in every sense of the word. Finally, be aware of a community's history of social action and the degree to which individuals and organizations have engaged and can now engage in risk-taking (and around what issues). Be clear on how you are defining risk. Your concept of risk may be very different from that of the community members with whom you are working.

Interorganizational Relationships

Interorganizational relationships in community practice assume a variety of forms, including coalitions, cooperatives, collaborations, campaigns, networks, and social movements. Each of these entities involves working with diverse individuals and groups that have a common interest in order to share information, take joint action on issues of mutual concern, or participate in an advocacy effort or political campaign (see Chapter 9). They range from informal ties—often based on personal connections—to semiformal networks, which have a loose organizational structure and allow participating organizations to maintain full autonomy, and formal coalition structures with elected officers, bylaws, clear decision-making processes, and separate budgets.

Participating in coalitions, networks, and collaborative projects has both potential benefits and potential problems. It can help community organizations obtain difficult-to-find information, access powerful decision-makers, learn from the experiences of other groups, build relationships for future campaigns, avoid political and social isolation, "borrow" power, acquire strength through increased diversity, share resources and work, enhance intergroup solidarity and avoid harmful divisions, and—at best—create in miniature a model of a just society.

Many community groups, however, hesitate to join or help build such inter-organizational efforts. They fear that the inevitable differences that will arise could lead to paralysis around pressing issues and make it more difficult for organizations to work together in the future. They often believe that the investment of finite time, energy, and resources is not worth the potential gains and that attempts to forge a coalition will be a drain on their organization. They are concerned that working with other groups will lead to a loss of control over goals, strategies, and tactics and that it will restrict their organization's autonomy and options. Finally, in a society that promotes competition in all aspects of our lives, they are skeptical that disparate groups, even those that espouse a social justice agenda, will be able to cooperate, particularly during a long-term effort. Therefore, it is understandable for community groups to ask, "When it is advisable to join with other organizations rather than work independently?" The following is a useful guide for making this decision:

When to Join a Social Justice Coalition, Network, or Campaign

- Genuine *common interests* exist among the potential partners.
- Your organization lacks sufficient resources to produce change alone.
- The members of your organization are aware of the need for change.
- Potential partners have resources.
- Leadership links already exist.
- The political and social environment supports the formation of new relationships.
- Your organization has already developed a power base.
- You have not yet initiated a campaign or change efforts.

In forging interorganizational relationships, groups engage in a process somewhat similar to a courtship. They gather intelligence about each other before making direct contact. In the early stages of their relationship, they often exchange "paper contacts" such as endorsing a common issue or cosigning a letter. If things go well, key members of their organizations work on a specific time-limited project such as a press conference. Later, the organizations may engage in a short-term alliance on a single issue. Finally, they may create a formal, ongoing partnership that may last years, lead to an affiliation or merger, or be dissolved.

Successful coalitions possess several qualities. First and most important, they demonstrate a willingness to experiment and learn from their mistakes. They have skilled and diverse leaders and members and a democratic decision-making structure with clearly defined roles (Herzberg, 2013). They take the time and effort to build trust among their members through effective means of communication and conflict resolution. Both internally and externally, they state their mission, values, and goals distinctly and develop a common vocabulary and concise means of framing the issues about which they are concerned. Finally, they acquire resources to achieve their goals and are able to mobilize their constituencies.

It is important to keep in mind that working in coalitions or similar groups is foreign to most people, particularly in the United States. To overcome this strangeness, potential partners must build connections by their acts and not merely by their words. Leadership roles and responsibilities and organizational assets must be shared, either through rotation or through some other mutually agreeable and equitable means. Maintaining the independence of your own organization and the fiscal autonomy of the coalition is critical. It is also important to be careful with regard to the sources from which you receive funding.

These challenges are particularly difficult in efforts to forge multicultural groups or coalitions. The following are guidelines that may be helpful:

- Find an issue that unites people; this is not simple in an increasingly partisan and fractious environment (Conway & Lassiter, 2011).
- Be clear on why the coalition is needed to *resolve* this issue, *not* to create it.
- Identify common goals and short-term projects to "try out" your partnership.
- Identify the historical/contextual factors that *facilitate or impede* coalition formation.
- Assess each group's strengths and self-interests carefully, including your own.
- Be aware of the impact of race, gender, class, and sexual orientation on people's behavior.
- To avoid divisions based on identity, try to create a new identity or a multiple identity.
- Given the diverse strengths of group members, level the playing field (e.g., in the use of technology).
- Take risks with new strategies and tactics.
- Be particularly sensitive to process and leadership questions.
- Think "outside the box" regarding who might be potential allies and supporters.
- Make time to build trusting relationships, not just among leaders.
- Leave space for a shared agenda to be created or revised as others join the coalition.
- Remember: Diversity means differences. Address the issue of diversity up front (e.g., before an initial meeting), and plan how you will respond to differences when they arise.

- Be prepared to discuss the "undiscussables"—avoiding conflicts only intensifies them; create "safe spaces" through different formats; and make sure all voices are heard.
- Remember that most coalitions are not permanent.

Ethical Dilemmas in Community Practice for Social Justice

Since the late 19th century, social workers have engaged in social action around such issues as labor conditions; civil rights for racial minorities, women, and the LGBTQ population; civil liberties for political dissidents; children's welfare; and peace and economic conversion. The goal of social justice is currently reflected in the statements of principles and codes of ethics issued by leading professional organizations such as NASW, the Council on Social Work Education, and the International Federation of Social Workers. These values and the ethical imperatives derived from them are particularly salient for community practitioners who are committed to social justice and the pursuit of the common good.

Values and Ethical Principles for Community Practitioners	
National Codes of Ethics	Particular Values and Ethical Issues Critical for Community Practitioners
Example: Values noted in US National Association of Social Workers' *Code of Ethics* or the social work code of your nation	
Service	Interdependence
Social justice	Empowerment practice
Dignity and worth of the person	Reciprocity
Importance of human relationships	Partnerships and mutuality in work
Integrity	Citizen and community participation
Competence	Human rights and social justice Structural analyses and approaches (work toward changing programs, policies, and root causes, not just manifestations of problems)

Just as in practice with individuals, families, and groups, it is important that community practitioners be aware of how their personal and professional values influence all aspects of their work. In addition, to practice from a social justice perspective, social workers need to broaden their conceptualization of community practice beyond the goals of its activities to incorporate the social justice components of the processes involved as described previously. In other words, the dimensions of socially just practice in communities often parallel those of socially just practice with individuals and families. Both can reflect approaches to doing justice that are "profoundly collaborative and informed by decolonizing practice and anti-oppression activism . . . doing solidarity, addressing power, fostering collective sustainability, critically engaging with language, and structuring safety" (Reynolds, 2012, p. 18).

Despite their similarities, there are some important differences between community practice and practice with individuals. Social (not individual) transformation is the primary goal of community practice. The people with whom community practitioners work are considered constituents or allies, not clients. To be effective, most community interventions involve partnerships with different qualities from the relationships that social workers forge with individuals and families, such as mutual empowerment and development of enhanced critical consciousness.

Other differences include the following: Community practitioners are more likely to be members of the community; community members have greater freedom to withdraw from the practice relationship; ethical conduct is often situational (Alinsky, 1971); cultural differences often exist about the meaning of community, leadership, group roles, and work styles; and an organization's values and goals are often in dispute. In addition, certain key ethical concepts, such as informed consent, self-determination, and confidentiality, are applied differently in community practice.

Examples of situations in community practice in which ethical dilemmas arise include the following:

- Truth-telling versus group interests and organizational loyalty (e.g., whistleblowing)
- Allocation of scarce resources (material and nonmaterial)
- Conflicts of duties or loyalties (e.g., in coalition work)
- Conflicts between means and ends in the selection of tactics

Exercise: Selecting Ethical Tactics in Community Practice

Introduction

Activists often have to make difficult ethical decisions about the use of tactics in a social or political action campaign. The following questions ask about the "fit" of particular types of tactics with your personal values and ethics. Please indicate your responses to the following questions by checking the appropriate box. Write your comments in the spaces provided.

1. The use of confrontation is an acceptable tactic.
   Always _____   Sometimes _____   Never _____

2. Embarrassing opponents is an acceptable tactic.
   Always _____   Sometimes _____   Never _____

3. Whistleblowing is an acceptable tactic.
   Always _____   Sometimes _____   Never _____

4. Leaking information is an acceptable tactic.
   Always _____   Sometimes _____   Never _____

5. The use of exposés is an acceptable tactic.
   Always _____   Sometimes _____   Never _____

6. Lying is an acceptable tactic.
   Always _____   Sometimes _____   Never _____

7. Legal disruptive actions are acceptable tactics.
   Always _____   Sometimes _____   Never _____

8. Civil disobedience is an acceptable tactic.
   Always _____   Sometimes _____   Never _____

9. Violence against property is an acceptable tactic.
   Always _____   Sometimes _____   Never _____

10. Violence against persons is an acceptable tactic.
    Always _____   Sometimes _____   Never _____

Summary

Beginning with a definition of community and community practice, this chapter discussed theories, models, issues, goals, and challenges of socially just community practice. It complements the material presented in Chapter 7 on organizations and demonstrates the similarities and differences between the application of social justice principles at the micro and macro levels. Chapter 9 addresses how social workers can influence the policymaking process in a manner that combines the pursuit of socially just goals and socially just means.

Discussion Questions

1. How do you define "community"? In what ways are social justice concepts reflected in your definition?
2. To what communities do you belong? In what ways are these communities socially just?
3. How do theories of community change reflect social justice concepts? Which theories of change are most consistent with your view of social justice?
4. How would you apply social justice concepts to the different types and stages of community practice?
5. Which strategies and tactics of community practice do you consider most consistent with social justice principles? For what reasons?

Role Play Exercise: Initial Contacts

I. Individual contacts
  A. You are employed by a community mental health center that is attempting to expand its programs into low-income neighborhoods in a nearby community and wants to establish an advisory committee to assist in their development. You have learned that there are several community groups whose support and participation on the advisory committee would be critical. You have arranged to stop by the home of the president of a neighborhood-based anti-drug group, Ms. Wanda Blank, to invite her participation. Ms. Blank is a widow, in her mid-50s, who has partial responsibility for raising her grandchildren. She works as a secretary in the local high school and is very active in her church. She greets you at the door politely but suspiciously and invites you in.
  B. You are employed by a local tenants' action group and assigned to contact residents of low-income housing developments. The organization is interested in establishing tenants' councils in these housing developments. Your assigned task is to determine if the tenants have problems or grievances around which they would be ready to organize on their own behalf. If you learn that this is what the tenants want to do, you are to help them organize a tenants' council. Because you do not know any of the residents personally, you decide to knock on doors and explore tenants' awareness of problems

---

and readiness to act. You park your car, knock on a door, and a tenant opens it. She is a young, single parent who is a Temporary Assistance for Needy Families (TANF) program recipient currently involved in a job training program.

II. Group contacts

A. You are employed by a local community development corporation and assigned to work with parents who are concerned about the operation of the local elementary school. During the past 2 weeks, you have contacted a number of parents and, based on these discussions, you have arranged for a meeting of 8–10 parents to begin to address their problems. The meeting is being held in the basement of a local church tonight.

B. You are employed by a federated agency, such as the United Way, that raises funds for social service and community education projects. You have been asked to convene a meeting of individuals who have been major donors to the agency in the past. The purpose of the meeting is to enlist the support of these individuals in a major new campaign to address the needs of women and girls in the community. The individuals invited are expected not merely to be donors but also to attract other potential donors to the project.

Exercise: Leadership

Introduction

Our views of leadership are shaped, in part, by our personal experiences and how we interpret them. The views of our families, schools, and churches influence our thinking, as do direct encounters with leaders we have known or observed from a distance. This exercise is designed to reveal experiences that shaped your personal view of leadership and influence your current thinking about becoming a leader and/or improving your leadership skills.

Step 1 (5 Minutes)

Think about individuals from your past whom you remember and revere. Think about individuals whom you consider to be a leader in your current life.

A. List three (3) people who have been important leaders in your past.

1.

2.

3.

B. List three (3) people whom you respect and value as leaders in your current life.
1.
2.
3.

Step 2 (5 Minutes)

For each of the persons you listed, indicate briefly how they integrated social justice principles into their work and what attributes you think made them effective leaders.

Step 3 (10 Minutes)

In the following chart, list those qualities and attitudes/behaviors that characterize the leaders you identified previously and indicate briefly what you learned from them that has been valuable in your professional and personal life. Try to identify the qualities and attitudes/behaviors that are common to several individuals.

Qualities	Attitudes/Behaviors	Lessons
Example: Personal integrity	Constructive/outspoken	Speak your mind
1.		
2.		
3.		
4.		
5.		
6.		

Think about: What did you learn from this chart? How do you use what you have learned from these leaders in your daily life? (Note the patterns in your answers.)

Step 4 (20 Minutes): For class discussion

1. What similar and different insights about leadership did individuals have?
2. What leadership qualities were interpreted in different ways?
3. What factors may influence these disagreements? What are their implications?

Creating and Implementing Socially Just Policies

Introduction

During the past three decades, economic globalization and major demographic, technological, and sociocultural changes have transformed the process of policy development and implementation and made it increasingly complex. To a considerable extent, the locus of policymaking and implementation has shifted: in the United States, from the federal government to state and local governments (a process referred to as *devolution*); on the world stage, from the nation-state to supranational institutions, such as the International Monetary Fund, the World Bank, and various global trade organizations; and domestically, from the public to the nonprofit and for-profit sectors (a process sometimes called the *privatization* of services). In a multipolar world, dominated by market-driven goals and neoliberal ideology, social workers must now respond effectively both to international issues and to the distinctive character of local needs and concerns. However, this has become increasingly challenging. Although from a social justice perspective the development of socially just policies requires broader democratic participation, critical policy decisions are increasingly made through nondemocratic means that bypass long-standing political processes, for example, by international financial institutions and multinational corporations.

To discuss the potential role of social workers in this increasingly complex environment, this chapter is divided into three parts. The first part discusses the relationship between the concept of social justice and social policy, including the role of the state, and the relationship between social justice and equality. It examines the impact of policies in terms of their redistributive effects and specific consequences for excluded and marginalized populations, such as women, people of color, LGBTQ persons, children, the aged, and individuals with disabilities.

An underlying theme is how to combine universal and selective approaches in policy formulation in order to achieve the goal of "justice for all."

The second part of the chapter explores how social workers can promote socially just policies through "case" and "cause" advocacy and other forms of community-based social action. It analyzes the phases of policy formulation that are most accessible to the application of social justice principles, even in structures with seemingly antithetical goals. It discusses how to increase the participation of individuals and groups, especially from low-power communities, in the policymaking process. These methods include community-based policy advocacy, popular education, and participatory budgeting.

The third part of the chapter discusses how to evaluate the impact of efforts to promote policy change through socially just means. The importance of an informed population as a prerequisite for socially just policies is emphasized, as is the use of media and community-based research as critical tools to achieve this result. Finally, the chapter discusses the challenges, risks, and ethical dilemmas that advocates for social justice face (Chisholm, 2013). As in other chapters, this chapter provides examples of how social workers can develop and use their own critical consciousness throughout the policy development and implementation processes.

The State and Social Justice

The concept of social justice has been fundamental in the development of public policies and political institutions, in rhetoric if not in practice, for several centuries. Although this concept continues to be prominently displayed in the official documents of many national and international organizations, it is often expressed in ambiguous terms and without a shared understanding of its meaning (Reisch, 2002). Complicating matters further, until recently, mainstream discourse on social justice largely occurred apart from discussions of its implications for racial or gender equality, although it has long been acknowledged that issues of social justice inevitably involve conflicts over race, gender, citizenship, and culture. The emergence of multiculturalism as both an incontrovertible social fact and a controversial issue (in terms of how society should respond) has made the underlying connections and conflicts between these fundamental concepts of social welfare and human well-being more explicit (Caputo, 2000; Reisch, 2008a).

A critical aspect of contemporary debates over the meaning and application of social justice involves disputes concerning the role of government, or "the state." Throughout the past 2000 years, assumptions about the role of government have changed considerably, particularly in Western countries. In ancient Greece and for centuries thereafter, proponents of "natural theory," such as Plato

(2013), Aristotle (2009), and Aquinas (2002), regarded the state as a "natural phenomenon" whose features were preordained. When strong centralized monarchies developed in Europe approximately 400–500 years ago, proponents of "divine right theory" asserted that God was the sole source of political authority and that kings could rule with absolute power by "divine right" (Hobbes, 1996), thereby equating the hierarchical status quo with justice (see Chapter 2).

Beginning in the 18th century, the emergence of "contract theory" altered the prevailing view of the relationship between government and social justice. Political philosophers such as Locke, Rousseau, and Jefferson argued that the state governs not as an instrument of God's will but, rather, solely by the consent of the governed. It is therefore the creation of all the individuals and groups that comprise it and not of a divinity (Foner, 1998). Abraham Lincoln stated this view succinctly in the Gettysburg Address: Government was "of the people, by the people, for the people" (Wills, 1992). This concept of the state as a democratic institution, which mediated competing interests based on the principle of "popular sovereignty," persists today in the United States, although sometimes it is expressed more in rhetoric than reality.

During the past 200 years, two other views of the state have competed with this liberal idea. One, based on "force theory," asserts that the state is the most powerful and total form of human organization—an institution that is distinctly above the people. Originally developed by Hegel (1964) to rationalize the presence of a strong Prussian monarchy, and later expanded on by Nietzsche (1968), it was subsequently used by the Nazis in the 20th century to rationalize the creation of an all-powerful totalitarian state ruled by a single, tightly controlled political party that allegedly served as the instrument of the people. Marx and Engels (1848) originally proposed a contrary view of the state—that in capitalist societies the state was the "executive committee" of the ruling class, whose interests were identical to those of the elite, not the people. Unfortunately, the state created by the Soviet Union after the Russian Revolution often violated the Marxist principles on which it was originally founded.

Borrowing to different extents from each of these perspectives, for most of the past century, Western industrial societies have conceptualized the relationship between the state and the social welfare system in three distinct ways, each of which has different implications for the ability of government to develop and implement socially just policies. One perspective, derived primarily from 18th- and 19th-century liberalism, suggests that the state is a neutral or benevolent force that "balances" competing interests in a pluralist political system and uses modest interventions to ameliorate the inequalities, shortcomings, or unintended negative consequences of the socioeconomic system. In other words, government's role is to provide minimal regulation in a basically free market system.

This perspective is compatible with a "residual" view of social welfare that has little interest in achieving social justice. In fact, proponents of this view regard the status quo as intrinsically just.

A second perspective is that the state can be a positive, even paternalistic, force in society, which through its policies makes critical interventions to encourage economic and social development. In this conception, however, government's role is limited to correcting the excesses of modern, industrial society, such as unemployment. During the mid-20th century, this conception of government, which equates a just society with one in which equal opportunity exists, produced an "institutional" view of social welfare in which the role of the state gradually expanded. It provided the foundation for the social policies developed in the United States from the 1930s until the mid-1990s and for the welfare states that developed in some Western European nations. Its key features included a "social division of welfare" (Titmuss, 1976b); a focus on people's needs, not rights; a paternalistic, top-down concept of the "common good"; a belief that a society can achieve social justice without altering its basic structure; and the use of public policy to reconcile social conflicts and restore at least the façade of community. Occasionally, however, it led to an adversarial relationship between the state and service recipients that increased the importance of policy advocacy on their behalf (discussed later).

A third perspective produces a more expansive role for the state. It regards the state as a potential vehicle for economic and social transformation, the redistribution of resources, the promotion of human well-being and development throughout the life cycle, and more recently, the recognition of social identity (Fraser, 1995). This model provided the foundation for "cradle-to-grave" social welfare systems that are most commonly found in Scandinavian countries, based on a "developmental view" of social welfare. Only a few of its features, such as universal pre-kindergarten programs, have been adopted in the United States.

Exploring: Promoting Social Justice through Contemporary Social Policy

Just as there are many ways to define social justice (see Chapter 2), there are also widely varied interpretations of how the concept should be applied to the development, implementation, and evaluation of social policies. The evolution of 20th-century social welfare systems in Western nations obscured to some extent the persistence of these differences. On the surface, welfare state policies (e.g., Social Security, Medicare, and unemployment insurance in the United States) are based on justice-oriented values such as the equal worth of all citizens, the equal right of all persons to meet their basic needs, the expansion of people's opportunities and life chances as widely as possible, and the goal of reducing or eliminating unjustified inequalities (Katz, 2001). Advocates for these policies assumed that a social welfare system should not be merely a "safety net" but should also be a springboard for economic opportunity and social mobility.

This assumption also inspired greater governmental investment in human capital development, such as education and training programs; the promotion of policies that enable people to balance employment, family, education, leisure, and retirement across the life cycle; and policies that strengthen social institutions such as the family and community and create a more stable and secure social environment (Commission on Social Justice, 1994). They reflect the ideal of a socially just society in which all members have the same basic rights, protections, opportunities, obligations, and social benefits (Marshall, 1950; Sunstein, 2004).

In recent decades, welfare state policies have expanded beyond the guarantee of fundamental rights and equal opportunity to include principles of redress or compensation for historic injustices; in the United States, affirmative action policies are a prime example (Rawls, 1971/1999). In some instances, policies have been designed to produce a more equal or equitable distribution of societal "goods"— both tangible and intangible, material and nonmaterial (Nussbaum, 2003; Sen, 2009)—or to establish what Martin Luther King, Jr., and bell hooks termed a "beloved community" whose members participate fully in its self-governance (Alsup, 2009). Such a community would encourage and respect a variety of cultural modes of expression, norms, and values, and it would possess societal structures and processes that do not consistently "center" particular worldviews.

It is important to note that until the mid-20th century, different views of social justice existed in different regions and among different populations in the United States (Reisch, 2007). To some extent, these cultural and political differences still exist; state and local policies continue to reflect different conceptions of justice on such issues as health care (Daniels, 2001), education, welfare, criminal justice, and the rights of disabled persons and the LGBTQ population. For example, during the past 5 years, a majority of state governments in the United States have refused to implement vital components of the Affordable Care Act, such as the expansion of Medicaid (although it will be largely funded by the national government) and the establishment of insurance exchanges. In many areas of social policy in both public and private sectors, these differences appear in statutory language, stated policy priorities, models of service delivery, and organizational forms. As a result of these diverse cultural norms and political philosophies, the application of social justice to social policy in the United States varies widely.

The range of these diverse ideological perspectives can be briefly summarized as follows: *Libertarians* (Nozick, 1974) and, to a slightly lesser degree, *conservatives* (Hayek, 1976) emphasize the preservation of individual liberty, property rights, and the maintenance of the current social and cultural order. They distinguish between outcomes that are "unfair" and those that are "unfortunate" and argue that government should play a limited role in shaping these outcomes. They do not make clear, however, how we should determine which outcomes fall into which category. (Libertarians are more strongly opposed than conservatives to government intervention in people's lives, for example, on issues such as reproductive and privacy rights and drug use.) Senator Rand Paul and, to a somewhat lesser extent, Representative Paul Ryan are libertarians. Senators Marco Rubio and Ted Cruz are conservatives.

Modern *liberals* (whose philosophy differs considerably from that of 19th-century liberals such as John Stuart Mill) favor policies that ban discrimination, provide a more equitable distribution of social benefits and burdens, and expand civil rights and liberties. Influential liberal philosophers such as Rawls (1977/ 1999) base their idea of justice on two principles—equal liberty and the distribution of societal goods to aid the least advantaged. Senators Barbara Mikulski and Debbie Stabenow, who are both social workers, are contemporary examples of liberal politicians.

Communitarians (Sandel, 1998) stress greater cooperation, trust, and mutuality in our institutions and relationships, whereas *Social Democrats* (Gil, 1998; Titmuss, 1976a) believe that social justice requires both greater social and economic equality and more democratic political participation (George & Wilding, 1994). Senator Bernie Sanders is a social Democrat. Finally, proponents of the "capabilities approach" (Nussbaum, 2011; Sen, 2009), as well as postmodern and critical theorists, argue that a socially just system of social welfare must also involve marginalized individuals and excluded groups in socially just policymaking processes. This perspective incorporates a growing awareness of the impact of different cultural and historical contexts (Young, 2011), includes nonmaterial resources among the "goods" to be distributed (Nussbaum, 2011), considers the implications of multiple forms of power on policymaking (Hill Collins, 2000), and argues that policies should be specifically tailored to address different types of oppression and manifestations of privilege (Mullaly, 2010).

Despite their differences, most of these perspectives maintain that socially just social policies would include the eradication of injustice, an equitable distribution of power and resources, and some mechanisms to ensure a more equal distribution of opportunities. Of course, proponents of each perspective define terms such as justice, equity, equality, and opportunity quite differently. As a result, conflicts continue to exist among policymakers on the following questions:

1. Should socially just policies emphasize more equal opportunities or more equal outcomes—what Ryan (1981) referred to as "fair play" or "fair shares"?

2. Would socially just policies be based on a person's merit, productivity, individual needs, status, past contributions, or future potential? How will these qualities be calculated?

3. Should social policies compensate for past injustices? If so, which injustices and to what extent?

4. Should policies provide basic "minimums" or enhance people's capabilities (Sen, 2009)?

5. Should policies reflect universal or group-specific conceptions of social justice? Should they be targeted at individual justice or justice for groups?

6. How should policies reflect religious and secular views of justice, such as the conflict over requiring contraceptive coverage in the Affordable Care Act (Judd, 2013)?

7. Should policies promote social change or social stability?

8. How can policies balance the goals of equality and individual rights/freedom (e.g., the conflict over mandatory coverage under the Affordable Care Act)?

9. How can policies take into account both the fiscal costs of attempting to address a problem and the social costs that result from not doing so (e.g., environmental regulations to address pollution and climate change)?

10. To what extent should policies address special needs (e.g., people with disabilities)?

11. Is the achievement of a more just society a "zero sum game" or a "win/win" situation?

12. Is social justice identical to or in conflict with the promotion of universal human rights?

13. Can social justice be achieved in a single nation or community or must it be achieved globally or not at all (Nussbaum, 2004)? (See Chapter 2.)

In developing socially just responses to these difficult questions, social workers face a number of challenges, including the following:

1. Applying concepts based on individual rights to group needs and concerns
2. Reconciling conflicting views of social justice in a diverse society and world
3. Achieving social justice when governments lack their former power and influence because of phenomena such as economic globalization and technological changes
4. Implementing just policies within outmoded institutions

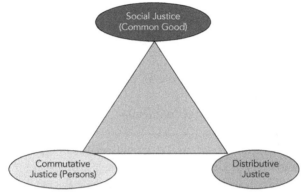

FIGURE 9.1   The Three Sides of Justice

Source: Daniel Maguire (2010). *Ethics: A complete method for moral choice*. Minneapolis, MN; Fortress Press.

Figure 9.1 illustrates this complexity.

Exercise: Different Approaches to Social Justice

1. Review the definitions in the following table. These represent some of the approaches commonly taken in relation to social justice. Add others important to you.

Ranking	Some Definitions of Social Justice
	A fair, equitable distribution of power and resources for the most people
	An equal opportunity to succeed and make life choices for everyone
	Freedom from threats of violence and being disparaged
	Challenging multiple ways that institutions, groups, and everyday practices create and perpetuate inequities and unearned privilege
	Norms, values, symbols, and customs that allow everyone to participate knowledgably and comfortably
	The right, obligation, and ability for everyone to participate fully in self- and societal governance
	Other:
	Other:

2. As a way to assess their relative importance in your thinking about social justice, please rank the importance of each definition for you, assigning a 1 to the one most important to you, a 2 to the next most important, and so forth.
3. Note briefly which criteria you used to make these rankings.
4. Think about some of the implications of different definitions for your field of practice and/or your practice setting (e.g., service delivery, larger environment, policy issues, your organization, staff issues, and the various constituencies your organizations serves).

Engaging: Working for Social Justice Today

During the past three decades, as a consequence of economic globalization, technological developments, and deliberate policy decisions, the gap in the distribution of income and wealth has significantly widened not merely in the United States but also between the Global North (industrialized nations) and the Global South (developing nations). As Figure 9.2 indicates, poverty in the United States persists, particularly in communities of color, with long-term negative consequences, especially for children and youth (Rank, 2004).

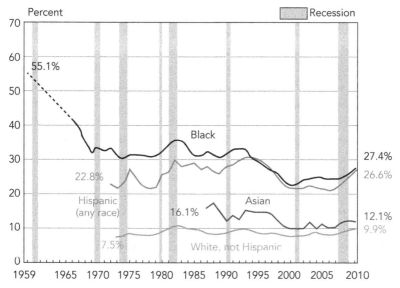

FIGURE 9.2 Poverty Rates by Race and Hispanic Origin, 1959–2010
Source: US Bureau of the Census, 2012.

In urging social workers to become more involved in recognizing and combating the effects of long-term poverty on children, Hernandez, Montana, and Clarke (2010) assert that

> ignoring children's health needs can compromise their educational preparedness, occupational pursuits, productivity, and longevity. . . . Poverty, restricted access to health insurance and health care services, cultural and linguistic barriers, neighborhood conditions, and racial and class inequalities exacerbate poor health outcomes and contribute to child health inequality. (p. 291)

In addition, the failure to address growing racial disparities in health, mental health, education, housing, and employment threatens the well-being and stability of our society (Stiglitz, 2013).

Attempts to address these serious and complex issues have recently been confounded by several factors. The focus on external "enemies," such as international terrorism, obscures the persistence of social inequality at home. The fragmented physical structure of many American communities often masks long-standing socioeconomic divisions, isolates the disadvantaged, and obscures the consequences of disproportionate privilege. Proponents of social justice are frequently attacked as unpatriotic and marginalized within the media, our political system, and even our helping professions. The fiscal consequences of economic globalization and the Great Recession have promoted budgetary austerity, an attack on "entitlement" spending, and a further weakening of the role of government in social policy formation (Reich, 2012).

In addition, heightened political polarization and changes in the distribution of political power have made it more difficult to reach consensual solutions to the nation's social problems (Blau, 2014). The privatization of social welfare, which has intensified during the past few decades, has often substituted market values for the social justice mission of social service organizations, particularly in the nonprofit sector (Salamon, 2012). Dramatic demographic changes—such as the aging of the US population, increased immigration, the shifting racial composition of urban areas, increases in the number of single-person households, and the movement of population from the heartland to the coasts—as well as new cultural norms about sexual orientation, marriage, work, family, and retirement have altered our perspective on long-standing issues.

At the same time, emerging issues, such as climate change, global epidemics, mass migration, the impact of wars and civil conflicts, the instability of employment, the impending financing crises of Social Security and Medicare, and increased social and economic stratification, create formidable policy challenges for the future. In an article in *Tikkun* magazine, Eisler (2010) argues that a holistic approach, which focuses on the care and protection of all people and the planet, is now required to address these interlocking problems. Caputo (2002) similarly emphasizes the link between individual and social caregiving—what he terms the "ethics of care"—and social justice.

Equality, Social Justice, and Social Policy

Debates concerning the application of justice principles to social policy are compounded further by disputes over the meaning of equality—an ideal that has long been enshrined in US political documents and institutions, if unrealized in practice—and over how the pursuit of equality is related to the goal of social justice. Persistent questions compound current political conflicts. They include the following:

- Why is equality a desirable goal?
- Equality of what?
- Is "true equality" attainable? If not, why not?
- Are all inequalities unjust?
- How do we distinguish between institutional and more subtle forms of inequality?
- To what extent should equality be measured in individual, group, or societal terms? How would group membership be established and by whom?
- How do we balance private needs and public concerns in the pursuit of equality?

Like social justice, equality or inequality can be conceived along several dimensions. For example, in addition to addressing the extent and effects of income inequality, it is also important to assess how inequalities of wealth (or assets), opportunities, access, rights, and status affect people's lives. In an affluent society such as the United States, it is worthwhile pondering why extensive poverty and inequality continue to exist and why, in some ways, they have become more severe during the past several decades. It is also important to ask the following: How can public policies reduce or eliminate these inequalities? To what extent can the "market" (the economic system) achieve these goals?

At the beginning of the 21st century, in response to the changing demographics of the United States, the 98th American Assembly (2001) published a number of recommendations to move the nation closer to racial equality by 2025 with the overall goal of eliminating persistent racial disparities. The report focused on long-standing concerns, such as economic opportunity and decent wages and working conditions, and emerging issues that have attracted intense media and political attention and require community-based reform efforts, including immigration (Lanning, 2012) and inequities in the educational and criminal justice systems (Arrigo, 2013; Cross, 2013). Like advocates in other industrialized nations, such as Australia and the United Kingdom (Carey & Riley, 2012; Goodman & Burton, 2012), the American Assembly suggested that policymakers employ a combination of "universal" and "particular" approaches to combat some of the challenges facing racial minority communities (p. 9). Ironically, the report indicated how little progress has been made in these areas during the past half century.

More than 40 years ago, the sociologist Herbert Gans (1971) argued that poverty (and, by implication, inequality) in the United States contributes to the maintenance of the social, political, economic, and cultural status quo. Consequently, we have tended to stigmatize poor and vulnerable people in order to rationalize societal inaction to address their problems. We have also tended to analyze issues in individual rather than structural ways to avoid an examination of the systemic causes of poverty and inequality. Unfortunately, since the publication of Gans's article, US social policies—such as new tax laws, cuts in social spending, and, until recently, the failure to increase the minimum wage to match the cost of living—have exacerbated inequality and made chronic and deep poverty more intractable. As Figure 9.2 illustrates, there is also a persistent racial dimension to poverty in the United States. African Americans and Latinos are two or three times more likely to be officially poor.

Other causes of growing poverty and inequality in the contemporary United States include the following:

1. Deindustrialization, technological change, and economic globalization, which have led to efforts to reduce the size of the welfare state in order to maintain a competitive advantage for US businesses in the international marketplace
2. A decline in unionization, particularly in the private sector, and an attack on workers' collective bargaining rights, which have contributed to lower average wages
3. The outsourcing of manufacturing and service jobs, which has resulted in higher rates of structural unemployment
4. Reductions in private pensions that have made retirement more precarious for millions of Americans (Madrick, 2006)
5. The emergence of "neoliberal" ideological rationales for reduced government intervention, lower spending on public programs, and individually focused policies that have transformed the norms of policy formulation, class relations, and institutional arrangements and processes (Abramovitz, 2012)

The consequences of growing inequality and poverty are experienced in every aspect of our society. They affect the people with whom social workers interact on a day-to-day basis as clients, constituents, and colleagues. They appear in fractured social relations and a more rigid separation of the population on the basis of class, race, and culture. They exacerbate hyperpartisanship in our politics and diminish the legitimacy of our political institutions, and they create growing apathy and hopelessness about the future (Reich, 2012; Stiglitz, 2013).This is why social justice advocacy today requires "the articulation of a coherent alternative ideology, through the mobilization of social forces, and through the institutionalization of non-neoliberal rules and norms within the apparatuses of the state" (Cahill, 2011, p. 479).

What, then, is to be done? Past strategies have alternated between a reliance on the private sector—for example, through the promotion of economic growth or "trickle-down" approaches to policymaking—and government intervention to reduce poverty and inequality through a combination of income supports (e.g., increases in the minimum wage, the passage of living wage laws, the expansion of cash assistance, the extension of unemployment benefits, and the earned income tax credit); assets development and protection programs (e.g., the creation of individual development accounts; the provision of universal demogrants or children's allowances; the removal of assets restrictions for Temporary Assistance for Needy Families (TANF) program recipients; and policies that would prevent home foreclosures, facilitate home ownership, protect private-sector pensions, and increase consumer protections in the finance and housing industries); redistribution through progressive taxation, public-sector employment, and supportive services (e.g., access to and subsidies for health care (Gorin & Moniz, 2014), child care (Palley & Shdaimah, 2014), pre-kindergarten programs, transportation, and housing); antidiscrimination legislation; and programs that emphasize human capital development (e.g., education and training).

In the future, it might be useful and more politically feasible to base policy initiatives on some combination of the previously mentioned strategies. Components of individual and community well-being could include guaranteed employment at a living wage; the opportunity to accumulate assets for future opportunities such as a college education, home ownership, or starting a small business; and services that would promote both human capital and social capital development. Given the increasing demographic and cultural diversity of our society, a consolidated strategy would also address the unique needs of specific populations, such as persons with disabilities and the LGBTQ community. It would provide the intangible supports people require to achieve their individual capabilities (Nussbaum, 2011).

An emerging area for the application of social justice is the physical environment. Here, too, clarity concerning the meaning of underlying concepts would help determine the direction of future policy developments. For example, advocates have framed the issues generated by increasing concern over the environment and the effects of climate change in three distinct ways. One is to focus on "environmental racism," including the deliberate targeting of racial minority or indigenous communities in the placement of toxic waste dumps, sewage treatment plants, incinerators, and manufacturing sites and also the differential enforcement of housing codes, noise pollution laws, and environmental regulations that affect air and water quality (Philip & Reisch, 2015).

Another way to frame the issue is in terms of "environment equality." This involves either equal protection of all communities through established laws (so-called "process equity") or greater balance in the spatial and temporal distribution of environmental benefits and burdens or "outcome equity" (Nweke et al., 2011). A third way to define the issue is in terms of "environmental justice." This approach emphasizes universal access to a high-quality physical environment, fair treatment of all communities, widespread participation by all groups in the policymaking process, and the emergence of sustainable economies and communities (Dominelli, 2012; Kuehn, 2014; Leuenberger & Wakin, 2007).

As a result of these different foci, recent policy initiatives to address environmental issues have ranged from the elimination of disparities of exposure to pollution, industrial toxins (Morrice & Colagiuri, 2013), and the impact of climate change to the achievement of minimum standards of safety. As in other policy arenas, current challenges include the following:

1. How can we assess the extent of present hazards?
2. How can we determine what constitutes a "disproportionately high and adverse effect" of environmental conditions?
3. How can we balance the social, fiscal, and economic costs involved in ameliorating or preventing environmental damages?
4. How should we decide on the most effective and equitable strategic approaches?
5. How can we integrate greater sensitivity to the social and cultural dimensions of affected communities into the policymaking process?
6. How can we develop policies that not only address immediate environmental issues but also establish equitable standards for the future (Garcia, 2013)?

Political Power and Social Policy

Two major issues influence the extent to which a society's political system affects the development of socially just policies and the impact of these policies on individuals, families, communities, and social service organizations. As discussed previously, one is the degree of responsibility that the government assumes for socioeconomic policy, human development, and social capital formation, including the degree to which government intervenes in the operations of the market economy and its supporting institutions such as banks. The other is the extent to which the state is biased or neutral as a regulating institution in its treatment of the conflicting interests and needs of individuals and groups in society—for example, in mediating differences between capital (corporations and financial institutions) and labor (unions and nonunionized workers).

The legitimacy of the government, its institutions, and the political process itself is also a major factor in determining how much influence the government has in shaping social policy. A half century ago, the Gallup poll found that the overwhelmingly majority of Americans believed government could be trusted to act on their behalf all or most of the time. Today, similar polls reveal that Americans' trust in their public institutions, such as Congress, and political parties is at an all-time low. If people no longer trust government to "do the right thing," any actions the government proposes to address social or economic problems will be regarded with suspicion. In today's hyperpartisan climate, ask yourself: How does the current antipolitics mood affect the development and implementation of policies that address the problems of your community, the organization where you work, and the clients or constituents with whom you work?

Political Equality and Social Justice

One of the assumptions of liberal contract theory is that a system of political equality could serve as a guarantor of a neutral state in which policy decisions were made in the best interests of society as a whole. Recently, however, increasing socioeconomic inequality combined with the growing political influence of elites (e.g., in the area of financing political campaigns) has undermined this assumption and produced a wide range of social policies that are antithetical to social justice goals. These developments raise such questions as the following:

- What are the components of political equality?
- Why is political equality important for the attainment of social justice?
- What is the relationship between political equality and other forms of equality?
- What should be the goals of political equality? Should they be equality of rights and equality of opportunity to participate in the political process? Or, should they be equality of outcomes (e.g., equal representation)?
- How can policy be used to level the political playing field?

Underlying these questions are several assumptions about political equality that provide the foundation for social justice-oriented policy advocacy. One is that political equality has intrinsic value because political participation is an educational process that helps strengthen our sense of community, builds character (what the ancient Greeks and the Founding Fathers referred to as "virtue"), and raises people's critical consciousness. Another assumption is more pragmatic— that political equality increases the legitimacy of our political institutions. It is not surprising that faith in our institutions has declined as political inequality has increased.

Finally, political equality furthers equal protection of the diverse interests in our complex society by providing every constituency with the opportunity to influence policy outcomes (Bates & Swan, 2010; Wolff, 2008). In the United States, both constitutional provisions (e.g., the 1st, 14th, and 19th amendments) and legislation (e.g., the 1965 Voting Rights Act) have established the right to vote, hold elective or appointive office, express one's political opinions or join a political party, petition the government, and contribute to a political campaign. In summary, these policies assume that political equality is a precondition for the creation of a socially just society.

It would be naïve, however, for proponents of social justice to assume that political equality exists in the contemporary United States. There are numerous ways in which US institutions, current policies, and contemporary social conditions undermine both the principle of equality and the goal of social justice, underscoring the reciprocal relationship between socioeconomic inequality and political inequality. For example, socioeconomic inequality restricts access to information about the issues underlying policies and to the political process itself. As a result of the Supreme Court's decision in *Citizens United*, wealthy individuals and corporations can spend virtually unlimited sums of money on elections, enhancing their influence not merely on the outcome of elections but also on the policies that elected officials enact. The lack of equal capacity and opportunity also produces diminished motivation to vote, become informed about issues, or engage in any form of legitimate civic participation. This explains, in part, the remarkably low voter turnout in the United States, particularly in nonpresidential elections.

Recent changes in the political process—such as the diminished role of political parties; the gerrymandering (redrawing) of political districts, which reduces the number of competitive electoral races; and persistent discrimination against racial minorities, low-income communities, and youth through policies designed to suppress the vote (e.g., voter identification requirements)—also erode political equality in the United States. Finally, the increasing complexity of issues and of the policy process, the simplistic ways in which the media frame the policy agenda (especially in regard to complex issues), and the time commitment required for meaningful political engagement restrict the ability of most people to engage in a democratic decision-making process. This is why, despite its problems, social workers still need to engage in policy advocacy if the profession's social justice goals are to be achieved.

Planning: Policy Advocacy for Social Justice

There are five major types of advocacy: case advocacy, cause or class advocacy, legislative or political advocacy, judicial advocacy, and administrative advocacy (Hoefer, 2012). *Case advocacy* refers to an intervention on behalf of an individual, family, or small group that is in conflict with an organization with regard to a needed service or resource. *Class advocacy* involves efforts on behalf of multiple groups of current or potential clients or constituents that address collective issues and seek to produce more responsive policies. *Legislative advocacy* consists of activities focused on creating or changing legislation or government budgets to benefit some category of clients or citizens. These range from letter writing to working on an advocacy campaign and testifying before a legislative committee or meeting with individual legislators. *Judicial advocacy* tries to influence the outcome or implementation of court decisions, for example, by providing research data through expert testimony. *Administrative advocacy* focuses on altering policies (e.g., regulations) developed by agency boards, public commissions, and the executive branch of government.

Advocacy can serve many social justice purposes. It can

- influence another individual or group to make a decision (that would not have been made otherwise) that concerns the welfare or interests of a third party;
- secure existing services that clients are entitled to but unable to obtain on their own; and
- take social action to secure or expand people's rights and entitlements.

In each of its forms, advocacy for social justice involves the strategic use of information to democratize unequal power relations. Its overall purpose is to empower excluded and marginalized populations through the transfer of information, other tangible and intangible resources, and practical tools (skills) and the enhancement of people's critical consciousness. In the process of working toward specific policy outcomes, advocates also strive to enhance people's self-respect, improve their self-efficacy, and promote intragroup and intergroup trust (bonding and bridging social capital). Advocacy organizations use different models to achieve these ends and rely on diverse operating principles. For example, the model currently used by the Industrial Areas Foundation, originally established by Saul Alinsky (1971), is based on the primacy of faith communities and the fusion of religious traditions of justice with power politics. This model allows leaders from different racial backgrounds to collaborate and expands the notion of leadership to include laypersons and not merely established organizational leaders. Other advocacy organizations, such as Health Care for the Homeless, involve clients and constituents in their efforts in a variety of roles.

Social justice advocacy has two other fundamental purposes: to influence political, economic, and social *outcomes* that directly affect people's lives and to change the *processes* by which decisions are made and create the capacity for new actors to be involved in making them. It also provides oppressed and marginalized populations with new ways of understanding their life circumstances; strengthens community-building efforts; and, at the international level, helps forge "caring relationships among people within and across borders" (Bisman & Koggel, 2012, p. 213). Advocacy is a clear expression of social work's values of social justice and inclusion (Morrow, 2011) and a means of strengthening people's ability to be self-determining. There is evidence that merely participating in advocacy enhances people's subjective well-being (Sun & Xiao, 2012).

The specific goals of social justice advocacy can also vary widely—from heightening the awareness of community members, the media, or the general public about a particular issue to changing people's attitudes and behaviors and acquiring power in order to promote policy change or to make those who possess power more accountable. Whatever its goals, all justice-oriented advocacy campaigns have certain common elements: a clear statement of their principles and goals, the resources needed to achieve these goals, defined constituencies, institutional targets, and a range of tactics. They reflect a concept of power that goes beyond the ability to effect or prevent a change to include the ability to shape the policy agenda (Bottomore, 1991).

Because the concept of advocacy originated in the legal system as a means by which (legal) advocates did things *on behalf of* people, advocates today must make special efforts to integrate a bottom-up, participatory, social justice orientation into their practice. In this regard, four core components are essential: genuine participation, representation, accountability, and transparency. Successful advocacy also involves working at the intersection of three distinct but overlapping cycles of change: people's problem-solving cycle, the life cycle of an issue in the public domain, and the life cycle of the advocacy organization.

The Cycles of Change

As discussed in Chapter 8, in the policy arena, the problem-solving cycle reflects the process by which a "private trouble" becomes a public issue (Mills, 1959)—that is, a situation comes to the attention of the public, the need to change that situation becomes clear, alternative solutions are debated, and, at best, a solution is adopted and implemented. A group's ability to have its private troubles redefined as a public issue is directly related to the degree of power it is able to exercise collectively. Examples include the recent experiences of the LGBTQ community in the United States regarding marriage equality and of Aboriginal Australians on a range of justice issues (Nakata, 2013).

The life cycle of an issue is analogous to human development; it describes the process by which an issue emerges in the public consciousness, a mature understanding of the issue develops through the nurturance and support of advocates and their allies, awareness of the issue and its importance reaches fruition (in a meaningful policy response), and the issue is either renewed (i.e., the policy is expanded) or it dies (the policy is revoked or defunded) because of diminished public support. Today's "24/7" news cycle speeds up this process considerably and shortens the attention span of the public about social justice issues. The impact of neoliberal ideology, which diverts attention away from the structural sources of people's problems toward individually focused solutions, also complicates contemporary social justice advocacy (Myers & Goddard, 2013), as demonstrated by the brief life cycle of the global "Occupy" movement.

Finally, the life cycle of an advocacy organization defines what roles it can effectively play in promoting social justice goals. It is difficult for a new organization to advocate successfully for policy change because it lacks the requisite skills, resources, reputation, and connections. After a period of experimentation—of testing out its ideas—it can take a leadership role, form alliances with others, and produce positive changes for its constituents. The evolution of civil rights organizations during the 20th century provides a vivid illustration of this process (Morris, 1984). A critical factor in the organizational life cycle is the extent to which it involves constituents in leadership roles and in the strategy development process. This presents a constant challenge to advocacy groups because of the tension that exists between producing just outcomes and creating just processes.

Advocates also need to recognize that in today's political climate, the change process is invariably incremental and multidimensional, particularly in the United States, because its political system (and Constitution) is designed to make major changes difficult (Wilentz, 2005). In order to be effective, therefore, each advocacy organization needs to match its life cycle stage to the issue life cycle stage. A contemporary example is the relationship between environmental advocacy organizations and the issue of climate change. Until recently, proponents of environmental advocacy, particularly "environmental justice," were scarcely heeded and even marginalized in the media and political discourse. It took the impact of major storms, droughts, and floods to increase public awareness and support for these organizations' cause.

Participatory change is at the heart of social justice advocacy. It is based on recognition that advocacy involves changing multiple components of complex systems through a major dislocation of the status quo. The challenge for advocates is to find a way to mobilize constituents around a large enough sphere of activities to make a difference in their lives but to avoid making these activities so extensive or so complicated that they constitute an impossible task and contribute to the further demoralization and withdrawal of community members. From experience, one of the authors learned how people's busy lives often preclude sustained participation in advocacy efforts, even around issues about which they feel passionate. Just as clinical practitioners need to "start where the client is at" in order to help each person produce the change she or he desires, advocates must also make the change process accessible and feasible for their constituents—something they can accommodate within their already stressful lives.

In summary, social justice advocacy combines elements of grassroots organizing, popular education, and participatory organizational development. It assumes people have wisdom based on their lived experiences and can learn from each other through dialogue and mutual problem-solving and decision-making. It reflects an idea of justice that focuses on means as well as ends, by insisting that the community "drives" the change process. Finally, it strives to create alternative organizational structures through which people articulate and meet their own needs and work to gain collective power to improve the functioning of existing systems. Its core values, therefore, include broad participation, an expansive definition of justice, an emphasis on individual and group capacity-building, the need to "put the last first" (in the words of Rawls (1971), to prioritize the needs of the least advantaged), the centrality of community control, a notion of power and leadership as collective rather than individual attributes, and the importance of taking the long view. Advocates for social justice also believe in people's ability to learn and grow, listen and participate, and build self-confidence and lasting interpersonal relationships (Reisch, 2015b).

To accomplish these goals, social justice advocates must identify—in themselves—and help constituents identify in themselves the beliefs, attitudes, misinformation, and imagery that underlie the status quo and then neutralize and counter these ideas by replacing them with alternatives. This requires advocates to cultivate active listening skills similar to those needed by clinical social workers because ignorance of other cultures is a serious obstacle to social justice work in an increasingly diverse society (Burghardt, 2013). In combination with the development of critical consciousness, advocates and constituents engage together in a process of discovery.

Implementing: The Strategy, Tactics, and Tools of Social Justice Advocacy

In each of its five forms, social justice advocacy can be done directly or indirectly. Examples of direct advocacy include oral or written testimony before a legislative body or commission, participation in a task force or formation of a coalition, writing interagency memoranda of understanding, analyzing or drafting legislation, and filing a lawsuit in state or federal court (Lens, 2014). Methods of indirect advocacy include volunteering to work for a hotline or action network, training clients or constituents in action research or public speaking, disseminating reports that analyze public policies or "grade" legislators and administrators, engaging in action research, and providing technical assistance to legislators in the drafting of a bill or to attorneys in drafting a legal brief (Healy & Sofer, 2014; Hoefer, 2012; Lens, 2014).

In selecting an effective advocacy strategy, there are several guidelines to keep in mind. Social justice advocacy, in particular, is a synthesis of appeals to the head (ideas), heart (emotions), and pocketbook (self-interest) of the target audience. In presenting their arguments, successful advocates overcompensate and emphasize the strongest elements of their position. Although facts are always useful, they need to be cast in ways that appeal to people's objective needs and that simplify often complex data. For example, a proposal to increase taxes to support universal pre-kindergarten programs could emphasize how little it would cost taxpayers each day to enable a larger, widely accepted social good to be accomplished. Or, it could be emphasized that a bill to aid TANF beneficiaries and their children would increase welfare payments by only 50 cents/day/person. This type of appeal is called "social math." It addresses people's objective needs and attempts to manipulate widely known symbols of the dominant culture.

An important part of developing advocacy strategy is determining its short-term and long-term goals. This is not as simple as it seems, particularly for social justice-oriented issues. Advocacy does not always focus on a specific policy change. Sometimes, the goal is to educate the public, policymakers, or constituents in order to heighten awareness of a condition in need of change or to increase receptivity to a change in the future. At other times, the goal might be mobilization of the population affected by a particular problem. Proponents of marriage equality or immigration reform, for example, focused on public education and mobilization before they promoted specific policy changes through judicial and legislative advocacy. Other short-term advocacy goals might include locating supporters, developing coalitions or strengthening existing alliances, selecting future targets, and testing which tactics (e.g., demonstrations, testimony, and popular education) are most effective.

Recent studies have identified a number of additional components of successful social justice advocacy. Kuilema (2013) notes the importance of becoming more familiar with how social media, especially access to broadband technology, can be an effective advocacy tool at the grassroots level. In addition, in both domestic and international arenas, it is critical that advocates integrate the consumer or constituent perspective into policy-oriented research (Buck, 2007). McCarthy (n.d.) suggests some tactics to overcome the growing mistrust of the nation's political institutions and the democratic process among Americans. These include reasserting the right to petition the government to address specific grievances and emphasizing the eradication of official corruption through a variety of means, including legislative testimony and meeting with members of the executive branch of government, legislators, and their staffs. Linhorst (2002) argues that advocacy efforts tend to be more successful when they begin at the local or state level. The history of social justice advocacy in social work provides some support for this assertion (Reisch & Andrews, 2002). (For further discussion, see Chapter 3.)

Under most circumstances, a combination of "inside" and "outside" advocacy strategies is most effective. The former may involve nurturing supportive relationships with key policymakers; the latter may include protests to raise public awareness of the issue. During the 1980s and 1990s, organizations that focused on the HIV/AIDS epidemic, such as ACT-UP, used this tactical combination effectively. The failure of advocacy organizations to adapt to changing external circumstances can diminish their stature and influence (Bordoloi, O'Brien, Edwards, & Preli, 2013); conversely, the ability of advocates to expand upon traditional approaches, such as antidiscrimination legislation, can increase their constituents' access to justice and equality before the law (Flynn, 2013). The work of advocates for marriage equality is an excellent recent example of the latter.

In this regard, an effective strategy that is particularly appealing to proponents of social justice is called "value-based advocacy." This approach can be implemented in three different ways and often relies on symbolic appeals. Advocates can present a stark contrast to hierarchical dominant culture values and point out the undesirable consequences of these values—for example, the primacy of profit enhancement over community well-being in the location of toxic waste facilities. Advocates might also demonstrate how their goals actually contribute to the fulfillment of their opponents' values, albeit in different ways—for example, how paid sick leave for workers helps promote public health or how the provision of maternity leave helps strengthen families.

Finally, advocates could assert that the solutions their opponents propose to a particular issue are not consistent with their espoused values. Social justice advocates have criticized policymakers who resist minimum wage increases but assert the importance of work.

Advocacy Campaigns

Sustained advocacy efforts are often referred to as campaigns. Whatever the issue, all campaigns follow a similar four-step pattern: (1) problem identification and issue framing, (2) determining whether it is feasible and desirable for an organization to engage in advocacy around this issue, (3) devising a solution to the issue, and (4) developing a strategy to achieve stated goals. Following this four-step process is particularly important for social justice advocates because they are attempting to alter the institutional status quo and must work in often inhospitable political and cultural environments—for example, advocating for gun control in rural areas or for reproductive rights in communities in which there is strong religious opposition to abortion.

Throughout a campaign, advocates need to reflect continuously on the following questions:

1. What do we want to accomplish?
2. Who possesses the resources, power, or influence to assist us in this effort?
3. What do we need to communicate to obtain their support? Who needs to communicate it? What means of communication would most likely be effective?
4. What resources do we have or need to engage in a successful advocacy effort?
5. What should we do first?
6. How can we involve clients or constituents in this effort?
7. How will we determine if our strategy is working?

Framing an Advocacy Message

The message advocates wish to communicate to the public, policymakers, and opinion leaders is the central organizing idea of their strategy. To be effective, the "frame" of the message should be simple, clear, focused, and consistent. Language, images, tone, content, and context all play key roles in shaping public opinion about the causes and cures of the problems that advocates address. The objectives of framing are to make an issue resonate most effectively with the advocate's most likely supporters by appealing to their values and to convince others of the virtue of the advocate's cause.

To frame an effective message, advocates should keep several guidelines in mind. First, each issue needs a separate frame because of the population affected, the nature of the policies involved, and the context in which it is raised. Although hunger and low wages affect similar populations, advocates would not frame their arguments in favor of nutrition programs or a "living wage" in the same way. Second, it is important to target the audience that needs to be persuaded, not the audience that is already supportive. Too many advocates "preach to the choir" rather than to groups that may be opposed to or skeptical about the issues they raise.

In this regard, social justice advocates face two persistent dilemmas in framing issues: the "dilemma of perception" and the "dilemma of power." The former refers to the problem that the most "realistic" framing of an issue potentially has the most negative impact on how the public assigns responsibility for its emergence. For example, if an issue is framed in terms of its impact on a specific, often stigmatized population, such as people who are homeless, there is the danger that the framing will weaken rather than strengthen public support. The dilemma of power refers to the need for social justice advocates to persuade the wealthy and powerful that the change being sought is in their self-interest. Because elites largely control the institutions in which policy is made, the views of constituents and clients are frequently excluded or ignored. Recent efforts to garner corporate support for immigration reform or removal of symbols of the Confederacy from public buildings, however, are examples of how powerful economic forces can be harnessed for social justice purposes.

The following are important guidelines to keep in mind when framing an advocacy message.

1. Develop a clear message for *every issue.*
2. Target the audience you need to persuade, *not* the audience that already supports you.
3. Keep the focus on the needs of clients/constituents, *not* on your organization.
4. Test your framing approach and reframe it if necessary.
5. Put a *face* on the issue (i.e., humanize it), and connect each issue to a specific solution.
6. Base your message on credible data.
7. Maintain a consistent theme, but shape the theme to the audience.
8. Whenever possible, use unlikely allies to help reframe or communicate the message.

In addition to crafting a clear, consistent message, advocates need to determine who will be the targets of that message. Increasingly, they use sophisticated methods such as polls, surveys, focus groups, and media trend analyses to make these decisions. In both message framing and targeting, it is also important to frame issues differently for each group being addressed and to use a different method of presenting the message for each group. Context is critical in this regard; different messages are not only required for different audiences but also more effective at different times. For example, messages need to be framed differently during times of prosperity or recession, when external crises exist, and during an election period.

Exercise: Framing Your Advocacy Argument

Introduction

Through discussion, the class as a whole will select an issue around which social justice advocacy could occur. The class is then divided into groups of three to five students depending on its overall size. Each group will address the following questions in regard to the advocacy issue(s) determined by the class through the previous discussion. At the conclusion of small group discussions, each group will present its answers and the process by which it reached its conclusions. The class then compares and critiques each group's responses.

Questions

1. How would you frame the issue(s) to the public and key decision-makers?
2. What are your goals/purposes in framing the issue in this way?
3. At what target(s) would you direct your efforts?* For what reasons?
4. How might you frame your argument to connect with the target(s)?**
5. What other avenues for policy advocacy might you pursue to address the issue(s)?
6. Who are your potential allies or opponents?
7. What elements of the "community" would you seek to involve? How would you enable them to participate in the advocacy process?
8. What skills/knowledge would you need to engage in effective advocacy around the issue(s)? How would you try to acquire or communicate them (to others)?
9. What obstacles might you encounter? How would you attempt to overcome them?

* *Think about*: Which of the following categories best characterizes your target(s)?

- The Active Ally—*Goal*: Keep engaged and provide supportive information
- The Committed Opponent—*Goal*: Redirect arguments to the real target
- The Uninvolved—*Goal*: Get small commitments as the basis for larger ones
- The Ambivalent—*Goal*: Get public agreement on the existence of the problem

** *Think about*: Under which category does your argument best fit?

- A (re)definition of the issue
- A reinterpretation of cause–effect regarding the issue
- An incitement to take action on an issue already recognized

Assess whether your argument addresses the following basic concerns:

- Is there a need for change?
- Does your proposed solution address this need?
- Is your proposed solution feasible?
- Would the benefits of your solution outweigh any harmful consequences?

For group discussion: How did the issues themselves shape how they were framed?

Features of Effective Advocacy Organizations

Social justice-oriented advocacy organizations possess certain common essential characteristics. The definition of the problems they address begins with those who are most affected; they involve their core constituents in the research and analysis of issues and the formation of strategies and tactics. This ongoing engagement with the issues provides constituents with a sense of ownership in the organization's vision and goals. By participating in problem analysis, people acquire a more in-depth understanding of the issues and are better able to connect their self-interest with that of others who may be affected by the issue in different ways. The evolution of the environmental justice movement is an example of these effects (Bullard, 2004).

In order for this to occur in a sustainable way, an advocacy group needs to forge those organizational mechanisms and structures, such as new networks of people and systems of peer education and communication, that facilitate a systematic group or collective approach to problem-solving, a clear scope and road map for decision-making, and a straightforward definition of principles and rules of participation that can transform the complexity of interests into a sense of common purpose. This enables constituents to establish their own goals and objectives for the change effort and to identify desired solutions to their problems. Although ongoing dialogue is critical to successful justice-oriented advocacy, a group must also take action steps to test its goals and objectives in the crucible of reality. This also puts into practice the "story for change" that it is drafting. Finally, through praxis—the dynamic relationship between reflection and action—the organization engages in ongoing evaluation of its work rather than waiting until the advocacy effort has succeeded or failed to assess its efficacy.

Engaging: Community Participation in Social Justice Advocacy

There are numerous reasons why people engage in social justice advocacy. Sometimes they are inspired by a sense of violation or a specific injustice, current or historic, or a recent loss or fear of loss. The "Black Lives Matter" campaign is an example of such efforts. At other times, people are motivated to act in response to a threat or a perceived threat to their community's well-being (e.g., efforts to protest fracking), to prevent a crisis or problem from occurring, or to prevent an existing problem from getting worse. A catastrophic event (e.g., a hurricane), the desire for material gain or political access, and the need to build community can all initiate advocacy efforts. As Arnstein (1969) notes and Figure 9.3 reflects, there are numerous levels of community participation, from tokenism to genuine expressions of political and social power.

The objectives of community participation in social justice advocacy include creating a constituency for change, framing issues in a way that increases public support, expanding the involvement of those most affected by problems and policies in the advocacy process, holding policymakers more accountable for their actions, and monitoring the media's portrayal of the issues affecting one's constituents. The ability of constituents and clients to participate effectively in advocacy efforts is also determined by such factors as the community's values and norms about political participation and the change process, the community's diversity, the type of participation that is required, the community's history of participation, the intensity of the problems it is experiencing, the degree of consensus or conflict regarding the causes of or solutions to the problem, the presence or absence of actual or potential leaders and formal organizations in the community, and the degree of bonding and bridging social capital that exists.

In promoting greater participation by clients and constituents, social justice advocates play a variety of roles, including *animateur* (one who inspires or motivates), organizer, facilitator, intermediary, or liaison. Advocates initiate dialogue, create a sense of common purpose, think "outside the box" for

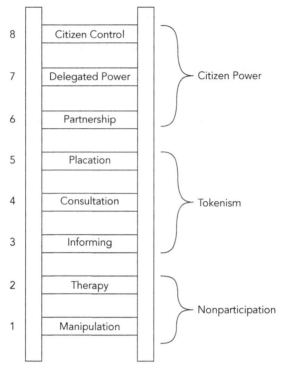

FIGURE 9.3   Arnstein (1969) A Ladder of Citizen Participation

problem solutions and encourage people to do the same, construct a database of allies and potential supporters in order to develop new networking vehicles and mobilize networks of people, help constituents articulate their decisions, and create a road map for change. The roles of community members complement those of advocates. Community members identify the issues and problems they experience, who is affected by them, and in what ways. They suggest the causes of their problems, propose solutions, and help select and implement strategies. Finally, they help advocates evaluate the outcomes of their efforts.

Advocates can promote this type of meaningful community participation in several ways. They can stimulate people's critical awareness through processes such as *popular education* (Kane, 2001), including the use of theater, art, poetry, and cinema (Boal, 2008; Clarke, 2014; Sakamoto, 2014; Sim, 2014; Taylor, 2014); critical consciousness-raising through dialogue or what Freire (1970) referred to as *conscientization*; and through what the French call *animation* (Reisch, Wenocur, & Sherman, 1981–1982). By using clients' or constituents' narratives, they can create a process of inquiry that enables excluded populations to connect their perceptions of their lives with an analytic framework that helps them interpret it. This helps transform them from objects being acted upon to subjects who can "name the world" (Freire, 1970).

In addition, through the development of democratic participatory structures, advocates can forge internal cohesion and solidarity among diverse groups and provide them with the means to express common cause. The participatory budget movement, in cities such as Brooklyn, New York, and Porte Alegre, Brazil, is an example of this approach. By facilitating the decision-making and problem-solving processes, advocates can also assist constituents in undertaking specific actions such as strategy development and tactical selection.

Outside the organization, advocates can serve as intermediaries to policymakers, experts, and opinion leaders by establishing contacts and introducing people to unfamiliar political processes. Using their existing relationships, they can help constituents identify allies, join networks, and build coalitions. At times, they can serve as "lightning rods" to draw attention and hostility away from their constituents (Alinsky, 1971).

In summary, participatory social justice advocacy organizations have the following 10 core characteristics:

1. They make ongoing efforts to democratize knowledge, thereby breaking down the barrier between "experts" and constituents. The Center for Third World Organizing (CTWO) has done excellent work in this area with immigrant groups and youth (Sen, 2012).

2. They adapt to the culture of the community in the development of both formal and informal structures. For example, environmental justice advocates in the Curtis Bay neighborhood of Baltimore have integrated youth culture (hip-hop and poetry) into their organizing efforts (Philip & Reisch, 2015).

3. They use various means of internal and external communication, including informal dialogue and social media, as efforts by the "Black Lives Matter" movement reflect.

4. They encourage shared work and collective responsibility for the success or failure of the organization, as the work of a parents' group (Parent Advocates for Youth) and a youth group (Youth Making a Change) created by Coleman Advocates for Children and Youth in San Francisco demonstrates (Brodkin, 1993).

5. They establish clear accountability mechanisms.

6. They develop processes for dealing with conflict *before* it inevitably occurs.

7. They make a conscious effort to address inequalities and avoid reproducing the forms of inequality that exist in the society they are attempting to change.

8. They promote and celebrate community in all its forms.

9. They emphasize the importance of relationships even as they focus on tangible outcomes.

10. They engage in ongoing reflection and evaluation.

> ### The Ingredients of Sustained Community Participation
>
> 1. Knowledge of the issue(s) and the change process
> 2. A democratic decision-making structure
> 3. Varied and culturally sensitive means of communication
> 4. Clear distribution of responsibilities
> 5. Accountability mechanisms
> 6. Means for resolving conflicts
> 7. Concerted efforts to address inequalities
> 8. A sense of community and common purpose
> 9. Developing ways to sustaining trust
> 10. Engaging in praxis: The dialectic of action and reflection

Models of Social Justice Advocacy

As Figure 9.4 shows, social justice advocates use a number of innovative practice models in pursuit of a wide range of causes. These innovations have taken several forms: Some integrate advocacy into traditional practice methods by building an advocacy component into long-standing social service programs or by using long-standing advocacy tools, such as legislative testimony, in new ways (Hoefer, 2012). The Kensington Welfare Rights Organization in Philadelphia

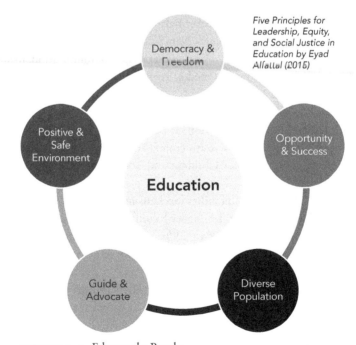

FIGURE 9.4   Educate the People

and Health Care for the Homeless in Baltimore are excellent examples of organizations that use this approach. A related innovation is the deliberate effort to transform former *objects* of advocacy—such as youth, women, and immigrants—into active *subjects* who play major roles in the advocacy process, as the work of Coleman Advocates and CTWO illustrates. Nongovernmental organizations, such as Oxfam (Bryer & Magrath, 1999), have helped create atypical coalitions that cross organizational or national boundaries by sharing vital information and facilitating the formation of strategic alliances. These transnational relationships have become critical in combating problems as diverse as climate change and child trafficking (Davy, 2013). Advocates have also focused on new dimensions of social justice, such as environmental justice and sustainable development (Dominelli, 2012; Stricker, 2010), and have used social media creatively to empower frequently excluded populations (Kanter & Fine, 2010).

Several other examples of new models of social justice advocacy are of interest. Clinical practitioners in the United States and the United Kingdom have developed Anti-Oppression Advocacy, which focuses on two interrelated goals: (1) promoting individual growth and change in clients and (2) achieving economic justice, particularly for marginalized persons (Ali & Lees, 2013). Social workers within the juvenile justice system in Philadelphia have used participatory advocacy to build a youth-led movement—the Youth Art & Self-Empowerment Project—whose goals are to keep young people out of the criminal justice system and expand their opportunities for a better future (Ford et al., 2013). Several law schools have created programs to empower youth emancipated from the foster care and juvenile justice systems to engage in self-advocacy (Krebs, Pitcoff, & Shalof, 2013). Similar programs have been established in Oakland, California, and Baltimore. In Pittsburgh, New York, and San Francisco, grassroots organizations have expanded the participation of children and youth in advocacy through the use of social media coupled with conscious efforts to acknowledge the agency of those most affected by changes in the nation's educational system (Ramey, 2013). In Porte Alegre, Brazil, and on a smaller scale in some US cities, participatory budgeting has been used to involve neighborhood residents in promoting social justice at the local level (Santos, 1998). Figure 9.5 illustrates how this works in New York.

In Serbia, Bosnia–Herzegovina, and Kosovo, regional and local women's organizations have based their organizing and advocacy on United Nations' resolutions to expand women's participation in decision-making processes, particularly with regard to issues of security and transitional justice (Irvine, 2013). In the United States, Latino mothers have joined with teachers to fight for a more socially just education for their children through the use of participatory action research (PAR) (Rodriguez, 2012). (For further discussion of PAR, see Chapter 10.) Professionals in the public health field have partnered with faith-based organizations and corporations in numerous communities to address

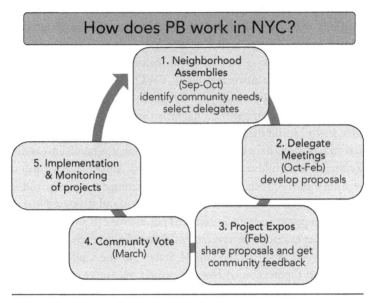

FIGURE 9.5   Participatory Budgeting in Action

the social determinants of health, such as poverty (Levin, 2013; Simon, 2006). Finally, throughout the world, advocacy groups have revitalized movements for justice among public-sector workers, nongovernmental employees, and individuals experiencing homelessness by emphasizing the participation of individuals and groups that are most affected by deteriorating workplace conditions and the lack of affordable housing (Rotumann, 2012; Zufferey, 2011)

Challenges of Social Justice Advocacy

Engaging in social justice advocacy is not without its risks—both to advocates and to the people with whom they work. In addition to the political obstacles cited previously and the usual challenges of advocacy work—insufficient resources and time, the complexity of many issues, lack of awareness within the public and among key decision-makers, and the danger of reverting to top-down approaches to promoting change—advocates for social justice also confront a unique set of problems. For example, a study of rural mental health practitioners engaged in social justice advocacy found that "in rural communities, becoming involved in social justice could be beneficial, damaging, and at time both, depending on the various contextual circumstances" (Bradley, Werth, Hastings, & Pierce, 2012, p. 356).

Advocates for social justice also have to address a number of persistent challenges and ethical issues. Among these challenges are finding a way to balance the efforts involved in promoting community mobilization with political feasibility within a political climate characterized by hyperpartisanship and fiscal austerity; determining how residents of a diverse community can work together when they may have little experience in such intergroup cooperation; sustaining constituents' or clients' involvement in the advocacy process in the context of busy and stressful lives; combining civic and political participation; balancing "doing the right thing" (i.e., what is consistent with social justice values) and doing things the right way (i.e., what is most likely to achieve defined goals); and, recently, using technology effectively in order to "do politics" in virtual communities.

Although they work toward the goal of social justice, advocates still have to confront ethical dilemmas that are present in all forms of social work practice, such as the unequal relationship that exists between them and their clients and constituents. This is particularly significant in determining the degree of risk that clients and constituents can be expected to take. Another ethical dilemma reflects the danger of paternalism—specifically, whether efforts to mobilize constituents or clients involve a degree of manipulation. A third issue revolves around the principle of self-determination. For example, what should advocates for social justice do when the people with whom they are working decide (i.e., self-determine) to advocate for an unjust goal, such as opposing the construction of affordable housing or the establishment of a halfway house for deinstitutionalized mental health clients in their neighborhood? Finally, because the process of policy advocacy inevitably involves compromise, advocates must decide which types of compromise are necessary to achieve their goals and which betray social justice principles.

Among the other challenges social justice advocates occasionally confront is the emergence of organizational rivalries or mistrust among coalition partners because of different organizational priorities or personality conflicts (Carlisle, 2010; Jordan & Van Tuijl, 2000). Other barriers to effective advocacy include a lack of practice experience in the advocacy arena or sufficient knowledge about the issues that vulnerable populations, such as the elderly, confront (Kwong-Leung & Jik-Joen, 2006); the difficulty of integrating advocacy with social and/or health care services because of the presence of different professional cultures, staffing patterns, and organizational priorities (Wiggins et al., 2013); and different conceptions among racial and ethnic minorities and indigenous people about the purposes and processes of advocacy (Bowes & Sim, 2006; Weaver & Congress, 2009). The struggles within the environmental justice movement are vivid, often painful examples of the latter (Bullard, 2004; Kuehn, 2014). As with practice with individuals and communities (see Chapters 5 and 6), social justice advocacy is impossible if it is based on notions of deficit (Fitzgerald, 2009). This point is particularly important because studies have found the following (Strolovitch, 2006):

> Organizations are substantially less active when it comes to issues affecting disadvantaged subgroups than they are when it comes to issues affecting

more advantaged subgroups. In spite of sincere desires to represent disadvantaged members, organizations downplay the impact of such issues and frame them as narrow and particularistic in their effect, while framing issues affecting advantaged subgroups as if they affect a majority of their members and have a broad and generalized impact. Consequently, issues affecting advantaged subgroups receive considerable attention regardless of their breadth of impact, whereas issues affecting disadvantaged subgroups do not. (p. 894)

Consequently, at both micro and macro levels, social justice advocates must adjust their strategies and tactics to the particular issues and context rather than adopt a "one-size-fits-all" approach (Jordan & Van Tuijl, 2000).

Social justice advocates face all these challenges because the changes they seek are often controversial and highly politicized. Consequently, they need to decide if their campaigns will focus on a single issue or make multiple, often broader demands and how explicitly they should highlight the ideological dimensions of their goals. Will their demands be considered incremental reforms that are consistent with existing policies, or will they be regarded as a radical change that diverges from widely held values and goals? Is the campaign intended to influence policy, shape public opinion, or change policy actors? On a practical level, advocates need to determine if their issue is winnable and if a sustained campaign is feasible in the current context. The latter is particularly important because of the two basic rules of policy advocacy:

1. Nothing happens overnight
2. You cannot change rule No. 1.

The work of social justice advocates is particularly difficult in politically conservative times. Nevertheless, by modifying their strategies and tactics, advocates for social justice can still achieve some successes, as recent victories in such diverse arenas as the courts (the Supreme Court decisions on marriage equality and affordable housing policies), the executive branch (new rules on immigration, overtime pay, and environmental pollution), and legislatures (the creation of universal pre-kindergarten programs) demonstrate. They can distinguish between minimum and optimum changes and focus on winnable battles that do not deplete their organization's resources or the hopes of their constituents. They can reduce the cost of proposed policy changes or demonstrate their economic or fiscal benefits to society. They can use an advocacy campaign to build for future efforts in a more fertile political environment. This involves strengthening their reputations as realistic, informed, principled, credible, and trustworthy advocates in the eyes of clients, constituents, policymakers, and the media.

Like clinical social workers, advocates must also be aware of how their personal conduct, their conscious use of self, affects their practice. Effective advocacy requires the exercise of self-control and the ability to separate personal feelings and professional judgment. Policymakers often posture or bait advocates with whom they disagree. Rather than take this bait, effective advocates are self-critical, admit their ignorance if necessary, educate rather than lecture those with whom they disagree, strive to build relationships rather than attack and alienate their opponents, stay focused on the long term, and are consistent and constant in their efforts.

Media Advocacy

Increasingly, advocates for social justice use various forms of media strategically "to advance public policy by applying pressure to policymakers and opinion leaders" (Wallack & Dorfman, 1996, p. 293). Media advocacy today is an essential tool to sustain movements for social justice. Given the increased importance of the media in shaping today's policy environment, it is important for advocates to remember that the main goal of media advocacy is not media coverage alone but, rather, to change policy or public awareness of an issue. Media advocacy is also an effective tool to position one's organization as a credible source of vital and sometimes unique information; maintain positive relationships with media contacts; advance long-term advocacy goals; and communicate one's message clearly and consistently to diverse audiences.

Media advocacy can also be an effective way to use established institutions to promote nonestablishment or even antiestablishment goals. Positive media coverage can confer legitimacy on social justice efforts; conversely, it can undermine or misinterpret them through selective and subjective reporting or through a blackout of coverage. The power of media has a direct impact, therefore, on the strategic choices of social justice organizations and has significant implications for how they motivate constituents to participate in social change efforts.

It is thus useful for social justice-oriented organizations to keep the following points in mind: News media do not mirror the world; they constitute it. Their subjective, often biased presentation of events not only shapes people's perceptions of their environments but also becomes reality. If an organization is perceived as a serious threat to the status quo, rather than as a legitimate proponent of an issue, mainstream media could withdraw coverage. If this occurs, like the proverbial tree falling in an otherwise empty forest, the "sounds" the advocacy organization makes will simply not be heard.

Consequently, social justice organizations must balance their interests and the interests of their clients and constituents with those of the media. This is increasingly difficult in a global economy in which corporate control of media has increased. Despite their self-interests, media have cleavages that can provide social justice organizations with the openings to promote their agenda. In summary, attracting media attention is a calculated risk that requires thoughtful strategy.

Media are generally classified into three categories: paid media, "earned media," and social media. Paid media consists of advertising or public service announcements (PSAs) in newspapers and on radio, television, or the Internet. Many social justice organizations cannot afford advertising but can, with some effort, persuade media to run their PSAs on a pro bono basis. Earned media consists of items that appear in print, electronic, and digital sources, such as news stories, letters to the editor, op-ed essays, and reports on web-based blogs. This type of media is generally far more accessible to social justice organizations, although there are numerous obstacles to its effective use, such as ensuring that news stories are timely and accurate and that letters or op-ed pieces get published.

Social media includes Facebook, Twitter, YouTube, and Instagram. (More apps will definitely appear before this book is published.) Although social media is the most technologically "current" form of media, there are several challenges associated with its use, including digital literacy gaps that particularly affect the vulnerable populations with whom social justice organizations work, the difficulty of identifying and employing a single voice for the organization, boundary issues arising from the ways social media is used and interpreted, and the presence of weak ties between the media and its audience.

Given the complexity of the media environment, what can social justice advocates do to use media effectively? Here are a few general guidelines:

1. An organization's media strategy should be closely connected to its overall strategy. They should complement each other rather than pursue separate paths.
2. Organizations should be realistic in their assessment of the possible benefits of media and be careful not to overuse the media as a social change tactic. This includes being realistic about the use of the organization's resources.
3. Organizations should use media strategically by targeting their message differently to specific audiences. For example, policymakers pay more attention to op-ed pieces, editorials, letters to the editor, targeted press releases, media events, and (sometimes) blogs and social media such as Twitter. The general public usually responds better to TV stories and cable TV segments, newspaper articles, radio coverage, the publications of groups to which they belong, appealing Internet blogs, and social media such as Facebook or Instagram.

4. Given the abundance of items the media cover and the short attention span of the public, organizations need to be as creative as possible in both how they use media and what they communicate through media.
5. Organizations need to be aware that the manner in which an issue is framed is critical to whether it generates a positive response.

As discussed previously, framing an issue involves selecting "some aspects of a perceived reality and [making] them more salient" (Entman, 1993, p. 51). Frames express broad principles through "cues"—words or topics that trigger an emotional response. The language used to convey these frames is particularly important. Think of the different reactions you have to the following ways of formulating an issue: urban sprawl versus suburban development, pro-choice versus pro-abortion advocates, insurgents versus terrorists, and estate tax versus death tax. No media story is framed on a "clean slate." Advocates need to be aware that each story, particularly those that address controversial issues, is based on certain assumptions or preconceptions about people and their problems.

Social justice organizations confront several other challenges in their efforts to obtain positive and consistent media coverage. Media tend to present social problems in episodic (individual and short-term) frames instead of in thematic (collective and long-term) ones. Media often regard news as a form of entertainment (for financial reasons); coverage of issues tends to focus on the game of politics, and the competition between players, instead of the substance of policies or whom they affect. In addition, media tend to construct issues in terms of opposing rights or moral principles, not their underlying economic or political causes. Finally, because they reflect the values of the dominant culture, media tend to frame issues in terms of their individual rather than group or social impact, which runs counter to a social justice approach.

According to the Center for Media Justice (2014), justice-oriented advocacy organizations can reframe media issues to the advantage of their clients and constituents by adopting one of two approaches. They can address the "big idea" behind an issue by raising new questions about its origins or consequences, explain why the issue matters or should matter, identify what is really at stake, and emphasize the values underlying the issue. Alternately, they can focus on how to frame the "back story" by selecting the best ways to illustrate their message; define the conflict at hand; and situate the story in its historical, social, political, or cultural context. They can also identify the heroes and villains in the story and interpret its meaning.

To sustain the social justice mission of your organization, it is important to involve constituents whenever feasible in crafting media messages. Use the creation of a media message to clarify the nature of the problem(s) constituents face, assign responsibility for the problem, indicate what is at stake if the problem is not addressed, and dismantle prevailing stereotypes about people affected by the problem or the nature of the problem. It is also important to include in the message how the organization's vision shapes the proposed problem solution and to identify what concrete action(s) you want those who hear your message to take.

How can social justice organizations get their message heard amid the cacophonous voices in today's media environment? There are several "tried and true" approaches that advocates should keep in mind which reflect themes that should be familiar to all social workers: Be careful in how issues are framed, convert the personal into the political, develop and use reciprocal relationships, target proposed interventions effectively, and use innovative means to address persistent problems. Some ways to apply these themes to media advocacy are discussed next.

The "24/7" news cycle requires advocacy organizations to respond rapidly to breaking news. If possible, designate regular spokespersons to be the primary, consistent media contacts or the individuals who post comments on the organization's website or Facebook or Twitter account. The media and the public resonate to stories that focus on people rather than statistics or ideas. It is important, however, not to lose sight of the larger social justice issues and to avoid presenting issues in a manner that might reinforce the tendency to blame people for their problems. It is also important not to exploit a situation and to address such issues with sensitivity, particularly if it involves a human tragedy that affects your clients or constituents (e.g., using a mass murder to advocate for gun control too soon after the event occurs). A timely op-ed essay or letter to the editor in an influential newspaper can be more effective in such circumstances.

Social justice organizations can get their "stories" heard in several different ways. Sometimes, they can create news through a press release (Figure 9.6). They can also "piggyback" on existing news or use the "hook" of an unexpected event. Assuming it reflects the social justice values and goals of the organization, a good issue to exploit has the following qualities: It is controversial; broad enough to link to the organization's specific cause (e.g., health care); reflects a clear injustice (e.g., the police killing of an unarmed youth); or involves a milestone, anniversary, or breakthrough. Other qualities of a good story include the participation of a celebrity or unusual messenger (e.g., Warren Buffett's support of changes in the tax code to address income inequality), the presence of humor or irony, and something with a local angle (Dorfman, 2003).

PRESS STATEMENT

FOR IMMEDIATE RELEASE 9/11/01

ACCESS—THE ARAB COMMUNITY CENTER FOR ECONOMIC AND SOCIAL SERVICES

Dearborn, Michigan. The Arab Community Center for Economic and Social Services (ACCESS) condemns the bombings as any right thinking group of people would. We believe this condemnation reflects the views of Arab-Americans universally.

We ask that our community neighbors not to jump to any conclusions as during the Oklahoma City bombing. During that crisis, many Arab groups were accused and in the end, it was a domestic terrorist act.

Today, many schools, religious institutions, and Arab-American organizations have received bomb threats. Arab-Americans families have been forced to take their kids out of school. We ask that the general public and the media in particular, keep in mind that we are Americans as well. We are devoted to our country and oppose violence.

Contact Person: Ismael Ahmed, Executive Director
Phone Number: (313) 842-7010
E-Mail-Iahmed@accesscommunity.org

FIGURE 9.6   Press Release Example
Source: Child Welfare League of America (http://www.cwla.org/newsevents/news20120607LGBTQ.htm).

Tips for Media Interviews

1. Control the agenda: Your media strategy must be linked to your organization's overall strategy and *specific* desired policy outcomes. *Remember*: An interview is not a conversation. It is an opportunity (or series of opportunities) to make a point. Here are some examples:
   - Policies should create/expand opportunity for all Americans.
   - Policies should enable all children to contribute to society.
   - Policies should reflect our shared values.

- Policies should reflect the diversity/reality of a multicultural society.
- Policies should reflect and reinforce social solidarity and interconnectedness.

Divide your message into three parts:

- What is the problem?
- What is the solution?
- Why does it matter that we address the problem? (the "so what" factor)

2. Stylistic tips

- Keep your sentences short. Use shorter words to convey complex ideas.
- Vary your cadence. *Slow down* (especially with print media). Wait for the next question. Restate the question for emphasis. Try to keep your style relaxed, especially on TV, which is a "cool medium."
- Restate powerful images/messages (e.g., "Our children are exposed to . . . ").
- Use colorful language and illustrations.
- Focus your interview on a specific goal. Do not tell everything at once.
- Focus on *one component of a problem* at a time.
- Do not list a range of issues/problems that affect your clients or constituents.
- Use research/action "bullets" (e.g., "We've learned that . . . ").
- Do not be afraid to express passion in your use of words (e.g., "We are *concerned* that . . . ").
- Use verbs that show ownership of the issues (e.g., "We *understand* or *know* or *have learned* that . . . ").
- Do not use jargon or name specific programs (that only policy wonks understand).
- Ask a rhetorical question ("Imagine if . . . ").
- Personalize your response—Use good examples to illustrate absurd possibilities of the issue you are addressing. Tell a good story.
- Focus on positives. Do not use terms that frame the issue solely in negative ways.
- Avoid statements that are too broad.
- Use powerful metaphors and "social math" (quantify the problem) to drive issues home and provide specific examples around emotion-laden issues.

Remember:

- *The press is not always an enemy.* Do not blame the media for unfavorable coverage or hold a grudge against a reporter. Try to maintain your sense of humor and move on.

- *Make the media's job easier.* Take the time to build ongoing personal relationships with media representatives; offer a service (new information) to help reporters and editors meet their deadlines; look for ongoing ways to help them do their jobs (e.g., briefings).
- Use a variety of media vehicles and find creative ways to reach journalists in different communities.
- Provide specific media contacts and outlets with consistent messages (preferably with a local angle) and information relevant to their respective audiences in formats they find most useful and timely. Understand how different media affect different audiences and how to use them. To ensure consistency and continuity, limit the number of organizational spokespersons.
- Be careful what you commit to paper. There is no such thing as "off the record."

Monitoring and Evaluating Advocacy Efforts

In today's accountability-oriented climate, social justice advocates must demonstrate the effectiveness of their efforts in order to maintain their credibility with clients, constituents, policymakers, the media, external funders, and the general public. Many advocates, however, resist evaluating their work for several reasons: It is time-consuming and resource intensive; it requires a degree of self-criticism that often feels uncomfortable, particularly among groups that have long been excluded and marginalized by the dominant culture; and it is difficult to develop clear measures of effectiveness (Homan, 2016). Ironically, although advocacy for social justice is an ethical imperative for social workers, there have been few attempts to determine whether such advocacy is effective in achieving its goals or whether it is cost-effective (McNutt, 2011).

Like the assessment of the impact of an intervention or a program, the evaluation of advocacy efforts has multiple purposes. The most obvious is to determine whether the effort achieved its immediate goals and objectives. Was a particular policy change adopted? Did funding for a specific program increase or was a proposed budget cut defeated? Has public awareness of and sympathy for an issue or constituency increased? Did a ballot measure pass or was one your organization opposed defeated? The more difficult part of evaluating an advocacy effort involves process evaluation—to determine what specific strategies and tactics worked and did not work. This is critical not only to demonstrate the efficacy of your organization or group to supporters but also to identify how to improve future advocacy efforts and to involve constituents and clients in sustainable and meaningful ways.

In evaluating social justice advocacy, there are three additional issues to consider: (1) whether socially just processes were used to achieve socially just outcomes, (2) whether meaningful changes in public opinion on an issue occurred (this can sometimes be measured through polling), and (3) whether the media advocacy strategies employed were effective. These types of evaluation, although costly in terms of time and resources, can be very helpful in determining how to frame and target future advocacy efforts.

Measuring process outcomes also requires social justice advocates to adopt a multiple frame perspective—that is, to consider short-term, medium-term, and long-term goals and consequences. This is particularly important because of the complexity and ambiguity of social justice goals and the challenge of translating social justice principles into actions due to the frequently unprecedented nature of what advocates are trying to achieve. In cooperation with constituents, advocates should ask the following questions in evaluating the processes used in their advocacy efforts:

1. How were decisions made?
2. Who made the decisions?
3. Were the processes used effective? Were they sufficiently participatory?
4. What actually happened in discussions of strategies and tactics?
5. Which targets were selected? By what means?
6. Who took action? To what extent? In what ways?

Through direct and indirect observation—that is, through a combination of self-reflection, candid group discussions, consultation with third parties, and review of media coverage—advocates should assess the impact of their efforts on the major contextual components of their current and future work. These include the advocacy organization, group, or coalition as a whole, both internally and in regard to its reputation within the public and the media, and among policymakers; its leadership and decision-making structure; its use of resources; the effectiveness of various strategies and tactics; and its external relationships with coalition partners, allies, and supporters. An important element of the evaluation process is clarifying the evolving meaning of "success" and translating this definition into both objective and subjective measures.

As discussed in previous chapters, applying the concept of praxis also requires advocates to engage in an honest assessment of what actually happened; determine what the advocacy efforts actually accomplished (and what would have occurred if nothing had been done); and, in situations involving multiple goals and objectives, estimate the impact of advocacy efforts on each outcome. The overall questions you want to answer are as follows: Was the advocacy effort worth the outcome? Which advocacy strategies and tactics helped achieve which goals and objectives, and at what cost? Should the organization replicate or revise these strategies and tactics in the future?

Measuring "Successful" Community Participation

There are four areas to evaluate in determining the extent to which a social justice advocacy effort was successful in promoting the participation of service users or constituents. First, what impact did the advocacy effort have on people's overarching values and behavioral norms? For example, was it successful in reorienting people's values toward more justice-centered principles? How inclusive was the advocacy effort at all stages of the process? To what extent did the advocacy effort remove barriers to people's participation and reflect the beliefs of constituents in its goals and processes?

Were the goals and objectives of the advocacy effort and the means to influence them clear and comprehensible to all potential actors? Did the advocacy process create incentives for building and strengthening community and promoting reciprocity of exchange (e.g., equality, mutuality, and sustained commitment)? The experience of the pioneering Mobilization for Youth organization in New York City during the early 1960s provides an excellent illustration of the gains, losses, problems, and pitfalls of community-focused advocacy (Purcell & Specht, 1965).

A second area to assess is the *structure* of the participation process. Was the process fair and inclusive? Did it emphasize partnership and collective decision-making rather than competition and hierarchy? To what extent did it foster community cohesion about vision, community identity, and the goals of the advocacy effort? Did it promote leadership development, particularly among elements of the community that have historically been ignored? Did it enable the community to acquire a greater sense of power and control over its destiny?

A third, related issue to assess is the *nature* of the participation process. Questions to address in this regard include the following: Did the advocacy organization or group emphasize genuine participation, or did it succumb to a more traditional task orientation that emphasized "efficiency" over empowerment? What was the extent of community participation in terms of breadth of participation (How many community members were involved?), depth of participation (Around what issues?), and frequency? Around what type of issues did community members play an active role (e.g., major strategic decisions or small, narrow questions)? What was the impact of the advocacy effort on intracommunity relationships, particularly in diverse communities and those with low levels of social capital or scant histories of community involvement? To what degree did community members take responsibility for the decision-making process and its outcomes (success or failure)? How did the advocacy effort enhance the knowledge, skills, and self-confidence that community members need to participate in the future?

Finally, the evaluation of an advocacy effort should reflect on its impact on the organization's external relationships with government agencies, influential nonprofit groups, and other professionals, inside and outside social work. With what levels or departments of government was the advocacy effort more or less successful? What are the constraints on future advocacy of existing policies and services? What external resources (money, alliances, etc.) will be needed in the future and from what sources? What role did professionals play and what impact did that have on the overall advocacy effort? How did the advocacy effort affect the community's future relationships with allies, competitors, or opponents?

The following is a framework to help advocacy organizations evaluate their level of success in promoting meaningful community participation:

A Framework for Assessing Community Participation

The following five-axis framework can be used to measure the extent to which clients, constituents, and community members have been involved in social justice advocacy efforts:

Axis 1—Community power and decision-making: This includes such factors as equal access to information; a common set of principles based on a clear definition of social justice and/or human rights; the right of everyone in the community to contribute to the community's agenda; transparency in all final decisions, which would be reached by consensus; rotating leadership roles; and a collective, nonhierarchical conception of leadership and power.

Axis 2—Community identification/boundaries: This contains such components as the presence of clear but permeable boundaries to identify who is or is not a community member; a positive, self-determined identity (accepted by external forces) in which every member has a sense of belonging, history, and continuity; and a culture that integrates, respects, appreciates, and embraces diversity in all its forms, which strives to empower members to find their unique place in the community, fosters sustainable relationships between individuals and groups, and establishes a common standard of behavioral norms.

Axis 3—Community needs and strengths: This refers to the importance of a community participating in identifying and defining its own needs, strengths, weaknesses, and goals. Supporters and allies from outside the community can become involved in advocacy efforts if they operate from an empowerment theory framework (as opposed to a deficit model) in making community assessments. Their role would be limited to consultation and technical assistance based on community input (Rivera & Erlich, 1998).

Axis 4—Community relationships and problem-solving: The features here reflect the community's culture and climate. In order for community members to be full participants in social justice work, the community must be a safe place, characterized by inclusivity and reciprocal, dynamic relationships between individuals and its organizations. The community needs to establish and maintain a common space that is designed, recognized, utilized, and "owned" by all members. Processes need to be established to handle internal and external conflicts effectively and in a manner that produces solutions that respond to the needs and interests of all stakeholders. Finally, in order for the change effort to be sustained, the community strives to meet its needs, as it defines them, through resources that are accessible and over which it can exercise some influence and control.

Axis 5—External structures and community well-being: This refers to the relationship between the community and the external institutions with which it interacts. Ideally, these institutions would take into consideration the wants, needs, and cultural diversity of the community. Open communication would exist, and a balance of power between the institutions and the community would be maintained. Decisions that affect the community would not be imposed unilaterally because the community's right to self-determination would be recognized. The community would have the ability to access external resources, and there would be a reciprocal sharing of knowledge, assets, resources, and power.

Question

What should be the limits of a community's power? For example, what happens when the community is biased or its leaders are corrupt?

Using Polls to Determine the Effectiveness of Advocacy

Increasingly, advocacy organizations, particularly those that are larger and better financed, are using opinion polls to determine the impact of their efforts on public opinion. Although such polls can be helpful in enhancing advocacy efforts, like all research methods, they must be used judiciously. Advocates should first ask: What do we really want to know? Why do we want this information? How will we use it now and in the future? To what extent might it influence our efforts to achieve socially just goals and engage in socially just processes? The last question is particularly important because of the powerful temptation to tailor advocacy efforts to the current climate of opinion, even when that climate is unsympathetic to social justice ends.

There are several potential pitfalls, therefore, in the preparation and use of opinion polls and in the analysis of their results. Advocates must take particular care in training volunteers, especially if inexperienced constituents are involved in the polling process, and in selecting outside consultants for technical assistance. They must also pay special attention to the wording of polling questions (which can significantly influence the outcome), the selection of the sample, and the methods used to maintain and secure polling data. Once data are collected, advocates must be wary of overanalyzing the results, focusing on meaningless relationships, overstating cause and effect, confusing respondents' attitudes and behaviors, and ignoring the context in which polling questions are posed.

There are several other obstacles to the use of polls to measure the effectiveness of advocacy efforts. One involves the development of a representative sample. Many individuals no longer possess landline telephones; others are difficult to contact due to their work schedules. In addition, many people are distrustful of pollsters, particularly if they ask questions about controversial issues. Finally, some people are reluctant to express opinions to pollsters that reflect their lack of knowledge about an issue or attitudes that may be considered prejudicial or discriminatory. Nevertheless, if adjustments are made for these potential problems, judicious use of polling can be a valuable tool to determine which advocacy strategies and tactics are most effective. Although polling is costly and time-consuming, when used wisely it can save advocacy organizations time and money in the future (Lake, 1987).

Evaluating Media Efforts

The process of evaluating media advocacy is similar. Its purpose is to make judgments about which media strategies worked and to generate knowledge about the media that can be helpful to an advocacy organization and its constituents in the future. As with any assessment process, it begins by asking the right questions: What do you want to know about the media? Is that information available? How will you get that information? How will you use that information?

In assessing social justice media advocacy, the following are important criteria to consider: the extent to which the advocacy effort has relied on media coverage to achieve its ends, the degree of "fit" between the social justice message the organization wishes to communicate and the media audience, and the nature and saliency of the issue. Another important factor is the sociocultural and political context at the time of the advocacy effort. In discussing advocacy on behalf of environmental issues, Liévanos (2012) asks, "How and why were aspects of the environmental justice frame institutionalized into regulatory policy while others were not?" (p. 481). Other examples include how media coverage of economic inequality evolved as a result of the "Occupy movement" and whether its coverage reflected or influenced public attitudes about the issue. The presence of other issues that are competing for the public's attention also affects media advocacy, particularly around complex and controversial topics that the media may be reluctant to cover or may cover only in superficial, often misleading ways.

In evaluating media advocacy efforts, other questions to consider include the following: Which media events were most effective in conveying your advocacy message or in changing or mobilizing public opinion? Did media attention match your original reasons for seeking coverage? How extensive (and in-depth) was the coverage? How was your issue framed by different types of media? What impact did the coverage have on building support among the public or policymakers? Did media advocacy strengthen or weaken your relationships with other groups?

Summary

This chapter focused on the relationship of social justice values to the substance of social policy and the policy development process. It discussed how social justice principles can influence the policy process, various methods of promoting social justice through policy advocacy, and how the strategic use of information in the media can help achieve social justice goals in a socially just manner. It concluded with a discussion of how advocacy efforts and attempts to expand the participation of clients and constituents in social justice work can be evaluated. Chapter 10 addresses various dimensions of social justice research, including evaluation and participatory action research—research methods that can also have a significant impact on practice, policy, and advocacy at the local and national level (Chapman & Schwartz, 2012).

Discussion Questions

1. How do different views about the role of government reflect different conceptions of social justice? Select an issue about which you are concerned. What are the implications of these views for policy development that addresses this issue?

2. What forces in the current environment create obstacles to the development of socially just policies that would address this issue? Which forces facilitate their development?

3. With which definition of a socially just policy do you most agree? How would you apply this definition to social policies that address an issue you care about?

4. Identify an issue that affects the people with whom you work or the organization in which you work. How does the framing of this issue (by government officials, the media, etc.) affect the policies that have emerged to address this issue? How might the issue be framed differently from a social justice perspective?

5. What advocacy strategies would you use to enhance current policies that address this issue? How would you integrate a social justice perspective into both your advocacy goals and the means through which you would attempt to achieve these goals?

Socially Just Research and Evaluation

Introduction: The Role of Research and Evaluation in Promoting Social Justice

This chapter discusses the role that research and evaluation play in the promotion of social justice. We agree with Clark and Hollander (2005) that

> for real opportunity and social justice in health research, two conditions must be present: A scientific community must produce relevant information through a rational deliberative process and groups affected by findings must be aware of and able to use the information. (p. 30)[1]

Several authors have considered this topic, such as Fraser (2009), Brown and Strega (2005), Denzin and Giardina (2006), Smith (2006), and Potts and Brown (2005). Furthermore, as Potts and Brown so eloquently state,

> Being an anti-oppressive researcher means that there is political purpose and action to your research work. Whether that purpose is on a broad societal level or about personal growth, by choosing to be an anti-oppressive researcher, one is making an explicit personal commitment to social justice. Anti-oppressive work involves making explicit the political practices of creating knowledge. It means making a commitment to the people you are working with personally and professionally in order to mutually foster conditions for social justice and research. It is about paying attention

---

1. We frequently refer to this article in this chapter because although it refers to health research, we find its points highly relevant to all social work research that seeks to make social justice issues central to all phases of the research process.

to, and shifting, how power relations work in and through the process of doing research. (p. 255)

The authors who write about social justice and research have also indicated their preferred methodologies: textual analysis (Newton, 1990; Woods & Kroger, 2000), sometimes "infused with feminist ideas" (Fraser, 2009, p. 92), narrative analysis (Riessman, 1993), or a scripting approach (Simon, 1996). We argue, specifically, that research and evaluation help to reduce power discrepancies among service users, providers of services, and all other stakeholders by providing each entity with information about the outcomes and processes that ensue from the service activity and the opportunity to fully participate in them. Possessed with the same information, if it is accepted as valid, each of these entities can use that information to point out whether it is "losing out" or in some way being disadvantaged by these outcomes and processes and to take action to rectify the situation. Danso's (2015) perspective is very similar to our own based on similar sources.

Needless to say, the research process can sometimes cause injury to persons and systems. At this point, ethical and value considerations enter the picture. For example, an outcome may be that service users have been awarded a resource (e.g., money, facilities, and policy changes) that impinges on the resources of the agency or some other organization or person.[2] A value position can be taken here that is derived from the concept of justice. The practitioner might argue that a just outcome is for the service users to have a "right" to the benefits obtained as a result of the social worker's research activities.

On the other hand, the service users may not have obtained their desired outcome. For example, parents may not have succeeded in obtaining a service from the school that they believed their children needed. They may argue this is an unjust outcome and seek further redress. Or, a service user may have been trying to reduce her anxieties and, when this is not achieved, may argue that the agency policy denied her the type or quantity of service she needed to attain this goal.

From the beginning of service, stakeholders should be involved in all aspects of the research and evaluation processes; this is discussed in more detail later. For example, investigators sought to determine the outcomes of a project to help patients with breast cancer cope with their illness and its consequences. The women were interested in determining whether they lived longer with this service than those who did not receive it, whether they were able to tolerate their treatment better, and whether their personal outlook was more optimistic and less depressed. These questions can be answered through evaluation processes.

---

2. For purposes of this chapter, we do not consider corporations to be persons as has been declared by the Supreme Court in cases such as *Citizens United*.

Service users may question any aspect of the evaluation or research process, such as the measures that will be evaluated to determine the effectiveness of a program or service; the measurement tools used; how data will be collected; who will have access to the data; how the outcomes will be disseminated; how much or little time will be allocated to the data collection procedures; whether the ways the data are collected reflect the biases and attitudes of the data collectors, especially if the data are collected by the service providers; what the consequences will be if their responses reflect negatively (or even positively) on the service providers; and how their responses will affect future services they may require.

Since the Flexner Report (Flexner, 1915), social work has been engaged in a quest for a knowledge base to legitimize its professional status (Ehrenreich, 1985; Wenocur & Reisch, 1989). Social work's master narrative has shaped the various components of this quest through its definition of the research process—from the formulation of a researchable question to the selection of appropriate methodologies, the development of suitable research instruments, the interpretation of data, and the assessment of its implications. This has had enormous impacts on the conceptualization, production, and dissemination of knowledge in the field of social welfare, with major implications for the theory and practice of social work (Fook, 2002; Kirk & Reid, 2002; Payne, 2005) and for the profession's ability to achieve its social justice goals.

The growing emphasis in schools of social work and professional journals on intervention research and "evidence-based practice" and the concomitant focus on increasingly sophisticated quantitative methodologies have been based on a dual rationale: the enhancement of the quality of social work scholarship to improve the effectiveness of social services and the need to strengthen the competitive position of the social work profession in the occupational and academic marketplace (Gambrill, 2004; Thyer, 2007). On a more subtle level, it may also be a means to reassert the master narrative in the face of theoretical, methodological, and political critiques (Elkins, 2005; Gibbs & Gambrill, 2002; Webb, 2001).

Power and knowledge are synthesized through the discourses produced by master narratives, including "the structure of statements, terms, categories and beliefs that are expressed through organizations and institutions" (Dominelli, 2002, p. 33). In these discourses, the preservation of binary oppositions—"difference"—helps maintain the existence of dominant/subordinate roles, including those between workers and clients. The master narrative's construction of our understanding of knowledge and research through a positivist tradition, which takes for granted that "practice can and should be based on 'proven facts' generated through [quantitative research] ... rather than 'less rigorous' research designs, intuition [i.e., analogical thinking], practice wisdom or theory" (Trinder, 2000, p. 41), has a direct impact on the practice of social work, the structure of social service agencies, and the application of social science (Laslett, 1998).

Changes in how the profession constructs the meaning of knowledge, research, and evidence have been introduced with little assessment of their effects on the long-standing mission of social work and the character of schools of social work and social service agencies. A peculiar feature of these current trends is how quickly they have been incorporated into social work's master narrative without regard for the intellectual and ideological contradictions involved, despite what Kirk and Reid (2002) refer to as an ill-suited application of physical sciences methods to social work. Although the debate between postpositivists and postmodernists has been instructive, evidence-based intervention research continues to be ascendant, and fundamental epistemological questions such as "What is knowledge?" "How do we know it?" and "Does truth equal validity?" remain unanswered (Witkin & Harrison, 2001).

In its current form, the definitions that underlie social work research reflect unacknowledged biases about such key terms as "evidence," "knowledge," and "knowing" (Collins, 2009; Fawcett, Featherstone, Fook, & Rossiter, 2000; Littell, 2008). Finally, by promoting research on the effectiveness of established interventions as a means of addressing contemporary social problems, rather than analyzing their structural roots, social workers implicitly accept these problems as inevitable—as conditions to be managed rather than eliminated. Indirectly, this new emphasis contradicts the profession's focus on social justice.

Critique of Research Methodologies

Epistemology

This issue concerns whether the concepts and theories underlying the approach to research and evaluation are valid. Essentially, it examines how "knowledge" in a particular situation is being defined. From a social justice perspective, this involves the assessment of the research methods being used to determine whether they reflect cultural biases, structural inequities, or unquestioned and potentially erroneous assumptions. For example, when service users are asked to indicate their gender, a classification of male/female leaves out a range of possible ways people identify their gender. Or a question regarding what degree the service users view the service as satisfactory may not reflect that to them the word "satisfactory" may have many different meanings. These issues are particularly salient when questionnaires or other measurement instruments are translated into another language (Jani & DeForge, in press).

Given these issues, the debate over whether investigators should utilize qualitative or quantitative measures may oversimplify the challenges of research and pay insufficient attention to how the service users being studied perceive their realities. This is not to be construed as an argument for using only qualitative data; quantitative measures may provide insights into an important component of a complex situation. For example, service users in a group setting may be asked about the proportion of other group members they thought listened to what they have said; this may offer valid information about how they perceived this aspect of the group situation.

The Purpose of Knowledge Development

We also subscribe to the general notion that social work practice should have an evidence base. The important question here is what constitutes evidence. Ultimately, data are filtered through the minds of each person examining the data. This interpretation is affected by each person's current and past experiences such as interactions with others, cultural beliefs, and ways of perceiving experience.[3] Knowledge is also cumulative and will be stored in many ways for future use in what may be a very different context. Although comparisons between past and present data can support the validity of a hypothesis or theory, a social justice perspective demands that the cultural context and power relationships at the time the data were collected and analyzed and at the time they are reviewed be considered.

Criteria for Valid and Useful Knowledge

From a social justice perspective, this means that knowledge used to inform practice incorporates the perspectives and interests of the service users. Although the perspectives of other systems must be considered at times, the needs and interests of the service users are paramount. These different perspectives must be considered in the following circumstances:

- When it is necessary to provide a context that explains the roles of these other systems in the processes and outcomes
- When these other systems possess power that has been a source of the oppression of the service users
- When the views held by individuals in these other systems help to explain the views and experiences of the service users

---

3. We, however, do not deny the idea that the personal experiences of the worker and the service users are also relevant data. In addition, the memory and understanding of these experiences will affect how these persons view and utilize other data. This idea is highly compatible with, and may be intrinsic to, a social justice approach that seeks to empower all actors. In summary, determining how knowledge is integrated with experience is important to this consideration.

An example of this series of issues is a research-evaluation project of a family violence prevention program in a not-for-profit family service agency. The outcomes were measured by observations of family interactions during sessions, individual reports from the abused family members, and reports from the police of calls from abused family members requesting police protection. The program had special components for the abuser, usually a male in the family, and the abused persons were predominantly women and children. A comprehensive social justice approach requires that the families concerned determine whether family observations are appropriate; where, when, and how these observations would occur; how the data obtained from these observations are interpreted; and what conclusions and practice implications are drawn from them.

Because the program sought to empower as well as protect the women in these families, when the men were treated in the men's program, their wives were also interviewed as to whether they continued to experience abuse.[4] The women were also asked about their experiences with the police and about the responsiveness of the police. Finally, the women and men were both interviewed with respect to their experiences with program staff. In addition, the investigators interviewed a sample of police to ascertain their attitudes toward the women who were abused. The agency's staff members were also interviewed to determine their attitudes toward the program. Admittedly, all of these interviews added to the cost of the research. Nevertheless, the investigators believed that unless they secured funding for all these activities, they would not have a valid picture of the program from a social justice perspective.

Power Relationships: Researcher–Subjects

Social justice-oriented investigators will consider the impact of likely power differentials among themselves, research subjects, and others who are interested in, involved in, and affected by either the research process or its outcomes. The following are specific examples:

- Investigators have power by virtue of their knowledge, organizational sanction, and linkage to an educational institution or to the organization sponsoring the research. If the research is funded by the government, this may also be a source of influence in such situations. An example of this kind of power was demonstrated when one of the authors conducted his doctoral research. He asked a group of teenagers for permission to record their group

---

4. The men were fully informed that this was an element of the program when they entered it and had a chance to react to and question this.

meeting and then asked them to complete questionnaires about the session. They gave permission, with one member commenting, "Who are we to stand in the name of science?!"

- Subjects may fear that their responses will cause harm to themselves although the investigator pledges confidentiality. This fear may even extend to situations in which individual data are not revealed but the aggregated data will have consequences when persons in authority learn, for example, that some subjects are critical of the services provided or persons in authority.

Evidence-Based Practice

Evidence-based practice (EBP) is a term that is very widely used in social work, as well as in other professions (e.g., medicine). According to Jenson and Howard (2008), this practice

> is a five-step process used to select, deliver, and evaluate individual and social interventions aimed at preventing or ameliorating client problems and social conditions. At its most basic level, EBP seeks to systematically integrate evidence about the efficacy of interventions in clinical decision-making. (p. 158)[5]

From a social justice standpoint, we do not take issue with the concept of EBP, as such, but how it is sometimes interpreted and applied. The following are some concerns we have in this regard:

1. What constitutes evidence? Some scholars tend to restrict evidence to quantitative studies, although this restriction is seldom specified in definitions of EBP.
2. Practitioners' anecdotal evidence or so-called "practice wisdom" is seldom used to supplement other findings, thus negating the power of the practitioner.
3. Service users' opinions are seldom elicited in the choice of interventions and the selection and evaluation of the evidence, thus negating their power. Their views on the effects of the intervention may not be considered, and outcomes may be measured by other evidence such as of behavior change or of the views of significant others, which may reflect different values and underlying cultural norms and assumptions.

---

5. These authors seem to emphasize clinical decision-making here, but we view the concept of evidence-based practice as applicable to any level of social work practice.

4. Although researchers today are likely to assess the evidence in terms of its applicability to the ethnicity, gender, religion, age, and geographical location of the service users, this standard may not be utilized in the selection of the evidence or the means by which it is collected and analyzed.

5. The ongoing involvement of service users in the determination of how the evidence is to be defined and utilized, or in assessing the services offered them, is not often found in articles relating to specific instances of EBP, thus further disempowering service users in the research process.

Tenets of Research Activity That Promote Social Justice

Brown and Strega (2005) view socially just research as "research from, by, and with the margins" (p. 6). They use the term "marginalization" as a "context in which those who routinely experience inequality, injustice, and exploitation live their lives" (p. 6). The work of these scholars has heavily influenced our point of view, and we are indebted to them for the following discussion. Brown and Strega (2005) assert,

> Being marginalized refers not just to experiences of injustice or discrimination or lack of access to resources. In the research context, it acknowledges that knowledge production has long been organized, as have assessments of the ways producing knowledge can be "legitimate," so that only certain information, generated by certain people in certain ways is accepted or can qualify as "truth." Historically, this has meant that those on the margins have been the objects but rarely the authors of research, and the discomfort that those on the margins feel about adopting traditional research processes and knowledge creation has been interpreted as their personal inability or failings. (p. 7)

Related to this point of view, we have developed a number of principles that we believe should be observed in socially just social work research:

• Marginalized groups should have a role in the formulation of the research, research design, measurement of variables, collection and interpretation, and dissemination of research results whenever the research has specific relevance for these groups.[6]

---

6. It can be argued that all research not directed at a specific nonmarginalized population (e.g., male managers of NGOs) will not be affected by this principle. In addition, some research is intended to be a sample of a very large population containing people of many different backgrounds for which this principle is legitimately modified. Nevertheless, many

- The researcher should draw on the insights that are offered by critical approaches to knowledge development, such as critical race theory and feminism.
- When indigenous peoples or people of different cultures and ethnicities are involved in the research, their ways of knowing should be understood and incorporated in the research processes and procedures.
- Research processes should be adopted that explicitly and implicitly challenge relations of domination and subordination when these exist.[7] These will be enhanced if researchers consider who will benefit from the outcomes of the research.[8]
- Researchers should engage in praxis by moving back and forth between theory and practice, reflecting on how innovative and critical research theories might be applied, and then modifying theories as a result of their practice experience.
- Research should relate to the enhancement of "empowerment," particularly in terms of its analysis of power relations and recognition of systemic oppressions (Brown & Strega, 2005, pp. 9-10).

Brown and Strega (2005)

challenge a broad range or currently popular research methodologies, across the range of positivism to postmodernism, by noticing that they all draw from a narrow foundation of knowledge based on the social, historical, and cultural experiences of White men: the dominant and hegemonic ideology under which we all live and in whose image the academy is constructed. (p. 10)

They argue (and we agree) that

research cannot challenge relations of dominance and subordination unless it also challenges the hegemony of current research paradigms. In order to make overt how power relations permeate the construction and

---

research grant-awarding entities require that the proposal for research address this issue, and if the principle has not been observed or only observed partially, they require an explanation as to why this is the case.

7. The worker will have to be able to recognize these, and this will require regular efforts for the workers to raise their own consciousness.

8. It is, of course, possible that those in power may legitimately benefit from the results. This does not mean the research should not be done. This is a complex issue that merits more consideration than it has received.

legitimation of knowledge, the question of the researcher's location and political commitments, which are obscured by methodological claims to objectivity, neutrality, and gender and race blindedness, must be taken up. (p. 11)

The Qualitative–Quantitative Issue in Research

There is no doubt that many researchers committed to fighting injustice and furthering justice favor qualitative approaches. There are a number of reasons for this, although qualitative approaches can also present problems from a social justice perspective.

One reason for preferring qualitative research is that the persons who are the subjects of qualitative research have more power and control over the data. In interviews, for example, they can determine the nature and content of their responses, increasing the likelihood that they will influence the frames of reference through which their lives and experiences will be interpreted. This reduces the possibility that the interviewer will bias the responses by the questions posed and by verbal and nonverbal indications of how much attention is being paid to each issue. Even the identities of the interviewer (e.g., gender, color, and physical appearance) will influence what the interviewee says. It is also unlikely that the interviewees will be fully forthcoming if they have little or no acquaintance with the interviewer or if they speak a different language. For these reasons, many social justice-oriented researchers spend time establishing a connection with the interviewees before engaging in the research process. This further empowers interviewees as they learn the skills necessary for this task.

Qualitative approaches may also involve the researchers in observing natural settings in which potential interviewees interact, such as group meetings and informal settings (e.g., while people are standing in line or sitting in a waiting room). Biases can also enter here, as researchers decided what and how to record, store, and analyze information. These may involve the persons who review the raw data, analyze its meaning, and draw implications from the results. In some research projects, it may also involve research subjects in recording their observations and comparing them to those of the researcher(s). This process, of course, is time-consuming and can be costly, but it is more likely to collect reliable information.

Another qualitative approach is the collection of life histories (narratives) or biographies. This can involve collecting information from the members of the group being studied and/or from significant persons in their lives. The information collected may or may not be valid or complete on its own, but this limitation can be minimized by having the individuals being studied review the data and how it is analyzed or reported. Although the data may not reflect an accurate and complete story, if they are reported carefully, they can reflect the perceptions of the individual(s) and add richness to the findings (Musson, 1998).

The data from any type of qualitative research (or any research for that matter) must be recorded, analyzed or interpreted, and presented to an "audience." The greatest fidelity, perhaps, is when an audiovisual recording is made. Even then, the intrusiveness of this process may have an impact on the events being observed. The analysis of such recordings, however done, can also be expensive and time-consuming.

The researcher committed to the principles of social justice espoused in this book will consider particularly how power differentials and differing cognitive perspectives (some of which are privileged) affect all research processes. As stated throughout this chapter, the involvement of the people in the population being studied is essential in resolving these issues or diminishing their impact. Their participation can influence the design of the observation process, how results are interpreted, and how findings are disseminated. It is also important that participants be informed in advance that any collection of data by whatever means can be discontinued at the request of the participants.

Qualitative research may also be iterative in nature in that the researchers and participants may examine data, revise or expand their research findings on the basis of this analysis, and return to gather more data by similar or different means as a result of questions raised by this examination. This underscores the need for a close partnership between researchers and participants.

Some qualitative research approaches use existing documents such as reports, letters, social histories (Andrews, 2007), newspaper articles, and even literature in the form of books, short stories, and poetry. A poor example of this is a study by Cmiel (1995) that purported to provide the history of a Chicago children's institution that began as a residence for children of Civil War widows (Chicago Nursery and Half Orphan Asylum) and later became a residential treatment agency. The author attributed the changes in the institution largely to societal changes in the field of child welfare.

One of the authors of this book had an intimate knowledge of this children's institution because it was his field placement and an agency at which he had been hired as a consultant. His personal information was that the agency hired a new director in 1949, after many examinations of its program, partially due to the extensive changes in child welfare that were occurring but also due to child abuse of the residents. Cmiel (1995) largely relied on written reports and board minutes and did not contact many living persons who had a different perspective on the agency. Chapin Hall closed in 1984, and Cmiel again attributes this to deinstitutionalization and other policy and funding shifts. Although that is true, this author was also aware (although no longer connected to the agency) of child abuse occurring in the institution. None of these occasions were reported in any of the documents examined by Cmiel.

This example illustrates the limits of relying on selected documents (especially those created by powerful persons) to determine cause and effect. The use of such documents should be supplemented—through a process referred to as "triangulation"—by other sources of information, such as interviews with people who had knowledge of the situation or reports on the situation written by outsiders. This is a social justice issue because the powerless and the oppressed (especially the children and their families) were not given a voice in interpreting developments that affected them.

Another important issue in both qualitative and quantitative research is cultural consciousness and reflexivity. This issue has received much attention and is particularly related to the concept of cultural humility (National Association of Social Workers, 2008). The issue here goes beyond the idea that the researcher should have knowledge of the culture of participants in the research. It is equally important to recognize that people from different cultures may have different ways of knowing, imparting what they know, and even viewing reality. The researcher must acquire knowledge of these matters and use this knowledge to develop a trusting relationship with participants. An example of these issues with reference to research with indigenous Canadian peoples is provided by Kovach (2005), Absolon and Willett (2005), and Thomas (2005).

The previous discussion is not intended to imply that quantitative approaches are inherently unjust. Our main argument is that qualitative approaches are more likely than quantitative ones to express the voices of oppressed peoples in ways that enable them to take ownership of their views in their own languages, ways of viewing their realities, and to express their own thoughts and feelings relevant to the matter at hand. Sometimes, with the understanding of all the stakeholders, researchers will need to sample the views and experiences of large populations. In such cases, quantitative instruments can ensure that all respondents are responding to the same stimuli (e.g., instrument questions). There are also data that are obtained which represent an almost universally recognized variable (e.g., age, area of residence, length of time an event occurred, and country of birth), although these data do not represent what these "facts" mean to the respondent. An example of such a variable that has recently been recognized as more complex than previously considered is gender. Persons such as transsexuals may view themselves as having unique gender attributes with regard to how their physical attributes, psychological sense of themselves, and gender history relate to their environment.

From a social justice perspective, there are strong advantages to using so-called "mixed methods" research in which some aspects of the views and experiences of people are identified through quantitative methods, whereas the personal meaning of these findings is discovered through qualitative methods. In socially just research, however, all of the data are gathered, recorded, analyzed, and interpreted by various stakeholders, especially participants.

Community-Based Participatory Action Research

An approach that is frequently utilized by investigators committed to social justice principles is "community-based participatory action research." This approach draws heavily on research approaches developed much earlier by Lewin (1947) and many of his associates. Action research involved processes to design research, to examine the outcomes and the utilization of these outcomes in changing social situations, and in an iterative manner to design and implement new research activity in the light of such changes or lack of change. The participatory aspect is integrated with the action research when the stakeholders (certainly including those whose behavior is examined in the research) are involved in full partnership with the researchers in all phases of the investigation. Social justice issues will be an essential feature of such research if the goals of the research are to promote social justice or ameliorate social injustice. According to Sohng (1996, as quoted in Gouin, Cocq, & McGavin, 2011), "PR (participatory research) was originally designed to resist the intellectual colonialism of Western social research into the Third World development process" (p. 80). Gouin et al. state, "The central concern in PR is the production and ownership of knowledge by oppressed groups with the intention of defining their own realities and mobilizing for action (p. 264).

An excellent example of socially just participatory action research is presented by Gouin et al. (2011). The authors are staff members of what is described as "a not-for-profit and nonhierarchical Canadian social justice organization" called Inter Pares. They were mandated to conduct research on the practice of this organization. They note that the staff members were committed to "process and consensus." The focus of the organization was on changing the way Canada engaged in international development. This led to the organization's financial and political support to "organizations in the Global South acting on issues of common concern: reproductive rights and women's health, violence against women, civil liberties, migration, human rights, resource extraction, and food sovereignty" (p. 262).

Gouin et al. (2011) observed the principles of this kind of research in all aspects of their research activity as follows:

- They specified that the purpose of their research is to determine "how Inter Pares' feminism informs its day-to-day functioning and programming and how it relates to results achieved" (p. 263). Specifically, they sought to "learn, affirm, and question: Where is the organization now? How did it get here? Where is it going?" (p. 263).

- A small group of staff members from various positions within the organization were referred to as the "research cluster." Members of this cluster arrived at all decisions by consensus and presented them to the full Inter Pares staff for discussion and final decision-making.
- Data were collected through multiple methods, including interviews, focus groups, and workshops "carried out with current and former staff, current and former board members, counterparts in Canada, Latin America, Asia, and Africa, funders, and other collaborators" (p. 266).

Phases of Social Justice Research

We can more specifically identify social justice issues in research and evaluation by discussing them in relation to what we view as *phases* of the research process.

Planning

Due to practical limitations in funding and sponsorship, choices must be made regarding which research questions are addressed. In addition, in a democracy concerns about social justice should guide research choices. Thus, how practitioners choose the problems that become the focus of their research is an important component of efforts to achieve social justice.

Clark and Hollander (2005) amplify this assumption by addressing such questions as how research is distributed and measured and how democratic societies can ensure a just distribution of research. Social justice requires that the voices of women and members of minority groups be heard when determining what problems should be researched. This means that the input from such groups requires greater transparency in the research process that goes well beyond "informed consent."

Data Collection

The process of data collection raises many social justice issues. One is that the choice of a sample may reflect biases. Various funding bodies now insist that the sample be representative with regard to race, ethnicity, color, gender, and age. Often, research limits the involvement of one or another of these groups in the research sample but claims that the findings are universally applicable. Even the choice of data collectors should be considered because research subjects may respond differently to people they view as similar or different from themselves on the basis of cultural or social characteristics.

Data Analysis

The analysis of data has important consequences for how research is used to inform practice and program development. As Montague (1964) states,

> The scientist is put in the position of having to make available the facts, for the benefit of those who may wish to judge the evidence for themselves. . . . Facts do not speak for themselves but are at the mercy of whoever chooses to give them meaning. (p. 137)

Thus, from a social justice perspective, the investigator should disclose to relevant audiences, especially the people whose views and experience have been studied, the approach that was taken in the analysis, why it was chosen, and how the research design is appropriate for the "subjects" and the issues being studied. Some analytic approaches seek to account for variations in responses from members of different social groups, whereas others do not. The researcher may indicate that too few (or no) members from a given group have been included in the research sample, but he or she must then explain why this occurred and how it was factored into the analysis of the findings. The federal government, in fact, usually insists that this question must be addressed in funding proposals and the exclusion of some groups justified. The response of the researcher to this question should also be included in explanations of the analysis. As Clark and Hollander (2005) state,

> Despite the well-trod territory of minority suspicion of public health based on the Tuskegee Syphilis Study (Gamble, 1997; Reverby, 2000) and other unethical "scientific" undertakings, an unspoken and perhaps greater danger is the unaddressed research questions, uncollected data, and the misinterpreted and/or underestimated findings. . . . The data we do not have and the questions we do not ask deprive various publics of relevant life-giving and life-saving information. A question for deliberation is why are "we" (disciplines) complacent with incomplete health knowledge, poor understanding, and inadequate dissemination of findings, even as yet another study of White males confirms what is already known. (p. 36)

Interpretation of Findings

In research, in addition to analyzing data, the findings are typically "interpreted"—that is, explained often by reference to previous research and established theories. There are ways in which findings that are unacceptable to the researchers, funders, or audiences may be explained away. For example, in a hypothetical study that examined alcohol use, the researchers may "explain away" a finding that did not meet their expectations and biases by claiming that the analysis was biased, the instruments were inaccurate, or the significance level was too large (i.e., there was too great a chance that the result was due to variation among samples and not an indication of a strong likelihood of the truth of the findings).

Dissemination of Findings

A major issue in this regard is how results are reported to "underserved poor groups" (Clark & Hollander, 2005). As Clark and Hollander state,

> Many underserved poor groups desperately need critical skills to interpret data. However, in the absence of such skills, cannot researchers be more mindful of delivering . . . information in a way that is useful, persuasive, and understandable? This is really a challenge of interpretation, translation, and dissemination. (p. 40)

Socially just research should be reported in a form that is readable and understandable to all persons to whom the research is relevant. If the study produces extensive statistical data, these might be included in an appendix for those who are interested. It might be appropriate to give oral presentations with useful diagrams to some audiences. Socially justice-oriented research is also likely to be related to social change efforts, and this relationship should be explicated and included in oral and written presentations.

Evaluation

The following are principles that apply to research whose purpose is to evaluate a particular form of intervention or program. A socially just evaluation will include both an evaluation of the outcomes and the processes utilized to attain these outcomes. The former answers the question as to whether the outcomes desired by the researchers, participants, and other stakeholders have or have not been achieved. The methods used to study this question will be consistent with all of the research principles discussed throughout this chapter. Often, the outcomes desired by those with less or more power will differ. For example, participants may have desired, as one of their goals, that certain discriminatory social policies be changed. The policymakers in the agency or higher levels may have desired to maintain the status quo. Presumably, this issue will have been negotiated before the evaluation began but should again be recognized in the evaluation process.

In addition to measuring the outcomes of a service or program, the evaluation should analyze the processes through which it was delivered. This will help answer such questions as the following:

- To what extent and how were the voices of participants heard and heeded in designing and implementing the evaluation?
- To what extent and how were the voices of participants heard and heeded in the interpretation of the data that were collected?
- To what extent and how were the voices of participants heard and heeded in the dissemination of the results?
- To what extent and how were the voices of participants integrated into efforts to achieve social and personal change as a result of the evaluation and in planning future research to carry the process of change forward?

Any evaluation also raises a series of power issues. An evaluation process may also help empower the recipients of service because their assessment of existing services or programs (if not suppressed) can have major consequences for the sponsoring organization or staff. On the other hand, the organization is likely to have more power than the recipients of service in determining how the evaluation will be disseminated (and to whom) and to what extent its recommendations will be implemented. Thus, to conduct a socially just evaluation, the power of the organization(s) involved should be considered in advance.

It is not often done, but we suggest that those who supplied the data are able to use the findings to promote social change whether or not the agency or organization approves their use of data about themselves and their situations. This is a difficult issue because the organization should also have some rights regarding the reliability and validity of the data and how they are presented as well as the ability to negotiate with other stakeholders regarding such issues. How researchers can create a "level playing field" in these contested and sometimes conflict-ridden circumstances is a matter that requires further exploration.

Unintended Consequences

The research process can also produce so-called "unintended consequences." For example, the process of data collection may uncover additional issues besides the ones that led to the evaluation; this process may also stimulate any of the parties to take other actions as a result of what is being said or written. The following are brief examples of this phenomenon:

- While knowing that an evaluation is underway, a worker or an agency perceives that the might uncover evaluation negative aspects of the service before the evaluation is completed. This might lead the worker or the agency to alter the evaluation process. The participants can be helped to recognize and oppose this.
- The service may be modified in other ways (e.g., as a result of unexpected developments or external pressures) while the evaluation is being conducted, and the impact of these changes should be considered in the assessment of the evaluation.
- The presence of researchers observing the agency may have a variety of consequences, such as the agency hiding practices, altering practices, or failing to cooperate with the investigators.
- One of the authors of this book had the experience of being invited to help evaluate a child protection program. He worked diligently with a team from the agency to conduct the evaluation. At the completion of the project, he wrote a final report that was provided to the agency. He was not as committed then to the ideas of social justice as he is today. Thus, participants in the evaluation (families referred to the agency because of allegations of abuse) were in no way involved in the research, although relevant staff were fully involved at each stage of the process. After he completed work with the agency as an outside researcher, he discovered through his perusal of journals that the agency staff had written and published an article based on the research. His participation was noted nowhere, and the agency authors presented a totally positive interpretation of the data; only data that supported favorable views of the agency were included. This example illustrates that good faith is not sufficient and that carefully drafted agreements that describe in detail which parties have the right to do what with the data should be developed before the evaluation begins. Ideally, this agreement would incorporate the socially just research principles described in this chapter.
- The other author was hired to conduct an evaluation of the youth services bureaus of a suburban county. Although the evaluation involved the active participation of all the relevant service actors (e.g., police, probation officers, social workers, and county administrators), none of the recipients of services were included. The evaluation identified both positive and negative features of these agencies, but the study's conclusions did not reflect the views of the youth or their families. Because service providers from different professions

varied in their assessment of the programs, the inclusion of service users could have had a decisive impact on what the evaluation found and how the results were interpreted.

In the best of circumstances, the findings of an evaluation can be used to promote positive changes in programs and services. For example, Baumann, Domenech Rodriguez, and Parra-Cardona (2011) conducted community-based applied research with Latino immigrant families according to ethical and social justice principles. Their intention was to culturally adapt, implement, and evaluate an evidence-based parenting intervention known as PMTO. PMTO has been culturally adapted for dissemination among Spanish-speaking Latino families in the United States, Mexico, and Puerto Rico. This investigation conformed to most of the social justice principles in research discussed throughout this chapter. To show how they did this, we list the ways that the research was conducted:

1. *Recognizing the social and political context of the research*: The researchers recognized that Latinos comprise a large proportion of the foreign-born citizens of the United States; this has led to recent changes in the social and political context of the country, and these changes have produced resistance such as exclusionary legislation. The authors state that these changes have deeply affected their own research, their practice, and their personal well-being. Their article discusses the challenges these developments posed to their research studies and how they "negotiated these political, contextual, and social challenges from within socially just social paradigms, which combined a community-based orientation with rigorous scientific traditions" (p. 132).

2. *Community-based orientation*: The authors' community-based orientation is "built on the nuanced and critical analysis forwarded by community-based participatory research (CBPR)." They indicate that "CBPR is a collaborative approach that prescribes equal participation from researchers and community members in all dimensions of the research process" (p. 132).

3. *Contingencies affecting practice in the environment*: The authors saw the parenting issue as affected by contingencies outside the home, such as their immigration status and existing immigration laws, institutional discrimination, and the need for language and other forms of cultural adjustment. They emphasize that "neither parents or children are pathologized, rather the problem is situated in the interaction between them" (p. 133).

4. *Cultural adaptation of instruments*: The investigators engaged in a process of cultural adaptation of existing materials with the help of a mentor who was knowledgeable and skillful in this process. The adaptation involved learning about the most pressing needs from community members regarding issues

of parenting and general life challenges. This took place with the help of key community leaders and members in the research enterprise.

5. *Replications*: There were several replications of the project. In one, performed in Utah, the principal investigator and three research associates were first-generation immigrants and another was the daughter of international immigrants; the implications of this issue were carefully considered.

6. *Researchers' roles*: In some ways, the researchers went beyond the usual roles of researchers—for example, buying groceries and supplies for participants. In obtaining data, families were seen in their own homes when this was required to enhance their sense of comfort and safety.

7. *Awareness of how participants coped with oppression*: At times, participants were arrested or deported, and parents in the study stepped forward to care for their children.

8. *Gaining access to participants*: In the project's implementation in Michigan, community leaders introduced the researchers at key community events. At these events, researchers asked parents where they would be comfortable meeting for the project; the parents clearly indicated they would prefer to meet in churches or private homes and not in schools or community centers.

9. *Protection of participants*: One of the research procedures involved tape recording of sessions. Participants were very quiet when they learned of this, and they indicated that if they said certain things, there could be repercussions from immigration authorities. This led to a very lengthy discussion of the role of the researchers and the protection of information, which ultimately led to participants' assent to the recording process.

10. *Ethics*: The investigators regularly consulted appropriate codes of ethics regarding the roles they assumed in obtaining resources, making referrals to agencies, and providing other services, and they were comfortable that they had not violated any of these.

11. *Justification for combining science and actions for social justice*: The authors conclude that "exclusively maintaining a sole focus on strong science can become a sophisticated oppressive tool for scientific imperialism" (p. 147). They also "confirmed that delivering strong science by listening to the voices of the families . . . and sharing their struggles constitutes a bona fide strategy to help them increase their quality of life" (p. 147).

Summary

In this chapter, we discussed the important role played by research and evaluation in socially just practice. An important dimension of this is the principle that individuals and groups affected by the research must play a role in designing the research and must be aware of and able to use the information derived through the research. We discussed and gave example of the types of research often utilized by researchers committed to the principles of social justice. We also discussed the epistemologies drawn upon by these researchers. This included a discussion of what we consider to be valid and useful knowledge and research.

We then discussed the various ways the research had an impact upon those affected by the consequences of the research or who were included as "subjects" in the process itself. This includes the power relationships between those studied and those doing the studying. Current practice/research models were discussed, such as evidence-based practice, and we considered what such practice should entail to be considered socially just.

In addition, specific details of the research process that promote social justice were reviewed, including the role of marginalized groups, the use by the researchers of critical theories, the different ways of knowing that are exhibited by people from different cultures, the degree to which the research questions relations of domination, and how the concept of praxis is applied to the research process.

We also raised the issue of whether qualitative or quantitative research is more compatible with socially just principles. The chapter also included a description of the phases of the research process from planning to dissemination and how socially just issues are reflected in each of these phases. We provided a discussion of a particularly important method of socially just research—community-based participatory action research. Finally, we examined the issues involved in evaluation research. We explored such tenets as the study of both process and outcome, the effect of power disparities on the research process, and the impact of the social and political context.

Discussion Questions

1. Choose a social work practice issue in which you are interested. How might you use research to help address the social injustices that the issue reflects?
2. Choose a practice issue about which you might engage in research. How would you integrate a social justice approach into that research?
3. Using the Internet, a refereed journal article, or a published report, select a piece of social work research that addresses an issue about which you are concerned. Discuss how this research did or did not concern itself with social justice in the way it was conceptualized or conducted.

Glossary

Action system: The individuals, groups, organizations, families, or others with whom practitioners interact to accomplish the purposes defined by the worker and the **client system**.

Alienation: Alienation is a concept that refers both to an individual psychological condition—often characterized as estrangement from the self and from society as a whole—and to the social conditions that underlie and promote it. Marx believed that general alienation was rooted in the loss of control on the part of workers over the nature of the labor task and over the products of their labor.

Animation/animateur: Social *animation* is a process of social and community change developed in French-speaking Canada that attempts to increase community participation by focusing on a specific issue. It combines features derived from the confrontational approaches developed by Saul Alinsky and the more consensual approaches described by Murray Ross. In France and Francophone Canada, community organization is taught in schools of *animation sociale*.

Apartheid: Apartheid was the system of rigid racial separation and oppression in South Africa that ended officially with the first multiracial national elections in 1994. It is an Afrikaans word meaning "separation" or literally "aparthood" (or "apartness"). In English, it has come to mean any legally sanctioned system of ethnic segregation.

Bhagavad Gita: The *Bhagavad Gita* is perhaps the most popular and most loved religious text in Hinduism, written between 200 BCE and 200 CE. In its 18 chapters, a variety of perspectives on religion and faith are discussed. The most prominent theme is the idea of faith and devotion being the primary means of salvation.

Capabilities approach: An approach to social justice developed by the economist Amartya Sen and the political philosopher Martha Nussbaum. They argue that a socially just system of social welfare must also involve marginalized individuals and excluded groups in socially just process policymaking processes. This perspective incorporates a growing awareness of the impact of different cultural and historical contexts, includes nonmaterial resources among the "goods" to be distributed, considers the implications of multiple forms of power on policymaking, and argues that policies should be specifically tailored to address different types of oppression and manifestations of privilege.

Case advocacy: Advocacy efforts designed to improve the situation of one or a limited number of individuals, families, or communities, for example, to obtain benefits for which they are eligible.

Casework: The method of social work practice with individuals to help them achieve their goals. The term has been enlarged to include work with couples and families; the term sometimes used in these circumstances is family casework.

Caste system: A caste system is a social system that divides people into a hereditary hierarchy. Each caste has its own customs that restrict the occupations and dietary habits of its members and their social contact with other castes. Some believe that the caste system in India was originally based on color distinctions between the conquering Aryans and the darker, native Dravidians. Some scholars have characterized the racial hierarchy in the American South as a caste system.

Charity organization societies (COS): Nonprofit organizations established in the last quarter of the 19th century in the United States that applied principles of "scientific charity" to the organization and distribution of public and private relief. These organizations later developed the method of social work practice known as social casework.

Class or cause advocacy: Advocacy efforts to improve the situation of many individuals, families, or communities that share common characteristics or needs at one time, usually by changing laws or policies.

Client system: The individuals, families, groups, or larger systems with whom practitioners contract to provide social work services and whose goals and needs are primarily taken into account.

Code of Hammurabi: The Code of Hammurabi was developed in Mesopotamia (modern Iraq) in approximately 1686 BC. It is one of the earliest sets of laws found and is often considered the first example of the legal concept that some laws are so basic as to be beyond the ability of even kings to change. This concept lives on in most modern legal systems and has given rise to the phrase "written in stone."

Collectivism: A view that people are social beings who depend on one another for the satisfaction of primary and social needs.

Community action programs: Neighborhood programs created by the Economic Opportunity Act of 1964 that were required to provide "maximum feasible participation" by community residents in the development and implementation of social services.

Conscientization: Conscientization is a popular education and social concept developed by the renowned Brazilian pedagogue and educational theorist Paulo Freire and is grounded in critical theory. Conscientization means breaking through prevailing mythologies to reach new levels of awareness—in particular, awareness of oppression and being an "object" in a world in which only "subjects" have power.

Constructivism/social construction: Constructivism is the application of the idea that reality is socially and psychologically constructed through social interactions. Social construction is a concept developed by postmodernists that postulates that reality is neither fixed nor objectively determined but, rather, is a subjective reflection of the cultural values and beliefs, primarily of dominant groups. The use of this lens provides a different interpretation of contemporary approaches to individual and social problems.

Critical consciousness: Continuous examination of one's own positionalities (social positions) in order to recognize one's own standpoints and to continue to learn about the ways in which our life experiences are shaped by our status and identities.

Critical theory/critical race theory: Critical theory is a sociological theory that originated in critical legal studies in the late 1970s. It aims to uncover the assumptions and masks that keep us from a full and true understanding of how the world works. A major goal of critical theory is to reveal how surface reality often contradicts the underlying reality. Learning to critically examine race relations is a key part of critical race theory. Examining everyday interactions, and finding the racial component in them, can help move the cause of racial equality beyond a simplistic "color-blind" approach.

Cultural humility: A cultural humility perspective invites an experience of "not knowing," curiosity, and openness to the wide range of cultural lenses that guide, sustain, and reinforce our individual uniqueness. It frees social workers from the need to possess knowledge of a range of cultural differences. Cultural humility subverts the professional impulse to maintain power and control and encourages awareness of the cultural experiences and internalized cultural meanings of others.

Devolution/policy devolution: The transfer of responsibility for the funding and delivery of social policies and programs from the federal government to the states and from state governments to local governments that began in the United States in the 1970s.

Dharma: In Hinduism, *dharma* is the doctrine concerning the religious and moral rights and duties of each individual; it generally refers to religious duty, but it may also mean social order, right conduct, or simply virtue. In Buddhism, dharma has two distinct meanings: It refers to religious truth, namely Buddhist teaching as the highest truth; it is also used as a technical term to denote a constituent element of experience or any existing thing or phenomenon.

Dialectical: A process that includes an original state (a thesis), contradictions or conflicts that arise within that state (its antithesis), and a resolution (or synthesis) that creates a new state. This process may occur in the world as well as in thought processes.

Dialogue: A process of conversation between and among people in which each person listens carefully and thoughtfully to what others say and contributes one's own ideas only after listening to others and fully considering the implications of what one has heard.

Dichotomous thinking: Creating false categories and choices that omit consideration of the full range of possibilities and in which such thinking reflects the position of privilege of the speaker.

Economic globalization: The transformation of the world economy that began in the 1960s and 1970s. It is characterized by the dominance of market values, increased power of financial institutions, the rapid mobility of capital, greater interdependence of national economies, and a widening gap between rich and poor nations. See **neoliberalism**.

Empirical: Knowledge that relies or is based solely on experiment and observation rather than theory, intuition, experience, and other ways of drawing conclusions.

Empowerment: A process and goal through which individuals, singly and in groups, gain mastery and control over their lives and become active in efforts to change their environments. It contains both political–economic and psychosocial components.

Engagement: The process in which practitioners and others (usually the client system) develop a relationship involving a mutual effort to define and accomplish agreed-on purposes.

Enlightenment: The Age of Enlightenment (or the Age of Reason) was a European intellectual movement of the 17th and 18th centuries in which ideas concerning God, reason, nature, and man were blended into a worldview that inspired revolutionary developments in art, philosophy, and politics. Central to Enlightenment thought were the use and celebration of reason. The Enlightenment produced modern secular theories of psychology and ethics and radical political theories. One of the Enlightenment's enduring legacies is the belief that human history is a record of general progress.

Environmental justice: A concept that emerged in the 1980s and 1990s that merged a civil rights approach to environmental activism. The US Environmental Protection Agency defines environmental justice as "the fair treatment and meaningful involvement of all people regardless of race, color, national origin, or income with respect to the development, implementation, and enforcement of environmental law, regulations, and policies." The environmental justice movement takes different forms in different areas of the world and is often linked to efforts to eradicate poverty and environmental racism.

Environmental set: The context in which communities and organizations are situated and with which they must interact. It includes the physical environment, the demographics of the community, the political and cultural climate, the nature of technology, and the availability and location of the material and nonmaterial resources they need to fulfill their goals.

Epistemic privilege: Immediate subtle cultural knowledge and affective experience of the oppression of others and one's favored position.

Epistemology: The study or theory of the nature, sources, and limits of knowledge.

Eurocentric/Eurocentrism: Eurocentrism is the practice, conscious or otherwise, of placing emphasis on European (and, generally, Western) theories and ideas at the expense of those of other cultures. Implicit in this definition is the assumption that Western concepts, such as individualism, human rights, freedom, social justice, and the separation of church and state, are universal.

Feminism: On the most basic level, feminism is the principle that women should have political, economic, and social rights equal to those of men. More broadly, it refers to the movement to win such rights for women and to end oppression against women in all forms. Within feminism, there are many approaches to the application of this principle, including radical, Marxist, and liberal.

Feminist planning/feminist process: An egalitarian model or organizational structure and decision-making that originated within the feminist movement during the 1960s and 1970s. In this model, there are no formally recognized leaders, and all decisions are made by consensus. It has later been adopted in whole or in part by environmental justice, peace organizations, and antinuclear groups. One advantage of this model is that it empowers staff and members through its collective conception of leadership. It tends to be more effective in smaller organizations and within organizations that possess a high degree of demographic and ideological homogeneity.

Founder's syndrome: A phenomenon in which an organization increasingly becomes defined primarily by the leader or leaders who established it rather than by its stated mission and goals. This creates a quasi "cult of personality" in which the organization becomes overidentified with the personal qualities and rivalries of its leader(s). This distorts the organization's focus, strategy development, external relationships, and public image.

Fraternity: Originally, brotherhood among a disparate body of people united in their interests, aims, beliefs, and goals. Although the concept emerged during the French Revolutionary era when politics was dominated by men, no contemporary contrast with "sisterhood" is intended by most of those who today embrace fraternity. The goal, rather, is to establish in the wider community the sorts of feelings and behaviors for each other that brothers and sisters are assumed to possess. It suggests a sense of belonging to a unit with which one can readily, if not naturally, identify.

Fundamentalism/fundamentalist: "Fundamentalist" describes a movement to return to what adherents consider the defining or founding principles of their religion. Recently, it has come to refer to any religious enclave that intentionally resists identification with the larger religious community in which it originally arose, on the basis that fundamental principles on which the larger religious group is supposedly founded have been displaced by alternative principles hostile to its identity.

Religious fundamentalism is a modern phenomenon characterized by a sense of embattled alienation in the midst of the surrounding culture.

General will: A theory of Jean-Jacques Rousseau, an 18th-century French political philosopher, that in a democratic society the state represents the general will of its citizens and that in obeying its laws each citizen is pursuing his or her own individual and collective interest. All citizens, therefore, are equal and have no more power or influence than any other citizens.

Generalist practice: A form of social work practice in which practitioners seek to help a client system achieve its goals through a variety of methods, which may include work with individuals, families, groups, communities, and organizations, as well as efforts to influence social policy.

Group process: The changes that occur over time in group conditions, including the interactions among members, group structures, group norms, group climate, and emotional expressions in the group. It also refers to the ways in which a specific group operates to achieve its goals.

Group structure: The pattern of relationships in a group such as communications, division of labor, and attraction or rejection of members to each other.

Hegemony/hegemonic: As developed by Italian Marxist Antonio Gramsci, hegemony is a concept referring to a particular form of dominance in which a ruling class legitimates its position and secures the acceptance if not outright support of those below it through the use of a range of social and cultural mechanisms. The concept of hegemony underscores how dominance and subordination become defined as part of the normal structure of society and are woven into the institutional frameworks of major aspects of social life, from the family to education and organized religion.

Historicism/historicity: Historicism has three meanings. In its first sense, it encompasses the idea that history can be explained in terms of fixed laws or principles. Knowledge of such patterns enables us to understand the past and predict the future. In its second sense, historicism is a perspective that argues that any aspect of social life can be understood only in the context of the historical period in which it exists. This implies that everything from cultural ideas to the structural character of social relationships and institutions is historically "relative" and cannot be compared across historical periods. The concept has been used by postmodernist thinkers to assert that there is no absolute truth about deep philosophical questions that should stand for all time. Finally, the term is used by some Christian fundamentalists to refer to that form of Biblical exegesis that holds that the Bible is able to predict the future, especially the "end of times."

Indigenous people/indigenous culture: The people who were the earliest inhabitants of a given area, prior to the formation of a nation-state, and their descendants who continue to live in that area. They do not belong to the dominant nation of that nation-state and are sometimes referred to as First People or First Nations.

The United Nations defines indigenous peoples as "those which, having a historical continuity with pre-invasion and pre-colonial societies that developed on their
territories, consider themselves distinct from other sectors of the societies now prevailing in those territories, or parts of them."

Influence: The use of power to affect the behavior of others. Influence may be the
result of expertise, status, formal authority, or personal charisma.

Internalized oppression: This describes the conscious and unconscious adoption of
beliefs, attitudes, and cultural messages that distorts the self-concept of members
of oppressed groups. It is an internal (psychological) manifestation of the external
conditions of oppression that is often associated with the inability of members of
oppressed groups to realize their potential.

Intersectionality: A concept that reflects the understanding that power and oppression exist on many levels and are not based solely on one's race, gender, and class but
often are the result of compounded layers of each acting in concert. It also refers to
the idea that everyone has multiple identities related to the statuses one occupies
and that the combination of these multiple identities determines one's perspective on and action in the world. Some scholars and activists have criticized the use
of the concept because it lacks a specific focus on oppressed populations and may
undermine efforts to focus on their unique conditions.

Involuntary clients: Clients who are compelled to participate in a social work service
under threat of some negative consequence if they fail to do so (e.g., expulsion from
school, incarceration, and loss of benefits). In recent years, the number of clients
who are involuntary has increased considerably. This has challenged the underlying
premises of social work practice.

Iron law of oligarchy: A concept developed by the political scientist Roberto
Michels. He postulated that within hierarchically structured organizations, a
small group would ultimately come to dominate all decision-making. This oligarchy often develops over time, based on personal relationships, access to power and
resources, and/or ideological compatibility. It excludes most staff and all clients
and constituents from the process of establishing organizational goals and evaluating the organization's work.

Justice/social justice: In the simplest sense, justice is a concept largely based on social
contract theory that refers to fairness or equity and to the process of people getting
what they deserve. In a legal sense, for example, justice consists of treating everyone according to the law—of guaranteeing civil rights and following prescribed
procedures in a consistent and evenhanded way. Distributive or social justice, however, involves less precise notions of what is fair, especially in the distribution of
resources and rewards such as wealth. In a highly influential work, philosopher
John Rawls argued that equality and equal liberty should prevail unless inequality
serves the best interests of everyone. Robert Nozick, on the other hand, argues
that justice is done when interference with individual freedom is minimized,

especially in relation to the state. Recently, the concept has been synonymous with the application of human rights, although this linkage has been criticized for its Eurocentric focus.

Karma: The doctrine of Karma states that one's state in this life is a result of actions (both physical and mental) in past incarnations, and action in this life can determine one's destiny in future incarnations. Although the action of karma may be compared with the Western notions of sin and judgment by God or gods, Karma is held to operate as an inherent principle of the Universe without the intervention of any supernatural being. Most teachings state that for common mortals, having an involvement with Karma is an unavoidable part of day-to-day living. Karmic law is universally applicable, and only those who have attained liberation from rebirth, called nirvana, can transcend it.

Leadership, group: The acts of an individual that increase the effectiveness of the group. This is sometimes divided into task leadership (aiding the group to accomplish its tasks or concrete goals) and social–emotional leadership (aiding the group's members to develop and maintain relationships and/or deal with their affects).

Liberation theology: Liberation theology is an important and controversial theological school in the Roman Catholic Church that emerged after the Second Vatican Council. It has had particularly widespread influence in Latin America and among the Jesuits. Liberation theology seeks to express religious faith by helping the poor and working for social justice, human rights, and political and social change. Liberation theologians have sometimes been criticized as purveyors of Marxism, and the Vatican has sought to curb their influence by appointing more conservative prelates.

Marxism/Marxist: Marxism is a political practice and social theory based on the works of Karl Marx, a 19th-century philosopher, economist, journalist, and revolutionary. Marx drew on Hegel's philosophy, the political economy of Adam Smith, the economics of David Ricardo, and the ideas of 19th-century French socialism to develop a critique of society that he claimed was both scientific and revolutionary. The Marxist theory of history posits class struggle as history's driving force, and it views capitalism as the most recent and most critical historical stage. There have been many conflicting interpretations and definitions of Marxism, and it has influenced the scholarship of both Marxists and non-Marxists and a wide range of political and social movements since the 19th century.

Maternalism/maternalist: Maternalism has three meanings. First, it refers to social practices grounded in women's concern for children, especially when those practices extend beyond the home into community and/or political arenas. Maternalism has been used particularly to describe the activities of Progressive Era social reformers in the United States who shaped the emerging welfare states' policies concerning mothers and children. Second, maternalism refers to discourse that highlights women's connection to and responsibility for children and that emphasizes differences (which may be conceived either as biologically based or as socially conditioned) between men's and women's contributions to family and society. Third, maternalism is sometimes used to describe feminist theory that critiques the cultural devaluation of mothering and that articulates the contributions of maternal practice to social and political life.

Mau Mau: A militant Kikuyu-led nationalist movement of the 1950s in Kenya that advocated violent resistance to British domination in Kenya. Kikuyu resistance spearheaded the independence movement, and Jomo Kenyatta, jailed as a Mau Mau leader in 1953, became prime minister of independent Kenya in 1963.

Meta- or master narrative: A way of thinking that unites knowledge and experience to seek to provide a definitive, universal truth. The concept of a master narrative emerges out of postmodernism. A master narrative reflects the ideology of the dominant culture and, as the sum of all culturally available narratives, it reflects the dominant discourse of a society. One of the key functions of master narratives is the construction of an assumed normative experience. A meta-narrative is an attempt to explain a broad range of historical or contemporary phenomena within one overarching framework. It can be a religious doctrine (e.g., Christianity) or a secular one (Marxism). Postmodernists reject all meta-narratives on the grounds of their inherent subjectivity.

Modern/modernism: In Western culture, modernism refers to the necessity of an individual rejecting previous tradition and, by creating individual techniques, produces work that is original to that artist. In general, the movement, especially in the arts, constituted a radical break with the past and concurrent search for new forms of expression. Modernism fostered a period of experimentation in the arts from the late 19th to the mid-20th century, particularly in the years following World War I. In an era characterized by industrialization, rapid social change, and advances in science and the social sciences, modernists felt a growing alienation incompatible with Victorian morality, optimism, and convention. They sought a more authentic response to a much-changed world.

Monitoring: The act of examining the processes through which individual, group, community, and societal interventions are implemented and the outcomes they produce. It may utilize such approaches as collecting critical incidents, administering structured instruments, and obtaining the views of participants.

Multiculturalism: Multiculturalism refers to the historical evolution of cultural diversity within a community, organization, or society; to the policies that embrace and support or reject and restrict that diversity; and to a cultural and political climate that promotes that diversity. Some critics of multiculturalism express concern that by amalgamating all forms of diversity, the concept obscures the particular challenges and forms of oppression that different groups experience.

Mutual aid: The process in which people help one another to accomplish individual and social goals through such activities as support, supply of resources, emotional expression (e.g., empathy), awareness of common conditions, affirmation of the ideas of others, and provision of information. Mutual aid organizations emerged in the United States in virtually every immigrant and racial/ethnic/religious minority community to aid their members by filling in gaps in services provided by government and mainstream nonprofit organizations.

NAFTA: The North American Free Trade Agreement (NAFTA) was negotiated between the United States, Mexico, and Canada between 1991 and 1993. It is the largest free trade area in the world. The agreement facilitates cross-border investment, and it includes side agreements addressing cooperation on labor and the environment. NAFTA has become a controversial domestic politics issue, being opposed mainly by unions and environmentalists.

Negritude: A literary and ultimately political movement that emerged from the intellectual environment of Paris in the 1930s and 1940s and from Black writers, such as Aimé Césaire, Léon Damas, and Léopold Sédar Senghor, joining together through the French language to assert their cultural identity, protest French colonial rule and forced assimilation, and respond to the alienated position of Blacks in history. From a political standpoint, negritude was an important aspect to the rejection of colonialism. Emerging at the cusp of African independence movements, negritude made an impact on how colonized people viewed themselves. The movement faded in the early 1960s after its objectives had been achieved in most African countries.

Neoliberalism: Neoliberalism is a political philosophy and movement that emerged concurrent with economic globalization during the 1960s and 1970s. Its main points include the elimination of government restrictions on the market (deregulation), the reduction of government's role in social welfare (the dismantling of the welfare state), privatization of services (in the interest of "efficiency"), and replacing the concept of "the public good" or "community" with "individual responsibility." Neoliberals prefer market-oriented and individually focused solutions to people's problems.

Nirvana: In Indian religious thought, the transcendent state of freedom and enlightenment achieved by the extinction of desire and individual consciousness. Nirvana is the supreme goal of the disciplines of meditation, particularly in Buddhism. This state is in opposition of suffering in which all greed, aversion, delusion, ignorance, craving, and ego-centered consciousness are extinguished.

Outcome: The change in individuals, groups, or larger systems as a result of an intervention. It may be measured immediately after the intervention or at a later time. It should be distinguished from **output**, which refers to the extent of effort but not the impact of that effort.

Pan-Africanism/Pan-African Movement: A political, philosophical, and cultural movement founded in approximately 1900 to secure equal rights, self-government, independence, and unity for African peoples. Despite variations in its application, the concept has a set of shared assumptions. Pan-Africanists tend to view all Africans and descendants of Africans as belonging to a single "race" with a shared cultural unity and historical fate. Cultural and intellectual manifestations of Pan-Africanism have focused on recovering or preserving African traditions and emphasizing the contributions of Africans and those in the African diaspora to the modern world. Politically, Pan-Africanists have invariably fought against racial discrimination and for the political rights of Africans and descendants of Africans. Some of the concepts of Pan-Africanism have influenced the social work field in the form of **Afrocentrism**.

Participatory action research (PAR): This approach to research design, implementation, and evaluation involves processes to adapt to changing social situations and, in an iterative manner, to design and implement new research activity in the light of such changes. The participatory aspect is integrated with the action research when the stakeholders (certainly including those whose behavior is examined in the research) are involved in full partnership with the researchers in all phases of the investigation. It is a particularly popular and effective approach among social justice organizations.

Participatory budgeting: A policymaking and planning process that has been adopted at the local level in the United States and Latin American nations. Through local councils, it attempts to enhance and make more meaningful the participation of community residents in determining the fiscal priorities of local government.

Pathologized: Alluding to some behavior or attribute of another as an aspect of mental illness. Some behaviors that are socially or culturally based have been "pathologized" as a means of denying or ignoring their environmental origins.

Popular education: An approach to community organizing and mobilization that has been particularly influential in shaping practice in Latin America and has been used throughout the world by labor unions, faith-based organizations, self-help organizations, and cooperatives. It emphasizes helping people redefine their place in the social structure and modify norms, role expectations, and community self-identification. The approach is consistent with social work's emphases on a strengths perspective and empowerment.

Popular sovereignty: The concept developed during the late 18th and 19th centuries that the "people" should rule. In theory, it has been a basic principle of Western political systems for the past two centuries. Some critics argue, however, that increasing economic inequality has undermined the concept and replaced it with an oligarchy of wealth.

Positionalities: The various statuses one occupies (e.g., class, gender, and race); one may be aware of these or oblivious to them.

Positivism: A system of philosophy developed by August Comte that knowledge is based solely on observable facts and their relationship to each other.

Postmodern/postmodernism: A diffuse cultural and artistic trend or movement that emerged in the 1950s. Philosophically, postmodernists question or reject claims of absolute certainty and objective truth that they regard as assertions of privilege or political power. The central premise of postmodernism is the rejection of all "meta- narratives." Postmodernism is largely a reaction to the assumed certainty of "modern" scientific efforts to explain reality. For this reason, postmodernism is highly skeptical of explanations that claim to be valid for all groups, cultures, traditions, or races and instead focuses on the relative truths of each person. It relies on concrete experience and interpretation rather than abstract principles and a fixed view of reality. Postmodernism is "post" because it is denies the existence of any ultimate principles, and it lacks the optimism of there being a scientific, philosophical, or religious truth that will explain everything for everybody—a characteristic of the so-called "modern" mind. The paradox of postmodernism is that by scrutinizing all principles with skepticism, even its own principles are not beyond questioning.

Power: Having the influence, position, ability to punish, personal attributes, and resources to determine the behavior of other individuals and systems or to define the alternative courses of action available to them.

Power analysis: A full examination of the power of individuals, groups, and larger systems active in a given situation.

Practice: In social work, practice is understood to mean the actions of social workers with client systems based on a foundation that synthesizes knowledge derived from research, the experiences of self and others, and the profession's values and ethics.

Practice principle: A prescription about the actions of social workers that combines a propositional statement (based on knowledge and theory) and a commendation providing guidelines for appropriate actions (which are derived from ethical imperatives).

Praxis: A dynamic process in which the practitioner engages in an action based on principles, examines the consequences of the action, and revises the principles and components of the action based on this examination. This is done in an iterative manner.

Privatization: The transfer of responsibility for social policy and program implementation and funding from government to either for-profit or nonprofit organizations. It is an important component of **neoliberalism**. Although usually done in the name of greater efficiency, privatization has primarily concentrated wealth in fewer hands and shifted the social costs of the market onto those segments of the population least able to pay for them.

Privilege: The unearned advantages of an individual or group associated with social categories that have higher status in society.

Process: The moment-to-moment changes in ideas, actions (verbal and nonverbal), and interactions between persons or within a group.

Progressive Era: A period of reform in US history (~1890–1917) in which the first major government and nonprofit social welfare and social service programs were created and the social work profession emerged.

Rank and file movement: A social movement of radical social workers from public- and private-sector organizations that emerged in the early and mid-1930s. It both promoted the interests of social workers as workers and engaged in coalition work and advocacy on behalf of the needs of all workers in US society. It reached the peak of its influence in the mid- to late 1930s when its membership exceeded that of the mainstream American Association of Social Workers.

Reflection: The review of one's actions, engagement in social processes, and social context that provides increased awareness of the effects of these factors on one's practice.

Reflexivity: The experience of ourselves in relation to our practice, social roles, ideas, historical context, and assumptions. It is an important component of socially just practice.

Satygraha: (Sanskrit for truth + path/way) The philosophy of nonviolent resistance most famously employed by Mohandas Gandhi in forcing an end to British rule in India. It has also been translated as "civil disobedience," "passive resistance," "truth force," or "the willingness to endure great personal suffering in order to do what's right." It is considered the philosophy behind nonviolent protest. Satyagraha seeks to conquer through submission. It involves refusing to submit to or cooperate with anything perceived as wrong, while adhering to the principle of nonviolence in order to maintain the tranquility of mind required for insight and understanding. The principle played a significant role in the US civil rights movement led by Martin Luther King, Jr.

Scientific charity: The application of principles of scientific management (e.g., efficiency and bureaucracy) by the **charity organization societies** to the administration of private charities and public relief programs in the late 19th and early 20th centuries.

Small group: A set of two or more individuals in face-to-face interaction such that the behavior of each person has the potential of having an impact on the other individuals in the set.

Social capital: A concept that refers to the combination of interpersonal, intergroup, and interorganizational relationships that exist in a community. Scholars refer to two types of social capital. "Bonding" social capital refers to long-standing social ties that often exist within tightly knit, homogeneous, insular communities, whose relationships are characterized as "horizontal" (i.e., more egalitarian). "Bridging" social capital refers to the connections that exist between a community and individuals, groups, organizations, and institutions outside the community that possess material and nonmaterial resources the community needs. These relationships are generally referred to as "vertical" because they are largely between groups with unequal power. In general, whereas low-income and low-power communities may possess considerable "bonding" social capital, privileged communities possess considerably more "bridging" social capital.

Social Gospel movement: A religious movement among American Protestants that developed after the Civil War. It emphasized New Testament teachings that addressed the needs of the poor and vulnerable in society. It inspired the activism of some early social work leaders such as Jane Addams, the cofounder of the social settlement Hull House in Chicago.

Social settlements: Agencies first created in the United States and Great Britain in the late 19th century, some of which still exist today. Settlements initially involved persons (called "residents") living in a neighborhood facility (called a "settlement house") through which they offered concrete services needed by the community, including education, recreation, child care, health care, and job training. Settlement house workers also engaged in advocacy efforts on behalf of a wide range of social reforms.

Social structure: The social components (individuals, groups, and institutions) of a particular situation, usually in interaction with each other. Social structure also reflects issues of power, status, resource distribution, cultural knowledge, and access to these "goods." These components may interact in collaborative, cooperative, or conflict-ridden relationships to each other.

Social system: A society or component of a society composed of interacting individuals embedded in larger structures and incorporating smaller structures. The component entities may engage in setting goals, using various forms of interaction, and granting rewards, while having more or less possession of resources and other sources of power.

Social–ecological model. A model of practice that views practice situations as embedded in a system that consists of the situations as well as their social, biological, and physical environments. According to this model, there is constant interaction among these entities; a change in one is likely to produce changes in others. Practitioners should examine these interactions and use this examination as the basis of action.

Stakeholder: Each individual involved in an interaction who, by virtue of his or her status, roles, and power, is invested in the preferred outcomes of that interaction.

Standpoints: The views and preferences of individuals involved in interactions based on their roles, power, values, history, culture, and understanding of the interaction.

Subjugation: The denial of resources, power, self-determination, freedom, employment, educational choice, or means of expression by one group in society to another based on such attributes as ethnicity, race, age, national origin, class, gender, religion, or sexual orientation.

Swaraj: The title of the first definitive writing of Mohandas Gandhi literally means "self-rule in India." In its more mature forms, it expresses many of Gandhi's basic ideas and philosophies of life. Gandhi believed that only nonviolent means could achieve Swaraj.

Target system: This is the system that practitioners attempt to change through their work with and on behalf of the client system.

Totalitarian/totalitarianism: Totalitarianism is a political system in which all citizens are subject to state authority in all aspects of day-to-day life. It goes well beyond authoritarian regimes, dictatorships, or typical police state measures, and even beyond those measures required to sustain total war with other states. It involves constant brainwashing achieved by propaganda to erase any potential for dissent, by anyone, especially the state's agents, and to achieve complete control over people's inner and outer lives. It is, perhaps, most vividly depicted in George Orwell's novel, *1984*.

Transparency: The act of making one's ideas and affects visible to others.

Unintended consequences: The outcomes of an action that were not the original purposes of the action and, in some instances, could not have been foreseen.

Universalist/universalism: Philosophically, the belief that all principles and norms are "universally" applicable to humanity. The United Nations' *Universal Declaration of Human Rights* is an example of the application of this idea. In the policy arena, universal policies are those whose benefits are made available to all citizens or all members of a particular demographic group (e.g., the aged) regardless of income. In the United States, examples of universal policies include public education, Social Security retirement benefits, and Medicare.

Varna: The ancient culture of India was based on a system of social diversification according to spiritual development. Four orders of society were recognized based on the four main goals of human beings and established society accordingly. These four groups were the Brahmins, the priests or spiritual class; the Kshatriya, the nobility or ruling class; the Vaishya, the merchants and farmers; and the Shudras or servants. These four orders of society were called "*varna*," which has two meanings: "color" and a "veil." As color, it does not refer to the color of the skin of people but, rather, to the qualities or energies of human nature. As a veil, it shows the four different ways in which the Divine Self is hidden in human beings.

Vatican II: The Second Vatican Council was convened by Pope John XXIII in October 1962 and ended on December 8, 1965. Its announced purpose was spiritual renewal of the Church and reconsideration of its position in the modern world. The most spectacular innovation of the Council was the invitation extended to Protestant and Orthodox Eastern churches to send observers. Another obvious feature was the diversity of national and cultural origins among those who attended. Unlike the previous 20 ecumenical councils, Vatican II was not held to combat contemporary heresies or deal with awkward disciplinary questions. Among its most important achievements were the vernacularization of the liturgy and promotion of greater lay participation, acknowledgment of the need for the

Church to adapt to the contemporary world, the Decree on Ecumenism, and the Declaration on Religious Freedom.

War on Poverty: The policy initiatives of the Johnson administration during the mid- to late 1960s that focused on the needs of low-income Americans. It included the Job Corps, Head Start, the Older Americans Act, and **community action programs**.

Way of Jain: Jainism is the smallest and one of the oldest of the 10 major world religions; it has been a significant force in Indian culture, philosophy, art, architecture, sciences, and politics. At the heart of right conduct for Jains lie the five great vows: nonviolence (*Ahimsa*)—not to cause harm to any living beings; truthfulness (*Satya*)—to speak the harmless truth only; nonstealing (*Asteya*)—not to take anything not properly given; chastity (*Brahmacharya*)—not to indulge in sensual pleasure; and nonpossession/nonattachment (*Aparigraha*)—complete detachment from people, places, and material things.

Worker system: The professional entity contracted with by the client system to enable the client system to achieve change in the target system. The worker system may be an individual, coworkers, or a team.

Zapatistas: The Zapatista Army of National Liberation (*Ejército Zapatista de Liberación Nacional* (EZLN)) is an armed revolutionary group based in Chiapas, one of the poorest states of Mexico. The EZLN claims to represent the rights of the indigenous population, but it also considers itself and is considered by others to be part of the wider anticapitalist movement, fighting for democracy, peace, and justice for all Mexicans and for all people. The Zapatistas are consciously opposed to **neoliberalism**. The group takes its name from the Mexican revolutionary Emiliano Zapata; its members view themselves as his ideological heir and the heir to 500 years of indigenous resistance against imperialism.

References

Abbott, E. (1924). *Immigration: Select documents and case records*. Chicago, IL: University of Chicago Press.

Abramovitz, M. (1999). *Regulating the lives of women: U.S. social policy from colonial times to the present* (Rev. ed.). Boston, MA: South End Press.

Abramovitz, M. (2012). Theorizing the neoliberal welfare state for social work. In M. Gray, J. Midgley, & S. Webb (Eds.), *The Sage handbook of social work*. Thousand Oaks, CA: Sage.

Absolon, K., & Willett, C. (2005). Putting ourselves forward: Location in aboriginal research. In L. Brown & S. Strega (Eds.), *Research as resistance: Critical, indigenous and anti-oppressive approaches* (pp. 97–126). Toronto, Ontario, Canada: Canadian Scholars' Press.

Ackerman, N. W., Beatman, F. L., & Sherman, S. N. (1961). *Exploring the basis of family therapy*. New York, NY: Family Service Association of America.

Acuña, R. F. (2007). *Occupied America: A history of Chicanos* (6th ed.). New York, NY: Pearson Longman.

Addams, J. (1902). *Democracy and social ethics*. New York, NY: Macmillan.

Addams, J. (1912). *The spirit of youth and the city streets*. New York, NY: Macmillan.

Aeschylus. (1956). *The Oresteian trilogy* (P. Vellacott, trans.). Baltimore, MD: Penguin.

Afro American Information Service (Ed.). (1975). *The tasks ahead: Selected speeches of Samora Machel*. New York, NY: Author.

Aguilar, L. E. (1978). The history of Marxist ideas in Latin America, 1890–1977. In *Marxism in Latin America*. Philadelphia, PA: Temple University Press.

Aguilar, M. I. (2007). *The history and politics of Latin American theology*. London, UK: SCM Press.

Ahluwalia, B. K., & Ahluwalia, S. (1982). *Netaji and Gandhi*. New Delhi, India: Indian Academic Publishers.

Akimoto, T. (2014). Social justice in an era of globalization: Must and can it be the focus of social welfare policies? Japan as a case study. In M. Reisch (Ed.), *The Routledge international handbook of social justice* (pp. 48–60). London, UK: Routledge.

Alban-Metcalfe, J., & Alimo-Metcalfe, B. (2009). Engaging leadership part two: An integrated model of leadership development. *International Journal of Leadership in Public Services, 5*(2), 5–13.

Alexander, M. (2010). *The new Jim Crow: Mass incarceration in the age of colorblindness.* New York, NY: New Press.

Alexander, M. G., & Levin, S. (1998). Theoretical, empirical, and practical approaches to intergroup conflict. *Journal of Social Issues, 54*(4), 629–639.

Alexander-Floyd, N. G. (2012). Disappearing acts: Reclaiming intersectionality in the social sciences in a post-Black feminist era. *Feminist Formations, 24*(1), 1–25.

Ali, A., & Lees, K. E. (2013). The therapist as advocate: Anti-oppression advocacy in psychological practice. *Journal of Clinical Psychology, 69*(2), 162–171.

Alinsky, S. D. (1971). *Rules for radicals: A practical primer for realistic radicals.* New York, NY: Random House.

Allyn, D. (2011). Mission mirroring: Understanding conflict in nonprofit organizations. *Nonprofit and Voluntary Sector Quarterly, 40*(4), 762–769.

Alperovitz, G. (2011). *America beyond capitalism: Reclaiming our wealth, our liberty, and our democracy* (2nd ed.). Boston, MA: Democracy Collaborative Press.

Alston, M. (2013). Environmental social work: Accounting for gender in climate disasters. *Australian Social Work, 66*(2), 218–233.

Alston, R. J., Harley, D. A., & Middleton, R. (2006). The role of rehabilitation in achieving social justice for minorities with disabilities. *Journal of Vocational Rehabilitation, 24*(3), 129–136.

Alsup, R. E. (2009). Liberation psychology: Martin Luther King, Jr.'s beloved community as a model for social creativity. *Journal of Humanistic Psychology, 49*(4), 388–408.

American Assembly. (2001). *Racial equality: Public policies for the twenty-first century. The ninety-eighth American Assembly* (4th ed.). Harriman, NY: American Assembly, Columbia University.

Anderson, J., & Carter, R. W. (2003). *Diversity perspectives for social work practice.* Boston, MA: Allyn & Bacon.

Andrews, J. (2001) Group work's place in social work: A historical analysis. *Journal of Sociology and Social Work, 28,* 45.

Andrews, J. L. (Ed.). (1993). *From vision to action: Social workers of the second generation.* St. Paul, MN: University of St. Thomas.

Andrews, J. L. (1997). Helen Hall and the settlement house movement's response to unemployment: Reaching out to the community. *Journal of Community Practice, 4*(2), 65–75.

Andrews, M. (2007). Exploring cross-cultural boundaries. In D. J. Clandinin (Ed.), *Handbook of narrative inquiry: Mapping a methodology* (pp. 489–511). Thousand Oaks, CA: Sage.

Appiah, K. K. (2006). *Cosmolitianism: Ethics in a world of strangers*. New York, NY: Norton.

Aquinas, T. (2002). *On law, morality, and politics* (R. J. Regan, Trans.). Indianapolis, IN: Hackett.

Arceo, S. M. (1985). *Compromiso cristiano y liberación* [*Christian compromise and liberation*]. México, DF: Ediciones Nuevomar, Centro de Estudios Ecuménicos.

Aristotle. (1980). *The Nicomachean ethics* (D. Ross, Trans.; Revised by J. L. Ackrill & J. O. Urmson). New York, NY: Oxford University Press.

Aristotle. (2009). *The politics* (E. Barker, Trans.). New York, NY: Oxford University Press.

Armstrong, F. (2012). Landscapes, spatial justice and learning communities. *International Journal of Inclusive Education, 16*(5–6), 609–626.

Arnold, F. (1974). *Kenyatta and the politics of Kenya*. London, UK: Dent & Sons.

Arnstein, S. R. (1969). A ladder of citizen participation. *Journal of the American Institute of planners, 35*(4), 216–224.

Arredondo, P., & Perez, P. (2003). Expanding multicultural competence through social justice leadership. *The Counseling Psychologist, 31*(3), 282–289.

Arrigo, B. A. (2013). Recognizing and transforming madness, citizenship, and social justice: Toward the revolution in risk management and the overcoming of captivity—A response to Brown and Ward. *International Journal of Offender Therapy and Comparative Criminology, 57*(6), 712–719.

Asmal, K., Chidester, D., & James, W. (Eds.). (2003). *Nelson Mandela: From freedom to the future, tributes and speeches*. Jeppestown, South Africa: Jonathan Ball.

Augustine of Hippo. (2005). *City of God* (P. G. Walsh, Trans.). Oxford, UK: Oxford University Press.

Austin, A. (2006). *Achieving Blackness: Race, Black nationalism and Afrocentrism in the 20th century*. New York, NY: New York University Press.

Babkina, A. M. (2004). *Affirmative Action: An annotated bibliography*. New York, NY: Nova Science.

Badawi, J. (1995). *Gender equity in Islam*. Burr Ridge, IL: American Trust Publications.

Bailey, M. J., & Danziger, S. (Eds.). (2013). *Legacies of the War on Poverty*. New York, NY: Russell Sage Foundation.

Baldwin, M. (2010). *Towards a social work of resistance: Social work as political activity—Resisting the status quo*. Unpublished paper presented at the Joint World Conference on Social Work and Social Development, Hong Kong.

Banks, S. (2011). Ethics in an age of austerity: Social work and the evolving new public management. *Journal of Social Intervention: Theory and Practice, 20*(2), 5–23.

Baronov, D. (2000). *The abolition of slavery in Brazil: The "liberation" of Africans through the emancipation of capital*. Westport, CT: Greenwood.

Barr, S., & Smith, R. (2009). Towards educational inclusion in a transforming society: Some lessons from community relations and special needs education in Northern Ireland. *International Journal of Inclusive Education, 13*(2), 211–230.

Barusch, A. S. (2006). Social justice and social workers. In *Foundations of social policy: Social justice in a human perspective* (2nd ed., pp. 3–23). Belmont, CA: Thomson Brooks/Cole.

Bates, K. A., & Swan, R. S. (2010). You can get there from here, but the road is long and hard: The role of public, private, and activist organizations in the search for social justice. In *Through the eye of Katrina: Social justice in the United States* (2nd ed., pp. 439–449). Durham, NC: Carolina Academic Press.

Bateson, G., Jackson, D. D., Haley, J., & Weakland, J. (1956). Toward a theory of schizophrenia. *Behavioral Science, 1,* 251–264.

Bauer, J. R., & Bell, D. A. (Eds.). (1999). *The East Asian challenge for human rights.* London, UK: Cambridge University Press.

Baumann, A., Domenech Rodriguez, M., & Parra-Cardona, J. R. (2011). Community-based applied research with Latino immigrant families: Informing practice and research according to ethical and social justice principles. *Family Process, 50,* 132–148.

Bauman, Z. (2001). *Conversations with Zygmunt Bauman.* Cambridge, UK: Polity Press.

Bauman, Z. (2000). *Liquid modernity.* Cambridge, UK: Polity Press.

Bauman, Z. (2004). *Wasted lives.* Cambridge, UK: Polity Press.

Baynton, D. C. (2001). Disability and the justification of inequality in American history. In P. K. Longmore & L. Umansky (Eds.), *The new disability history: American perspectives* (pp. 33–57). New York, NY: New York University Press.

Beck, E. (2012a). Strategies for preventing neighborhood violence: Toward bringing collective efficacy into social work practice. *Journal of Community Practice, 20*(3), 225.

Beck, E. (2012b). Transforming communities: Restorative justice as a community building strategy. *Journal of Community Practice, 20*(4), 380.

Beck, E. L., & Eichler, M. (2000). Consensus organizing: A practice model for community building. *Journal of Community Practice, 8*(1), 87–103.

Beito, D. (2001). *From mutual aid to the welfare state: Fraternal societies and social services, 1890–1967.* Chapel Hill, NC: University of North Carolina Press.

Bell, D. A. (2004). *Race, racism, and American law* (5th ed.). New York, NY: Aspen.

Bell, L., & Desai, D. (2011). Imagining otherwise: Connecting the arts and social justice to envision and act for change: Special issue introduction. *Equity & Excellence in Education, 44*(3), 287–295.

Bender, T. (1975). *Toward an urban vision.* Baltimore, MD: Johns Hopkins University Press.

Bennett, L., & Segerberg, A. (2012). The logic of connective action: Digital media and the personalization of contentious politics. *Information, Communication & Society, 15*(5), 739–768.

Bentley-Williams, R., & Morgan, J. (2013). Inclusive education: Pre-service teachers' reflexive learning on diversity and their challenging role. *Asia-Pacific Journal of Teacher Education, 41*(2), 173–185.

Berger, M. T., & Guidroz, K. (2009). A conversation with founding scholars of intersectionality—Kimberlé Crenshaw, Nira Yuval-Davis, and Michelle Fine. In M. T. Burger & K. Guidroz (Eds.), *The intersectional approach: Transforming the academy through race, class, & gender* (pp. 61–78). Chapel Hill, NC: University of North Carolina Press.

Berlin, I. (1978). *Concepts and categories*. London, UK: Hogarth.

Berlin, I. (1996). *Karl Marx: His life and environment* (4th ed.). New York, NY: Oxford University Press.

Berlin, I. (2002). Two concepts of liberty. In H. Hardy (Ed.), *Isaiah Berlin, liberty*. New York, NY: Oxford University Press.

Berman-Rossi, T., & Miller, I. (1994). African Americans and the settlements during the late nineteenth and early twentieth centuries. *Social Work with Groups, 17*(3), 77–94.

Bernard, B. (2006). Using strengths-based practice to tap the resilience of families. In D. Saleeby (Ed.), *The Strengths Perspective in Social Work Practice*, 4th ed. (pp. 197–215). Boston: MA: Pearson Education, Inc.

Bernard, S. M. (1995, September). *Catolicismo y democracia*. Paper presented at the meeting of the Latin American Studies Association, Washington. Retrieved May 10, 2008, from http://lanic.utexas.edu/project/lasa95/benard.html.

Berry, J., & Portney, K. (1997). Mobilizing minority communities. *American Behavioral Scientist, 40*(5), 632–644.

Bertalanffy, L. V. (1969). *General system theory: Foundations, development, applications*. New York, NY: Braziller.

Bethell, L. (1991). The decline and fall of slavery in nineteenth century Brazil. *Transactions of the Royal Historical Society, 1,* 71–88.

Bettez, S. (2011). Critical community building: Beyond belonging. *Educational Foundations, 25*(3–4), 3–19.

Bettez, S., & Hytten, K. (2013). Community building in social justice work: A critical approach. *Educational Studies: Journal of the American Educational Studies Association, 49*(1), 45–66.

Bieler, D. (2012). Possibilities for achieving social justice ends through standardized means. *Teacher Education Quarterly, 39*(3), 85–102.

Bisman, C., & Koggel, C. (2012). Gender justice and development: Local and global. *Ethics and Social Welfare, 6*(3), 213–215.

Blau, J. (2014). The political-economy of U.S. social policy. In M. Reisch (Ed.), *Social policy and social justice* (pp. 101–123). Thousand Oaks, CA: Sage.

Blitz, L., & Kohl, B. (2012). Addressing racism in the organization: The role of white racial affinity groups in creating change. *Administration in Social Work, 36*(5), 479–498.

Boal, A. (2008). *Theatre of the oppressed*. London, UK: Pluto.

Boer, R., & Okland, J. (Eds.). (2008). *Marxist feminist critiques of the Bible*. Sheffield, UK: Sheffield Phoenix Press.

Bolland, J. (2002). Neighboring and community mobilization in high-poverty inner-city neighborhoods. *Urban Affairs Review, 38*(1), 42–69.

Bordoloi, S., O'Brien, N., Edwards, L. L., & Preli, R. (2013). Creating an inclusive and thriving profession: Why the American Association of Marriage and Family Therapy needs to advocate for same-sex marriage. *Journal of Feminist Family Therapy, 25*(1), 41–55.

Bottomore, T. (Ed.). (1991). *A dictionary of Marxist thought* (2nd ed.). Cambridge, MA: Blackwell.

Bourdieu, P. (2003). *Firing back against the tyranny of the market 2* (L. Wacquant, Trans.). New York, NY: New Press.

Bowes, A., & Sim, D. (2006). Advocacy for Black and minority ethnic communities: Understandings and expectations. *British Journal of Social Work, 36*(7), 1209–1225.

Boyd, L., Gupta, F., & Kuzmits, F. (2011). The evaporating cloud: A tool for resolving workplace conflict. *International Journal of Conflict Management, 22*(4), 394–412.

Boyte, H. C. (1980). *The backyard revolution: Understanding the new citizens' movement*. Philadelphia, PA: Temple University Press.

Bradley, J. M., Werth, J. R., Hastings, S. L., & Pierce, T. W. (2012). A qualitative study of rural mental health practitioners regarding the potential professional consequences of social justice advocacy. *Professional Psychology: Research and Practice, 43*(4), 356–363.

Branom, C. (2012). Community-based participatory research as a social work research and intervention approach. *Journal of Community Practice, 20*(3), 260.

Braveman, P. A., Kumanyika, S., Fielding, J., Laveist, T., Borrell, L. N., Manderscheid, R., & Troutman, A. (2011). Health disparities and health equity: The issue is justice. *American Journal of Public Health, 101*, 149–155.

Bravo, C. (1994). *En busqueda de la paz* [In search of peace]. In C. Bravo (Ed.), *Chiapas: El evangelio de los pobres: Iglesia, justicia, y verdad*. México, DF: Ediciones Temas de Hoy Para, Espasa Calpe Mexicana S.A.

Brawley, E. A., & Martinez-Brawley, E. E. (1999). Promoting social justice in partnership with the mass media. *Journal of Sociology and Social Welfare, 26*(2), 63–86.

Braxton, E. T. (2010). Healing the wounded organization: The role of leadership in creating the path to social justice. *Tamara Journal for Critical Organization Inquiry, 8*(3–4), 89–118.

Briones, R., Jin, Y., Kuch, B., & Liu, B. (2011). Keeping up with the digital age: How the American Red Cross uses social media to build relationships. *Public Relations Review, 37*(1), 37–43.

Brodie, J. M. (2009). Little cases on the middle ground: Teaching social justice lawyering in neighborhood-based community lawyering clinics. *Clinical Law Review, 15*(2), 333–385.

Brodkin, M., & Coleman Advocates for Children and Youth. (1993). *Every kid counts: 31 ways to save our children.* San Francisco, CA: Harper San Francisco.

Brower, A., Garvin, C., Hobson, B., Reed, B., & Reed, H. (1987). The effects of the gender and the race of the leader in group process. In *Proceedings of the 1984 annual group work symposium.* New York, NY: Haworth.

Brown, L., & Strega, S. (Eds.). (2005). *Research as resistance: Critical, indigenous, and anti-oppressive approaches.* Toronto, Ontario, Canada: Canadian Scholar's Press.

Brown, M. (1999). *Race, money, and the American welfare state.* Ithaca, NY: Cornell University Press.

Brown, W. W. (1847). *Narrative of William W. Brown, a fugitive slave: Written by himself.* Boston, MA: Anti-Slavery Office.

Bryan, J., & Henry, L. (2012). A model for building school–family–community partnerships: Principles and process. *Journal of Counseling & Development, 90*(4), 408–420.

Bryer, D., & Magrath, J. (1999). New dimensions of global advocacy. *Nonprofit and Voluntary Sector Quarterly, 28*(1), 168–177.

Buck, A. (2007). The policy-demand for social research in civil justice: The UK perspective. *Zeitschrift für Rechtssoziologie, 28*(2), 165–178.

Bullard, R. D. (Ed.). (2004). *The quest for environmental justice: Human rights and the politics of pollution.* San Francisco, CA: Sierra Club Books.

Burdick, J., & Hewitt, W. E. (Eds.). (2000). *The church at the grassroots in Latin America: Perspectives on thirty years of activism.* Westport, CT: Praeger.

Burghardt, S. (2013). *Macro practice in social work for the 21st century: Bridging the macro–micro divide.* Thousand Oaks, CA: Sage.

Burke, E. (2001). *Reflections on the revolution in France* (J. C. D. Clark, Ed.). Stanford, CA: Stanford University Press. (Original work published 1790)

Burnes, T., & Ross, K. (2010). Applying social justice to oppression and marginalization in group process: Interventions and strategies for group counselors. *Journal for Specialists in Group Work, 35*(2), 169–176.

Butcher, H. L., Banks, S., Henderson, P., & Robertson, J. (2007). *Critical community practice.* Bristol, UK: Policy Press.

Butz, D. A., & Plant, E. A. (2006). Perceiving out group members as unresponsive: Implications for approach-related emotions, intentions and behavior. *Journal of Personality and Social Psychology, 91*(6), 1066–1079.

Cabral, A. (1966). *The weapon of theory.* Paper presented at the Tricontinental Conference of the Peoples of Asia, Africa, and Latin America, Havana, Cuba. Retrieved July 25, 2008, from http://www.marxists.org/subject/africa/cabral/1966/weapon-theory.htm.

Cabral, J., Chavan, A., Clarke, T., Greacen, J., Hough, B., Rexer, L., . . . Zorza, R. (2012). Using technology to enhance access to justice. *Harvard Journal of Law & Technology, 26,* 241ff.

Cahill, D. (2011). Beyond neoliberalism? Crisis and the prospects for progressive alternatives. *New Political Science, 33*(4), 479–492.

Calma, T., & Priday, E. (2011). Putting indigenous human rights into social work practice. *Australian Social Work, 64*(2), 147–155.

Campbell, J. (with Moyers, B.). (1991). *The power of myth.* New York, NY: Anchor Books.

Campbell, T. (1989). *Seven theories of human society.* Oxford, UK: Clarendon.

Canfield-Davis, K., Gardiner, M. E., & Joki, R. A. (2009). Social justice leadership in action: The case of Tony Stewart. *Journal of Ethnographic & Qualitative Research, 3*(4), 205–217.

Caputo, R. (2000). Multiculturalism and social justice in the United States: An attempt to reconcile the irreconcilable within a pragmatic liberal framework. *Race, Gender, and Class, 7*(4), 161–182.

Caputo, R. K. (2002). Social justice, the ethics of care, and market economies. *Families in Society, 83*(4), 355–364.

Carey, G., & Riley, T. (2012). Fair and just or just fair? Examining models of government—Not for-profit engagement under the Australian Social Inclusion Agenda. *Health Education Research, 27*(4), 691–703.

Carli, L. L., & Eagly, A. H. (2001). Gender, hierarchy and leadership: An introduction. *Journal of Social Issues, 37*(4), 629–636.

Carlisle, S. (2010). Tackling health inequalities and social exclusion through partnership and community engagement? A reality check for policy and practice aspirations from a social inclusion partnership in Scotland. *Critical Public Health, 20*(1), 117–127.

Carlton-Laney, I. B. (Ed.). (2001). *African American leadership: An empowerment tradition in social welfare history.* Washington, DC: NASW Press.

Carmichael, S., & Hamilton, C. V. (1967). *Black power: The politics of liberation in America.* New York, NY: Random House.

Carson, E. D. (1993). *A hand up: Black philanthropy and self-help in America.* Washington, DC: Joint Center for Political Studies.

Carson, M. J. (1990). *Settlement folk: Social thought and the American settlement movement, 1885–1930.* Chicago, IL: University of Chicago Press.

Castelloe, P., Watson, T., & White, C. (2002). Participatory change: An integrative approach to community practice. *Journal of Community Practice, 10*(4), 7–32.

Center for Media Justice. (2014, October 9). *Echoing justice: Communications strategies for community organizing in the 21st century.* Retrieved from http://centerformediajustice.org/resources.

Chakrabarty, B. (2006). *Social and political thought of Mahatma Gandhi.* Abingdon, Oxon, UK: Routledge.

Chambers, C. A. (1963). *Seedtime of reform: American social service and social action, 1918–1933.* Minneapolis, MN: University of Minnesota Press.

Chan, S. (1991). *Asian Americans: An interpretive history.* Boston, MA: Twayne.

Chapman, S., & Schwartz, J. P. (2012). Rejecting the null: Research and social justice means asking different questions. *Counseling and Values, 57*(1), 24–30.

Chaskin, R. J., & Joseph, M. L. (2010). Building 'community' in mixed-income developments: Assumption, approaches, and early experiences. *Urban Affairs Review, 45*(3), 299–335.

Chen, Y. (2014). Public engagement exercises with racial and cultural "others": Some thoughts, questions, and considerations. *Journal of Public Deliberation, 10*(1).

Cheung, F. M., & Halpern, D. F. (2010). Women at the top: powerful leaders define success as work+ family in a culture of gender. *American Psychologist, 65*(3), 182.

Chew, L. (2004). Reflections on Buddhism, gender and human rights. In K. L. Tsomo (Ed.), *Buddhist women and social justice: Ideals, challenges and achievements.* Albany, NY: State University of New York Press.

Chisholm, L. (2013). Exploring the future of lifelong learning: Advocacy, research and footprinting. *International Review of Education/Internationale Zeitschrift Für Erziehungs wissenschaft, 59*(3), 373–382.

Clark, M. D., & Hollander, R. B. (2005). Addressing equity in health research: Applying a democratic education framework for social justice. *Journal of Negro Education, 74*(1), 30–42.

Clarke, C. (2014). By its absence: Literature and the attainment of social justice consciousness. In M. Reisch (Ed.), *The Routledge international handbook of social justice* (pp. 480–491). London, UK: Routledge.

Cmiel, K. (1995). *A home of another kind: One Chicago orphanage and the tangle of child welfare.* Chicago, IL: University of Chicago Press.

Coatsworth, J., Santisteban, D., McBride, C., & Szapocznik, J. (2001). Brief strategic family therapy versus community control: Engagement, retention, and an exploration of the moderating role of adolescent symptom severity. *Family Process, 40,* 313–331.

Cohen, A. (2009). Many forms of culture. *American Psychologist, 64*(3), 194–204.

Cohen, B., & Austin, M. (1997). Transforming human services organizations through empowerment of staff. *Journal of Community Practice, 4*(2), 35–50.

Cohn, F. M. (1943). *Workers' education in war and peace.* New York, NY: Workers' Education Bureau of America.

Collins, P. H. (2000). Toward a politics of empowerment. In *Black feminist thought: Knowledge, consciousness, and the politics of empowerment* (2nd ed., pp. 273–290). New York, NY: Routledge.

Collins, P. H. (2009). *Black feminist thought* (2nd ed.). New York, NY: Routledge.

Combahee River Collective. (1982). *All the women are white, all the blacks are men, but some of us are brave.* Cambridge, MA: Author.

Commission on Social Justice. (1994). *Social justice: Strategies for national renewal— The report of the Commission on Social Justice.* New York, NY: Vintage/Ebury.

Connelly, J. B. (2014). *The Parthenon enigma: A new understanding of the West's most iconic building and the people who made it.* New York, NY: Vintage.

Conrad, R. (1972). *The destruction of Brazilian slavery, 1850–1888.* Berkeley, CA: University of California Press.

Conway, P., & Lassiter, K. (2011). Opportunity knocks: The intersection of community social work and food justice praxis. *Arete, 32*(2), 5–32.

Conze, E. (Ed.). (1964). *Buddhist texts through the ages.* New York, NY: Harper Torchbooks.

Cooper, C., Riehl, C. J., & Hasan, A. (2010). Leading and learning with diverse families in schools: Critical epistemology amid communities of practice. *Journal of School Leadership, 20*(6), 758–788.

Coser, L. A. (1956). *The functions of social conflict.* Glencoe, IL: Free Press.

Council on Social Work Education. (2008). *Educational policy and accreditation standards.* Alexandria, VA: Author.

Council on Social Work Education. (2015). *Educational policy and accreditation standards—Revised.* Alexandria, VA: Author.

Craig, K. M., & Rand, K. A. (1998). The perceptually "privileged" group member: Consequences of solo status for African Americans and Whites in task groups. *Small Group Research, 29*(3), 339–358.

Crenshaw, K. (1990–1991). Mapping the margins: Intersectionality, identity politics, and violence against women of color. *Stanford Law Review, 43,* 1241–1299.

Crenshaw, K. (1995). The intersection of race and gender. In K. Crenshaw, G. Peller, & K. Thomas (Eds.), *Critical race theory* (pp. 357–383). New York, NY: New Press.

Cross, J. (2013). Gifted education as a vehicle for enhancing social equality. *Roeper Review, 35*(2), 115–123.

Cullen, A. (1976). *Harambee! The prime minister of Kenya's speeches, 1963–1964.* Nairobi, Kenya: Oxford University Press.

Curseu, P. L., Schruijer, S., & Boros, S. (2007). The effects of groups' variety and disparity on groups' cognitive complexity. *Group Dynamics: Theory, Research, and Practice, 11*(3), 187–206.

Dai, H. (2011). Surviving in "localistic communitas": Endogenous multicultural community organizing among migrant workers in post-socialist China. *Journal of Social Service Research, 37*(2), 165–179.

Daloz, L. (2004). *Chrétiens dans une Europe en construction.* Paris, France: Harmattan.

Daniels, D. (1989). *Always a sister: The feminism of Lillian D. Wald.* New York, NY: Feminist Press at the City University of New York.

Daniels, N. (2001). *Justice, health and healthcare.* Cambridge, MA: MIT Press. Available online at http://www.hsph.harvard.edu/benchmark/ndaniels/pdf/justice_health.pdf.

Danso, R. (2015). An integrated framework of critical cultural competence and anti-oppressive practice for social justice social work research. *Qualitative Social Work, 14*(4), 572–588.

Davies, N. (1980). *The Toltec heritage: From the fall of Tula to the rise of Tenochtitlan.* Norman, OK: University of Oklahoma Press.

Davies, N. (1987). *The Aztec empire.* Norman, OK: University of Oklahoma Press.

Davis, A. F. (1967). *Spearheads for reform: The social settlements and the progressive movement, 1890–1917.* New York, NY: Oxford University Press.

Davy, D. (2013). Understanding the motivations and activities of transnational advocacy networks against child sex trafficking in the greater Mekong subregion: The value of cosmopolitan globalisation theory. *Cosmopolitan Civil Societies: An Interdisciplinary Journal, 5*(1), 39–68.

Day, P. J. (with Schiele, J. H.). (2013). *A new history of social welfare* (7th ed.). Boston, MA: Pearson.

DeChant, E. (Ed.). (1996). *Women and group practice: Theory and practice.* New York, NY: Guilford.

Delgado, G. (1994). *Beyond the politics of place: New directions in community organizing in the 1990s.* Oakland, CA: Applied Research Center.

Denzin, N. K., & Giardina, M. D. (Eds.). (2006). *Qualitative inquiry and the conservative challenge.* Walnut Creek, CA: Left Coast.

Dessel, A., Rogger, M. E., & Garlington, S. B. (2006). Using inter-group dialogue to promote social justice and change. *Social Work, 51*(4), 303–315.

Dewees, M., & Roche, S. E. (2001). Teaching about human rights in social work. *Journal of Teaching in Social Work, 21*(1–2), 137–155.

Dierendonck, D. (2011). Servant leadership: A review and synthesis. *Journal of Management, 37*(4), 1228–1261.

Dominelli, L. (2002). *Anti-oppressive social work theory and practice.* London, UK: Palgrave Macmillan.

Dominelli, L. (2007). Human rights in social work practice: An invisible part of the curriculum? In E. Reichert (Ed.), *Challenges in human rights: A social work perspective* (pp. 16–43). New York, NY: Columbia University Press.

Dominelli, L. (2010). *Social work in a globalizing world.* Malden, MA: Polity.

Dominelli, L. (2012). *Green social work: From environmental crises to environmental justice.* Cambridge, UK: Polity.

Dorfman, L. (2003). Using media advocacy to influence policy. In R. J. Bensley & J. Brookins-Fisher (Eds.), *Community health education methods: A practical guide* (2nd ed., pp. 383–409). Boston, MA: Jones & Bartlett.

Douglass, F. (1847, May 11). *The right to criticize American institutions.* Speech before the American Anti-Slavery Society, 1817–1849.

Douglass, F. (2014). *Narrative of the life of Frederick Douglass: A narrative of a slave written by himself.* Boston, MA: Anti-Slavery Office. (Original work published 1845)

Douzinas, C. (2000). *The end of human rights: Critical legal thought at the turn of the century.* Oxford, UK: Hart.

Dover, G., & Lawrence, T. (2012). The role of power in nonprofit innovation. *Nonprofit and Voluntary Sector Quarterly, 41*(6), 991–1013.

Dover, M. (2009, September 11). *Putting social justice back into social work.* Plenary Panel presentation, National Social Work Action Network. Lecture conducted from University of Bath, UK.

Downey, K. (2010). *The woman behind the New Deal: The life and legacy of Frances Perkins—Social Security, unemployment insurance, and the minimum wage.* New York, NY: Anchor Books.

Dubois, L., & Garrigus, J. (2006). *Slave revolution in the Caribbean, 1789–1804: A brief history with documents.* New York, NY: Palgrave Macmillan.

Du Bois, W. E. B. (1901). The problem of the twentieth century is the problem of the color line. In *On sociology and the black community* (pp. 281–289). Chicago, IL: University of Chicago Press.

DuBois, W. E. B. (1999). *The souls of Black folk.* New York, NY: Norton. (Original work published 1903)

Dyck, B., Kleysen, R., Lawrence, T., & Mauws, M. (2005). The politics of organizational learning: Integrating power into the 4I framework. *Academy of Management, 30*(1), 180–191.

Eagly, A. H. (2007). Female leadership advantage and disadvantage: Resolving the contradictions. *Psychology of Women Quarterly, 31,* 1–12.

Edmonds-Cady, C., & Sosulski, M. R. (2012). Applications of situated learning to foster communities of practice. *Journal of Social Work Education, 48*(1), 45–64.

Ehrenreich, J. H. (1985). *The altruistic imagination: A history of social work and social policy in the United States.* Ithaca, NY: Cornell University Press.

Eichler, M. (2007). *Consensus organizing: Building communities of mutual self-interest.* Thousand Oaks, CA: Sage.

Eisenbeiss, S. (2012). Re-thinking ethical leadership: An interdisciplinary integrative approach. *Leadership Quarterly, 23*(5), 791–808.

Eisler, R. (2010, April 12). Roadmap to new economics: Beyond capitalism and socialism. *Tikkun.* Retrieved from http://www.democraticunderground.com/discuss/duboard.php?az=view_all&address=103x529697.

Elkins, J. (2005). *Master narratives and their discontents.* New York, NY: Routledge.

Ellacuria, I. (1976). *Freedom made flesh: The mission of Christ and His church* (J. Drury, Trans.). Maryknoll, NY: Orbis Books.

Ellis, A. P. J., Ilgen, D. R., & Hollenbeck, J. R. (2006). The effects of team leader race on performance evaluations: An attributional perspective. *Small Group Research, 37,* 295–332.

Elshtain, J. B. (2002). *Jane Addams and the dream of American democracy: A life.* New York, NY: Basic Books.

Emejulu, A. (2011). The silencing of radical democracy in American community development: The struggle of identities. *Community Development Journal, 46*(2), 229–244.

English, L., & Peters, N. (2011). Founders' syndrome in women's nonprofit organizations: Implications for practice and organizational life. *Nonprofit Management and Leadership, 22,* 159–171.

Entman, R. M. (1993). Framing: Toward clarification of a fractured paradigm. *Journal of Communication, 43*(4), 51–58.

Epstein, M. (2007). *Psychotherapy without the self: A Buddhist perspective.* New Haven, CT: Yale University Press.

Estacio, E. (2013). Health literacy and community empowerment: It is more than just reading, writing and counting. *Journal of Health Psychology, 18*(8), 1056–1068. doi:10.1177/1359105312470126

Esteves, A. M. (2014). Decolonizing livelihoods, decolonizing the will: Solidarity economy as a social justice paradigm in Latin America. In M. Reisch (Ed.), *The Routledge international handbook of social justice* (pp. 74–90). London, UK: Routledge.

Etzioni, A. (1993). *The spirit of community.* New York, NY: Crown Books.

Evans, S. D., Prilleltensky, O., McKenzie, A., Prilleltensky, I., Nogueras, D., Huggins, C., & Mescia, N. (2011). Promoting strengths, prevention, empowerment, and community change through organizational development: Lessons for research, theory, and practice. *Journal of Prevention & Intervention in the Community, 39*(1), 50–64.

Ewalt, P., Freeman, E., Kirk, S., & Poole, D. (Eds.). (1996). *Multicultural issues in social work.* Washington, DC: NASW Press.

Fanon, F. (1967). *Toward the African revolution* (H. Chevalier, Trans.). New York, NY: Evergreen.

Fanon, F. (2004). *The wretched of the earth* (Rev. ed.; C. Farrington, Trans.). New York, NY: Grove Press.

Fanon, F. (2008). *Black skin, white masks* (Rev. ed.; R. Philcox, Trans.). New York, NY: Grove Press.

Farnsworth, V. (2010). Conceptualizing identity, learning and social justice in community-based learning. *Teaching and Teacher Education: An International Journal of Research and Studies, 26*(7), 1481–1489.

Fawcett, B., Featherstone, B., Fook, J., & Rossiter, A. (Eds.). (2000). *Practice and research in social work: Post-modern feminist perspectives.* New York, NY: Routledge.

Fellin, P. (2000). Revisiting multiculturalism in social work. *Journal of Social Work Education, 36,* 261–278.

Festinger, L. (1950). Informal social communication. *Psychological Review, 57,* 271–282.

Figueira-McDonough, J. (1993). Policy practice: The neglected side of social work intervention. *Social Work, 38*(2), 179–188.

Filler, L. (1960). *The crusade against slavery.* New York, NY: Harper & Brothers.

Finn, J., & Jacobson, M. (2008). *Just practice: A social justice approach to social work* (2nd ed.). Peosta, IA: Eddie Bowers.

Fisher, J. (1980). *The response of social work to the depression.* Cambridge, MA: Schenkman.

Fisher, R. (1994). *Let the people decide: Neighborhood organizing in America* (Rev. ed.). New York, NY: Twayne.

Fisher, R. J. (2000). Inter-group conflict. In M. Deutsch & P. T. Coleman (Eds.), *The handbook of conflict resolution: Theory and practice* (pp. 166–184). San Francisco, CA: Jossey-Bass.

Fisher, S., Abdi, D. I., Ludin, J., Smith, R., Williams, S., & Williams, S. (2000). *Working with conflict: Skills and strategies for action.* London, UK: Zed Books.

Fitzgerald, T. (2009). Just leading? Social justice and socially just outcomes. *Management in Education, 23*(4), 155–160.

Flexner, A. (1915). Is social work a profession? In *Proceedings of the National Conference of Charities and Correction* (pp. 575–590). Chicago, IL: Hildman.

Flynn, E. (2013). Making human rights meaningful for people with disabilities: Advocacy, access to justice and equality before the law. *International Journal of Human Rights, 17*(4), 491–510.

Flynn, F., & Wiltermuth, S. (2010). Who's with me? False consensus, brokerage, and ethical decision-making in organizations. *Academy of Management, 53*(5), 1074–1089.

Flynn, N. (2011). The economic, social and political context of the local community approach to integrated offender management: Theory and practice, rhetoric and reality. *British Journal of Community Justice, 9*(1–2), 81–92.

Foldy, E., & Ospina, S. (2010). Building bridges from the margins: The work of leadership in social change organizations. *Leadership Quarterly, 21*(2), 292–307.

Foner, E. (1998). *The story of American freedom.* New York, NY: Norton.

Foner, E. (1999). Expert report of Eric Foner to the Federal Court of Appeals, 6th Circuit, in the cases of *Gratz, et al. v. Bollinger, et al.* and *Grutter, et al. v. Bollinger, et al.* Retrieved from http://www.umich.edu/~urel/admissions/legal/expert/foner.html.

Foner, E. (2002). Who is an American? In *Who owns history? Rethinking the past in a changing world* (pp. 149–166). New York, NY: Hill & Wang.

Foner, E. (2015). *Gateway to freedom: The hidden history of the underground railroad.* New York, NY: Norton.

Fook, J. (2002). *Social work: Critical theory and practice.* London, UK: Sage.

Fook, J. (2014). Social justice and critical theory. In M. Reisch (Ed.), *The Routledge international handbook of social justice* (pp. 160–172). London, UK: Routledge.

Ford, R., Hershberger, S., Glenn, J., Morris, S., Saez, V., Togba, F., & Williams, R. (2013). Building a youth-led movement to keep young people out of the adult criminal justice system. *Children & Youth Services Review, 35*(8), 1268–1275.

Forsythe, D. (2010). *Group dynamics* (5th ed.). Belmont, CA: Wadsworth Cengage.

Forum Organizing Project. (2009). *Forum organizer's guide.* Jamaica Plain, MA: Author.

Foucault, M. (1995). *Discipline and punish: The birth of the prison* (A. Sheridan, Trans.). New York, NY: Vintage Books. (Original work published 1975)

Fraser, N. (1989). *Unruly practices: Power, discourse, and gender in contemporary social theory.* Oxford, UK: Polity.

Fraser, N. (1995). From redistribution to recognition? Dilemmas of justice in a "post-socialist" age. *New Left Review, 212,* 68–93.

Fraser, N. (1997). *Justice interruptus: Critical reflections on the "postsocialist" condition.* London, UK: Routledge.

Fraser, N. (2000). Rethinking recognition. *New Left Review, 3,* 107–120.

Fraser, N. (2008). Reframing justice in a globalising world. In K. Olson (Ed.), *Adding insult to injury: Nancy Fraser debates her critics.* London, UK: Verso.

Fraser, N. (2009). Feminism, capitalism and the cunning of history. *New Left Review, 56,* 97–117.

Freire, P. (1970). *Pedagogy of the oppressed.* New York, NY: Seabury.

Freire, P. (1973). *Education as the practice of freedom for critical consciousness.* New York, NY: Continuum.

French, J., & Raven, B. (1959). The bases of social power. In D. Cartwright (Ed.), *Studies in social power* (pp. 150–167). Ann Arbor, MI: Institute for Social Research, University of Michigan.

Freston, P. (2004). Evangelical Protestantism and democratization in contemporary Latin America and Asia. *Democratization, 11*(4), 21–41.

Friendly, A. (2013). The right to the city: Theory and practice in Brazil. *Planning Theory & Practice, 14*(2), 158–179.

Fuentes, C. (1968). *A change of skin* (S. Hileman, Trans.). New York, NY: Farrar, Straus, & Giroux.

Fuentes, C. (1992). *The buried mirror: Reflections on Spain and the New World.* Boston, MA: Houghton Mifflin.

Furman, G. (2012). Social justice leadership as praxis: Developing capacities through preparation programs. *Educational Administration Quarterly, 48*(2), 191–229.

Gago Guerrero, P. F. (n.d.). Los principios de la justicia. *Cuadernos de Trabajo Social, 7,* 87–108.

Gal, J. (2001). The perils of compensation in social welfare policy. *Social Service Review, 75*(2), 225–244.

Galeano, E. (1997). *Open veins of Latin America: Five centuries of pillage of a continent.* New York, NY: Monthly Review Press.

Galeano, E. (2010). *Century of the wind, volume 3 of a trilogy* (C. Belfrage, Trans.). New York, NY: Nation Books.

Gamble, D. N. (2012). Well-being in a globalized world: Does social work know how to make it happen? *Journal of Social Work Education, 48*(4), 669–689.

Gamble, V. (1997). Under the shadow of Tuskegee: African Americans and health care. *American Journal of Public Health, 87,* 1773–1778.

Gambrill, E. (2004). Contributions of critical thinking and evidence-based practice to the fulfillment of the ethical obligations of professionals. In H. E. Briggs & T. L. Rzepnicki (Eds.), *Using evidence in social work practice: Behavioral perspectives* (pp. 3–19). Chicago, IL: Lyceum.

Gandhi, M. (1917). *Mahatma Gandhi: His life, writings and speeches.* Madras, India: Ganesh.

Gans, H. (1971, May/June). The uses of poverty: The poor pay all. *Social Policy,* 20–24.

Garcia, R. (2013). Social justice and leisure. *Journal of Leisure Research, 45*(1), 7–22.

Garrison, W. L. (Ed.). (1836, May 21). A call to the New England Anti-Slavery Convention. *The Liberator, 6*(21), 83.

Garvin, C. (1997). *Contemporary group work* (3rd ed.). Boston, MA: Allyn & Bacon.

Garvin, C., Glasser, P., Carter, B., English, R., & Wolfson, R. (1985). Group work intervention in the social environment. In M. Sundel, P. Glasser, R. Sarri, & R. Vinter (Eds.), *Individual change through small groups* (2nd ed., pp. 277–293). New York, NY: Free Press.

Garvin, C. D., & Tropman, J. (1998). *Social work in contemporary society* (2nd ed.). Boston, MA: Allyn & Bacon.

Gates, H. L., & McKay, N. Y. (Eds.). (1997). *The Norton anthology of African American literature.* New York, NY: Norton.

Gay, P. (1966). *The enlightenment* (2 vols.). New York, NY: Knopf.

Geggus, D. P. (2002). *Haitian revolutionary studies.* Bloomington, IN: Indiana University Press.

George, J. (1999). Conceptual muddle, practical dilemma: Human rights, social development, and social work education. *International Social Work, 42*(1), 15–26.

George, V., & Wilding, P. (1994). *Welfare and ideology.* London, UK: Routledge.

Gerstle, G. (2001). *American crucible: Race and nation in the twentieth century.* Princeton, NJ: Princeton University Press.

Gibbs, L. E., & Gambrill, E. (2002). Evidence-based practice: Counterarguments to objections. *Research on Social Work Practice, 12*(3), 452–476.

Gibelman, M. (2000, March). Affirmative action at the crossroads: A social justice perspective. *Journal of Sociology and Social Welfare, 27*(1), 153–174.

Gil, D. (1998). *Confronting injustice and oppression: Concepts and strategies for social workers.* New York, NY: Columbia University Press.

Gilbert, N. (1989). *The enabling state: Modern welfare capitalism in America.* New York, NY: Oxford University Press.

Gilbert, N. (1995). *Welfare justice: Restoring social equity.* New Haven, CT: Yale University Press.

Gill, A. (2004). Weber in Latin America: Is Protestant growth enabling the consolidation of democratic capitalism? *Democratization, 11*(4), 42–65.

Glasius, M., & Pleyers, G. (2013). The global moment of 2011: Democracy, social justice and dignity. *Development & Change, 44*(3), 547–567.

Goddard, T., & Myers, R. R. (2013). Youth justice innovation on the West Coast: Examining community-based social justice organizations through a left realist lens. *Western Criminology Review, 14*(1), 51–62.

Goldberg, G., & Elliott, J. (1980). Below the belt: Situational ethics for unethical situations. *Journal of Sociology and Social Welfare, 7,* 478.

Goode, J. (2006). Faith-based organizations in Philadelphia: Neoliberal ideology and the decline of political activism. *Urban Anthropology & Studies of Cultural Systems & World Economic Development, 35*(2–3), 203–223.

Goodman, D. (2001). *Promoting diversity and social justice.* Thousand Oaks, CA: Sage.

Goodman, R., & Burton, D. (2012). What is the nature of the achievement gap, why does it persist and are government goals sufficient to create social justice in the education system? *Education 3-13, 40*(5), 500–514. doi:10.1080/03004279.2010.550586

Gordon, L. (1991, September). Black and white visions of welfare: Women's welfare activism, 1890–1915. *Journal of American History, 78,* 559–590.

Gordon, L. (2002). Who deserves help? Who must provide? In R. Albelda & A. Withorn (Eds.), *Lost ground: Welfare reform, poverty and beyond* (pp. 9–25). Cambridge, MA: South End Press.

Gorin, S., & Moniz, C. (2014). Health and mental health policy. In M. Reisch (Ed.), *Social policy and social justice* (pp. 405–430). Thousand Oaks, CA: Sage.

Gouin, R. R., Cocq, K., & McGavin, S. (2011). Feminist participatory research in a social justice organization. *Action Research, 9*(3), 261–281.

Graden, D. T. (2006). *From slavery to freedom in Brazil: Bahia, 1835–1900.* Albuquerque, NM: University of New Mexico Press.

Gramsci, A. (2007). *Prison notebooks* (edited with an introduction by J. A. Buttigieg; A. Callari, Trans.). New York, NY: Columbia University Press.

Gray, M., Agglias, K., & Davies, K. (2014). Social justice feminism. In M. Reisch (Ed.), *The Routledge international handbook of social justice* (pp. 173–187). London, UK: Routledge.

Grayson, J. (2011). Organising, educating, and training: Varieties of activist learning in left social movements in Sheffield (UK). *Studies in the Education of Adults, 43*(2), 197–215.

Green, J. (1999). *Cultural awareness in the human services* (3rd ed.). Boston, MA: Allyn & Bacon.

Greenberg, J. (2007). Positive organizational justice: From fair to fairer—and beyond. In J. D. Dutton & B. Rose Ragins (Eds.), *Exploring positive relationships at work: Building a theoretical and research foundation* (pp. 159–178). New York, NY: Psychology Press.

Greenwald, G. (2014). *No place to hide: Edward Snowden, the NSA, and the U.S. surveillance state.* New York, NY: Henry Holt.

Greenwood, D. J., Foote Whyte, W., & Harkavy, I. (1993). Participatory action research as a process and as a goal. *Human Relations, 46*(2), 175–191.

Gronbjerg, K., & Salamon, L. M. (2002). Devolution, marketization, and the changing shape of government–nonprofit relations. In L. M. Salamon (Ed.), *The state of nonprofit America* (pp. 447–470). Washington, DC: Brookings Institution.

Guo, C., & Saxton, G. (2011). Accountability online: Understanding the web-based accountability practices of nonprofit organizations. *Nonprofit and Voluntary Sector Quarterly, 40*(2), 270–295.

Gupta, M., Boyd, L., & Kuzmits, F. (2011). The evaporating cloud: A tool for resolving workplace conflict. *International Journal of Conflict Management, 22*(4), 394–412.

Gutierrez, G. (1973). *A theology of liberation*. Maryknoll, NY: Orbis Books.

Gutierrez, L., & Lewis, E. A. (Eds.). (1999). *Empowering women of color*. New York, NY: Columbia University Press.

Gutierrez, L., Parson, R. J., & Cox, E. O. (Eds.). (1998). *Empowerment in social work practice: A sourcebook*. Belmont, CA: Brooks/Cole.

Gutierrez, L. M. (2001). Working with women of color: An empowerment perspective. In J. Rothman, J. Erlich, & J. Tropman (Eds.), *Strategies of community intervention* (7th ed., pp. 209–217). Itasca, IL: Peacock.

Gutierrez, L. M., GlenMaye, L., & DeLois, K. (1995). The organizational context of empowerment practice: Implications for social work administration. *Social Work, 40*(2), 249–258.

Gutierrez, L. M., Nagda, B., Raffoul, P., & McNeece, A. (1996). The multicultural imperative in human service organization. In *Future issues in social work practice* (pp. 203–213). Needham Heights, MA: Allyn & Bacon.

Haijing, D. (2013). Social inequality in a bonded community: Community ties and villager resistance in a Chinese township. *Social Service Review, 87*(2), 269–291.

Haley, J. (1984). *Ordeal therapy: Unusual ways to change behavior*. New York, NY: Jossey-Bass.

Hamilton, D. C., & Hamilton, C. V. (1997). *The dual agenda: The African American struggle for civil and economic equality*. New York, NY: Columbia University Press.

Hammond, L. H. (1920). *Interracial cooperation: Helpful suggestions concerning relations of White and colored citizens*. New York, NY: National Board of the YWCA.

Hammond, N. (2013). Developing a community psychology service in one local community through a practitioner–researcher pilot study. *Educational & Child Psychology, 30*(1), 50–60.

Hammond, N. S. (1993). Warriors and kings: The city of Copan and the ancient Mayan. *History Today, 43*, 54ff.

Hancock, A. (2007). Intersectionality as a normative and empirical paradigm. *Politics and Gender, 3*(2), 248–254.

Hardina, D. (2005). Ten characteristics of empowerment-oriented social service organizations. *Administration in Social Work, 29*(3), 23–42.

Harding, S., & Simmons, L. (2010). Community practice and organizing in a time of reaction. *Journal of Community Practice, 18*(4), 413–416.

Hare, I. (2004). Defining social work for the 21st century: The International Federation of Social Workers' revised definition of social work. *International Social Work, 47*(3), 407–424.

Harkavy, I., & Puckett, J. L. (1994). Lessons from Hull House for the contemporary urban university. *Social Service Review, 68*(3), 299–321.

Harms, L., Middleton, J., Whyte, J., Anderson, I., Clarke, A., Sloan, J., & Smith, M. (2011). Social work with aboriginal clients: Perspectives on educational preparation and practice. *Australian Social Work, 64*(2), 156–168.

Harrison, D. A., & Klein, K. J. (2007). What's the difference? Diversity constructs as separation, variety or disparity in organizations. *Academy of Management Review, 32*, 1199–1228.

Hasenfeld, Y. (1987). Power in social work practice. *Social Service Review, 61*, 469–483.

Hayek, F. A. (1976). *The mirage of social justice.* Chicago, IL: University of Chicago Press.

Haynes, G. E. (1912). *The Negro at work in New York City: A study in economic progress.* New York, NY: Longmans, Green.

Haynes, K. S., & Mickelson, J. S. (2010). *Affecting change: Social workers in the political arena* (7th ed.). Boston, MA: Allyn & Bacon.

Hays, D., Arredondo, P., Gladding, S., & Toporek, R. (2010). Integrating social justice in group work: The next decade. *Journal for Specialists in Group Work, 35*(2), 177–206.

Healy, M., & Sofer, G. (2014). Advocacy at the federal level: A case study of Americorps—How the little guys won. In M. Reisch (Ed.), *Social policy and social justice* (pp. 237–258). Thousand Oaks, CA: Sage.

Hegel, G. W. F. (1964). *Hegel's political writings* (T. M. Knox, Trans.). Oxford, UK: Clarendon.

Held, V. (1984). *Rights and goods: Justifying social action.* New York, NY: Free Press.

Held, V. (1995). *Justice and care: Essential readings in feminist ethics.* Boulder, CO: Westview.

Hepworth, D., Rooney, R., & Larson, J. (2010). *Direct social work practice* (8th ed.). Belmont, CA: Brooks/Cole.

Hernandez, J. A. (1983). Principles and ideals of Chicano mutualism. In *Mutual aid for survival: The case of the Mexican American.* Malabar, FL: Krieger.

Hernandez, V., Montana, S., & Clarke, K. (2010). Child health inequality: Framing a social work response. *Health & Social Work, 35*(4), 291–301.

Herzberg, L. (2013). Shared decision-making: A voice for the Lakota people. *Child & Family Social Work, 18*(4), 477–486.

Hibbing, J., & Theiss-Morse, E. (2005). Citizenship and civic engagement. *Annual Review of Political Science, 8*, 227–249.

Hill Collins, P. (2000). *Black feminist thought: Knowledge, consciousness, and the politics of empowerment* (2nd ed.). New York, NY: Routledge.

Hilmers, A., Hilmers, D. C., & Dave, J. (2012). Neighborhood disparities in access to healthy foods and their effects on environmental justice. *American Journal of Public Health, 102*(9), 1644–1654.

Hine, D. C. (1990). "We specialize in the wholly impossible": The philanthropic work of Black women. In K. McCarthy (Ed.), *Lady bountiful revisited: Women, philanthropy, and power* (pp. 70–95). New Brunswick, NJ: Rutgers University Press.

Ho, M. K., Rasheed, J., & Rasheed, M. N. (2004). *Family therapy with ethnic minorities.* Thousand Oaks, CA: Sage.

Hobbes, T. (1996). *Leviathan.* New York, NY: Oxford University Press.

Hoefer, R. (2012). *Advocacy practice for social justice* (2nd ed.). Chicago, IL: Lyceum.

Holder, A. C. (1922). *The settlement idea: A vision of social justice.* New York, NY: Macmillan.

Homan, A. C., van Knippenberg, D., Van Kleef, G. A., & De Dreu, C. K. (2007). Bridging faultlines by valuing diversity: Diversity beliefs, information elaboration, and performance in diverse work groups. *Journal of Applied Psychology, 92*(5), 1189–1199.

Homan, M. S. (2016). *Promoting community change: Making it happen in the real world,* 6th ed. Belmont, CA: Brooks/Cole.

Horwitt, S. D. (1989). *Let them call me rebel: Saul Alinsky, his life and legacy.* New York, NY: Knopf.

House, R. J., Hanges, P. J., Javidan, M., Dorfman, P. W., & Gupta, V. (Eds.). (2008). *Culture, leadership, and organizations: The GLOBE study of 62 societies.* London, UK: Sage.

Huddleston, J. (1989). *The search for a just society.* Oxford, UK: George Ronald.

Hull, G. T., Bell-Scott, P., & Smith, B. (Eds.). (1982). *All the women are White, all the Blacks are men, but some of us are brave.* Old Westbury, NY: Feminist Press at CUNY.

Hunter, R. (1904). *Poverty.* New York, NY: Grosset & Dunlap.

Hyde, C. (1996). A feminist response to Rothman's "'The interweaving of community intervention approaches'." *Journal of Community Practice, 3*(3–4), 127–145.

Ife, J. (2001). *Human rights and social work: Toward rights-based practice.* New York, NY: Cambridge University Press.

Ife, J. (2007). Cultural relativism and community activism. In E. Reichert (Ed.), *Challenges in human rights: A social work perspective* (pp. 76–96). New York, NY: Columbia University Press.

Ife, J. (2010). *Human rights from below.* New York, NY: Cambridge University Press.

Iglehart, A. P., & Becerra, R. M. (2011). *Social services and the ethnic community: History and analysis* (2nd ed.). Long Grove, IL: Waveland.

Ignatieff, M. (2001). The attack on human rights. *Foreign Affairs, 80*(6), 102–116.

Imber-Black, E. (2011). Towards a contemporary social justice agenda in family therapy research and practice. *Family Process, 50*(2), 129–131.

Imoh, A. T. (2012). From central to marginal: Changing perceptions of kinship fosterage in Ghana. *Journal of Family History, 37*(4), 351–363.

International Defense and Aid Fund for Southern Africa. (1986). *Nelson Mandela: The struggle is my life*. London, UK: Author.

International Federation of Social Workers (2010). Definition of social work. Retrieved June 6, 2010 from http://www.eassw.org/definition.asp.

Irele, A. (1965). Negritude—Literature and ideology. *Journal of Modern African Studies, 3*(4), 499–526.

Irvine, J. A. (2013). Leveraging change. *International Feminist Journal of Politics, 15*(1), 20–38.

Israel, J. I. (2001). *Radical enlightenment: Philosophy and the making of modernity, 1650–1750*. New York, NY: Oxford University Press.

Ivey, A. E., & Collins, N. M. (2003). Social justice: A long term challenge for counseling psychology. *The Counseling Psychologist, 31*(3), 290–298.

Jack, H. (Ed.). (1961). *The wit and wisdom of Gandhi*. Bombay, India: Perennial Press.

Jackson, B. W. (2006). Theory and practice of multicultural organization development. In B. B. Jones & M. Brazzel (Eds.), *The NTL handbook of organization development and change* (pp. 139–154). San Francisco, CA: Pfeiffer.

Jackson, D., & Weakland, J. (1959). Schizophrenic symptoms and family interaction. *Archives of General Psychiatry, 1*, 618–621.

Jacobs, H. (2010). *Incidents in the life of a slave girl: Written by herself* (J. Fleischner, Ed.). Boston, MA: Bedford/St. Martin's. (Original work published 1861)

James, C. L. R. (1963). *The Black Jacobins*. New York, NY: Vintage.

Jani, J. S., & DeForge, B. R. (2014). Contextually appropriate measurement as the basis for culturally appropriate intervention. *Social Work in Public Health, 30*(2), 1–18.

Jani, J. S., & Reisch, M. (2011). Common human needs, uncommon solutions: Applying a critical framework to perspectives on human behavior. *Families in Society, 92*(1), 13–20.

Jansson, B. (2005). *The reluctant welfare state* (5th ed.). Pacific Grove, CA: Brooks/Cole.

Jaskyte, K. (2012). Exploring potential for information technology innovation in nonprofit organizations. *Journal of Technology in Human Services, 30*(2), 118–127.

Jean-Marie, G. (2006). Welcoming the unwelcomed: A social justice imperative of African-American female leaders at historically Black colleges and universities. *Educational Foundations, 20*(1–2), 85–104.

Jensen, J. M. (2008). Reflections and future directions for social work research. *Social Work Research, 32*(3), 131–134.

Johnson, A. G. (2001). *Privilege, power and difference*. Mountain View, CA: Mayfield.

Johnson, C. (2005). *Meeting the ethical challenges of leadership: Casting light or shadow.* Thousand Oaks, CA: Sage.

Johnson, C., Dowd, T. J., & Ridgeway, C. L. (2006). Legitimacy as a social process. *Annual Review of Sociology, 32,* 53–78.

Johnson, L. R., & Rosario-Ramos, E. M. (2012). The role of educational institutions in the development of critical literacy and transformative action. *Theory Into Practice, 51*(1), 49–56.

Jones, P., & Waters, R. (2011). Using video to build an organization's identity and brand: A content analysis of nonprofit organizations' YouTube videos. *Journal of Nonprofit & Public Sector Marketing, 23*(3), 248–268.

Jones, R. (1984, February). Four churches in one: Latin American Catholicism. *Christian Century,* 199.

Jordan, L., & Van Tuijl, P. (2000). Political responsibility in trans-national NGO advocacy. *World Development, 28*(12), 2051–2065.

Judd, R. G. (2013). Social justice: A shared paradigm for social work and religion? *Journal of Religion & Spirituality in Social Work: Social Thought, 32*(2), 177–193.

Kallen, E. (2004). *Social inequality and social injustice: A human rights perspective.* New York, NY: Palgrave Macmillan.

Kamal, M. (2014). *Achieving development outcomes through technology interventions in a nonprofit organization.* Paper presented at the 47th Hawaii International Conference on System Sciences (HICSS), Waikoloa, HI. IEEE, pp. 4245–4253.

Kane, L. (2001). *Popular education and social change in Latin America.* London, UK: Latin American Bureau.

Kanter, B., & Fine, A. H. (2010). *The networked nonprofit: Connecting with social media to drive change.* San Francisco, CA: Jossey-Bass.

Karakowsky, L., McBey, K., & Miller, D. (2004). Gender, perceived competence, and power displays: Examining verbal interruptions in a group context. *Small Group Research, 35*(4), 407–439.

Karenga, M. (2007, February 8). Boukman and the voice for freedom: Standing in solidarity with Haiti. *Los Angeles Sentinel,* p. A-9.

Karger, H. J. (1988). *Social workers and labor unions.* Westport, CT: Greenwood.

Kasius, C. (Ed.). (1950). *A comparison of diagnostic and functional casework concepts, report.* New York, NY: Family Service Association of America.

Kaslow, F. (2010). A family therapy narrative. *American Journal of Family Therapy, 38,* 50–62.

Kasmir, S. (1996). *The myth of Mondragon: Cooperatives, politics, and working class life in a Basque town.* Albany, NY: State University of New York Press.

Katiuzhinsky, A., & Okech, D. (2014). Human rights, cultural practices, and state policies: Implications for global social work practice and policy. *International Journal of Social Welfare, 23*(1), 80–88.

Katz, M. B. (2001). *The price of citizenship: Redefining the American welfare state.* New York, NY: Metropolitan Books.

Kaushik, A. (2001). *Politics, symbols and political theory.* Jaipur, India: Rawat.

Keevers, L., Sykes, C., & Treleaven, L. (2006). The policy space as a catalyst for the push to partnership and participation.

Keevers, L., Treleaven, L., Sykes, C., & Darcy, M. (2012). Made to measure: Taming practices with results-based accountability. *Organization Studies, 33*(1), 97–120.

Kelley, P. (2011). Narrative therapy and social work treatment. In F. J. Turner (Ed.), *Social work treatment: Interlocking theoretical approaches* (5th ed., pp. 315–326). New York, NY: Oxford University Press.

Kellough, J. E. (2006). *Understanding affirmative action: Politics, discrimination, and the search for justice.* Washington, DC: Georgetown University Press.

Kelly, J. J., & Clark, E. J. (Eds.). (2009). *Social work speaks: National Association of Social Workers' policy statements, 2009–2012.* Washington, DC: NASW Press.

Kelsey, B. L. (1998). The dynamics of multicultural groups: Ethnicity as a determinant of leadership. *Small Group Research, 29*(5), 602–623.

Kennedy, R. (2013). *For discrimination: Race, affirmative action, and the law.* New York, NY: Pantheon.

Kenyatta, J. (1968). *Suffering without bitterness: The founding of the Kenyan nation.* Nairobi, Kenya: East African Publishing House.

Kickbusch, I., & Nutbeam, D. (1998). *Health promotion glossary.* Geneva, Switzerland: World Health Organization.

Kim, J. F. (2006). Youth as important civic actors: From the margins to the center. *National Civic Review, 95*(1), 3ff.

Kim, S., Mankoff, J., & Paulos, E. (2014). Exploring the opportunities of mobile technology use in nonprofit organizations. *CHI '14 Extended Abstracts on Human Factors in Computing Systems, 1939–1944.*

Kim. S.-M., & Sherraden, M. S. (2014). The capability approach and social justice. In M. Reisch (Ed.), *The Routledge international handbook of social justice* (pp. 202–215). London, UK: Routledge.

Kirk, S. A., & Reid, W. J. (2002). *Science and social work.* New York, NY: Columbia University Press.

Kirkpatrick, S. A., & Locke, E. A. (1991). Leadership: Do traits matter? *The Executive, 5,* 48–60.

Klein, N. (2014). *This changes everything: Capitalism vs. the climate.* New York, NY: Simon & Schuster.

Kline, M., Dolgon, C., & Dresser, L. (2000). The politics and knowledge in theory and practice: Collective research and political action in a grassroots community organization. *Journal of Community Practice, 8*(2), 23–38.

Knight, L. W. (2005). *Citizen: Jane Addams and the struggle for democracy.* Chicago, IL: University of Chicago Press.

Koch, S. C. (2005). Evaluative affect display toward male and female leaders of task-oriented groups. *Small Group Research, 36*(6), 678–703.

Kochman, T. (1981). *Black and white styles in conflict*. Chicago, IL: University of Chicago Press.

Krebs, B., Pitcoff, P., & Shalof, A. L. (2013). SELF-advocacy education for youth: The role of law school communities in expanding opportunities for system-involved youth. *Family Court Review, 51*(4), 698–711.

Kropotkin, P. (1902). *Mutual aid*. Boston, MA: Porter Sargent.

Kuehn, R. (2014). Environmental justice. In M. Reisch (Ed.), *The Routledge international handbook of social justice* (pp. 319–338). London, IL: Routledge.

Kuilema, J. (2013). Social workers and broadband advocacy: Social justice and information communications technologies. *Social Science Computer Review, 31*(3), 291–305.

Kurasawa, F. (2007). *The work of global justice: Human rights as practice*. Cambridge, UK: Cambridge University Press.

Kvasny, L., Ortiz, J., & Tapia, A. (2011). A critical discourse analysis of three US municipal wireless network initiatives for enhancing social inclusion. *Telematics and Informatics, 28*(3), 215–226.

Kwong-Leung, T., & Jik-Joen, L. (2006). Global social justice for older people: The case for an international convention on the rights of older people. *British Journal of Social Work, 36*(7), 1135–1150.

Lacey, A., & Ilcan, S. (2006). Voluntary labor, responsible citizenship, and international NGOs. *International Journal of Comparative Sociology, 47*(1), 34–53.

Lai, H. M. (2004). *Becoming Chinese-American: A history of communities and institutions*. Walnut Creek, CA: AltaMira.

Lake, C. C. (1987). *Public opinion polling: A handbook for public interest and citizen advocacy groups*. Washington, DC: Island Press.

Lanning, K. (2012). Social psychology and contemporary immigration policy: An introduction. *Analyses of Social Issues and Public Policy (ASAP), 12*(1), 1–4.

Larrabure, M., Vieta, M., & Schugurensky, D. (2011). The "new cooperativism" in Latin America: Worker-recuperated enterprises and socialist production units. *Studies in the Education of Adults, 43*(2), 181–196.

Lasch-Quinn, E. (1993). *Black neighbors: Race and the limits of reform in the American settlement house movement, 1880–1945*. Chapel Hill, NC: University of North Carolina Press.

Laslett, B. (1998). Gender and the rhetoric of social science: William Fielding Ogburn and early twentieth-century sociology in the United States. In J. Cox & S. Stromquist (Eds.), *Contesting the master narrative: Essays in social history* (pp. 19–49). Iowa City, IA: University of Iowa Press.

Lauffer, A. (1978). *Social planning at the community level*. Englewood Cliffs, NJ: Prentice Hall.

Lavalette, M. (Ed.). (2011). *Radical social work today: Social work at the crossroads.* Bristol, UK: Polity.

Le Baron, B. (1966). Negritude: A pan-African ideal. *Ethics, 76*(4), 267–276.

Lee, E. (2003). *At America's gates: Chinese immigration during the exclusion era, 1882–1943.* Chapel Hill, NC: University of North Carolina Press.

Lee, J. (2001). The empowerment approach: A conceptual model. In *The empowerment approach to social work practice: Building the beloved community* (pp. 30–55). New York, NY: Columbia University Press.

Lens, V. (2014). The judiciary and social policy. In M. Reisch (Ed.), *Social policy and social justice* (pp. 281–304). Thousand Oaks, CA: Sage.

Leonard, P. (1995). Postmodernism, socialism, and social welfare. *Journal of Progressive Human Services, 6*(2), 3–19.

Leonard, P. (1997). *Postmodern welfare: Reconstructing an emancipatory project.* Thousand Oaks, CA: Pine Forge Press.

LeRoux, K. (2007). Nonprofits as civic intermediaries. *Urban Affairs Review, 42*(3), 410–422.

Leuenberger, D., & Wakin, M. (2007). Sustainable development in public administration planning: An exploration of social justice, equity, and citizen inclusion. *Administrative Theory & Praxis, 29*(3), 394–411.

Levin, J. (2013). Engaging the faith community for public health advocacy: An agenda for the Surgeon General. *Journal of Religion & Health, 52*(2), 368–385.

Lewin, K. (1948). *Resolving social conflicts: Selected papers on group dynamics* (G. W. Lewin, Ed.). New York, NY: Harper & Row.

Lewis, H. (1982). *The intellectual base of social work practice: Tools for thought in a helping profession.* New York, NY: Haworth.

Lewis, H. (2004). The cause in function. In M. Reisch (Ed.), *For the common good: Essays of Harold Lewis* (pp. 10–14). New York, NY: Routledge.

Lewis, J. A. (2011). Operationalizing social justice counseling: Paradigm to practice. *Journal of Humanistic Counseling, 50*(2), 183–191.

Li, J., Karakowsky, L., & Siegel, J. P. (1999). The effects of proportional representation on intragroup behavior in mixed-race decision-making groups. *Small Group Research, 30*(3), 259–279.

Libby, M., Sedonaen, M., & Bliss, S. (2006). The mystery of youth leadership development: The path to just communities. *New Directions for Youth Development, 109,* 13–25.

Lieberman, R. (1998). *Shifting the color line: Race and the American welfare state.* Cambridge, MA: Harvard University Press.

Liévanos, R. S. (2012). Certainty, fairness, and balance: State resonance and environmental justice policy implementation. *Sociological Forum, 27*(2), 481–503.

Linhorst, D. M. (2002). Federalism and social justice: Implications for social work. *Social Work, 47*(3), 201–208.

Littell, J. H. (2008). Evidence-based or biased? The quality of published reviews of evidence-based practices. *Children and Youth Services Review, 30,* 1299–1317.

Lizarraga, F. (2006). *La justicia en el pensiamiento de Ernesto Che Guevara* [*Justice in the thoughts of Ernesto Che Guevara*]. Havana, Cuba: Editorial de Ciensias Sociales.

Lonne, B., McDonald, C., & Fox, T. (2004). Ethical practice in the contemporary human services. *Journal of Social Work, 4*(3), 345–367.

Lorenz, W. (2014). The emergence of social justice in the West. In M. Reisch (Ed.), *The Routledge international handbook of social justice* (pp. 14–26). London, UK: Routledge.

Lubove, R. (1968). *The struggle for Social Security, 1900–1935.* Cambridge, MA: Harvard University Press.

Lum, D. (1999). *Culturally competent practice: A framework for growth and action.* Pacific Grove, CA: Brooks/Cole.

Lundblad, K. S. (1995). Jane Addams and social reform: A role model for the 1990s. *Social Work, 40*(5), 661–669.

Luttrell, W. (2013). Children's counter-narrative of care: Towards educational justice. *Children and Society, 27*(4), 295–308.

Lyotard, J.-F. (1984). *The postmodern condition: A report on knowledge.* Minneapolis, MN: University of Minnesota Press.

Lyotard, J.-F. (1988). *The differend: Phrases in dispute.* Minneapolis, MN: University of Minnesota Press.

Lyotard, J.-F. (1992). *The postmodern explained: Correspondence 1982–1985.* Minneapolis, MN: University of Minnesota Press.

Lyotard, J.-F. (with Thebaud, J.-L.). (1985). *Just gaming.* Minneapolis, MN: University of Minnesota Press.

Madrick, J. (2006, January 12). The way to a fair deal, *New York Review of Books,* No. 1, 37–40.

Maguire, D. C. (2010). *Ethics: A complete method for moral choice.* Minneapolis, MN: Fortress Press.

Maguire, D. C. (2014). Religious influences on justice theory. In M. Reisch (Ed.), *The Routledge international handbook of social justice* (pp. 27–38). London, UK: Routledge.

Maimonides, M. (1949). *The code of Maimonides.* New Haven, CT: Yale University Press.

Mann, R. D. (1959). A review of the relationship between personality and performance in small groups. *Psychological Bulletin, 56,* 241–270.

Mann, S. A., & Huffman, D. J. (2005). Decentering of second wave feminism and the rise of third wave. *Marxist–Feminist Thought Today, 69*(1), 56–91.

Marable, M., Steinberg, I., & Middlemass, K. (Eds.). (2007). *Racializing justice, disenfranchising lives: The racism, criminal justice, and law reader.* New York, NY: Palgrave Macmillan.

Marbley, A., Bonner, F., Wimberly, C., Stevens, H., & Tatem, B. A. (2006). Harambee: Working together to engender change in communities of color. *Educational Forum, 70*(4), 320–336.

Marbley, A. F. (2004). His eye is on the sparrow: A counselor of color's perception of facilitating groups with predominantly White members. *Journal for Specialists in Group Work, 29*(3), 247–258.

Margolin, L. (1997). *Under the cover of kindness: The invention of social work.* Charlottesville, VA: University of Virginia Press.

Marshall, T. H. (1950). *Citizenship, social class, and other essays.* Cambridge, UK: Cambridge University Press.

Martin, P. Y. (2004). Gender as social institution. *Social Forces, 82*(4), 1249–1273.

Marx, K. (1844/1964). *Economic and philosophic manuscripts of 1844* (D. J. Struik, Ed.; M. Milligan, Trans.). New York, NY: International Publishers.

Marx, K., & Engels, F. (1848). *The communist manifesto.* New York, NY: International Publishers.

Massey, D. S., & Denton, N. A. (1993). *American apartheid: Segregation and the making of the underclass.* Cambridge, MA: Harvard University Press.

May, R. A. B. (2007). Introduction: Era(c)ing and (Re)constructing race and the racialized self. *Symbolic Interaction, 30*(3), 293–295.

Mays, V. M., Cochran, S. D., & Barnes, N. W. (2007). Race, race-based discrimination, and health outcomes among African Americans. *Annual Review of Psychology, 58,* 201–225.

McCarthy, M. (n.d.). The ethics of political advocacy and the integrity of the democratic process. *Woodstock Project on Ethics and Public Policy.*

McGoldrick, M., Giordano, M., & Garcia-Preto, N. (Eds.). (2005). *Ethnicity and family therapy* (3rd ed.). New York, NY: Guilford.

McGoldrick, M., & Hardy, K. V. (2008). *Revisioning family therapy: Race, culture, and gender in clinical practice.* New York, NY: Guilford.

McIntosh, P. (1988). White privilege and male privilege: A personal account of coming to see correspondences through work in women's studies. Reprinted in M. L. Anderson & P. H. Collins (2000), *Race, class, and gender: An anthology.* Belmont, CA: Wadsworth.

McJimsey, G. (1987). *Harry Hopkins: Ally of the poor and defender of democracy.* Cambridge, MA: Harvard University Press.

McKay, C. L. (2010). Community education and critical race praxis: The power of voice. *Educational Foundations, 24*(1–2), 25–38.

McKnight, J., & Kretzmann, J. (2008). Mapping community capacity. In M. Minkler (Ed.), *Community organizing & community building for health* (pp. 157–172). New Brunswick, NJ: Rutgers University Press.

McNutt, J. (1997, December). New communitarian thought and the future of social policy. *Journal of Sociology and Social Welfare, 24*(4), 45–56.

McNutt, J. (2011). Is social work advocacy worth the cost? Issues and barriers to an economic analysis of social work political practice. *Research on Social Work Practice, 21*(4), 397–403.

McWilliams, W. C. (1973). *The idea of fraternity in America*. Berkeley, CA: University of California Press.

Mead, L. (1986). *Beyond entitlement: The social obligations of citizenship*. New York, NY: Free Press.

Mead, L. (1992). *The new politics of poverty*. New York, NY: Basic Books.

Mead, L. (1997). *The new paternalism: Supervisory approaches to poverty*. Washington, DC: The Brookings Institution.

Merry, S. E. (2006). Trans-national human rights and local activism: Mapping the middle. *American Anthropologist, 108*(1), 38–51.

Merry, S. E., & Levitt, P. (2008). *Law, human rights and social movements: Exploring the justice scaffold*. Unpublished paper presented at "Women and the Law" seminar, April 3–4, 2008, University of Michigan, Ann Arbor, MI.

Michels, R. (1915). *Political parties; A sociological study of the oligarchical tendencies of modern democracy* (E. C. Paul, Trans.). London, UK: Jarrold & Sons.

Miley, K. K., O'Melia, M., & DuBois, B. (2009). *Generalist social work practice: An empowering approach* (6th ed.). Boston, MA: Pearson/Allyn & Bacon.

Miller, D. (1976). *Social justice*. Oxford, UK: Clarendon.

Miller, D. (2001). *Boundaries and justice: Diverse ethical perspectives*. Princeton, NJ: Princeton University Press.

Miller, J. B. (1982). *Women and power*. Wellesley, MA: Stone Center for Developmental Services and Studies, Wellesley College.

Mills, C. W. (1956). *The power elite*. New York, NY: Oxford University Press.

Mills, C. W. (1959). *The sociological imagination*. New York, NY: Oxford University Press.

Minkler, M. (2004). Ethical challenges for the "outside" researcher in community-based participatory research. *Health Education Behavior, 3*(6), 684–697.

Minuchin, S., Montalvo, B., Guerney, B. G., Jr., Rosman, B. L., & Schumer, F. (1967). *Families of the slums*. New York, NY: Basic Books.

Mondlane, E. (1969). *The struggle for Mozambique*. Baltimore, MD: Penguin.

Mondros, J. B., & Wilson, S. M. (1994). *Organizing for power and empowerment*. New York, NY: Columbia University Press.

Montague, A. (1964). *Man's most dangerous myth: The fallacy of race* (4th ed.). Cleveland, OH: World Publishing.

Moreau, M. J. (1979). A structural approach to social work practice. *Canadian Journal of Social Work Education, 5*(1), 75–94.

Morrice, E., & Colagiuri, R. (2013). Coal mining, social injustice and health: A universal conflict of power and priorities. *Health & Place, 19*, 74–79.

Morris, A. D. (1984). *The origins of the civil rights movement: Black communities organizing for change*. New York, NY: Free Press.

Morris, P. M. (2002). The capabilities perspective: A framework for social justice. *Families in Society, 83*(4), 365–373.

Morris, R., & Freund, M. (Eds.). (1966). *Trends and issues in Jewish social work in the United States, 1899–1952*. Philadelphia, PA: Jewish Publication Society of America.

Morrow, H. (2011). Integrating deliberative justice theory into social work policy and pedagogy. *Journal of Social Work Education, 47*(3), 389–402.

Moshe Grodofsky, M. (2012). Community-based human rights advocacy practice and peace education. *International Social Work, 55*(5), 740–753.

Mosley, J. E. (2013). The beliefs of homeless service managers about policy advocacy: Definitions, legal understanding, and motivations to participate. *Administration in Social Work, 37*(1), 73–89.

Mullaly, R. P. (2007). *The new structural social work*. Toronto, Ontario, Canada: Oxford University Press.

Mullaly, R. P. (2010). *Challenging oppression and confronting privilege: A critical social work approach*. New York, NY: Oxford University Press.

Mullender, A., Ward, D., & Fleming, J. (2013). *Empowerment in action: Self-directed group work*. Basingstoke, UK: Palgrave Macmillan.

Mulroy, E. A., & Austin, M. J. (2004). Towards a comprehensive framework for understanding the social environment: In search of theory for practice. *Journal of Human Behavior and the Social Environment, 10*(3), 25–59.

Murray, C. (1984). *Losing ground: American social policy, 1950–1980*. New York, NY: Basic Books.

Musson, G. (1998). Life histories. In G. Symon & C. Cassell (Eds.), *Qualitative methods of analysis in organizational research: A practical guide* (pp. 10–27). Thousand Oaks, CA: Sage.

Myers, R. R., & Goddard, T. (2013). Community-driven youth justice and the organizational consequences of coercive governance. *British Journal of Criminology, 53*(2), 215–233.

Nabuco, J. (1883). *O abolicionismo*. London, UK: Abraham Kingdon & Co.

Nagda, B. A. (2006). Breaking barriers, crossing borders, building bridges: Communication processes in intergroup dialogues. *Journal of Social Issues, 62*(3), 553–576.

Nagda, B. A., Kim, C., & Truelove, Y. (2004). Learning about differences, learning with others, learning to transgress. *Journal of Social Issues, 50*(1), 195–214.

Nakata, M. (2013). The rights and blights of the politics in indigenous higher education. *Anthropological Forum, 23*(3), 289–303.

Napier, A. Y., & Whitaker, C. A. (1978). *The family crucible*. New York, NY: Harper & Row.

Narayan, U. (1999). Working together across differences. In B. Compton & B. Galaway (Eds.), *Social work processes* (6th ed., pp. 243–252). New York, NY: Brooks/Cole.

Narayan, U., & Harding, S. G. (Eds.) (2000). *Decentering the center: Philosophy for a multicultural, post-colonial, and feminist world*. Bloomington, IN: Indiana University Press.

National Association of Social Workers. (1998). *Code of ethics* (Rev. ed.). Washington, DC: Author.

National Association of Social Workers. (2008). *Code of ethics—Revised*. Washington, DC: Author. Retrieved January 4, 2015, from http://www.socialworkers.org/pubs/code/default.asp.

National Association of Social Workers (1981). *Working statement on the purpose of social work*. Washington, DC: Author.

National Gender Equity Campaign. (2009). *Building organizational capacity for social justice*. San Francisco, CA: Author.

Nelson, M. C. (1997). *Beyond fear: A Toltec guide to freedom and joy: The teachings of Miguel Angel Ruiz*. San Francisco, CA: Council Oak Books.

Nenga, S. (2014). Volunteering to give up privilege? How affluent youth volunteers respond to class privilege. *Journal of Contemporary Ethnography, 40*(3), 263–289.

Nietzsche, F. W. (1968). *Basic writings of Nietzsche* (W. Kaufmann, Ed. & Trans.). New York, NY: Modern Library.

Nkrumah, K. (1961). *I speak of freedom*. London, UK: Heinemann.

Nkrumah, K. (1963). *Africa must unite*. London, UK: Heinemann.

Northouse, P. (2007). *Leadership: Theory and practice*. Thousand Oaks, CA: Sage.

Nozick, R. (1974). *Anarchy, state, and utopia*. New York, NY: Basic Books.

Nussbaum, M. C. (1999). *Sex and social justice*. New York, NY: Oxford University Press.

Nussbaum, M. C. (2003). Capabilities as fundamental entitlements: Sen and social justice. *Feminist Economics, 9*(2–3), 33–59.

Nussbaum, M. C. (2004). Beyond the social contract: Capabilities and global justice. *Oxford Developmental Studies, 32*(1). (Lecture originally given June 19, 2003, in Oxford, UK)

Nussbaum, M. C. (2006). *Frontiers of justice: Disability, nationality, species membership*. Cambridge, MA: Belknap.

Nussbaum, M. C. (2011). *Creating capabilities: The human development approach*. Cambridge, MA: Belknap.

Nweke, O. C., Payne-Sturges, D., Garcia, L., Lee, C., Zenick, H., Grevatt, P., & Dankwa-Mullan, I. (2011). Symposium on integrating the science of environmental justice into decision-making at the Environmental Protection Agency: An overview. *American Journal of Public Health, 101*(Suppl. 1), S19–S26.

O'Grady, J. (1931). *Catholic charities in the United States: History and problems*. Washington, DC: National Conference of Catholic Charities.

Ohmer, M. L. (2008). Assessing and developing the evidence base of macro practice interventions with a community and neighborhood focus. *Journal of Evidence-Based Social Work, 5*(3–4), 519–547.

Olkkonen, M., & Lipponen, J. (2006). Relationships between organizational justice, identification with organization and work unit, and group-related outcomes. *Organizational Behavior & Human Decision Processes, 100*(2), 202–215.

Ortega, R. M., & Faller, K. C. (2011). Training child welfare workers from a cultural humility perspective. *Child Welfare, 90*(5), 27–49.

Ottinger. G. (2011). Environmentally just technology. *Environmental Justice, 4*(1), 81–85.

Oxfam. (2006, Spring). Challenging injustice. *Oxfam Exchange.*

Paley, J. (2001). *Marketing democracy: Power and social movements in post-dictatorship Chile.* Berkeley, CA: University of California Press.

Palley, E., & Shdaimah, C. S. (2014). *In our hands: The struggle for U.S. child care policy.* New York, NY: New York University Press.

Pardeck, J. T. (1996). *Social work practice: An ecological approach.* Westport, CT: Auburn House.

Parker, L. (2008). The cultural context model: A case study of social justice-based clinical practice. *Social Justice in Context, 3*, 25–40.

Patterson, F. M. (2004). Motivating students to work with elders: A strengths, social construction, and human rights and social justice approach. *Journal of Teaching in Social Work, 24*(3–4), 165–181.

Patterson, J. (2001). *America's struggle against poverty in the 20th century.* Cambridge, MA: Harvard University Press.

Payne, M. (2005). *Modern social work theory* (3rd ed.). Chicago, IL: Lyceum.

Payne, M. (2014). *Modern social work theory* (4th ed.). London, UK: Palgrave Macmillan.

Pazey, B. L., & Cole, H. A. (2013). The role of special education training in the development of socially just leaders: Building an equity consciousness in educational leadership programs. *Educational Administration Quarterly, 49*(2), 243–271.

Peabody, C. G. (2013). Using photo-voice as a tool to engage social work students in social justice. *Journal of Teaching in Social Work, 33*(3), 251–265.

Pelton, L. (2005). *Frames of Justice.* New Brunswick, NJ: Transaction Publishers.

Perdue, T., Prior, M., Williamson, C., & Sherman, S. (2012). Social justice and spiritual healing: Using micro and macro social work practice to reduce domestic minor sex trafficking. *Social Work & Christianity, 39*(4), 449–465.

Perlman, H. H. (1971). Putting the social back in social case work. In H. H. Perlman (Ed.), *Perspectives on social case work* (pp. 124–136). Philadelphia, PA: Temple University Press.

Petrella, I. (Ed.). (2005). *Latin American liberation theology: The next generation.* Maryknoll, NY: Orbis.

Philip, D., & Reisch, M. (2015). Rethinking social work's interpretation of "environmental justice": From local to global. *Social Work Education: An International Journal.*

Piketty, T. (2014). *Capital in the twenty-first century.* Cambridge, MA: Belknap.

Pincus, A., & Minahan, A. (1973). *Social work practice: Model and method.* Itasca, IL: Peacock.

Pinderhughes, E. (1983). Empowerment for our clients and ourselves. *Social Casework, 64*, 331–338.

Piven, F. F. (2002). Welfare policy and American politics. In F. F. Piven, J. Acker, M. Hallock, & S. Morgen (Eds.), *Work, welfare and politics: Confronting poverty in the wake of welfare reform* (pp. 19–33). Eugene, OR: University of Oregon Press.

Piven, F. F., & Cloward, R. (1995). *Regulating the poor: The functions of public welfare*, revised ed. New York: Vintage.

Plato (1974). *The republic* (G. M. A. Grube, Trans.). Indianapolis, IN: Hackett.

Plato (2013). *Republic* (C. Emlyn-Jones & W. Preddy, Eds. & Trans.). Cambridge, MA: Harvard University Press.

Plough, A., Fielding, J. E., Chandra, A., Williams, M., Eisenman, D., Wells, K. B., & Magaña, A. (2013). Building community disaster resilience: Perspectives from a large urban county department of public health. *American Journal of Public Health, 103*(7), 1190–1197.

Polack, R. J. (2004). Social justice and the global economy: New challenges for social work in the 21st century. *Social Work, 49*(2), 281–290.

Poole, D. L., Ferguson, M., DiNitto, D., & Schwab, A. J. (2002). The capacity of community-based organizations to lead local innovations in welfare reform: Early findings in Texas. *Nonprofit Management & Leadership, 12*(3), 261–276.

Prasant, J. P. (2014). The Gandhian concept of social justice. In M. Reisch (Ed.), *The Routledge international handbook of social justice* (pp. 39–47). London, UK: Routledge.

Prigoff, A. (2000). *Economics for social workers: Social outcomes of economic globalization, with strategies for community action*. Belmont, CA: Brooks/Cole Thomson.

Purcell, F. P., & Specht, H. (1965). The house on Sixth Street. *Social Work, 10*(4), 69–76.

Pyke, K. D., & Johnson, D. L. (2003). Asian American women and racialized femininities: "Doing" gender across cultural worlds. *Gender and Society, 17*(1), 33–53.

Rambaree, K. (2013). Social work and sustainable development: Local voices from Mauritius. *Australian Social Work, 66*(2), 261–276.

Ramey, J. B. (2013). For the public good: Urban youth advocacy and the fight for public education. *Children & Youth Services Review, 35*(8), 1260–1267.

Randel, A. E. (2002). Identity salience: A moderator of the relationship between group gender composition and work group conflict. *Journal of Organizational Behavior, 23*(6), 749–769.

Rank, M. R. (2004). *One nation underprivileged: Why American poverty affects us all*. New York, NY: Oxford University Press.

Rank, O. (1936). *Will therapy: An analysis of the therapeutic process in terms of relationship*. New York, NY: Knopf.

Rank, O. (1958). *Beyond psychology*. New York, NY: Dover.

Ratts, M., Anthony, L., & Santos, K. N. T. (2010). The dimensions of social justice model: Transforming traditional group work into a socially just framework. *Journal for Specialists in Group Work, 35*(2), 160–168.

Rawls, J. (1999). *A theory of justice*. Cambridge, MA: Harvard University Press. (Original work published 1971)

Rawls, J. (2001). *Justice as fairness: A restatement*. Cambridge, MA: Belknap.

Reamer, F. G. (1998). The evolution of social work ethics. *Social Work, 43*(6), 488–499.

Reamer, F. G. (2013). *Social work values and ethics* (4th ed.). New York, NY: Columbia University Press.

Reed, B., Ortega, R. M., & Garvin, C. (2010). Small group theory and social work: Promoting diversity and social justice or recreating inequities? In R. R. Greene & N. Kropf (Eds.), *Human behavior theory: A diversity framework* (2nd ed.). Piscataway, NJ: Transaction Publications.

Reed, B. G., & Garvin, C. (1995). Feminist psychodynamic group psychotherapy: The applications of principles. In B. DeChant (Ed.), *Women and group psychotherapy: Theory and practice* (pp. 127–156). New York, NY: Guilford.

Reich, R. B. (2012). *Beyond outrage: What has gone wrong with our economy and our democracy, and how to fix it*. New York, NY: Vintage.

Reichert, E. (2011). *Social work and human rights: A foundation for policy and practice* (2nd ed.). New York, NY: Columbia University Press.

Reichert, E. D. (2004). Ethics: Human rights and social work. *New Social Worker, 11*(4), 4–6.

Reichert, E. D. (Ed.). (2007). *Challenges in human rights: A social work perspective*. New York, NY: Columbia University Press.

Reisch, M. (1998). The socio-political context and social work method, 1890–1950. *Social Service Review, 72*(20), 161–181.

Reisch, M. (2002). Defining social justice in a socially unjust world. *Families in Society, 83*(4), 343–354.

Reisch, M. (2007). Social justice and multiculturalism: Persistent tensions in the history of U.S. social welfare and social work. *Studies in Social Justice, 1*(1), 67–92.

Reisch, M. (2008a). From melting pot to multiculturalism: The impact of racial and ethnic diversity on social work and social justice in the U.S. *British Journal of Social Work, 38*(4), 788–804.

Reisch, M. (2008b). The democratic promise: The impact of German Jewish immigration on social work in the United States. In *Yearbook of the Leo Baeck* (Vol. 53, pp. 169–190). London, UK: Berghahn.

Reisch, M. (2009). Social workers, unions, and low wage workers: An historical perspective. *Journal of Community Practice, 17*(1–2), 50–72.

Reisch, M. (2012a). Radical community organizing. In M. O. Weil, M. Reisch, & M. Ohmer (Eds.), *The handbook of community practice* (2nd ed., pp. 361–381). Thousand Oaks, CA: Sage.

Reisch, M. (2012b). The challenges of health care reform for hospital social work in the U.S. *Social Work in Health Care, 51*(10), 873–893.

Reisch, M. (2013). What is the future of social work? *Critical and Radical Social Work, 1*(1), 67–85.

Reisch, M. (2014a). Introduction to Part I. In M. Reisch (Ed.), *The Routledge international handbook of social justice* (pp. 9–13). London, UK: Routledge.

Reisch, M. (2014b). Introduction to Part II. In M. Reisch (Ed.), *The Routledge international handbook of social justice* (pp. 125–131). London, UK: Routledge.

Reisch, M. (2014c). Social justice and liberalism. In M. Reisch (Ed.), *The Routledge international handbook of social justice* (pp. 132–146). London, UK: Routledge.

Reisch, M. (2015a). Legislative advocacy to empower oppressed and vulnerable groups. In K. Corcoran (Ed.), *Social workers' desk reference* (3rd ed.). New York, NY: Oxford University Press.

Reisch, M. (2015b). The boundaries of justice: Addressing the conflict between human rights and multiculturalism in social work practice and education. In K. Libal, L. Healy, M. Berthold, & R. Thomas (Eds.), *Advancing human rights in social work education* (pp. 177–195). Alexandria, VA: Council on Social Work Education.

Reisch, M. (2015c). Coalizione o conflitto: Lavoro sociale e classe lavoratrice negli Stati Uniti, (U.S. social work and the working class: Coalition and conflict.) *Zapruder*, *37*, (Odradek, Rome), 40–57.

Reisch, M., & Andrews, J. L. (2002). *The road not taken: A history of radical social work in the United States.* New York, NY: Brunner-Routledge.

Reisch, M., & Guyet, D. (2007). Communities as "big small groups": Culture and social capital. In R. Cnaan & C. Milofsky (Eds.), *Handbook of community movements and local organizations* (pp. 163–178). New York, NY: Springer.

Reisch, M., Ife, J., & Weil, M. O. (2012c). Social justice, human rights, values, and community practice. In M. O. Weil, M. Reisch, & M. Ohmer (Eds.), *Handbook of community practice* (2nd ed., pp. 73–103). Thousand Oaks, CA: Sage.

Reisch, M., & Jani, J. S. (2012d). The new politics of social work practice: Understanding context to promote change. *British Journal of Social Work, 42*(6), 1132–1150.

Reisch, M., & Lowe, J. I. (2000). 'Of means and ends' revisited: Teaching ethical community organization in an unethical society. *Journal of Community Practice, 7*(1), 19–38.

Reisch, M., Wenocur, S., & Sherman, W. (1981–1982). Empowerment, conscientization, and animation as core social work skills. *Social Development Issues, 5*(2–3), 108–120.

Reverby, S. (Ed.). (2000). *Tuskegee's truths: Rethinking the Tuskegee syphilis study.* Chapel Hill, NC: University of North Carolina Press.

Reynolds, B. C. (1951). *Social work and social living.* New York, NY: Citadel Press.

Reynolds, B. C. (1963). *An uncharted journey: Fifty years of growth in social work.* New York, NY: Citadel Press.

Reynolds, V. (2012). An ethical stance for justice-doing in community work and therapy. *Journal of Systemic Therapies, 31*(4), 18–33.

Richmond, M. E. (1917). *Social diagnosis.* New York, NY: Russell Sage Foundation.

Richmond, M. E. (1922). *What is social casework?* New York, NY: Russell Sage Foundation.

Ridgeway, C. L. (1991). The social construction of status values: Gender and other nominal characteristics. *Social Forces, 70*(2), 367–386.

Ridgeway, C. L. (2001). Gender, status and leadership. *Journal of Social Issues, 57*(4), 637–655.

Ridgeway, C. L. (2006). Linking social structure and interpersonal behavior: A theoretical perspective on cultural schemas and social relations. *Social Psychology Quarterly, 69*(1), 5–16.

Ridgeway, C. L., Boyle, E. H., Kuipers, K. J., & Robinson, D. T. (1998). How do status beliefs develop? The role of resources and interactional experience. *American Sociological Review, 63*(3), 331–350.

Ridgeway, C. L., & Diekema, D. (1989). Dominance and collective hierarchy formation in male and female task groups. *American Sociological Review, 54, 79–93*.

Ridgeway, C. L., Diekema, D., & Johnson, C. (1995). Legitimacy, compliance, and gender in peer groups. *Social Psychology Quarterly, 58*(4), 298–311.

Ridgeway, C. L., & Erickson, K. G. (2000). Creating and spreading status beliefs. *American Journal of Sociology, 106*(3), 579–615.

Ridgeway, C. L., & Johnson, C. (1990). What is the relationship between socioemotional behavior and status in task groups? *American Journal of Sociology, 95*(5), 1189–1212.

Rivera, F., & Erlich, J. (1998). *Community organizing in a diverse society* (3rd ed.). Boston: Allyn & Bacon.

Rivera, J. A. (1987). Self help as mutual protection: The development of Hispanic fraternal benefit societies. *Journal of Applied Behavioral Science, 23*(3), 387–396.

Rodriguez, R. A. (1998). Challenging demographic reductionism: A pilot study investigating diversity in group composition. *Small Group Research, 29*(6), 744–759.

Rodriguez, V. R. (2012). Review of "Mothers United: An Immigrant Struggle for Socially Just Education." *Hispanic Journal of Behavioral Sciences, 34*(2), 368–371.

Roemer, J. E. (1996). *Theories of distributive justice.* Cambridge, MA: Harvard University Press.

Rogge, M. (1997). Toxic risk, community resilience, and social justice in Chattanooga, Tennessee. In M. D. Hoff (Ed.), *Sustainable development: Studies in economic, environmental, and cultural revitalization* (pp. 105–118). Boca Raton, FL: Lewis.

Rooney, R. (2009). *Strategies for work with involuntary clients* (2nd ed.). New York, NY: Columbia University Press.

Rorty, R. (1989). *Contingency, irony, and solidarity.* Cambridge, UK: Cambridge University Press.

Rorty, R. (1991). *Objectivity, relativism and truth: Philosophical papers* (Vol. 3). Cambridge, UK: Cambridge University Press.

Rorty, R. (1998). *Truth and progress: Philosophical papers* (Vol. 3). Cambridge, UK: Cambridge University Press.

Rose, N. E. (1994). *Out to work: Relief programs in the great depression.* New York, NY: Monthly Review Press.

Rose, S. (1984). Use of data in identifying and resolving group problems in goal oriented treatment groups. *Social Work with Groups, 7*, 23–36.

Rothman, J. (1970). Three models of community organization practice. In J. Rothman, J. Erlich, & J. Tropman (Eds.), *Strategies of Community Organization* (pp. 20–35). Itasca, IL: Peacock Publishers, Inc.

Rothman, J. (1996). The interweaving of community intervention approaches. *Journal of Community Practice, 3*(3–4), 69–99.

Rottmann, C. (2012). Forty years in the Union: Incubating, supporting, and catalyzing socially just educational change. *Journal of Educational Change, 13*(2), 191–216.

Rousseau, J.-J. (1994). *Discourse on the origins of inequality*. New York, NY: Oxford University Press.

Rowe, M. P. (1990). Barriers to equality: The power of subtle discrimination to maintain unequal opportunity. *Employee Responsibilities and Rights Journal, 3*(2), 153–163.

Roysircar, G. (2008). A response to "Social Privilege, Social Justice, and Group Counseling: An Inquiry": Social privilege: Counselors' competence with systematically determined inequalities. *Journal for Specialists in Group Work, 33*(4), 377–384.

Ruether, R. R. (2005). *Goddesses and the divine feminine: A Western religious history*. Berkeley, CA: University of California Press.

Ruiz, M., & Valverde, M. (2012). Transformative Hispanic-serving institutions: Realizing equity praxis through community connections and local solutions. *Journal of Latinos and Education, 11*(3), 189–194.

Ryan, W. (1981). *Equality*. New York, NY: Pantheon.

Sabbagh, L. (2011). The paradox of decategorization: Deinstitutionalizing race through race-based affirmative action in the United States. *Ethnic and Racial Studies, 34*(10), 1665–1681.

Saint-Just, A. L. L. de (1968). *Oeuvres choisies, discours, rapports, institutions republicaines, proclamations, letters*. Paris, France: Gallimard.

Sakamoto, I. (2014). The use of the arts in promoting social justice. In M. Reisch (Ed.), *The Routledge international handbook of social justice* (pp. 463–479). London, UK: Routledge.

Salamon, L. M. (Ed.). (2012). *The state of nonprofit America* (2nd ed.). Washington, DC: Brookings Institution.

Saleeby, D. (2002). *The strengths perspective and social work practice* (3rd ed.). Boston, MA: Allyn & Bacon.

Salem, D. (1990). *To better our world: Black women in organized reform, 1890–1920*. Brooklyn, NY: Carlson.

Sample, T. S. (2001). Consensus v. conflict strategies. In J. Rothman, J. Erlich, & J. Tropman (Eds.), *Strategies of community intervention*, 7th ed. Itasca, IL: Peacock.

Sandel, M. J. (1998). *Liberalism and the limits of justice* (2nd ed.). New York, NY: Cambridge University Press.

Sander, R. (2005.). *Social work and community initiatives: Does social justice matter?* Baltimore, MD: University of Maryland School of Social Work.

Santos, B. de S. (1998). Participatory budgeting in Porto Alegre: Toward a redistributive democracy. *Politics & Society, 26*(4), 461–510.

Scanlan, M. (2013). A learning architecture: How school leaders can design for learning social justice. *Educational Administration Quarterly, 49*(2), 348–391.

Schein, E. H. (2010). *Organizational culture and leadership* (Vol. 2). New York, NY: John Wiley & Sons.

Schiele, J. (2000). *Human services and the Afrocentric paradigm.* New York, NY: Haworth.

Schmidtz, D., & Goodin, R. E. (1998). *Social welfare and individual responsibility.* New York, NY: Cambridge University Press.

Schneider, J. A. (2009). Organizational social capital and nonprofits. *Nonprofit and Voluntary Sector Quarterly, 38*(4), 643–662.

Schram, S. F., Soss, J., & Fording, R. C. (2014). Welfare and welfare reform in the age of neoliberal paternalism. In M. Reisch (Ed.), *Social policy and social justice* (pp. 377–404). Thousand Oaks, CA: Sage.

Schrecker, E. (1998). *Many are the crimes: McCarthyism in America.* Boston, MA: Little, Brown.

Schulman, L. (1999). *The skills of helping individuals, families, groups, and communities.* Itasca, IL: Peacock.

Schwartz, W. (ed.) (1961). The social worker in the group. In *New perspectives on service to groups* (pp. 7–29). New York, NY: Columbia University Press.

Seabury, B., Seabury, B., & Garvin, C. D. (2011). *Theoretical foundations of interpersonal practice in social work: Promoting competence in generalist practice* (3rd ed.). Thousand Oaks, CA: Sage.

Seebohm, P., Chaudhary, S., Boyce, M., Elkan, R., Avis, M., & Munn-Giddings, C. (2013). The contribution of self-help/mutual aid groups to mental well-being. *Health & Social Care in the Community, 21*(4), 391–401.

Segal, R. (1995). *The Black diaspora: Five centuries of the Black experience outside Africa.* New York, NY: Farrar, Straus, & Giroux.

Sekhon, J. (2006). Engendering grassroots democracy: Research, training, and networking for women in local self-governance in India. *NWSA Journal, 18*(2), 101–122.

Sen, A. (1992). *Inequality reexamined.* New York, NY: Russell Sage Foundation.

Sen, A. (1999). *Commodities and capabilities.* New York, NY: Oxford University Press.

Sen, A. (2009). *The idea of justice.* Cambridge, MA: Harvard University Press.

Sen, A., & Muellbauer, J. (1988). *The standard of living.* Cambridge, UK: Cambridge University Press.

Sen, R. (2012). New theory for new constituencies: Contemporary organizing in communities of color. In M. O. Weil, M. Reisch, & M. L. Ohmer (Eds.), *The handbook of community practice* (2nd ed., pp. 249–264). Thousand Oaks, CA: Sage.

Senghor, L. S. (1965). *Prose and poetry* (J. Reed & C. Wake, Trans.). London, UK: Oxford University Press.

Shaw, T. (2013). Is social work a green profession? An examination of environmental beliefs. *Journal of Social Work, 13*(1), 3–29.

Shields, C. (2010). Transformative leadership: Working for equity in diverse contexts. *Educational Administration Quarterly, 46*(4), 558–589.

Shippen, M. E., Patterson, D., Green, K. L., & Smitherman, T. (2012). Community and school practices to reduce delinquent behavior: Intervening on the school-to-prison pipeline. *Teacher Education and Special Education, 35*(4), 296–308.

Sim, G. (2014). Social justice and cinema. In M. Reisch (Ed.), *The Routledge international handbook of social justice* (pp. 502–512). London, UK: Routledge.

Simon, A. (2006). Reflections on promoting social justice: An interview with Art Simon, founder and president emeritus of Bread for the World. *Review of Business, 27*(2), 4–6.

Simon, B. L. (1994). *The empowerment tradition in American social work*. New York, NY: Columbia University Press.

Singh, A. A., & Salazar, C. F. (2010). Six considerations for social justice group work. *Journal for Specialists in Group Work, 35*, 308–319.

Singh, V. (2014). Qualitative and quantitative methods in libraries (QQML): Special Issue— Social Justice. *Social Inclusion, 2*(1), 49–57.

Singleton, G. E., & Linton, C. (2006). *Courageous conversation about race: A field guide for achieving equity in schools*. Thousand Oaks, CA: Corwin.

Sklar, K. K. (1995). *Florence Kelley and the nation's work: The rise of women's political culture, 1830–1900*. New Haven, CT: Yale University Press.

Sklar, K. K. (1998). *Social justice feminists in the U.S. and Germany: A dialogue in documents, 1885–1933*. Ithaca, NY: Cornell University Press.

Skurnick, W. (1965). Leopold Sedar Senghor and African socialism. *Journal of Modern African Studies, 3*(3), 349–369.

Smith, A. M. (2008). Neoliberalism, welfare policy, and feminist theories of social justice. *Feminist Theory, 9*(2), 131–144.

Smith, L. C., & Shin, R. Q. (2008). Social privilege, social justice, and group counseling: An inquiry. *Journal for Specialists in Group Work, 33*(4), 351–366.

Smith, R. M. (1997). *Civic ideals: Conflicting visions of citizenship in U.S. history*. New Haven, CT: Yale University Press.

Smith-Lovin, L., & Brody, C. (1989). Interruptions in group discussions. *American Sociological Review, 54*(3), 424–435.

Smyth, P., Reddel, T., & Jones, A. (Eds.). (2005). *Community and local governance in Australia*. Sydney, Australia: University of New South Wales Press.

Sohng, S. (1996). A Korean gay man in the U.S.: Toward a cultural context for social work practice. In J. F. Longres (Ed.), *Men of Color: A Context for Service to Homosexually Active Men* (pp. 115–137). New York, NY: Harrington Park/Haworth Press.

Solomon, B. B. (1976). *Black empowerment: Social work in oppressed communities.* New York, NY: Columbia University Press.

Soltis, S. M., Agneessens, F., Sasovova, Z., & Labianca, G. (2013). A social network perspective on turnover intentions: The role of distributive justice and social support. *Human Resource Management, 52*(4), 561–584.

Spano, R. (1982). *The rank and file movement in social work.* Washington, DC: University Press of America.

Specht, H. (1969). Disruptive tactics. *Social Work, 14*(2), 5–15.

Specht, H., & Courtenay, M. (1994). *Unfaithful angels: How social work abandoned its mission.* New York, NY: Free Press.

Speight, S., & Vera, E. (2003). Multicultural competence, social justice, and counseling psychology: Expanding our roles. *The Counseling Psychologist, 31*(3), 253–272.

Spleth, J. (1985). *Leopold Sedar Senghor.* Boston, MA: Twayne.

Stephan, W. G. (2008). Psychological and communication processes associated with intergroup conflict resolution. *Small Group Research, 39*(1), 28–41.

Stephens, C., & Gillies, A. (2012). Understanding the role of everyday practices of privilege in the perpetuation of inequalities. *Journal of Community & Applied Social Psychology, 22*(2), 145–158.

Sterba, J. P. (2009). *Affirmative action for the future.* Ithaca, NY: Cornell University Press.

Stern, M. J., & Axinn, J. (2013). *Social work: A history of the American response to need* (8th ed.). Boston: Allyn & Bacon.

Stiglitz, J. E. (2013). *The price of inequality.* New York, NY: Norton.

Stoesz, D. (2014). Conservatism and social justice. In M. Reisch (Ed.), *The Routledge international handbook of social justice* (pp. 147–159). London, UK: Routledge.

Stoesz, D., Karger, H. J., & Carrilio, T. E. (2010). *A dream deferred: How social work education lost its way and what can be done.* Herndon, VA: AldineTransaction.

Stokamer, S. (2013). Pedagogical catalysts of civic competence: The development of a critical epistemological model for community-based learning. *Journal of Higher Education Outreach and Engagement, 17*(1), 113–121.

Stone, D. A. (2008). *The Samaritan's dilemma: Should government help your neighbor?* New York, NY: Nation Books.

Stricker, P. (2010). Bringing social justice back in: Cuba revitalises sustainable development. *Local Environment, 15*(2), 185–197.

Strolovitch, D. Z. (2006). Do interest groups represent the disadvantaged? Advocacy at the intersections of race, class, and gender. *Journal of Politics, 68*(4), 894–910.

Suarez, Z. E., Newman, P. A., & Reed, B. G. (2008). Critical consciousness and cross-cultural social work practice: A case analysis. *Families in Society, 89*(3), 407–417.

Sue, D. (1981). *Counseling the culturally different.* New York, NY: Wiley.

Sugrue, T. J. (2005). *The origins of the urban crisis: Race and inequality in postwar Detroit.* Princeton, NJ: Princeton University Press.

Sun, F., & Xiao, J. (2012). Perceived social policy fairness and subjective wellbeing: Evidence from China. *Social Indicators Research, 107*(1), 171–186.

Sunstein, C. R. (1997). *Free markets and social justice.* New York, NY: Oxford University Press.

Sunstein, C. R. (2004). *The second bill of rights: FDR's unfinished revolution and why we need it more than ever.* New York, NY: Basic Books.

Swalwell, K. (2013). "With great power comes great responsibility": Privileged students' conceptions of justice-oriented citizenship. *Democracy & Education, 21*(1), 1–11.

Swenson, C. R. (1998, November). Clinical social work's contribution to a social justice perspective. *Social Work, 43*(6), 527–537.

Takacs, D. (1993, Summer). How does your positionality bias your epistemology? *Thought & Action (NEA Higher Education Journal),* 27–38.

Talmon, J. L. (1970). *The origins of totalitarian democracy.* New York, NY: Norton.

Tannen, D. (1990). *You just don't understand: Women and men in conversation.* New York, NY: HarperCollins.

Taylor, J. (2014). Music and social justice. In M. Reisch (Ed.), *The Routledge international handbook of social justice* (pp. 492–501). London, UK: Routledge.

Telushkin, J. (1994). Let the law cut through the mountain: Jewish principles of justice. In J. Telushkin (Ed.), *Jewish wisdom: Ethical, spiritual, and historical lessons from the great works and thinkers.* New York, NY: Morrow.

Tervalon, M., & Murray-García, J. (1998). Cultural humility versus cultural competence: A critical distinction in defining physician training outcomes in multicultural education. *Journal of Health Care for the Poor and Underserved, 9*(2), 117–125.

Thakur, S. (1996). *Religion and social justice.* New York, NY: St. Martin's Press.

Theoharis, G. (2007). Social justice educational leaders and resistance: Toward a theory of social justice leadership. *Educational Administration Quarterly, 43*(2), 221–258.

Thomas, H. (1997). *The slave trade: The story of the Atlantic slave trade, 1440–1870.* New York, NY: Simon & Schuster.

Thomas, K. W., Fann Thomas, G., & Schaubhut, N. (2008). Conflict styles of men and women at six organization levels. *International Journal of Conflict Management, 19*(2), 148–166.

Thomas, M., O'Connor, M., & Netting, F. (2011). A framework for teaching community practice. *Journal of Social Work Education, 47*(2), 337–355.

Thomas, R. R., Jr. (1991). *Beyond race and gender: Unleashing the power of your total work force by managing diversity.* New York, NY: American Management Association.

Thompson, E. F. (2014). Social justice in the Middle East. In M. Reisch (Ed.), *The Routledge international handbook of social justice* (pp. 61–73). London, UK: Routledge.

Thyer, B. (2010). *Cultural diversity and social work practice.* Springfield, IL: Charles C Thomas.

Thyer, B. A. (2007). Evidence-based practice in the U.S. In B. A. Thyer & M. A. F. Kazi (Eds.), *International perspectives on evidence-based practice in social work* (pp. 9–27). Birmingham, UK: Venture Press.

Tilly, C. (1978). *From mobilization to revolution.* Reading, MA: Addison-Wesley.

Titmuss, R. M. (1968). *Essays on the welfare state.* Boston, MA: Beacon Press.

Titmuss, R. M. (1976a). *Commitment to welfare* (Rev. ed.). London, UK: Allen & Unwin.

Titmuss. R. M. (1976b). *Essays on the welfare state* (3rd ed.). London, UK: Allen & Unwin.

Todd, N. R., & Allen, N. E. (2011). Religious congregations as mediating structures for social justice: A multilevel examination. *American Journal of Community Psychology, 48*(3–4), 222–237.

Tomasi, J. (2001). *Liberalism beyond justice: Citizens, society, and the boundaries of political theory.* Princeton, NJ: Princeton University Press.

Toplin, R. B. (1972). *The abolition of slavery in Brazil.* New York, NY: Athaneum.

Torres-Harding, S. R., Carollo, O., Schamberger, A., & Clifton-Soderstrom, K. (2013). Values and religiosity as predictors of engagement in social justice. *Journal of Prevention & Intervention in the Community, 41*(4), 255–266.

Towle, C. (1945). *Common human needs.* Washington, DC: Social Security Administration.

Townsend, J., Zapata, E., Rowlands, J., Alberti, P., & Mercado, M. (1999). *Women and power: Fighting patriarchy.* New York, NY: Zed Books. (See especially J. G. Townsend & E. Zapata, Introduction (pp. 1–18); J. G. Townsend et al., Empowerment matters: Understanding power (pp. 19–45); and E. Zapata, Levels of power: From the person to the world (pp. 150–163).)

Trinder, L. (2000). Reading the texts: Postmodern feminism and the "doing" of research. In B. Fawcett et al. (Eds.), *Practice and research in social work: Postmodern feminist perspectives* (pp. 39–61). New York, NY: Routledge.

Tucker, F. (1913). Presidential address: Social justice. In *Proceedings of the National Conference of Charities and Corrections* (Vol. 40, pp. 1–13). Chicago, IL: University of Chicago Press.

Tucker, W. J. (1903). *The progress of the social conscience.* Boston, MA: South End House Association. (Reprint from the *Atlantic Monthly, 116*(3), 289–303)

Turbett, C. (2014). Review of "Radical Social Work Today—Social Work at the Crossroads." *Journal of Social Work, 14*(1), 96–97.

Turner, J. (2010). Seeing the poor and moving toward justice: An interactive activity. *Social Work & Christianity, 37*(2), 142–160.

Turner, K., Hayes, N., & Way, K. (2013). Critical multimodal hip pop production: A social justice approach to African American language and literacy practices. *Equity & Excellence in Education, 46*(3), 342–354.

Twill, S., & Fisher, S. (2010). Economic human rights violations experienced by women with children in the United States. *Families in Society: The Journal of Contemporary Social Services, 91*(4), 356–362.

Tyson, G. (Ed.). (1973). *Toussaint L'Ouverture*. Englewood Cliffs, NJ: Prentice Hall.

United States Bureau of the Census (2012). Income, poverty, and health insurance coverage in the United States, 2011. *Current Population Reports*, P60-243. Washington, DC: U.S. Government Printing Office.

US Conference of Catholic Bishops. (1986). *Economic justice for all: Pastoral letter on Catholic social teaching and the U.S. economy*. Washington, DC: National Conference of Catholic Bishops.

Van Kleeck, M. (1915). *Facts about wage-earners in the United States census* [instructional materials]. New York, NY: The New York School of Philanthropy.

Van Kleeck, M. (1932). Social research and industry. In *Proceedings of the Second International Conference of Social Work, Frankfurt Main, Germany* (4th section, pp. 1–20). Archives of the University of Pennsylvania School of Social Work, Philadelphia)

Van Kleeck, M. (1934). *Miners and management*. New York, NY: Russell Sage.

Van Knippenberg, D., Haslam, S. A., & Platow, M. J. (2007). Unity through diversity: Value-in-diversity beliefs, work group diversity, and group identification. *Group Dynamics: Theory, Research, and Practice, 11*(3): 207–222.

Van Soest, D. (1992). *Incorporating peace and social justice into the social work curriculum: Curriculum materials and suggestions for faculty and students*. Washington, DC: NASW, Peace and Social Justice Committee.

Van Soest, D. (1994). Strange bedfellows: A call for reordering national priorities from three social justice perspectives. *Social Work, 39*(6), 710–717.

Van Soest, D. (1997). *The global crisis of violence: Common problems, universal causes, shared solutions*. Washington, DC: NASW Press.

Van Soest, D., & Garcia, B. (2003). *Diversity education for social justice: Mastering teaching skills*. Alexandria, VA: Council on Social Work Education.

Verschelden, C. (1993). Social work values and pacifism: Opposition to war as a professional responsibility. *Social Work, 38*(6), 765–769.

Vosler, N. R. (1996). *New approaches to family practice: Confronting economic stress*. Thousand Oaks, CA: Sage.

Wakefield, J. C. (1988a). Psychotherapy, distributive justice, and social work—Part 1: Distributive justice as a conceptual framework for social work. *Social Service Review, 62*(2), 187–210.

Wakefield, J. C. (1988b). Psychotherapy, distributive justice, and social work—Part 2: Psychotherapy and the pursuit of justice. *Social Service Review, 62*(3), 353–382.

Wakefield, J. C. (2014). Psychological justice: Distributive justice and psychiatric treatment of the non-disordered. In M. Reisch (Ed.), *The Routledge international handbook of social justice* (pp. 353–384). London, UK: Routledge.

Waldegrave, C. (1998). The challenges of culture to psychology and postmodern thinking. In M. McGoldrick (Ed.), *Revisioning family therapy: Race, culture, and gender in clinical practice* (pp. 404–413). New York, NY: Guilford.

Walker, A. (2002). The right to life: What can the White man say to the Black woman? *Seattle Journal for Social Justice, 1*(1), Article 1.

Walker, D. (2000). *Walker's appeal, in four articles; Together with a preamble to the colored citizens of the world, but in particular, and very expressly to those of the United States of America* (P. P. Hinks, Ed.). University Park, PA: Pennsylvania State University Press. (Original work published 1829)

Wallack, L., & Dorfman, L. (1996). Media advocacy: A strategy for advancing policy and promoting health. *Health Education & Behavior, 23*(3), 293–317.

Wallerstein, N. B., Yen, I. H., & Syme, S. (2011). Integration of social epidemiology and community-engaged interventions to improve health equity. *American Journal of Public Health, 101*(5), 822–830.

Wallis, J. (2008). *The great awakening: Reviving faith and politics in a post-religious right America.* New York, NY: HarperOne.

Walsh, F. (2009). *Spiritual resources in family therapy* (2nd ed.). New York, NY: Guilford.

Warren, C. J. E. (1954). Brown v. Board of Education. *United States Reports, 347,* 483.

Warren, R. (1983). *New perspectives on the American community* (4th ed.). Homewood, IL: Dorsey.

Warren, R. L. (1970). The good community—What would it be? *Journal of the Community Development Society, 1*(1), 14–24.

Wasonga, T. A. (2009). Leadership practices for social justice, democratic community, and learning: School principals' perspectives. *Journal of School Leadership, 19*(2), 200–224.

Weaver, B. (2011). Co-producing community justice: The transformative potential of personalisation for penal sanctions. *British Journal of Social Work, 41*(6), 1038–1057.

Weaver, H., & Congress, E. (2009). Indigenous people in a landscape of risk: Teaching social work students about socially just social work responses. *Journal of Ethnic & Cultural Diversity in Social Work, 18*(1–2), 166–179.

Weaver, H. N. (2014). Indigenous struggles for justice: Restoring balance within the context of Anglo settler societies. In M. Reisch (Ed.), *The Routledge international handbook of social justice* (pp. 111–122). London, UK: Routledge.

Webb, S. A. (2001). Some considerations on the validity of evidence-based practice in social work. *British Journal of Social Work, 31*(1), 57–79.

Weber, M. (2009). *From Max Weber: Essays in sociology* (H. H. Gerth & C. W. Mills, Ed. & Trans.). New York, NY: Routledge.

Weil, M. O., Gamble, D. N., & Ohmer, M. L. (2012). Evolution, models, and the changing context of community practice. In M. O. Weil, M. Reisch, & M. L. Ohmer (Eds.), *The handbook of community practice* (2nd ed., pp. 167–194). Thousand Oaks, CA: Sage.

Wells-Barnett, I. B. (1970). *Crusade for justice: The autobiography of Ida B. Wells* (A. M. Duster, Ed.). Chicago, IL: University of Chicago Press.

Wenocur, S., & Reisch, M. (1989). *From charity to enterprise: The development of American social work in a market economy.* Urbana, IL: University of Illinois Press.

White, J. E. (2000). *Democracy, justice, and the welfare state: Reconstructing public care.* University Park, PA: Pennsylvania State University Press.

Whitman, W. (1855). *Leaves of grass.* New York, NY: Viking.

Wiggins, N., Kaan, S., Rios-Campos, T., Gaonkar, R., Morgan, E., & Robinson, J. (2013). Preparing community health workers for their role as agents of social change: Experience of the Community Capacitation Center. *Journal of Community Practice, 21*(3), 186–202.

Wilentz, S. (2005). *The rise of American democracy: Jefferson to Lincoln.* New York, NY: Norton.

Wills, G. (1992). *Lincoln at Gettysburg: The words that remade America.* New York, NY: Simon & Schuster.

Wise, S. S. (1909). The conference sermon: Charity vs. justice. In A. Johnson (Ed.), *Proceedings of the National Conference of Charities and Corrections* (Vol. 36, pp. 20–29). Fort Wayne, IN: Fort Wayne Publishing.

Withorn, A. (1986). What is progressive social work? *The Bertha Capen Reynolds Society Newsletter, 1*(2), 1–2.

Witkin, S. (1998). Is social work an adjective? *Social Work, 43*(6), 483–486.

Witkin, S. (1999). Identities and contexts. *Social Work, 44*(4), 293–297.

Witkin, S. (2000). Writing social work. *Social Work, 45*(5), 389–391.

Witkin, S. L., & Harrison, W. D. (2001). Whose evidence and for what purpose? [Editorial]. *Social Work, 46*(2), 293–296.

Witkin, S. L., & Irving, A. (2014). Postmodern perspectives on social justice. In M. Reisch (Ed.), *The Routledge international handbook of social justice* (pp. 188–201). London, UK: Routledge.

Wodarski, J., & Feit, M. D. (2009). *Evidence-based interventions in social work: A practitioner's manual.* Springfield, IL: Charles C. Thomas Publisher.

Wolff, J. (2008). Social justice and public policy: A view from political philosophy. In G. Craig, T. Burchardt, & D. Gordon (Eds.), *Social justice and public policy: Seeking fairness in diverse societies* (pp. 17–31). Bristol, UK: Polity.

Wood, G. G., & Middleman, R. R. (1989). *The structural approach to direct practice in social work.* New York, NY: Columbia University Press.

Woods, M. E., & Hollis, F. (2000). *Casework: A psychosocial therapy* (5th ed.). Boston, MA: McGraw-Hill.

Woods, R. (1905, October). Social work: A new profession. *International Journal of Social Ethics, 16.*

Wright, R. R. (1920). What does the Negro want in our democracy? In *Proceedings of the National Conference of Social Work* (pp. 539–545). Chicago, IL: University of Chicago Press.

Wronka, J. (2008). *Human rights and social justice: Social action and service for the helping and health professions.* Thousand Oaks, CA: Sage.

Wronka, J. (2014). Human rights as pillars of social justice. In M. Reisch (Ed.), *The Routledge international handbook of social justice* (pp. 216–226). London, UK: Routledge.

Wynne, L. C. (1984). The epigenesist of relational systems: A model for understanding family development. *Family Process, 23,* 297–318.

Young, D. (1999). Complementary, supplementary, or adversarial? A theoretical and historical examination of nonprofit-government relations in the United States. In E. Boris & E. Steuerle (Eds.), *Nonprofits and government: Collaboration and conflict* (pp. 31–67). Washington, DC: Urban Institute Press.

Young, I. M. (1990). *Justice and the politics of difference.* Princeton, NJ: Princeton University Press.

Young, I. M. (2008). Structural injustice and the politics of difference. In G. Craig, T. Burchardt, & D. Gordon (Eds.), *Social justice and public policy: Seeking fairness in diverse societies* (pp. 77–104). Bristol, UK: Polity.

Young, I. M. (2011). *Responsibility for justice.* New York, NY: Oxford University Press.

Young, S., McKenzie, M., Schjelderup, L., & Omre, C. (2012). The rights of the child enabling community development to contribute to a valid social work practice with children at risk. *European Journal of Social Work, 15*(2), 169–184.

Young, W. M. (1965). Civil rights—Unfinished business, part two· Civil rights and a militant profession. *Proceedings of the National Conference on Social Welfare* (pp. 42–54). New York, NY: Columbia University Press.

Yunus, M. (with Jolis, A.). (2007). *Banker to the poor: Micro-lending and the battle against world poverty.* New York, NY: PublicAffairs.

Zinn, H. (1980). *A people's history of the United States.* New York, NY: Harper & Row.

Zufferey, C. (2011). Homelessness, social policy, and social work: A way forward. *Australian Social Work, 64*(3), 241–244.

Index

Privatization of services, 279
Privilege. *See also* Inequalities
  epistemic, 170
  power and, 185
  unearned, 173
Proactive motives, 254
Problem conception, 104–105
Process. *See also specific types*
  group, 185–186
  social work practice, 7–8, 29
Process equity, 292
Progressive approaches, 137t, 141
Progressive Era, 76, 258
Psychoeducational model, 144, 149t
Psychosocial model, 134
Public service announcements
  (PSAs), 314
Purpose
  group work, 166–167, 168–169
  processes and procedures, 110–112
  *Working Statement on the Purpose of
  Social Work*, 79
Purposive change, 222
"Putting the Social Back in Social Case
  Work" (Perlman), 134

Qualitative–quantitative research,
  335–338
Qur'an, 35
  on forgiveness, 36
  on freedom, 40
  on gender inequality, 39
  unity and equality in, 38

Racial disparities, 287–288, 287f
Racism. *See also specific topics*
  environmental, 292
Racism, institutional
  post-World War II, 78
  1960s, NASW stance, 79
Radical approaches (model), 137t, 141

Rancorous conflict, 219, 237
Rank, Otto, 134
Rank and file movement, 77–78, 135
Raven, B., 183
Rawls, John, 44
  first principle, 7
  second principle, 7
  theory of justice, 6–7
  A Theory of Justice, 44–45, 83
Reactions, alternative, 14, 122
Reactive motives, 254
Reamer, Frederic G., 112
Redress
  policies, 283
  principle, 6–7
"Red Scare," 78–79
Referent power, 183, 247
Reflection
  definition, 107
  practitioner, 107
  worker, 107, 107f
Reflexive learning, 259
Reflexive process, circular, 107, 107f
Reflexivity
  practitioner, 107, 107f
  research, 337
Rehabilitation, group work, 169
Reid, William J., 329
Reisch, Michael, 227–228
Relational power, 248
Relations between social entities,
  unequal, 22
Relative needs, 231
Religious ideas, 31–42
  activists, modern, 31
  Bible, 33–36
  Buddhism, 33
  community, 41–42
  correcting wrongs, 32
  divine intervention, 32
  equality, 37–39